THE
LEGAL
ENVIRONMENT
OF
COMPUTING

IMPORTANT NOTE

The purpose of this book is not to give solutions to every legal problem. It is intended to be a guide as to the nature of legal issues in most countries, and the reader should be aware that although the issues may be the same, they may be dealt with in a different manner from country to country. In addition, the law in every country is subject to continual change and development. Although every effort has been made to be accurate, there is not substitute for obtaining professional legal advice in particular circumstances and this book does not purport and should not be relied upon to give advice on any legal issue.

THE
LEGAL
ENVIRONMENT
OF
COMPUTING

PETER KNIGHT
JAMES FITZSIMONS

ADDISON-WESLEY
PUBLISHING
COMPANY

Sydney • Wokingham, England • Reading, Massachusetts
Menlo Park, California • New York • Don Mills, Ontario
Amsterdam • Bonn • Singapore • Tokyo • Madrid • San Juan

Many of the designations used by manufacturers and sellers to distinguish their
products are claimed as trademarks. Addison-Wesley has made every attempt to supply
trademark information about manufacturers and their products mentioned in this
book. A list of the trademark designations and their owners appears on p. xiv.

Cover designed by Kiboh Kuki, Singapore,
Typeset by Times Graphics.
Printed in Singapore.
Index prepared by Jill Matthews, HiTech Editing, Australia.

First printed in 1990

British Library Cataloguing in Publications Data
Knight, Peter, 1953–
    The legal environment of computing.

    Bibliography.
    Includes index.
    ISBN 0 201 41701 4.

    1. Computers — Law and legislation —
    Australia. I. Fitzsimons, James, 1956–
    II. Title.

343.940999

Library of Congress Cataloging-in-Publication Data
Knight, William Peter.
    The legal environment of computing.

    Includes bibliographical references.
    1. Computers — Law and legislation. 2. Computer
contracts. I. FitzSimons, James McHarg. II. Title.
K564.C6K56   1989   343.099′9   89–18251
ISBN 0–201–41701–4   342.3999

343.0999
K71

Contents

Preface

There is no such thing as 'computer law'. At least, there is not enough of it to write a book about. It would be pretentious for lawyers to suggest that there is such a thing, or to profess expertise in such a phantom.

So what is this book about? It is about legal issues relevant to the computer industry, based upon a great body of well understood law but applied to a new industry, the computer industry, and its products. In essence, it is made up of the answers the authors have given to questions asked over and over again by people in the computer industry.

So this is not a legal treatise, and cannot go into detailed explanations of legal principles and exceptions to those principles. Also, we are not concerned with the operation of computers in the practice of law, the use of computer output in court proceedings, or of computers themselves to assist the business of courts and lawyers, all of which raise both legal and practical considerations.

This book is not, therefore, written for lawyers — except perhaps those who wish to gain more understanding of the computer industry. We have tried to explain in easily understood terms legal principles applicable with minor variations in most capitalist countries, and with which lawyers should already be familiar. Admittedly, there have been a few special changes in the law made as a result of the special demands of the computer industry, such as copyright and tax matters, but these are usually regarded as side issues in a greater body of law, and thus of interest only to specialists in the particular field they affect.

Notwithstanding this, we have included for lawyers interested in the subject a brief 'Summary of Basic Computer Technology' which was originally prepared to help judges and lawyers involved in the Apple Computer copyright cases — it is necessarily brief and does not pretend to be comprehensive. Those in the industry can skip over this summary, or read it to judge how we lawyers analyze computer products.

The first section of this book mainly consists of a summary of the principal legal issues affecting the computer industry, employment law, intellectual property, contract law and so on. We do not, however, deal with every area of law with which the computer industry may come into contact, such as the law of trusts and fiduciaries, company law and partnership law, constitutional law, or the law relating to real property.

The legal issues discussed are distinguished only by their impact on the computer industry — often in ways which are unexpected to those in the industry. An understanding of the details of any area of technology is not usually necessary to explain the law. More important is the experience of how the law interacts with an industry. It is for this reason that we have attempted in this book to explain relevant legal principles with examples, some facts from experiences in the computer industry, some derived from other industries. Some of the most striking examples of this are provided by the law of copyright. This has been a familiar topic for some years in the industry — a topic occasionally the subject of heated debate. The industry has for very good reasons sought to ensure copyright protection for computer programs and other products of the industry, that battle being fought by Apple Computer perhaps more than any other. However the industry has not been prepared for all the consequences of success — notably the special rules concerning ownership of and dealings with copyright materials. These matters are discussed in Chapters 2 and 3.

The second section of the book is dedicated to the most striking examples of the application of the law to the computer industry: computer industry contracts. As examples only, these do not attempt to be comprehensive statements of the necessary contents of the ideal contract, but a means of showing how issues are raised and dealt with in a legal framework. There are a number of books available today which are quite exhaustive in their treatment of important contract forms, licences, purchase agreements, maintenance agreements and so on. These examples are a guide to the issues only. There are, however, a few contract examples which are not so common: a reciprocal site backup agreement, facilities management and copyright assignment, for example. In addition, there is an explanation of the purposes behind the 'boilerplate' clauses of a contract, which are often overlooked, but can have a most significant impact on the workings of the main agreement between the parties.

In many ways, the examples in the first section typically deal with disputes between parties, while the contracts in the second section are examples of ways to avoid such disputes. The second section gains its purpose and justification from the first.

Knowledge of the law will not solve all the problems that arise between those in the computer industry and their customers, but will enable many such problems to be avoided. The difficulty for the industry (and for lawyers, too) is that due to inexperience, many people in the industry do not know enough of the law to ask the right questions, and lawyers do not understand enough of the computer industry to guide their clients to the rights answers. The purpose of this book then is to help in both these areas.

W. P. KNIGHT and J. M. FITZSIMONS
Sydney, Australia
April 1989

ACKNOWLEDGEMENT

The authors gratefully acknowledge the advice and assistance of members of Abbott Tout, Russell Kennedy and the Law Department of Apple Computer, Inc. However, the opinions expressed in this book are those of the authors and do not represent the opinions of Abbott Tout, Russell Kennedy or Apple Computer, Inc.

I SUMMARY OF LEGAL ISSUES

1   Introduction

Summary of basic computer technology

What is a computer?

A *computer* is a device which processes information. The information
with which it deals must first be transformed into simple sequential
instructions capable of operating the mechanisms of the computer, that
is, into 'digital information' or groups of ordered electronic impulses.
The information is then worked upon or 'processed' by the mechanisms
of the computer and then transformed back into information for the
benefit of the user of the computer.

The sources of information manipulated by the computer are:

- a keyboard or other user operated device (such as an electronic
  drawing board or a scientific instrument), a communications line
  (such as a telephone line) connected to the computer via a
  'modem' or 'multiplexor' or from some other source of data; these
  types of information are known as 'input';
- the computer programs available — both inbuilt (in ROMs, or
  'Read Only Memory' forms), and/or external to the computer
  (from magnetic diskettes, disks, or tapes in an appropriate disk or
  tape 'drive').

The principal 'mechanism' within the computer is the '*microprocessor*'
— this is the heart or 'motor' of the computer, the digital information
processing device around which all other parts of the computer: disk
drives, printers, multiplexors and all the other electric paraphernalia
operate. The information produced by the computer is called the
'output', which may be displayed on the monitors, or *VDUs* (visual
display units), to enable further manipulation by the user, or may be
printed on paper by a printer, or sent by some communication device
elsewhere. It may also be permanently stored in digital form (i.e., in a
form suitable for recall and further immediate use at a later time) by
'saving' it on a disk, diskette or tape using the 'drive' attached to the computer.

A computer carries out its tasks in accordance with the instructions of one or more computer programs, usually more than one, it being necessary to have various '*operating system*' *programs* to organize the computer's integrated functioning, under the higher direction of at least one '*application*' *program*.

What is a computer program?

Whatever its level, or function, a computer program is a series of instructions in a 'computer language' or 'code' (as distinct from mere data alone such as that created and stored by *use* of a computer program). These instructions and the language in which they are written are designed to direct the microprocessor to do the simple tasks required, tiny step by tiny step, to produce desired results. Of course the thousands of simple tasks required are done at such a great speed that the individual operations are not discernible.

Computer programs are written by those skilled in the art, using special 'languages' or codes of limited and defined vocabulary which are designed or adapted for various purposes, or are simpler, more complex or more to the taste of one programmer than another.

Computer languages

One group of such languages is that of the so called 'high level' languages. Examples of such languages are **BASIC** ('Beginners' All Purpose Instruction Code') and **Pascal**, developed as simple, easy to understand, flexible languages for all sorts of non-specialised programming tasks; **FORTRAN**, especially useful for technical, scientific or mathematical programming; and **COBOL**, supposedly designed for business programming. Another more recently developed program which has become fashionable is 'C'.

There is no limit to the number of words available in a high level language as long as those words can be transformed into the more limited number of instructions available in the 'assembly language' and 'object code' appropriate to the microprocessor of the computer being used.

The next group of programming languages is made up of assembly languages, codes devised specifically for the microprocessor upon which they must operate. For example, in the case of the Apple II computer which uses the 6502 microprocessor, the assembly language is called the '6502 Assembly Language'.

In typical assembly languages, each of the available instructions consists of just a few letters, known as 'mnemonics' as they are abbreviations of English words. In the case of 6502 Assembly Language, these mnemonics include:

- BRK which means Force Break,

- ADC which means Add memory to accumulator with Carry,
- AND which means 'AND' memory with accumulator,
- ASL which means Shift Left one bit (memory or accumulator),
- BCC which means Branch on Carry Clear,

and so on. Of course, the significance of these messages is only clear to those skilled in assembly language programming. However, the meanings in a general sense are not difficult to discern: 'break' forces a break in the program; 'accumulator shift left' causes a left-hand shift of one bit in the accumulator (a temporary memory device in the microprocessor); and so forth.

Object code

The expression 'object code' refers to the computer program as stored in some permanent form, either as an article external to the computer such as a magnetic tape or disk, or the inbuilt memory (ROM) of the computer. The former operates in a manner identical to sound recordings or tape, the latter is constituted by specially manufactured 'silicon chips' protectively encased in black plastic cases affixed to the computer's printed circuit boards (PCBs). The plastic encased silicon chips are referred to as 'ROMs' or, in the case of a special type of permanent memory device, 'EPROMs' (erasable programmable ROMs).

Although the object code never varies from one medium to another, electromagnetic storage media (diskette and tape) differ from electromechanical storage media (ROMs and EPROMs) in their *method of storage*. The former consist of an orderly array of magnetized and unmagnetized particles, the latter consist in one way or another of an orderly array of open or shut 'gates' (in older technology, these were minute fuses, fused or unfused, or in recent times layers of semi-conductive material such as silicon treated or 'doped' with impurities such as arsenic, patterned in such a way as to leave circuits or a grid of chargeable material fixed with a pattern or charges). In either case, the orderly array is a definite series of 'ONs' and 'OFFs'. Accordingly, an object code is a series of ONs and OFFs stored in one of these forms.

Object code can be read. If one could look closely enough at the physical state of the permanent memory form, one could ascertain whether, at any place, there was a magnetized or unmagnetized particle or an open or shut gate. However, this is extremely impractical and unnecessary. It is more convenient to read the machine code set out in binary or preferably hexadecimal notation.

Object code notations

By a universally accepted convention, the ONs and OFFs of object code may be represented as the numbers '0' and '1'.

Originally, microprocessors were designed to deal with a maximum of eight electrical impulses (coming to it along groups of eight electrical lines) at a time. Accordingly, such a microprocessor could process only eight ONs and OFFs at any one instant. Each of these eight ONs and OFFs were referred to as 'bits', and the basic unit of eight bits was referred to as a 'byte'. A byte may therefore be represented as, for example, 01001100, or any of 255 other arrangements of 1 and 0. Each one of these 256 arrangements may be the object code of an assembly language instruction. Thus, in the 6502 assembly language, 00100000 (all gates open except the sixth from the right) represent the instruction JSR (Jump to Subroutine). An assembly language does not require all 256 possible arrangements for its vocabulary — many may be 'NOPs', that is, 'no operation'.

Because a byte may be represented as a series of eight 0s and 1s, it may be treated as a *binary number* (that is, a number in the number system to the base of two) of eight digits. Just as the decimal system uses 10 digits, 0 to 9, the binary system uses two digits 0 and 1.

Any decimal number (that is a number in the number system to the base 10) from 0 to 255 may be represented by a byte, treating the byte as a binary number.

Example — Decimal Notation

The decimal number 65 385 is made up in the following manner:

10^4	10^3	10^2	10^1	10^0
10 000s	1000s	100s	10s	1s

$(6 \times 10\ 000) + (5 \times 1000) + (3 \times 100) + (8 \times 10) + (5 \times 1) = $ 65 385
(decimal)

Example — Binary Notation

The binary number 01001010 (which has the same numerical value as the decimal number 74) is made up in the following manner:

2^7	2^6	2^5	2^4
128s	64s	32s	16s

$(0 \times 128) \quad + \quad (1 \times 64) \quad + \quad (0 \times 32) \quad + \quad (0 \times 16) \quad +$

2^3	2^2	2^1	2^0
8s	4s	2s	1s

$(1 \times 8) \quad + \quad (0 \times 4) \quad + \quad (1 \times 2) \quad + \quad (0 \times 1) \quad = \quad$ 74
(decimal)

Thus the decimal number 0 may be represented as 00000000, the highest number that may be represented by eight digits is 255, that is, 11111111, and a number in between, say 36, is 00100100.

For each and every instruction in assembly language, or any computer language, there is one and only one equivalent binary number.

Using binary numbers as a representation of object code is cumbersome. Accordingly, when dealing with object code computer programmers usually refer to 'hexadecimal notation', or 'hex', for convenience. In other words, the same number representing an assembly language instruction can be written in decimal, binary or hexadecimal notation. Hexadecimal numbers have 16 digits, 0 and 9 and A to F, the letters A to F substituting for the decimal numbers 10 to 15.

Example — Hexadecimal Notation

The hexadecimal number 4A (which has the same numerical value as the decimal number 74) is made up in the following manner:

16^1	16^0
16s	1s
(4 × 16) +	(A [i.e., 10] × 1) = 74
	(decimal)

Source Code

The source program (in a high level language or assembly language) and object program (in ONs and OFFs) do not only consist of 'doing words', that is, verbs such as BRK (00000000), JSR (00100000), BCC (10010000). The programmers must also have subjects and objects of their verbs. These may be numbers, characters and/or 'addresses', and each of these must be converted to, transmitted, operated upon and stored, as groups of eight bits, that is, bytes.

As mentioned above, any (decimal) number from 0–255 may be represented by a byte, treating the byte as a binary number, and such number will also have a hexadecimal equivalent.

Characters, including letters of the alphabet and punctuation marks, must have object code equivalents. A common standard, that is 'built in' to be recognised by most computer microprocessors, is the ASCII (American Standard Code for Information Interchange) set. Thus the letter A is in object code 11000001 (hex C1), B is 11000010 (hex C2) and so on.

Finally, every byte in the memory of the computer, whether permanent (ROM, 'Read Only Memory') or temporary (RAM, or 'Random Access Memory') has an 'address', or 'location'. This is simply the number of the location, from 0 (the first) to whatever is the number of the last byte. The Apple II has, including the permanent memory, 65 536 locations (or 64K, 'K' being a unit of measurement of 2^{10}, or 1024), and thus has addresses numbered from 0 to 65 535.

Needless to say, these (decimal) numbers are too large to deal with in single bytes as a single byte can only represent decimal numbers up to 255. Accordingly addresses are dealt with by using two bytes. For example, location 65 385 (also referred to as −150 if counting from the end of the memory and not its beginning) is 11111111 01101001 (hex FF69).

Now we can see how a section of a program in 6502 Assembly Language is written and then converted into object code.

Example — A Computer Program

Assembly Language	English Meaning	Binary	Hexadecimal
LSR A	shift right one bit in the accumulator	01001010	4A
PHP	push processor status on stack	00001000	08
JSR GBASCALC	jump to the location of the 'GBASCALC'	00100000 00110011	
	routine saving return address	11111100 10	47F8
PLP	pull processor status from stack	00101000	28
LDA #$0F	load accumulator with memory number 15 (0F)	10101001 00001111	A9 0F
BCC RTMASK	branch on carry clear to location of the RTMASK routine	10010010 00000010	90 02
ADC #$E0	add memory number 224 (E0) to accumulator with carry	01101001 11100000	69 E0
STA MASK	store accumulator in for memory location called MASK	10000101 00101110	85 2E

As can be seen, the binary notation is very much analogous to Morse code. It should be noted that the 'source code', the information in assembly language in the first column in the above example, tends to contain a little more information in it than can simply be derived from 'disassembly' of the object code. Frequently, source code will include even more explanatory material concerning the function and direction of the program at any point, which may be difficult to unscramble from mere object code alone. This material is not translated into the object code. It is for this reason that source code is almost invariably regarded as highly confidential — it may be essential to effective support and development of the computer program over time.

Operation of a computer program

Why does the microprocessor not confuse instructions, numbers, characters and addresses?

The program always starts with an instruction, a verb. This instruction determines what is required to follow, whether a number (as in BCC), an address (as in JSR), or a character. Once the required number of bytes is obtained, the microprocessor automatically treats the next byte as an instruction.

When the computer is turned on, the computer is normally so designed that the beginning of the operating system program is automatically addressed, and then that program may be worked through to start the operations of the computer as a whole, as well as other available programs in the 'drives' of the computer.

If an instruction is issued from the keyboard, for example CALL −151 (in BASIC), by the user typing the characters on the keyboard and striking the RETURN key (or some other designated key that puts an end to the instruction, like a full stop, instructing the computer that the instruction is complete and is to be assembled into an object code instruction for the microprocessor), then, put simply, the necessary bytes are consecutively sent into the operating system's 'language' program which results in a series of instructions in machine code being issued to the microprocessor. The microprocessor acts upon the instruction CALL −151 in object code and transmits further electronic impulses to the address called, namely −151, or hexadecimal FF69 (in a small Apple II computer of 64K memory). The subroutine commencing at the location FF69 is then tripped off (this, by further instructions, results in a 'prompt' appearing on the screen, asking for the next appropriate instruction to be typed in to the computer.

Writing a computer program

Programmers write programs in much the same way as any word processor document is written: a draft may be written by hand on paper, and then typed into the computer and stored, or simply typed directly into the computer and edited before being stored.

At this stage the program is the merest data, stored in exactly the same fashion as it would be with a word processor. It may also be permanently saved on a diskette or tape. However, it cannot be operated upon and used by the microprocessor.

To make the assembly language source program 'machine readable' it must be 'assembled' into object code. This requires a computer program called an 'assembler' to convert, for example, the typed letters of 'JSR' into one byte, 00100000 (hex 20).

Once converted, the object code may again be stored on diskette or tape. Copies of the object code may then be made onto other disks or tapes, or into other forms of permanent storage like ROMs or EPROMs, by mechanical procedures.

When the source program is written in a high level language, it must first be 'compiled' into assembly language and then 'assembled' into object code. This procedure is invariably assisted by a *'compiler'* program, which works on the high level language source code stored in the temporary memory. There are a number of computer programs designed for different high level languages and microprocessors, and each will produce different assembly language/machine code results, both in the nature and order of instructions, from the same source code.

However, because of the close link between assembly language and object code, there is a one-to-one relationship between assembly language instruction and operational field, and the machine code equivalent. Assembly from assembly language to object code produces the same resultant object program every time, and the reverse process, 'disassembly', likewise.

A computer program does nothing. It is stored in a permanent form in, say, a ROM and there its instructions may be recreated in groups of electronic impulses which are sent to the microprocessor for action. In this sense, it is exactly the same as the printed page, which absorbs or reflects light to enable the eye to 'read' the page.

All programs are written to carry out certain tasks. The skill of the programmer lies in breaking up the steps necessary to achieve a desired end into the thousands of tiny steps the machine must take to achieve that end, using in aid any other programs available, either built into the computer, or external to it (on disk or tape).

We have spent a great deal of time on computer programs, their creation and operation. This is because computer programs are so commonly misunderstood by those not involved in the industry, as some kind of electrical engineering thing, rather than the product of a logical and literary art. With an understanding of computer programs, the purpose and function of computers and their peripheral devices — disk drives, printers, communications devices and terminals — become more apparent and are not difficult to appreciate. The law may be a more difficult thing to fathom.

Semiconductor chips

Silicon chips, or integrated circuits, are at the heart of the computer industry. They constitute many of the major components of computer devices, particularly the memory devices (ROMs and EPROMs) and the microprocessors (also referred to as 'central processing units', although this expression is also used of the whole computer) referred to above, but also any other circuitry which the hardware designer may wish to miniaturize by taking advantage of this technology. By and large, most attention in this area is focussed on the microprocessor, and to a lesser extent on the custom designed logic circuits, as these embody greater creative effort than do memory chips, or creative effort of a different kind, as memory chips are largely constituted by arrays of 'on/off' switches awaiting setting by data or programs.

Silicon chips are made possible by the use of substances known as 'semiconductors'. Semiconductors are so useful primarily because of their unusual physical properties. They can either conduct electricity or insulate from it, depending upon their physical state. By applying a voltage across the semiconductor, or by adding various elements or compounds known as impurities (by 'doping'), it is possible to alter this state. By doping small adjacent regions on and slightly below the surface of a semiconducting material with various materials, it is possible to suitably change the electrical properties of each of these regions. In this fashion an integrated circuit containing transistors, diodes, resistors and capacitors together with the electrical connections necessary to form a complete electronic device can be fabricated.

Transistors, the main building block of all electrical devices, were developed in the late 1940s to replace vacuum tubes in signal switching and amplification. Although transistors were a significant improvement on vacuum tubes, both in the amount of space and amount of power required (and they were more rugged and more reliable), they were originally manufactured as individual components which then had to be soldered together. This need to solder components together imposed limitations on size and reliability. This led to the development of *printed circuit boards* (PCBs), manufactured by laying out the connections on a standard 'board' instead of having to solder each connection. It was a development of this technique which led to the integrated circuit.

With permanent metalization patterns replacing soldered leads, the reliability, as well as the miniaturization, of integrated circuits greatly exceeds that of non-integrated circuit transistors. Integrated circuits containing up to a million separate transistors are today quite common.

An integrated circuit is made from layers of silicon crystal, bonded together and resting upon a silicon base, connected by gold filaments to the circuits accessing and using the chip. The whole is fixed in a protective plastic case which is connected to a printed circuit board by 'legs', or 'pins', which are in fact the conducting lines connecting with the gold filaments which are in turn connected to the silicon chip.

The circuits which comprise each layer of the chip are first designed and drawn onto a '*mask*'. Initially, this mask is of a size that is visible to the human eye — it is rather like a blueprint, a circuit diagram, or a printed circuit board drawing. The mask is then photoreduced until the circuits depicted are of the microscopic size used in chips. Each layer of silicon in the chip is manufactured by taking a wafer of silicon and coating it with a thin layer of silicon dioxide. This oxide layer is then coated with a light sensitive, acid resistant material known as a 'resist'. The mask work is then placed over the silicon wafer and an ultraviolet light is shone upon it. The ultraviolet light passes through the transparent portions of the mask and polymerizes the resist lying beneath these transparent portions. When the wafer is immersed in a solvent and the unpolymerized resist is removed, the polymerized resist on the wafer is in the same pattern as that of the transparent portions of the mask. Then follow several more steps in which various impurities may be added to form regions with a particular electronic property and an insulating layer before the next layer is added and a new mask for that layer used.

For those familiar with the methods of modern engraving, or even silk screen printing, the similarity between these forms of activity and the process of creating and using masks will be evident.

The final product, then, consists of a number of layers of doped silicon, silicon dioxide and metalizations in which each layer has been defined by a particular mask.

In the future, it may be possible to create a chip without using a mask, for instance, by use of an electron beam under the control of a computer. An existing development is 'magnetic bubble' technology which is really a new class of integrated circuit which uses only a single layer.

The development and exploitation of integrated circuits is crucial to the advance of information technology. By miniaturization, they have made possible the impossible in terms of speed, bulk, energy saving and cost — they are essential to robotics, artificial intelligence and 'super computers', as well as the millions of other devices from computers to calculators that are flooding the world.

How the law works

Common law and statutes

Not all the law is written down in the statutes of the legislature — whether a parliament, diet, or congress. Preceding all statutory law, and the background against which it is all written, is the general body of law built up by time, the traditional law expounded and interpreted by judges. In countries with an English legal tradition, this is called the 'common law'.

For example, most of the law of contract is common law, on which statutes have operated in a number of narrow, specialized ways. Centuries before anti-trust law in the United States, judges applying common law principles had ruled as illegal attempts to prevent employees and business people from exercising their skills and trades in competition with their former employers or purchasers of their businesses.

If common law is not written, how does one know what it is? The common law is to be found in the judgments of courts, which interpret the statements of courts before them, referred to as 'precedents'. The law of precedent is something of an art — sometimes a precedent is binding on a judge, if it is an opinion on the law which gave rise to the decision of an appeal court higher in the court hierarchy — unless it is considered too old to be meaningful for modern circumstances. Usually, however, precedents are merely a flexible guide to judges, showing how other judges have dealt with similar circumstances, which for the sake of consistency a judge will follow unless it would be an injustice to do so.

Sometimes the common law is codified. In one sense, this is what has happened when textbook writers have attempted a definitive statement of the law — and these, with time, are often very highly regarded. In more recent times there have been attempts to state the law in legal 'codes', such as the *Uniform Commercial Code* (UCC) and the *Restatement of the Law of Torts*, both of the United States, which have been largely ascribed to and have taken on more or less statutory force.

As well as providing the 'substantive law' — the law of contracts, torts, employment, confidentiality, restraint of trade, defamation (libel and slander), and so on — the common law is also the source of the '*procedural law*', that is the law governing procedures, and the granting of damages, injunctions and other remedies discussed below.

Upon this very large body of common law, governments and government authorities impose their statutes, ordinances, regulations and by-laws. By this means, the common law is either added to or changed. Examples of additions to the common law are the protection of publishers and authors by copyright law (in England dating from the beginning of the eighteenth century), and the protection of inventors by patent law. Examples of changes to the existing law are the operation of consumer protection law on contracts, and trade mark and unfair competition law on the old law of 'passing-off'.

Of course, judges must apply the statute law as well as the common law. Sometimes, statute law is far from easy to interpret and apply — as anyone who has read the taxation statutes will only too readily agree. In fact, some statutes are deliberately written in the vaguest terms, like the anti-trust laws, so that the complex and subtle social and economic principles they seek to express (and which are too difficult to write down) may be interpreted and put into effect by judges, perhaps aided by expert opinion and a common sense appreciation of the purposes of such laws.

For these reasons, rules of precedent are as important in the development of a body of interpretation around statute law, as with the common law.

All this makes interpreting the laws a combination of the common law, and the statutes and judgments of courts interpreting them. But one thing must be clearly understood — the body of law is a fixed 'data set', like a set of pigeon holes. It is not the case that there is a remedy for every perceived wrong — the rôle of lawyers is to find the right pigeon hole(s) for a given set of circumstances. The law is rarely 'made' to fit a new problem.

Remedies

Before talking about remedies, it should be understood that remedies are the orders a court may make to correct a wrong done. Such orders are usually preceded by protracted and grossly expensive court proceedings. The expense of litigation (fighting a dispute out in the courts), must be measured not only in huge legal costs, but in the administrative burden in lost time and personnel required for the proper management of litigation. For these reasons, the best remedy of all is one's own, preventing disputes. One of the principal ways of preparing for and preventing disputes is in writing sound and well considered contracts. It is for this reason that a great portion of this book is devoted to a few sample contracts, and the rest may be regarded as an explanation of why the contracts contain what they do.

Above all, the best time to write a contract is at the beginning of a commercial relationship when all the parties are friendly with one another. That is just the time to write down what should happen if, and when, friends fall out — this is not negative thinking, it is just commercial common sense. In addition, there is nothing wrong with planning ahead for any eventuality, not necessarily dispute, and writing a contract can help in this also.

The remedies the courts may give may be divided into two broad classes: damages and other monetary orders and injunctions and other mandatory orders.

Damages

Under the old common law, the courts in most circumstances could only make orders for payment of money, or damages. So for most legal wrongs — breach of contract, negligence, breach of a duty of confidentiality as well as breaches of statutory law — the courts will award damages unless persuaded they should exercise one of their other powers.

What damages can a court award? Damages are only compensation for actual and demonstrable financial loss arising from the wrong done. Except in rare cases, discussed below, damages are not punitive — if they were, this would amount to giving a successful litigant a financial windfall out of the wrong done. Nor do damages usually compensate for hurt feelings, or a sense of vexation or injustice done.

Damages are calculated in different ways, depending on the nature of the claim. They are always limited to losses directly flowing from the wrong done, but in the case of a breach of contract or similar commercial matters, even direct losses will not be compensated unless they are the sort of losses that would be regarded as the natural consequences in the usual course of events arising from a breach of the contract. 'Exceptional losses' will not be recoverable unless they could have been expected by the parties to the contract at the time of entering upon the contract.

By comparison, the measure of damages in the case of claims in tort (that is legal wrongs, such as negligence, not depending on a contractual relationship), the losses recoverable can be much greater, for damages extend to all losses of a kind reasonably foreseeable at the time of injury. In this method of compensation, exceptional losses may well be recoverable, as long as they are of the type considered to be 'reasonably foreseeable'.

Example — Contractual Damages

ABC Computer Systems, Inc. has agreed to supply high powered computer systems to a bank for its on-line banking transactions and commits itself to a fixed delivery date. Unknown to ABC, at the time of entering upon the contract, the bank has agreed with an insurance company to provide a highly profitable bureau service to commence on the date of expiry of the insurance subsidiary's present arrangements. After entering upon the supply contract, ABC fails to deliver.

Here ABC may well be liable for the losses the bank incurs in its banking business due to the delay in installation, but cannot be held liable for the loss of profits the bank suffers due to the failure of its undisclosed bureau plans. These losses are 'exceptional' and not contemplated at the time of entering the contract. Needless to say, the loss incurred by the insurance company is a perfect example of an economic loss not recoverable by it at all (except from the bank, that is, unless the bank has a 'force majeure' clause in its contract — see Chapter 7). It has no contractual relationship with ABC and so cannot sue in contract, and, for reasons discussed in Chapter 9 below, it is unlikely to find a remedy in 'tort' either. The insurance company has no legal 'pigeon holes' upon which to rely.

This example serves to illustrate yet a further point. Damages may also be limited by the bank's failure to 'mitigate its loss' — that is, even if ABC were aware of the bank's bureau arrangements with the insurance company at the time of entering upon the contract, the bank may still be denied part of its claim if the bank could have made other arrangements, such as an alternative bureau service, to minimise its liability to the insurance company, in which case the damages payable by ABC would be limited to the cost of providing such alternative service.

Example — Tortious Damages

XYZ Solutions Limited advertises its expert medical software which calibrates the administration of certain drugs to patients. Naturally, it has *professional indemnity insurance up to $ 1 000 000.00. Through the negligence of one of its programmers, there is a significant error in output in a certain combination of circumstances. Dr X uses the system to deal with his patients who, unknown to XYZ Solutions, consist mainly of Arab oil sheikhs. Due to XYZ's negligence, an injured sheikh makes a claim for $ 4 000 000.00. This is known to lawyers as the 'eggshell skull' problem — that is, XYZ is liable notwithstanding the exceptional susceptibility to loss of the victim of its negligence.*

A further point to note about tort law is that it does occasionally allow 'exceptional' damages. For example, in assault and defamation cases, 'aggravated damages', where monetary loss does not reflect the special circumstances of a victim, may be granted, but these are not often of relevance to the computer industry. More important are punitive or 'exemplary' damages. Such damages have been available in very exceptional circumstances in the common law from an early date but they have always been limited to conduct where a person has been guilty of malice, or such 'contumelious disregard' of another's rights that he should be punished. Accordingly, such damages again tend to be raised in matters such as deceit, defamation and assault — but have received statutory recognition in the law of copyright (see Chapter 3), and triple damages in the US anti-trust law (see Chapter 10).

It should be noted that a number of jurisdictions in the United States do allow much more substantial awards of aggravated and exemplary damages.

From the above it will be apparent that litigation is rarely worth the cost, the time, the uncertainty and the trouble, as one will never be as well off as if the wrong had never been done, or had been avoided.

Injunctions and other mandatory orders

There are cases where damages are not enough. Damages may repay what has been lost, but if the wrong doer continues the wrong there seems no point in suing over and over again.

For this reason, when damages are an inadequate remedy, the courts have devised mandatory orders, including the injunction. By such orders, the court may forbid the doing of an act, or, in certain special cases, order the doing of certain things, like the execution of the stipulations in documents, or delivery of goods. One thing, however, the court will never order, is the provision of personal services, into which category may fall a wide variety of activities of relevance to the computer industry, such as programming, training, maintenance and support services, and even 'consultation', such as is a common requirement of marketing and product development agreements.

The power of the injunctive order is that, unlike an order for damages, refusal to obey the order is regarded as contempt of court, punishable by immediate imprisonment until the contempt is 'purged', or by a fine, at the court's discretion.

It is by reason of this very power, and concern that courts should not lightly exercise authority that may be flouted, that courts require very good reasons to grant an injunction, and conduct of the applicant may disentitle it to the remedy. Thus if the applicant delays unduly in seeking the remedy, or is himself guilty of some wrongdoing which places the wrongdoer at a disadvantage, the court will refuse the remedy.

There are special categories of injunctions known as interim or interlocutory orders. These are issued, occasionally as urgent relief, even without the wrongdoer's presence, pending the final hearing of a claim for final orders. As indicated above, the course of litigation may be very protracted indeed, and if one of the parties shows that it should have the benefit of an order preserving the *status quo*, then the court will granting such an order. There is one very important condition often attached to the grant of such interim orders, that is, the person seeking it must guarantee to make good any damage suffered by the person subject to the order, in the event that the person to whom it is granted ultimately fails in the action.

Limitation periods

In the case of nearly all legal actions, legal proceedings must be commenced within a certain period from the time of the wrongdoing, or the damage suffered. The purpose of these rules is to prevent excessive delay, with the possibility of evidence 'going stale'. The effect of these limitation periods is that the right of action is completely lost after such a period has expired.

The length of such limitation periods varies — they can be as brief as six or twelve months in the case of claims against government bodies in some countries, but they are usually periods such as three, six or twelve years. In every case, a person who feels he or she has suffered a wrong should seek advice promptly in order to ensure that appropriate action is taken before the expiry of any relevant limitation period.

The courts

The court system can seem to be of byzantine complexity. As well as courts of appeal at various levels, the courts in which action must be commenced, 'courts of first instance', vary enormously.

There are 'all purpose' courts in which familiar claims — commercial matters, contracts, torts and so on — are brought, which are usually divided by the value of the claim — small debts courts on the lowest level, with a jurisdiction limited to a certain amount of money, up through various levels to the highest court, in which actions may not be commenced unless they are valued at over a certain amount. These courts may also be divided by their powers — the lesser courts often do not have powers to grant mandatory orders.

In addition, there are courts with special jurisdictions — industrial courts and tribunals dealing with patent and trade marks, special administrative courts and tribunals, and so on. Frequently, special statutory powers are administered solely by these separate courts.

Finally, to add the last complication, courts may be divided between state or provincial, and federal courts — each dealing with the laws of the special jurisdiction represented. It can be extremely difficult electing in which court or courts to commence, in order to optimize the remedies available in a given situation.

The frequently encountered difficulty with all courts is that the judges lack knowledge of the computer industry and its products. Frequently, this is of no concern, but in many cases the cost and uncertainties of litigation could be greatly reduced if some knowledge on the part of the tribunal could be relied upon.

Occasionally, judges may be assisted by specially appointed court experts, or by expert evidence (usually highly contradictory), but the rules governing this, and their efficacy, vary greatly from court to court, and country to country.

Arbitration

There is only one court which may be constituted by a decision maker by choice. That is an arbitration court.

The parties to a contract, or parties already in dispute, may agree that a dispute will be determined by an independent arbitrator appointed by them. By the same agreement they may decide not only who the arbitrator shall be, or how the arbitrator shall be selected, but also all the procedures to be adopted, even how evidence will be obtained and dealt with, the use of experts and lawyers, and even that neither party will go to court unless and until the dispute has been arbitrated and an award given. To save thinking out all this detail, there are a number of Arbitration Codes which may be referred to. These Codes are normally related to national and international bodies which may provide arbitrators and facilities for conducting arbitrations if called upon to do so.

In most countries there are statutes dealing with arbitrations, which often provide for enforcement of arbitration awards, and sometimes awards of foreign arbitrations under certain circumstances. These statutes also provide certain basic 'default options' in the event that parties to an arbitration agreement have failed to consider and deal with some important issues. In considering arbitration in any country, the presence of these laws must be carefully taken into account.

There is one warning to be observed in relation to arbitration.

Arbitrators may have knowledge of the industry, but frequently they are not as skilled in dispute resolution or determination as judges. Despite all the sets of rules to assist arbitrators in procedures for arbitrations, and the availability of arbitrators supposedly specially trained to deal with dispute resolution, arbitrations everywhere are vexed by a tendency to become grossly protracted and even more expensive than the courts by virtue of the inability of arbitrators to dispose of procedural issues before getting to the heart of the matter. The absence of legal representation frequently sought by arbitrators and the rules of arbitration can make this problem worse, not better. Finally, if one of the parties does not agree with the outcome of the arbitration (there is always someone, usually the loser), then often the dispute may end up in the courts anyway!

Notwithstanding these words of caution, arbitration should be considered in every contract, and the manner of selection of an arbitrator may be the most important issue in determining whether arbitration should apply. Properly run arbitration may well prevent litigation and assist in resolution or determination of a dispute between commercial parties.

International law

There is no system of international law. When lawyers speak of 'international law' they generally refer to two types of legal system, which are known as 'public international law' and 'private international law'.

Public international law

Public international law consists of a mass of multilateral and bilateral treaties and conventions among nations, on a diverse range of issues, some sponsored by the United Nations, the European Economic Commission and such bodies, others answering specific needs, which are adopted by member countries into their own law. Multilateral treaties include the familiar GATT (General Agreement on Tarriffs and Trade), the Geneva Convention (concerning conduct of war), the Warsaw Convention (concerning responsibility for loss during air transport), the Treaty of Rome (concerning trade between members of the EEC), the Bretton Woods Agreement (concerning international currency trade) and many others, concerning ownership of the seabed, taxation of foreign nationals and so on. Bilateral treaties can be of very broad significance, such as that between the United States and Taiwan concerning mutuality of treatment of nationals, or very specific, such as the many agreements concerning deportation of foreign criminals.

There are international treaties concerning the recognition of foreign arbitration awards, and judgements or court processes of other countries, which can be of great importance in deciding where to take action in a dispute. It is of little value getting a judgement or award in one country, if it will not be recognized in the country of the person against whom it has been made.

Most importantly for an international computer industry, there are treaties concerning the recognition of intellectual property, which are referred to in Chapters 3 and 5 below, and most recently a United Nations Convention on International Contracts for the Sale of Goods, referred to in Chapter 7.

The efficacy of such treaties depends upon their implementation in the national laws of each country acceding to them and, of course, the number of countries which decide to accede to them — membership of the treaty organizations is far from universal, and there can be some surprising omissions. For example, there are few parties as yet to the United Nations contract convention, and until recently, the United States refused to join the Berne Convention, the most important copyright treaty with the widest membership, notwithstanding its insistence upon foreign recognition of copyright in the works of its nationals.

Private international law

This branch of the law is not really international at all. Sometimes referred to as 'conflict of laws', it concerns those parts of national laws which deal with the application of foreign legal principles in a national court. For example, when a person in one country deals with another person in another country, with a view to entering a binding contract, *which* national laws apply in deciding whether a binding contract has been made, and which law applies in interpreting the contract? In one country, the contract may be illegal, but in the other it may not. In determining damages for breach of contract, one country may permit punitive damages, and the other's courts may not consider such a thing. If, in a contract, the parties choose to agree that Californian law will govern the contract, how much, if any, of the body of Californian law will be applied by the local court, assuming it has the expertise available to do so?

This is far too complex an area to examine here, as the laws of each country do vary. There are, however, some general principles. In general, procedural law, including the law of damages as well as other remedies, will be determined by the law of the country in which action is taken. Substantive legal issues will be determined by the law of the country with the closest connection to the cause of action — the place of the contract, the place of the wrong done and so on. Generally, the courts will not apply selective pieces of law, but will attempt to apply an entire, consistent body of law where appropriate.

General comments

As with computers themselves, the basic principles of operation of the law may be relatively simply described; however the actual operation of those principles in complex systems, or modern commercial communities, can be devilishly complicated.

When considering the legal issues described in this book, it is always wise to bear in mind that legal rights may be real enough, but their application in a legal system, with all the considerations of appropriate procedures and the availability of remedies to match the wrong suffered, with the legal costs associated, may be very uncertain. No better advice can be given than to arm oneself with awareness of the legal issues, and avoid dispute with the right questions to good legal advisers, and sound contractual procedures.

2 Employees and contractors

What's the difference?

There is a difference. Simply put, it is this: the employment relationship, the relationship of 'master' and 'servant', has for so long been an essential part of the fabric of society that there has evolved over time an enormous body of law concerning the benefits and obligations of each of the parties to the relationship. This law has tended to be coloured by the antique notion that 'servants' are of an inferior social order to 'masters'.

Lawyers have sought to characterize the employment relationship as being constituted by a '*contract of employment*'. In fact, it is in many ways very different from the normal contractual relationship, and far more like other legal relationships, such as marriage. Just as with marriages, there are very few expressly negotiated terms agreed between the parties. The law, not satisfied with such an absence of rules, has imposed a number of 'implied terms' on the contract of employment, even though most of them do not remotely comply with the rules of contract law relating to implied terms (see Chapter 7, 'Implied terms'). The law of contract arose from the transactions of the merchant middle classes and hence is ill equipped to deal with employment, a different area of human affairs.

Contractors, too, have been with us from early days. Artisans and tradespeople, such as stonemasons, painters, watchmakers and others, have always agreed to carry out specific tasks for a certain period, or until a certain result or product was produced. Such transactions however have always been regarded as being between social equals, at least, between two people capable of striking a bargain, and so fall squarely into the familiar realms of contract law.

Because of this, in comparison with the employment relationship, there are very few 'implied terms' invariably applied to contracts with contractors.

It has been a feature particularly of the software side of the computer industry that a number of important distinctions between the legal status of employees and contractors have been overlooked. In many countries there are the benefits of flexible income tax planning when receiving fees for services rendered as a contractor or consultant, instead of a salary or wages as an employee. However, just as important is the sense of independence in being a contractor, and status in a new found profession — just as surgeons in hospitals keep their independence while being retained by a particular hospital. There are many degrees of independence in fact; many 'contractors' in the computer industry are to all appearances 'employees' and behave accordingly.

In this chapter, we will discuss the implied terms of employment, and their consequences, and note the possible consequence of the entire absence of these from the contractors' agreement.

The employment relationship

In addition to the 'express' terms of the contract of employment, matters such as salary, fringe benefits, holidays and sick leave which are more or less negotiated, whether individually or collectively, the 'implied terms' incorporated in employment contracts in most countries, unless the contrary is agreed upon, include the following:

Duties of the employer

(a)   *The employer shall pay the employee at least the agreed wages at the agreed frequency.*

This may seem trite, but it is important to realize that, because as we shall see, the employment relationship is a '24 hour a day' one, as long as the employee holds himself or herself out for work, the employer cannot refuse or delay payment of the employee's wages if the employee refuses to do certain tasks. The employee may be responsible for reimbursing the employer for any losses suffered as a result of refusing to obey lawful instructions, but cannot be denied his or her wages.

(b)   *The employer shall provide a safe and secure working environment.*

The employer will be liable to any losses or injury suffered by an employee 'in the course of employment' arising from an unsafe or insecure working environment. Unfortunately, in many countries the view was taken that the employee was entitled to and had a duty to the employer and fellow employees to take steps to eliminate the danger or insecurity if it arose. So the effect of this duty on the employer often was only to require that the employer promptly summon medical attention or other assistance when necessary. It is for this reason that many countries have special 'Workman's Compensation' law, and compulsory insurance, to ensure that the responsibility at least for physical injury rests firmly with the employer.

(c)   *The employer shall indemnify the employee against liability and expenses incurred in the course of employment.*

This is a very important duty. It means that an employee must be reimbursed expenses incurred in carrying out his or her general duties or specific instructions, even if they were not contemplated by the employer as being necessary, so long as the employee behaved reasonably. Of course, this does not extend to travelling to and from the place of employment. It also means that an employee who causes loss or injury to someone in the course of employment can look to the employer to pay the cost, however alarming this may be. A word of caution to employees, however — breach of the duty to obey instructions may, in some countries, mean that the employer can look to the employee to help with paying the bills! This important matter is discussed further below.

(d)   *The employer shall at all times treat the employee with proper courtesy and respect.*

This is considered the corollary of the duty of 'fidelity', or good faith and honesty, discussed below. It entitles the employee to regard himself or herself as improperly dismissed if the employer insults or humiliates the employee. It is considered essential that an employee and an employer regard each other with confidence that inspires obedience, if not respect.

It will be observed that these general duties on the employer are rather sparse, and do not include a number of matters which employees often assume as their 'right'. For example, the employer has no duty to provide a reference to a meritorious employee.

Duties of the Employee

(a)   *The employee shall at all times show good faith and honesty to the employer.*

This is a 'catch-all' requirement that forbids such things as giving false time records or lying about the performance of any work, or even giving false references before employment, and has extended to matters such as seduction of employees. Duties to be diligent, competent and careful are positive aspects of this obligation.

(b)   *The employee shall at all times act in the best interests of the employer.*

This is a most important and often overlooked aspect of the employee's ' duty of fidelity'. At its most severe, this duty requires that every opportunity for gain offered the employee 'in the course of employment' should be exploited by the employee to the benefit of the employer. As all the proceeds of the employee's labours belong to the employer, including those gained in breach of this duty, the remedies of the employer are very severe, as we shall see.

(c)   *The employee shall at all times in the course of employment exercise due care and skill consistent with the responsibilities for which he was employed.*

When an employee takes on employment he or she effectively warrants that he or she possesses the skill called for to carry it out. This does not mean that a disappointing employee can be sued for damages, but it does mean that he or she may be held liable for negligence resulting in loss to the employer. This is discussed further below.

(d)   *The employee shall at all times and during working hours obey the reasonable and lawful instructions of the employer.*

The requirement of reasonableness is an objective, not subjective, standard. In other words, the standard is set by the courts, not by what either employer or employee may consider reasonable at the time. Very little guidance can be given because every circumstance is different. In the extreme case, of course, it is reasonable to refuse an instruction where it exposes the employee, or any other person, to risk of injury.

Depending on local laws protecting employment, breach of any of these duties by the employee may entitle the employer to summarily dismiss the employee, that is, with no period of notice. Furthermore, in certain cases the employer may sue the employee for damages. It goes without saying that the rights of the employee to terminate his or her own employment upon breach of one of the employer's duties is something of a hollow power, and the employer's duties do not lend themselves to legal claims on the part of employees for damages. This fact only emphasizes that much of this law has survived from the days of 'master and servant' into the modern employment relationship.

The 'course of employment'

It will be observed that each of the duties discussed above depends very much on the notion of 'the course of employment'. Under various names, this concept of 'work-related' activity is an important part of the definition of the duties of employment, particularly for the employee. It is a very broad concept in the law. One thing is clear, above the level of the unskilled worker, it extends far beyond the time the employee spends on the employer's premises, or is going about the employer's business, but how far it extends is not always clear.

It is in the nature of employment that it is a 24 hour a day relationship. So, for example, the traditional law would have it that 'mooonlighting', that is having a second job, is a breach of the employment contract because the employee's full time and skills should be devoted to the employer. However, 'moonlighting', is often accepted in unskilled workers. This illustrates that the 'course of employment' is not defined by mere time. Rather, it is defined in terms of the nature of the employee's skills, duties and seniority. A junior programmer or technician will only be acting in 'the course of employment' at a time when he or she is involved in programming of the nature he or she is employed to do, whether or not it is during office hours or for the benefit of the employer. A person at managerial level, however, may be regarded as being 'in the course of employment' *at all hours and places*.

Let us now consider how the implied terms of employment contracts affect the computer industry, and give some examples.

Conflict of interest

As suggested above, some of the most surprising consequences of employment arise under this duty. It is not limited to a duty not to deceive the employer, for example by putting in false time recording reports, but also a positive duty to disclose matters of importance to the employer.

So also, the employee has an obligation to act at all times in the interests of the employer, and this means that the employee cannot put himself or herself in a position of conflict with the interests of the employer.

Accordingly, an employee who gains information that would be valuable to the employer has an obligation not only to disclose it to the employer, but also not to use it to his own benefit or for anyone else's benefit unless the employer expressly permits it.

An employee who sees that his or her employer is not taking advantage of an opportunity cannot take up that opportunity, *even by leaving the employment*, unless he or she has first obtained the *express* permission of the employer without concealing any aspect of the opportunity. It is not enough for the employee simply to know, or be confident, that the employer would have no interest in the opportunity, or even that the employer is not in a position for any reason to take up the opportunity. The employee must actually take the matter to the employer first and seek the employer's permission.

Example —————————————————————————————————————

Richard Rowe is the Manager of Information Systems at XYZ Insurance Inc. As such, it is his responsibility to engage contractors, and call for tenders on software and hardware requirements of the insurance company.

The company requires the development of software supplied to its agents to allow them to use policy and premium data supplied by the company. He considers that he could do the job better and cheaper than most people, so he arranges with a friend who has a software development company that it will be contracted to supply the software and he will do the design work and they will share the profits. He is of the view that as a result, the insurance company will get a better, cheaper product.

Clearly, Mr Rowe and his friend are gaining the benefits of a 'secret profit' for which he is liable to account to his employer. He is liable even if the insurance company is getting a better deal than it would get by independent tender. Oddly enough, the software house is probably also liable to account.

This example illustrates something we shall see again, that an employer can in fact gain a windfall from the employee's conflict of interest. This arises from the notion that an employer is a master of his employee's time and the products of his labours.

Further examples are provided by customer lists and other confidential data acquired by employees and taken by them to their new work or to start their own business, and 'poaching' fellow employees to work on outside projects. Again, these cases show a conflict of interest arising where the employee is gathering information for his own benefit during his employment, albeit usually in its latter stages. We shall consider this problem again below.

Ownership of products

The employer owns all products of the employee produced in the course of employment.

It follows from the comments above that the employee devotes all his time and skill to the employer, that copyright in works created by the employee in the course of employment, and the right to secure patent rights in relation to inventions devised by the employee in the course of employment, belong to the employer.

Example

John Doe is an employee of ABC Systems Limited, a company engaged in licensing financial accounting packages for use on mini and mainframe computers. He is a programmer whose duties are to work in error correction and system development of the financial accounting package licensed by the company. He observes that this support and development program is not very well managed within ABC and he hits upon an idea for a project management system. As a hobby, in his spare time, he writes a suite of programs for the project planning, modelling and management to be used with a popular brand of microcomputer. When it is completed, he considers it highly marketable and resigns from ABC to devote more time to it.

It would dismay many in the computer industry to realize that John Doe should have disclosed his idea to his employer and his employer may be entitled to claim the proceeds or part of the benefit of John Doe's 'invention'. Even if John Doe had offered the package to ABC and it had refused, he still may not be 'off the hook' unless he expressly makes known what he intends to do and obtains ABC's permission to go ahead with it. This apparently harsh result arises from the fact that what John Doe did in his 'spare time' was in the nature of what he was employed to do — even though his 'homework' was on a micro and probably in a different language from that which he used at work — and furthermore, his idea was generated by problems he perceived in the project management at work — even though he was not employed as a project manager.

This conclusion would probably be different if John Doe's software were entirely unrelated to his work, such as a games package, but these cases would always be difficult to decide.

This example again shows the employer gaining a windfall benefit and it shows that this opportunity may well extend beyond the end of the employee's employment. It may seem unfair that this right on the part of the employer is not matched by any obligation to give the employee any compensation or royalty in return for ownership of the products of his 'extracurricular' efforts, but this is so in many countries.

Responsibility for misconduct and negligence

The characterization of the employment relationship as a contract has lead to one very strange consequence.

As mentioned above, on the one hand it is the responsibility of the employer to indemnify the employee against liability for loss and damage caused in the course of employment, but on the other, it is a term of the contract of employment that the employee shall exercise due skill and care, so that the employee can be sued for breach of contract not only if the employee is guilty of misconduct, but also if the employee fails to exercise due skill, that is, is negligent.

The strangeness of this result is best illustrated by an English case unrelated to the computer industry, *Lister* v *Romford Ice*.

This case concerned a humble employee, a driver of the Romford Ice van. Apparently he was negligent in backing his van over a relative, whereupon the relative made a claim on the employer for compensation for his injuries. Romford Ice was undoubtedly liable for the negligence of its employee, but sued its employee to indemnify it (or its insurers) for the amount payable to the relative. The English House of Lords found that the employee was in breach of his contract of employment — he was employed to drive the van carefully, and had failed to do so — and ordered that the employee reimburse the employer.

This was a case where two legal principles came into sharp conflict, the old law of liability of the master for the acts of the servant and the new law of the 'contract of employment'. Legislation has been introduced in a number of countries to counteract this result, although it should be borne in mind that it does not necessarily extend to deliberate breaches of employment, as when a specific directive of an employer is disobeyed.

Example

Credit Data Limited gathers credit data and supplies it to its shareholders which are banks, finance companies and the like. It gathers its information from its shareholders and also from sources such as debt collection agencies, court records and so on. All data entered into its database is backed by hard copy of the source of the data. All credit reports issued by the company must be approved by Jane Doe, a Manager of Credit Data, and it is an express instruction of Credit Data that she must have the hard copy verification of any adversely reported incident.

Through the negligence of a data entry operater, Richard Rowe, a code indicating that liquidation proceedings had been commenced against the ABC Industrial Company is entered against the name of ABC in the database.

Jane Doe is subsequently requested to approve a report including this adverse data and recommending against credit terms, which she does, without checking the hard copy which would have corrected the error. ABC finds itself financially in great difficulty as a result of this, and loses a substantial contract. ABC sues Credit Data for defamation, seeking substantial damages.

Credit Data may not be entitled to seek compensation from Richard Rowe, because he was merely negligent, but Jane Doe disobeyed a direct instruction, and it is a term of the contract of employment that the employee will obey such instructions. Accordingly, if Credit Data, or its insurer, is inclined to do so, it may seek compensation from Jane Doe. If there is no legislation protecting Richard Rowe from action, he may also be sued by Credit Data for his negligence.

Termination of employment and statute law affecting employment

Under the old law of master and servant, the employer has the right to dismiss an employee without notice or payment of wages in lieu, if the employee breaks the contract of employment. In addition, an employee's employment could be terminated at any time, for no reason, on 'reasonable notice'. What is 'reasonable notice' depends on a number of factors, usually a multiple or the normal payment period — weekly, fortnightly, monthly, or whatever it may be — and the seniority of the employee. An unskilled employee paid weekly may be entitled to only a week's notice, whereas a managing director paid monthly may be entitled to three to six month's notice, or in exceptional cases, twelve months.

Usually, no allowance would be made for the age of the employee, or years of service, or the difficulties of obtaining new employment, except in the most severe cases.

Of course, there being no duty on the part of the employer to provide work, the employer's duty to give reasonable notice of termination is equally satisfied by giving a payment of money equal to the wages for the same period as the required notice, and ordering the employee 'out of the door' — a very common occurrence where an employee occupies a sensitive position, such as a programmer, salesperson, or manager.

This state of the law has had many harsh consequences, particularly for less senior employees. For example, even if an employee were wrongfully dismissed without notice or payment in lieu, since he or she is probably only entitled to wages for a month, or at the most two, it is not worthwhile for the employee to undertake expensive and time consuming litigation for such a small sum.

This is still the law in many countries. However, in most cases the severity of the common law has been alleviated, although mainly for unionized labour and hence this is often of no relevance to the computer industry. For example, in the United Kingdom, an employer is obliged in all cases to give notice of termination in accordance with a formula which sets a minimum and increases that minimum according to years of service. In addition, there are legal controls on 'unfair dismissal', and there are established special tribunals with a simpler, cheaper procedure for dealing with employee disputes outside union–management collective bargaining arrangements. In the United States, the general law has developed so that the rigours of an unfair dismissal may result in higher awards of damages, taking into account not only a 'reasonable' period of notice, but also other factors such as the damage to the employee's reputation and the difficulty of obtaining substitute employment.

In this century, employment has been the subject of a great deal of legislative intervention. Many countries have statues regulating minimum terms and conditions of employment, in such matters as weekly earnings and other matters, but generally these are still of little relevance to the computer industry. In addition, there are employment protection laws, which affect all employees, which prescribe minimum annual leave, redundancy and such matters. Finally, many countries have sex and racial discrimination laws, workers' compensation, provident fund and superannuation provisions.

With the special tribunals and courts introduced to enforce these laws, employment can be a complex, difficult and costly matter for employers.

Contractors

Employees and contractors are quite different things. In the language of lawyers, which leads to endless confusion, employees commit all their services for an indefinite period — so this is a 'contract for services' — whereas contractors commit specific skills for a particular time or for a particular result — so this is a 'contract for service'.

There is very little statute law affecting contractors. In other words, by entering into a relationship of contractor and principal rather than employee and employer, the parties may inadvertently lose benefits as well as disadvantages of the law of employment.

Implied terms and conditions of a contractor

Except for an implied term to use reasonable skill and care, none of the terms implied in every contract of employment would be implied by the general law in a contract for service.

The consequences of this are worth noting. Unless there is a contract which specifies to the contrary, a contractor may have a conflict of interest: he may do work for competitors, both during and after his contract, and, subject to any special legislation concerning secret commissions, he may gain benefits from his engagement which an employee would not be entitled to. This is subject to special laws in most countries concerning 'secret commissions', some of it very old-fashioned. However, breach of these special laws generally involves conduct which by most moral standards would be clearly identified as underhand or sly, and they are by no means as far-reaching and demanding as the law of employment.

Furthermore, a contractor will own the copyright in work he writes, such as computer programs, and any inventions or other rights. Again, in many countries, this is subject to the 'work for hire' doctrine, particularly in relation to copyright. That is, where a *specific* work is commissioned, then copyright in that work will belong to the commissioner not the contractor. It is most important to note that this doctrine will *not* apply where a work is created pursuant to a general contract, as with most contractors. In many countries, there is no form of ' work for hire' doctrine, or it is extremely limited, so copyright will belong to the contractor in any event.

Example

Mr Andrews is a contract programmer. He is engaged by ABC Industries Inc. over some time to design, write and modify controller firmware for various animal toys. ABC is considered a leader in its field and in the use of controller firmware, which leadership has mainly been gained through Mr Andrews' expertise. ABC's biggest competitor, XYZ Amusements Limited, wishes to launch a competing range of toys and engages Mr Andrews to design the firmware controllers, hoping to benefit from his experience with ABC.

There is nothing to prevent Mr Andrews, or XYZ from engaging in this conduct, simply because ABC did not employ Mr Andrews nor were the programs specifically commissioned, but only produced pursuant to a more general retainer. The fact that the firmware programs created by Mr Andrews for XYZ are likely to be identical to those created by Mr Andrews for ABC is immaterial. Copyright in them almost certainly belongs to Mr Andrews in the absence of a written agreement to the contrary and, for reasons discussed below, any benefit of confidentiality is probably for the benefit of Mr Andrews, not ABC. Had ABC considered a more comprehensive agreement with Mr Andrews, the picture would have been very different.

From the point of view of the contractor, there may also be some detrimental consequences from the decision to remain an independent contractor.

For example, the contractor will not have the benefit of an implied obligation to indemnify him or her for negligence. Accordingly, unless the contractor has an express written agreement to the contrary, the principal may be able to exonerate itself from liability by pointing to the contractor's negligence, and the contractor will not be entitled to assistance from his or her principal.

In addition, contractors do not usually enjoy any benefit under the employment protection laws referred to above. Again, by way of example, unless there is an express written agreement setting out the grounds for termination and the period of notice to be given, the contractor's services may be terminated on 'reasonable' notice, often with reference to the harsh rules of the common law of employment.

Restraint of employee or contractor after the contract

The last example of Mr Andrews and ABC Industries raises a very important consideration, one that requires special attention.

It is frequently the wish of employers and principals of contractors in the computer industry to restrain programmers, engineers, sales staff and managers, individuals essential to the success of a product, after they have left the employment or service contract. Usually, such restraint is expressed in terms of a limitation on the right to work in a particular industry in a specified area for a particular period.

The common law imposes very special restrictions on these sorts of provisions. The law is concerned that persons who require special skills upon which they depend for a livelihood do not in a moment of weakness impose upon themselves an unreasonable limitation of their right to exercise that skill for the benefit of themselves and of society at large.

Accordingly, an unreasonable restraint of this type in a contract will be unenforceable — the employee or contractor will be entitled to ignore it altogether. In some countries, courts are entitled to give such a contractual restraint some limited effect, but such a possibility should not be relied upon for fear of disappointment.

It is far better at the time of the contract to do what a court must decide in the event of a dispute, that is:

- identify the legitimate commercial interest that needs to be protected;
- describe the prohibited services, having regard to the competitors who may take advantage of this person's skills;
- define the *geographical area* within which one will be damaged if the person takes up competitive work;
- set a time within which the restraint will operate, probably with regard to the relevant products' life cycles.

Consider, for example, a restraint of trade on a humble programmer. The commercial risk may be low, so any restraint of trade should be very limited, say three months in a very specific area of work upon which he or she is working, and may acquire product sensitive information. In the case of a senior manager, with long term product planning information, the restraint may be very wide in area and for as long as a year, although still limited to competing industries. A key product designer or manager may be somewhere in between these extremes.

In some cases, the provisions of anti-trust law may also be taken into account.

The following is a very brief example derived from the case of ABC and Mr Andrews.

Example — restraint of trade clause

'The contractor agrees that he shall not within the Crown Colony of Hong Kong be engaged in the provision of the services of hardware or software design for any supplier of children's toys or other amusements for a period of one year following the termination of this agreement.'

*The typical provision may go on to deal with what 'engagement'
means, for example, direct or indirect relationship with competitors.
In this example, a lawyer's analysis may run as follows:*

- *The area of Hong Kong may be small, but for some employees and
  contractors, it may be unreasonable to require them to leave their
  home in order to practise their skills. This concern would be
  lessened by a narrow definition of the prohibited activities, as some
  employees and contractors could work in another industry without
  difficulty.*

- *'Hardware or software design' and 'children's toys or other amusements' may be too broad if ABC is only involved in the manufacture
  of children's toys — 'other amusements' could extend to amuse-
  ment arcade machines, games or even gambling devices, only some
  of which may compete with ABC's products.*

- *The period of one year is probably too long in the case of children's
  toys, whose market life cycle may be short, say six months — Mr
  Andrews, however, may be a exceptionally key individual to justify
  this long period.*

- *Greater latitude may be given in the case of restrictions on
  contractors, because of, and to the extent of, the contractor's greater
  independence and the benefits discussed above.*

- *On balance, the limitations given may be excessive in most cases —
  although a decision must be made in each instance.*

Liability of employees and contractors

As between the parties to a contracting arrangement, the courts will
normally respect the parties' stated intention of independence, one from
the other. It is precisely this relationship of an independent adviser which
falls squarely within the definition of a professional or expert with a
special relationship to the 'employer'. Yet it is only in the case of the most
'genuine' independent contractors that one ever encounters arrangements relating to disclaimers of liability, or the provision of insurance.

The involvement of contractors in the computer industry raises
another complication. In the case of a genuine independent contractor,
that is, one who is not rightly perceived as an employee by third parties
measured against a bundle of criteria (whether within the organization,
engaged full-time, answerable to the direction of the principal, and so
on), as mentioned above, the principal is not liable for the contractor's
acts of negligence, except and to the extent that such acts of negligence
were directed to be carried out by the principal.

The classic cases in this area have concerned doctors working in
hospitals. Is a hospital responsible for the acts of the negligent surgeon

who is merely a visiting consultant? In other words, there is an encroaching dilemma that contractors may well be liable in negligence to third parties and not entitled to pass on any of that liability to the organization that engages them.

An interesting example may well be a provider of switching services in an ATM (Automatic Telling Machine) network, where there occurs through negligence a defect in the switching software causing customers to lose money from their accounts. The inherent difficulty is that here, unlike the case of the surgeon and the patient, whereas the provider of the switching service knows or is reasonably expected to know of the existence of the bank's customer, the bank's customer does not necessarily know of the existence of the provider of the switching services.

Written contracts

An important consequence of the matters discussed in this chapter is that more contractors in the computer industry — many of whom presently have made no provision for insurance, or no provision with their principals for insurance or a disclaimer of liability — have, by choosing the status of contractor, willingly excluded themselves from the benefits of employment, as well as its burdens.

Neither type of contract, employment or independent contractor, need be in writing. Written employment contracts are rare. Service contracts are more often in writing. However, in line with the recommendations of the rest of this book, if more employment contracts, and more contractors' agreements were in writing, many of the problems arising from uncertainty would be avoided.

The existence of a written agreement will usually be decisive on a number of issues.

First of all, it will decide, if there would otherwise be any doubt, whether the parties intended their relationship to be of employment or independent contractor character in the first place. If the parties have expressed the agreement in writing, fixing on the latter, then the courts will accept that with all its consequences. Usually this is advantageous to the would-be employer.

Secondly, the parties may vary what would otherwise be the legal consequences of their choice — for example specific agreements may be reached as to the ownership of copyright and software or other copyright works, or the 'ownership' of inventions. Without such written agreement, contractors may well own the copyright to works created by them during their engagement, whereas the opposite is so in the case of employees.

Note: For certain purposes a written contract or the understanding between the parties, may be of little relevance. Notably this is so in taxation statutes where legislatures have realized that extensive preference for 'independent contractor' status may be undermining the government's fiscal policies. In a number of such cases the definition of employment is so broad as to 'catch' many of the less independent contractors. In addition, when the issue of liability to third parties is raised, such as when a contractor causes injury or loss to a person outside the organization in which he or she works, the courts may ignore the contractor status to fix liability for injury on the contractor's 'employer'.

In these circumstances, the curious consequence will be that for certain purposes a person will be an independent contractor, whilst for others he will be treated as if he were an employee. One must not assume, then, that because a person is treated as an employee for one purpose, that he or she will be treated as an employee for all purposes.

There is one further consideration to be remembered. Whether the contract of service or services is in writting or not, to be effective it may need to be 'supported by consideration'. In other words, the employer or principal must give something in return for any promises given by the employee or contractor. As explained in Chapter 7, this may only be nominal (such as a coffee mug!), but without it, the undertakings of the employee or contractor may not be enforceable. It is not sufficient to offer the contract to the employee or contractor *after* work has commenced, on the basis that he or she may be fired unless it is signed. In other words, the contract must be entered *before* the employee or contractor is hired, or something must be given in return for the promises in addition to wages or fees.

3 Copyright

What is copyright?

There is a widespread misconception that the primary function of copyright is to protect the work of artists, sculptors, musicians and authors of novels and plays, with grudging concessions to films, records, radio and television. The creative people of the computer industry, and other new technologies, are seen by those sharing this misconception as 'carpetbaggers', unworthy opportunists in the world of garrets, studios and galleries. History shows this view to be largely unfounded.

Copyright is a benefit granted by statute, not by the 'common law'. In England, the source of one stream of copyright law, there was no copyright as we understand it today until 1709, when the first copyright law, the *Statute of Anne*, was introduced. This law related only to literary works — it was many years before music and the plastic arts were also recognized — but it was not passed for the benefit of authors. The motivating force of the law was to create a registration system to protect publishers, the owners of the new technology of that time — printing presses. This set a trend that has continued throughout the history of copyright — its primary purpose has always been the protection of the exploiters of information, not its creators.

The Statute of Anne provided for a Register of works to be kept at the Stationer's Office. Registration conferred approval to publish, and works which were registered could not be published by any person other than the registered publisher for a period of twenty-five years. The system was at that time both an instrument of censorship and a means of creating a publishers' monopoly. It is interesting to note that the Japanese copyright system followed a similar historic path.

Over time, in most countries registration requirements have been dropped or substantially weakened, authors have become recognized as the primary owners of the right, and the term of copyright has been substantially extended to ensure that an author can enjoy the benefit of his or her efforts throughout life, and his or her heirs can take advantage of that fame which appears to increase after death — usually for a period of fifty years. The main features of copyright protection were however established by the Statute of Anne, that is, copyright protection is an exclusive right in respect of only a limited class of acts, principally copying and publication, only for a set period of time, albeit a very long period.

In European based laws, there have developed a number of additional principles, called 'moral rights', which are intended to protect the integrity of the creator's work. These moral rights permit an author or artist to prevent his or her work from being altered, or his or her authorship from not being properly acknowledged, or, sometimes, permitting the author or artist to take a cut of the price on each dealing with the work, subsequent to its initial disposal. To this aspect of copyright law has been added in many countries protection of traditional and cultural works, and works of historic significance which do not concern us here.

With the increasing uniformity of copyright throughout the world, brought about by international treaties, some of these 'moral rights' have been introduced into the laws of other countries, but the fundamental links between copyright and industry remain unaltered.

The main features of modern copyright law are as follows:

(1)   Copyright extends to literary, artistic and musical works, as well as to films, records, and radio and television broadcasts. Varying from country to country, a number of other incidental embodiments of creative expression are also protected, such as satellite transmissions, the typesetting of pages, and performances. Protection for literary and artistic works is the most important aspect for the computer industry. Subject to comments in the next chapter concerning purpose-specific laws and industrial designs, computer programs, as well as manuals and other written materials, are the proper subject matter of the category of literary works, and mask works, PCB drawings, circuit diagrams and even case designs may be regarded as artistic and sculptural works.

(2)   Copyright is not a monopoly — not like a patent or registered design, or utility model. It is merely a 'bundle' of exclusive rights, including

   (a)   the exclusive right to reproduce, or copy the whole, or a significant portion of the work;

   (b)   the exclusive right to translate the work from one language to another, or to create a 'derivative work' whereby the substance of the work is taken, but converted into another form;

   (c)   the exclusive right to publish to subscribers on a cable network;

   (d)   the exclusive right to transmit the work or to broadcast the work, to which would probably be assimilated diffusion by microwave or other linking system;

To these are added in some countries other forms of commercial exploitation such as rental, discussed in the section on infringement of copyright, below.

(3)   These exclusive rights last for varying periods, depending on the nature of the work, and the country concerned. Most commonly, the copyright in a literary or artistic work, such as a computer program or engineering drawing, lasts for the life of the creator (the person who wrote or drew the work), plus fifty years. In some countries, the period may be as short as twenty-five years from the date of publication. Almost universally, for works that have not been published, copyright is perpetual, only publication 'triggers' the time limitation.

Example

Brokers Data Services Limited is an English company owned by a large firm of insurance brokers wishing to use it as a vehicle to exploit software for calculating premiums and other such activities, as well as keeping track of accounting and management information and other useful activities — software which had been created for its own business, as well as insurance data and information which was collected as part of the business but was seen as equally exploitable commercially. The company elects to create a total 'package' product and service based upon a personal computer solution, and sets about its task as follows:

(1)   it chooses a personal computer product and has the existing software recompiled, modified and rewritten to operate on this personal computer with its operating system, including a communications program to enable access to a database to be set up by the company;

(2)   it creates a database that can be accessed by the software with a suitable password or passwords depending upon the subscription status of the customer;

(3)   it has a cassette tape recording made to which new users can listen to be guided through the basics of the computer and the software (the speaker on the tape reads a scripted 'guided tour');

(4)   it has a manual written to show customers in more depth how to use the software, gain access to the data, and manipulate the data to best effect;

(5)   it creates a looseleaf book of selected data and information as hard copy backup, to be updated by regular monthly releases of both hard copy and files on diskette;

(6)   it engages an industrial designer to create artwork for the packaging;

(7)   it engages a solicitor to create a licence document for the software

and the data, including a separate warranty registration card and software support agreement; and

(8)   it engages an advertising agency to create advertising for an industry journal and a video extolling the virtues of the product and services offered, for display to potential customers.

Shortly after launch, the marketing manager writes a memo to the managing director summarizing some shortcomings in the product due to the usual time and budget shortfall, and suggesting an enhanced version be released in the near future.

Which of the articles created above are subject to copyright?

The answer is: all of them. The software, the database, the user manual, the looseleaf book (and all updates separately), the licence agreement, warranty registration card and software support agreement, the script for the audio 'guided tour' and the video, even the memo sent by the marketing manager, all enjoy copyright as literary works (except in some countries the software may have a limited copyright by virtue of special laws — leading to the anomaly that the manual, or the marketing manager's memo, may have a more long-lasting copyright than the software!). In addition, the audio and video have special 'sound recording' and 'cinematographic film' copyrights, the typesetting and any drawings and photographs in the manual will have their own copyright, and last, but not least, the artwork on the packaging will (subject to requirements in some countries of design laws — see the section on 'moral rights' relevant to the computer industry, below) enjoy copyright as one or more 'artistic work(s)'!

As can be seen from this example, a single article may have many separate copyright interests — a video may have music (musical copyright) and a script (literary copyright), as well as its separate copyright as a film. To make matters even more complicated, each of these copyright interests may belong to different people — these rules of ownership are looked at in a little more detail below, in the section on the ownership of copyright.

Another aspect of this complex of copyright interests is that different types of copyrights last for different durations. In the above example, all the literary, artistic and musical works will be subject to copyright for the life of the actual author, plus fifty years. However, the photograph, typesetting, video and audio copyrights will probably be for fifty years only, each period of fifty years probably commencing on a different date.

It is important to note from this example that copyright is not concerned with the question of whether the artistic or creative content of any particular work is high, only with the question of whether a work is original, in the sense that it is not itself copied from somewhere else.

Naturally enough, however, when it comes to a question of infringement of copyright, a court may be harder to convince that a relatively simple work, like the marketing manager's memo, has been copied, unless the copying is 'word for word', whereas in the case of software, proof of copying may involve substantially less than 'byte for byte' identity. The issue of the nature of copying is considered in the next section.

Some important copyright issues

Registration

Registration of the copyright work is another important feature of copyright protection in some countries, most notably in the United States. We first saw a requirement for registration in the Statute of Anne of 1709, which required registration of the work with the Stationer's Office in order to gain the protection afforded by the law.

The purpose of registration may well have been to create certainty — so that the author's work could be identified with certainty when an alleged plagiarizing copy was made. As mentioned above, the registration system in the English legal framework had two side affects — it was policed by publishers and hence became identified with the publishers' monopoly, and it could also be used as an instrument of political censorship. As a result of these side effects, the registration system has gradually fallen out of use in 'common law' countries and registration is now unnecessary, except in the law relating to 'industrial designs'.

In the United States, and also in countries such as Taiwan and Canada, registration has ceased to be a prerequisite for the *subsistence* of copyright, but can be a necessary condition of suing for *infringement* and/or recovering damages (as opposed to a restraining order alone). In Japan, there remain registration provisions, and the registration of an assignment of copyright may be required before the commencement of legal action by the assignee. In any event, registration is a relatively simple and inexpensive procedure, without the extensive delays and costs associated with other registration systems in patent, trade mark and designs law.

One problem of the registration system which has been raised by the computer industry is the requirement that a copy of the copyright work be lodged with the copyright office, with the consequent problem of maintaining of secrecy in source code. On the one hand, it may be argued that the source code is not published when software is released in object code form, so there should be no requirement to lodge it for registration. On the other hand, it is widely accepted that piracy of object code amounts to reproduction of the source code, and this militates in favour of registration of the source code. At the present time a compromise procedure has been adopted by certain countries requiring registration, whereby the source code may be lodged subject to a secrecy arrangement, by which only an object code listing is available for public inspection.

The copyright notice '©'

It is a requirement of the copyright law of the United States that on each copy of a work published in that country there is displayed a 'copyright notice', that is '©' accompanied by the name of the copyright owner, and the year of first publication. Failure to comply with this will not necessarily result in loss of copyright, at least under the current law, but will disentitle the copyright owner to claim damages. There are now special rules making allowance for the special requirements of computer products, for example permitting the copyright notice to be coded into a computer program so that it displays on 'power up', or allowing it to be placed on the outside of a silicon chip casing, or even engraved onto a silicon chip so that it will be obvious to any person interested enough in the topography of the chip to examine it closely.

The reasons for this requirement are very good ones. It is only reasonable that a person should not be penalized for copying and publishing a work if he or she has no reason to believe that the work is not in the 'public domain', or has no way of knowing who the copyright owner is in order to obtain a licence.

There are similar requirements in other legal systems, particularly those participating in the Universal Copyright Convention, an international copyright reciprocity arrangement discussed further, below. However English 'common law' countries and most European countries do not have such a requirement. In these countries it is argued very persuasively that in these days of high copyright awareness it would be obvious to all but the least intelligent that a work must be the subject of copyright, and it is not too difficult to trace a work back through its supplier in order to find out who is the owner of that copyright. For this reason, it is really incumbent on the copier to defend a copyright claim by showing that he or she did not know of the copyright claim and could not find out who was the copyright owner.

Whichever of the legal systems may be preferable, or wherever the work is published, it is good common sense to ensure a copyright notice in some form is displayed on the work — then there can be no debate on the subject in the event of an infringement.

Publication

'Publication' is an event critical to copyright. The right to first publish a work, as well as being one of the exclusive rights of the copyright owner, governs the period of the rights of the copyright owner, and the copyright itself in a particular country may depend on where, and sometimes when, a work is published.

Publication is the making available to the public of a sufficient number of copies of the work to meet reasonable demand. On the one hand, this is not the same test for 'publication' as is required under patent law (see Chapter 4), or the law relating to trade secrets (see Chapter 5), which tend to consider publication as supply to even an individual who is free to use the information as he or she chooses. What is required is the supply of such number as may be necessary to meet reasonable demand. On the other hand, this does not mean publication in the normal commercial sense, which means large scale distribution, 'pushing' the product by advertising and marketing. In other words, it is possible to meet the requirement of publication simply by placing the work on sale to the public, without advertising, and accordingly only requiring a small number of copies.

Adaptations, translations and derivative works

Another of the exclusive rights of the copyright owner is the right to make further works based upon the original.

In copyright systems based upon the English model, this is covered by a number of specific and quite narrow provisions, but the most important from our point of view is the right to make an 'adaptation', generally meaning in the context of computer programs 'a translation of the work'.

'Translation' is not defined at all, but prior to the decision of the High Court of Australia in the Apple case discussed below, it appeared that it was the use of this concept that overcame the difficulty of relating the object code of a computer program to its source code form, and this was certainly a view accepted by the Canadian Federal Court in the Apple case which came before it.

When any human language is translated into another, say English into German, then, as well as new arrangements of letters being substituted, the grammar, or order of words, is often changed, and new words are even introduced in order to translate accurately the sense of the original, or to introduce appropriate colloquialisms. We can say the same of the object code in relation to the source code, although the difference may be more like that between English and Russian than that between English and German.

In the United States law, these problems are not raised, as the copyright is expressed in much broader terms, as the sole right to make a 'derivative work', being any work based upon and taking material from the original.

In many non-European countries, it is presently being debated whether the notion of 'translation' also extends to the modification of a program's screen displays so that the program appears to the user in the local language — this is a question of particular significance in

Singapore, Korea and Taiwan, and potentially in the People's Republic of China, should the latter introduce a copyright system. The significance of this debate lies in the fact that local copyright laws permit translation of a copyright work into the local language under certain circumstances *without* there being a breach of copyright, in order that works not otherwise available may be usable by the people of those countries. Such provisions may have some justification in respect of printed matter, such as school textbooks, but are difficult to justify in the case of computer programs, where the screen displays are a small part of the program, indeed really only a set of data incidental to the program itself. It is improbable that 'translation' in this sense could apply to compilation or assembly of source codes, but this debate adds a level of complication to this discussion.

As to the ownership of the copyright in translations, or derivative works, see the section on ownership, below.

Infringement of copyright

It is an infringement of the copyright owner's statutory rights to do without his or her permission any of the things encompassed within the exclusive rights during the period of copyright in question, the most important being the right of copying, or 'reproduction'.

Reproduction — the protection of the work, not the ideas

Copyright is not concerned with 'mere ideas' in a work. Anybody can create another work using exactly the same ideas and not be in breach of copyright at all, but nobody can copy the actual words of the author.

Example

Charles Pascal is a programmer. He is particularly interested in a PC based communications program of PC Communications Inc., which he uses regularly, and is irritated by what he regards as unclear and slow entry procedures for its application. On analysis of the program, he decides that it makes inadequate use of the disk operating system and so he writes a short modification which fits into the place of one of the sections of the PC communications program, which significantly speeds the opening of the application and brings a clear entry screen onto the monitor on booting. His modification consists of only a dozen or so lines of code.

He sends the code to PC Communications with a letter describing the entry system and asking whether the company is interested in buying this improvement from him. He hears nothing further. Some time afterwards, a friend shows him a new version of the PC Communications program that he has just bought. Charles sees the entry screen he had devised and on inspection of the object code finds the code identical to his own. In addition, he finds that a paragraph of his letter has been used in the manual to describe the new entry procedure.

There can be no doubt that PC Communications has infringed the copyright of Charles, which he enjoys in both his code and his letter, both in reproducing it, and in publishing it. It does not matter that the code written, or the letter, was relatively insignificant or mundane — as long as it was Charles' original work. Copyright has been found to subsist in railway timetables, racing guides, pools coupons, examination papers and a host of commonplace articles.

The position here would be quite different if PC Communications had seen what Charles had written, and then used that idea to create something of its own, but it is unlikely to result in identical code, just as it is unlikely that a paragraph of PC Communication's manual would have accidentally contained a paragraph identical to one in Charles' letter.

'Look and feel' and 'reverse engineering'

Sometimes the dividing line between what is a new work that has only taken ideas, and a 'copy' that has in fact taken original material is very blurred. This is particularly so in the case of computer programs and other technology products, such as mask works. The grey area is best illustrated by 'look and feel' cases, and cases of 'reverse engineering'.

'Look and feel' claims relate to the adopting by a new program of successful procedures used by a prior program belonging to someone else. In the case of screen layouts, these may qualify as 'artistic works' in their own right, but many programs involve the interaction of various elements on screen in a particular manner, so that the screen's appearance may be quite different each time the user operates the program. In addition, the sequence of events may be an important element of the success of the program, which others will wish to emulate.

As we have seen, copyright requires something in a fixed form, and infringement involves the copying of a substantial element of that fixed form, not the ideas it expresses. Accordingly, 'look and feel' claims present a real difficulty to traditional legal concepts. There have been some successful claims in the United States, such as the *Jaslow* v *Dental Laboratories* and *Broderbund* v *Unison* cases, although each of these cases involved some more traditional copyright elements. However, in each of these cases the Courts accepted that the earlier computer program expressed a certain way of doing things, and the program was a fixed material form of that expression, so there was nothing inconsistent with traditional legal ideas in the 'look and feel' claim.

'Reverse engineering' presents quite different issues. It is essential in establishing infringement of copyright that the original work has been copied. In other words, if the second work only looks like the earlier one by accident, there is no breach of copyright, as copyright is not a monopoly in the same sense as patent or design law. For this reason, in the case of a computer program or mask work, if the original work is only used to extract its ideas and to create a specification of a completely new work, then the original has not been copied at all. However, the creators of the new work must be very careful that they do not save time, money and creative effort by taking elements or solutions to problems from the earlier work, as the more they do this the more likely it is that the later work will be an infringement after all.

Reproduction — copying a 'substantial part'

Copyright protection would be useless if the only conduct that amounted to infringement were reproduction of the entire work, or if slavish translation were required. In other words, if the pirate could avoid liability by changing or leaving out sections of the work that he or she did not need or like, then the computer industry, at least, would have no use for copyright.

For this reason, the test of infringement is one of *quality*, not *quantity*. Based upon a side by side comparison, the issue will depend upon whether what has been taken by the infringer was 'substantial' — bearing in mind that if the infringer thought that what was taken was clever enough for him or her not to wish to do it himself or herself, then it is more than likely that it is 'substantial'. A small fraction of the original may be sufficient in appropriate cases.

Example

Beta Computers, Inc. produces many computers and a full range of peripheral devices including disk and tape drives of its own design. Effective Peripherals, Inc. produces large capacity disk and tape drives and sees a market for selling its drives into the Beta Computers' user base and in competition with Beta selling its own drives. To do this, Effective obtained an interface board from a Beta customer, which included a small ROM based program, and logic diagrams and certain other information from service manuals published by Beta for its OEMs service organizations and distributors, without effective limitation. For use with its own drives, Effective reorganized the interface board and rewrote 75% of the code in the ROM based program to adjust for Effective's slightly different storage procedure, but was able to use the remainder, because to rewrite it would have involved a substantial design change in the product — the routines in the program were shuffled about. The result was an Effective drive transparent to the Beta computer and much cheaper. Needless to say, the logic diagram for the Effective interface board, issued to its distributors and service organizations, was very similar to the Beta circuit diagram for its equivalent part.

Notwithstanding the fact that Effective rewrote a great deal of the program, and reorganized the remainder, there has been a breach of Beta's copyright because what was kept was clearly substantial, and it is irrelevant that it was reorganized. There has also been infringement of the logic diagram, as there is a clear link between the work of Beta which was taken by Effective. Again, the case would have been a deal more difficult if Effective had not used the Beta components to design their own, but designed their logic and their code 'from scratch'. But then the design effort may have been so protracted and costly that Effective's product may not have been price competitive.

Can three-dimensional articles reproduce drawings?

It is plain that visual works such as drawings for casings, semiconductor chip masks and printed circuit board layouts must qualify as 'artistic works' to enjoy copyright.

In United States copyright law, however, a useful three-dimensional object cannot enjoy copyright as such, and so it cannot be a 'copy' of the drawings made for it. So if one computer manufacturer copies the casing of another, that would not be a breach of copyright, as copying even a small part of the manual for it would be. It is less clear whether a useful article which remains two dimensional, like a layer of a semiconductor chip, or a PCB, is affected by the same limitation. These articles, for example, are made by a process so similar to silk screen printing or photogravure, that it is not immediately apparent why they should be excluded from copyright protection simply because they serve a utilitarian purpose.

In English copyright systems, there has not until recently been any such difficulty in the articles being of an industrial nature. There have been many cases which confirm this. Recent examples in decided cases include the making of three-dimensional articles from drawings for parts of a hot water system, an exhaust pipe for a motor car, an electric kettle, the working parts of pumps, and various toys. The only genuine difficulties in English legal systems have arisen from the test for infringement by reproduction, that the three-dimensional article should appear the same as the drawing to an untrained observer, and from questions raised by the possible application of the law of industrial designs, which is further mentioned in the next chapter.

However, recent trends have swung sharply away from this liberal extension of copyright to useful articles, and laws limiting the use of copyright in this way, or at least full copyright lasting for the life of the designer plus fifty years have been introduced in the United Kingdom and elsewhere.

'Secondary' infringement — importation and distribution

A further aspect of infringement is that of certain 'secondary' rights of the copyright owner.

A copyright owner is entitled to prevent any person from importing, selling, distributing, displaying or otherwise dealing in 'infringing copies' of the work. 'Infringing copies' refers to copies of the work made without the permission of the copyright owner.

The practical importance of these powers in support of the copyright owner is immediately obvious. Copyright protection would be worthless if one could prevent unauthorized copying within a country, but not prevent cheap illegal copies coming into the country from overseas.

In some countries, this protection even extends to the preventing of the importation of legitimate copies of the work, in other words 'parallel importation' or 'grey marketing'. This is so in Australia and New Zealand, but not in Japan or the United States. In the United Kingdom (and its colony Hong Kong), this is so in respect of copies made by licensees of the copyright owner (including related corporations) restricted by the terms of their licences to particular territories outside the country into which the product is being imported — a very odd restriction indeed. Regrettably, in most countries this development of the law is not available.

The significance of these rights will not be lost on those who must expend considerable sums of money promoting a product in a small market (all of which moneys must be recovered in the price of goods sold or licensed), facing loss of that market to parallel imports from a cheaper market, which take advantage of that expenditure without having to recover it.

Can use of a copyright work amount to infringement?

Although publishers of computer programs would like to control use of computer programs and do their best with their licences, it is still not usually regarded as an infringement of copyright to use a computer program. Subject to the licence contract, any person can purchase and use the program on his or her own computer regardless of where it was intended to be used.

However, if computer programs in object code enjoy copyright, it is a most significant fact that computer programs on disk or tape (such as most application software and operating systems for all computers from micros to mainframes) operate by means of reproduction in whole or in part in the temporary memory of the computer. Accordingly, copyright would put in the power of the copyright owner the power to control use of the program other than by contract — a very important consideration in, say, limiting users to certain types of computer, or in limiting the number of terminals in certain types of terminal networks. Aware of this possibility, some of the more recent amendments to the copyright law have specifically qualified the definition of 'reproduction' so that it does not encompass normal use.

The most important consequence of this aspect of copyright law is the growing rental market, and the provision of bureau services.

When copyright was mainly concerned with books, the issue of rental and lending was mainly concerned with the rights of public libraries, but the video industry, and now the software industry, have shown how valuable the rental business is, and there is no obvious reason why copyright owners should not take a share of this further exploitation of their creative efforts.

Of course, the existing law already prohibits as primary and secondary infringement the making and dealing with (including rental) *illegal* copies, but there is no limit, other than in any valid licence, in most countries to the rental of legitimate copies, or their use in a bureau service. Japan is an interesting exception to this observation, and there are proposals in many countries to modify their copyright laws in the same fashion. In those countries which have chosen to place computer programs in a separate copyright category, great care must be taken to ensure that computer programs are not overlooked in this area.

Remedies for copyright infringement

The remedies available to the copyright owner are formidable. Not only can continued infringement be restrained by injunction but, in appropriate cases, the courts can award damages, or payment to the copyright owner of the ill-gotten gains, by way of an 'account of profits'.

In certain countries, there is a further remedy available in certain cases. That is, the 'infringing copies' are deemed to belong to the copyright owner — this can be a very harsh penalty indeed when the copyright component is only a fraction of the product, as in the case of a design on the outside, or when the materials in which the work is embodied are very valuable in their own right.

In addition, in some countries, local customs authorities and/or police are empowered to seize infringing copies being imported, or infringing copies being circulated within the country, as well as to bring criminal prosecutions in appropriate cases.

The difficulties in establishing copyright infringement as a practical matter are considered further below, in relation to the Apple cases.

Enforcing copyright — the Apple cases

Since the writing of a computer program is essentially a literary activity, albeit using a limited 'language' or code, usually a subset of English, it is natural to assume that it would be a 'literary work' protected by copyright law. However, until recent trends to amend the law, most copyright statutes predated computers, so it is to the interpretation of the existing law given by the courts that we must turn.

Of course, in those cases where the source code for a computer program is written or printed on a conventional medium, such as paper, it should be clear that such a source code qualifies as a literary work and enjoys copyright as such. Equally clearly in the case of data, all forms of data on media readable by the unassisted eye clearly enjoy protection as literary works or 'compilations'. However, some courts have exhibited a regrettable difficulty in dealing with forms of embodiment not comprehensible to the human eye, including all forms of computer storage.

With such advantages attaching to copyright, as opposed to other forms of protection, it is very important to know whether copyright does extend to computer programs, mask works, and technical drawings, not as they may be on paper, but in the forms of storage in which they are readily usable. This important question has focused attention on the Apple cases around the world, and these cases give an insight into the law, not only in relation to computer programs, but the way the law generally deals with the new information products of the computer industry.

In the United States, one of the earliest decisions concerning the 'copyrightability' of computer programs was the decision of *Data Cash Systems*, which doubted whether copyright under the United States law prior to 1978 could extend to computer programs, although the court clearly did not understand the nature of the work with which it was there dealing (the case was decided on another issue). Following upon the landmark decision of *Williams* v *Artic*, however, which found that the new law definitely did protect computer programs, the same court, the US Court of Appeals, confirmed in *Apple* v *Franklin* that the effect of the amendments to the United States Copyright Act (Title 17) 1976, which came into effect in 1978, gave complete and effective protection to computer programs.

However, in Australia, the same Apple case, *Apple* v *Computer Edge* was decided the other way. Australia is a 'common law' country, with a copyright law virtually identical to that of the United Kingdom. One finds substantially the same legislation in South Africa, India, New Zealand, Hong Kong and Singapore.

It was alleged that the ROMs of the Computer Edge computer embodied unlawful reproductions of Apple's source codes and/or the object codes.

Apple's case was, briefly, as follows:

(1)   Clearly, a source code written by pen on paper is a literary work. Even a list of meaningless codes is a literary work, as is a railway timetable, a television program and a pools coupon. How much more so a clearly articulated sequence of instructions consisting of abbreviations of English words such as 'jump', 'shift' and so on, and numbers. Furthermore, the program as such is clearly intended to be interpreted by human beings — at least the

operator of the device for keying the program into a computer for storage on an electromagnetic storage medium. Also, many programs in source code are published for enthusiastic hackers, or technicians, to employ in modification of the programs. Would so many source programs be closely held secrets if they could not be read by humans?

(2)   Furthermore, a 'work' first enjoys copyright from the time it is first reduced to writing 'or some other material form'. Clearly, then, the law contemplates that a work could be in some 'material form' other than writing. Indeed, that is the scheme of the Act.

(3)   Copyright is therefore a régime intended to protect creative expressions of the human mind, fixed in some material form. This was reinforced by the United Kingdom statute of 1956, which introduced for the first time protection in terms of abstracts such as 'sound recordings' rather than the protection for mechanical devices provided under the 1911 legislation.

So it was argued that a literary work could be materially embodied in object code — like a word processor document. Since a word processor document on disk or tape is no different from a computer program similarly embodied, it would appear illogical that copyright protection should not extend to a computer program in such a medium.

Likewise, since the exclusive right of the copyright owner is 'reproduction in a material form', wording apparently chosen to guarantee that an article not appearing to the eye the same as the original could nonetheless embody a reproduction, then data or object code on a disk or tape should be capable of being a reproduction of the original document or other electromagnetic medium from which it is derived.

It is a small further step to say that electromechanical forms of embodiment, such as silicon chips, can equally be the repository of literary works or reproductions of literary works.

The contrary argument was that literary works must be on a visible medium. So, according to this argument, if an author chose not to dictate his work, or write it, but chose to write his work with a word processor, the work is not created at all until it is printed out, prior to which, the disk or tape may be copied freely by others. Likewise, any literary work on paper could be keyed onto a disk or on tape and disseminated electrically without infringement.

Unexpectedly, at first instance, the copyright claim was dismissed at the threshold. The Court found that it was a necessary requirement of any literary work that it have the purpose or intention of affording 'either information or instruction, or pleasure in the form of literary enjoyment' and that a computer program in source code was merely a set of instructions for the operation of a machine not designed for human consumption.

If this decision had been allowed to stand, it would have resulted in the odd conclusion that copyright could subsist in a railway timetable but not a computer program, even one written by hand on paper!

On appeal, the Full Bench of the Federal Court of Australia found that the source codes of the subject programs were literary works, that the object programs were 'adaptations' and that the ROMs were 'reproductions in a material form' of Apple's object programs.

The High Court of Australia overturned this decision.

The majority of the Court found that the source codes, which in this case were written by human hand on paper, were literary works enjoying copyright under the Act, although this decision appears to be of no practical significance. However, the majority also found that the programs were not protected in the form of ROM and could, in effect, be copied by anyone in that, or any other, electronic form.

On the question of whether the object codes themselves could be literary works, the Chief Justice observed:

> It seems to me a complete distortion of meaning to describe electrical impulses in a silicon chip, which cannot be perceived by the senses and are not intended to convey any message to a human being and which do not represent words, letters, figures or symbols as a literary work; still less can a pattern of circuits be so described.

Of course, this entirely missed the point. Never would it be said that as ink flows from the pen and rests tantalizingly on the nib that it is there a literary work. So Apple did not claim copyright in transitory electrical impulses, the 'ink' of the computer. Equally, it would never be said that the ink scattered and dried on the paper is the 'literary work', nor did Apple claim copyright in the 'pattern of circuits' in any ROM. Rather, it is the fixed collocation of words ('words' in the sense of the abstract units of language) represented by the ink and paper that is the work, and likewise the fixed collocation of words in the source codes represented by the ROMs in which Apple claimed copyright. The 'work' is a thing distinct from the material form in which it is embodied.

Looking at the problem in another way, it is irrelevant that a disk, tape or silicon chip is a component part for the working of a machine, just as a printed page is not denied protection merely because it may be characterized as a device consisting of two planar surfaces connected to a central binding for display consecutively with a number of other such surfaces.

In other words, the Court made the error of fixing its attention upon the medium and not the message.

On this issue of 'translation' in the ROMs, the Chief Justice said:

> The ROMs did not in any way express or render the source programs; rather, the ROMs were the means of putting into action and making effective the instructions

written in the source programs. Just as a person does not (except in a metaphorical sense) translate the instructions for the working of a machine when, following those instructions, he sets the machine in motion, so the electrical charges in the ROMs effectuate, but do not translate, the instructions in the source program.

The Chief Justice, having concluded that the object code could not be a literary work, considered that Apple's claim could only be made out if the object code of the Computer Edge ROMs were a reproduction of the source code of the Apple programs. However, his Honour defined reproduction as follows:

> [There must be] 'a sufficient degree of objective similarity between the two works' . . . It is impossible to say that there is any objective similarity between the ROMs and EPROM on the one hand and the written source programs on the other. Neither the silicon chips nor the electrical impulses that may be generated in them have the slightest resemblance to the written source programs.

This is a most extraordinary test of reproduction. The cases relied on by the Court were all cases concerning artistic works, not literary works, and by 'objective similarity' the Court appears to have imposed a requirement of 'visual similarity' — a test of comparison of storage media, not of the works embodied in them.

It is this last conclusion which was most surprising. It appears to confuse the 'medium' and the 'message' in the same manner as the old cases which decided that piano rolls were not 'copies' of the music they played, a confusion which the legislators sought to overcome by the 1911 and subsequent re-enactments of the copyright law. This confusion is rather exacerbated by references to an old analogy that a pie is not a 're-production' of a recipe for a pie, but rather a product of acting upon the instructions in the recipe, by which it was suggested that the material embodiment of computer programs is somehow dictated by the program itself.

Just as in the case of the amendments to the United States law in 1976, the Australian law was amended in 1984 to overcome concerns that the High Court would decide the way it did, in order to provide certainty rather than await the outcome of the appeal to the High Court.

Apple has run similar cases in Canada, Hong Kong and Israel, in each case successfully, in each case the court accepting that programs on ROM chips were 'reproductions' of the source code, although expressing doubt as to whether they could be regarded as 'translations'.

The significance of this debate for the computer industry and for copyright law itself is profound. Not only is it a question of the tests of protection of the forms in which computer technology related products are stored and disseminated, having impact upon the law in India, New Zealand, Singapore, Hong Kong, Canada, and England as well as Australia. It is also a test of the capacity of courts and their legal practitioners in all countries to deal with new technologies.

Ownership of copyright

The copyright in a work belongs, in the first instance, to its author.

Every copyright work must have an author or authors, or a maker or makers and it is to such authors or makers that copyright belongs, with few exceptions. It should be remembered that almost invariably for legal purposes it is the programmer or designer, not the person directing the work and providing the logic but the person who actually 'puts pen to paper', who is the author or maker, and hence the owner, for the purposes of the law. There are exceptions, principally relating to works produced in the course of employment as well as the works of journalists, or photographs, portraits or engravings made pursuant to an agreement. A significant omission from this list of exceptions is that of literary and artistic works made under contract other than a contract of employment.

Naturally, this is subject to the existence of an assignment of copyright, discussed below.

Example

ABC Games Pty Limited is the maker of devices for poker machines and has developed a new, computerized poker machine called 'Jubilee' with the assistance of Mr Andrews, engaged as an independent contractor (not as an employee), writing the programs needed. Mr Andrews wrote for ABC very artful computer programs for the management of the poker machines' functions, monitoring coin input, spinning the reels, lighting the lights, making the noises and making sure that the players were paid the right amounts on the reel spins. Some little time after the introduction of the 'Jubilee' poker machine by ABC, XYZ Pty Limited commences refurbishing old Jubilee poker machines and, in the process, improving their functions, changing their appearance and upgrading their performance all for a much lower cost than purchasing a new poker machine. XYZ also engages Mr Andrews to provide them with computer programs to replace those in the Jubilee poker machine. ABC alleges that copyright in its computer programs has been breached.

Since copyright belongs to the author, unless the author signs a written assignment of copyright, Mr Andrews, not ABC, owns copyright to the programs. This is so notwithstanding the fact that ABC has paid Mr Andrews to prepare the programs and has instructed him in the requirements of the programs and the functions they should perform. Accordingly, Mr Andrews was free to walk away from that job and sell or license the identical programs to a direct competitor.

A further important exception to the general principle of ownership is the 'work for hire' doctrine, by which in certain countries it is conceded by the law that where a work is created under a contract specifically to create that work (not necessarily under a general contract), then copyright will automatically belong to the person who commissioned the work. This doctrine does not automatically apply to all copyright works — in some countries it applies only to some works, like films, portraits and industrial designs, but not to others, such as literary works — and it is always very carefully limited.

An interesting aspect of the application of these principles of ownership is that the authors or makers of 'derivative works', including translations, own the product of their creative efforts (subject to an assignment of their rights, of course). Naturally, the ownership of a person who modifies or translates another work is not absolute, it is subject to the underlying ownership of the original work. The result is that there are two owners of the derivative work, and an illegal copy of the derivative work infringes the copyright of both authors. It also means that one of the authors cannot deal with the translation without the permission of the other. This principle applies not only to translations, and other major reworkings of an original work, but applies equally to relatively small modifications — a matter well understood by the publishing industry, the members of which always ensure that authors who 'update' existing works for a new edition assign back the copyright in their adjustments and additions. The significance of this issue for those who engage contractors to carry out modifications to their software will be immediately apparent.

Example

Alphabetical Sorters Limited is the owner of copyright in software it had specially developed for its use in a mail addressing and dispatch business, the software maintaining lists of names and addresses, correcting spelling errors and adding postal codes in addresses, cross matching names and addresses, and keeping records of material sent to addresses on the lists.

Alphabetical resolves to improve efficiency, lower costs and reduce dependence on an aging minicomputer by having the software modified and recompiled for use by less skilled personnel on personal computers in its organization. For this purpose, it engages Ms Trumpeter as a contractor to create a modification of the main system, consisting of a cut down version with a 'user friendly' interface and enhanced speed, compiled for the personal computer. A letter of appointment is used by Alphabetical to Trumpeter, but this does not refer to ownership, only to the specifications and the hourly rate for the work to be done.

Some time after Trumpeter has successfully completed the work, Alphabetical sees an advantage in commercially distributing the software, and spends a considerable sum investigating the market, designing packaging and manuals and generally preparing for commercialization of the product. Trumpeter hears of this and threatens legal action to prevent the manufacture and sale, unless Alphabetical agrees to pay her a 15% royalty on gross receipts.

Can Alphabetical ignore this threat?

The answer is probably not. In most countries the copyright in the personal computer version belongs to both Alphabetical and Trumpeter, so she is entitled to forbid copying of her work. At best, because Alphabetical never raised with Trumpeter the possibility of commercial exploitation of her work, it has a licence, terminable on reasonable notice (whatever that may be), to use the software for its own internal purposes. Even in the case of the 'work for hire' doctrine there may be arguments as to whether the informal letter was sufficient, and even in countries such as Japan where it is possible to assign copyright by an 'implied term' of the contract (see Chapter 7), it may not be easy to prove in these circumstances that there was such an implied term.

The same issues may extend to quite minor changes in software.

Clearly, therefore, it is in the interests of every person who wishes to exploit data, programs or artistic works (such as semiconductor chip masks) to know whether he is governed by copyright and, if so, to ensure that such works are created by an employee or there is in existence a valid copyright assignment.

Assignments and licences

For a copyright assignment to be effective and binding, it must be unequivocally clear. In most countries, it must also be in writing and signed by the copyright owner. Although under normal circumstances a contract, including a contract to sell ordinary property (other than land) may be oral (see Chapter 7), this is not so in the case of copyright assignments in most countries, a notable exception being Japan, although in that country it is desirable to register assignments of copyright for the purposes of taking legal action, and a written assignment is clearly helpful in the registration process, especially if registration takes place some time after the original work was made.

A copyright assignment need not assign all the copyright. Copyright may be split up, both geographically and by reference to individual exclusive rights. So, for example, the owner of the copyright in a computer program can 'assign away' Japanese copyright, retaining United States copyright. In the case of computer programs, it is difficult to see how one could assign individual rights, as the right to make film, or the right to broadcast, are not very relevant (as they are not relevant to railway timetables!), but in the case of a conventional literary work, one could assign away the rights to, say, turn a book into a play and broadcast the play, whilst retaining absolutely the right to publish the book.

In addition, it is possible to assign away copyright in future works, that is, works yet to be written or made. This is a very important point which enables a contractor to be bound before he or she starts work, not only after the work has been finished when there may be some advantage to the contractor in refusing!

Licences, on the other hand, do not require the same degree of formality, but they must be clear. For this reason, and because what the licensee may do may adversely affect the copyright, it is very sensible to think carefully about copyright licences, and preferable that they be *written*, with all the terms, duration, royalties/fees, the inclusion of copyright notices, quality control, support, modification and ownership of modifications and other relevant matters clearly dealt with, and then *enforced*.

Examples of a copyright assignment and a software licence are to be found in Section II of this book.

International protection

A further benefit of copyright which is of general importance to the computer industry is its internationalization. Copyright is the only form of protection which can claim to be truly, effectively, international. Many works will automatically enjoy copyright, without any formality, in most significant world markets by virtue of the international and bilateral treaties that prevail, in particular the Berne and UCC (Universal Copyright Convention) conventions. The same cannot be said of patent and design protection.

Basically, as well as setting out minimum criteria for the copyright laws of each member country, these conventions provide a system whereby works made by citizens of member countries, and also works first published in or substantially created in member countries will be treated as if they were made by citizens of, first published in, or made in the other member country in which copyright may be claimed.

It is important to remember that this system of 'national treatment' means that it is a local country copyright that is owned, not a foreign copyright that is recognized. This means that the owner may have more, or fewer, rights than he or she has in his or her own country, or may be affected by local rules as to assignments, licences, or a host of other issues.

Example

Alphalock Systems Inc., an American company, manufactures modems. It engages a design firm, Crane Design, specifically to create an exciting new and distinctive modem case design, subject to a 'work for hire' contract in which it is assumed that Alphalock will own the copyright, but there is no express assignment.

The new product is launched in the United States. Alphalock has a small office in Canada and, within a week of the launch in the United States receives enquiries from interested purchasers to whom it supplies the product, and thereafter continues to sell in Canada. By a year after the launch the product has been sufficiently successful for Alphalock to receive its first enquiries from England and Australia. Also by this time Alphalock and Crane have fallen out, Crane saying that Alphalock let them down on another contract. Meanwhile, sales of the new product boom in all countries, to such an extent that replicas of the Crane design appear in England which are distributed in Australia.

What can Alphalock do about the replicas in England and Australia?

England is not a signatory of the UCC, but because both Canada and England are signatories of Berne, and the product was first published in Canada (that is, within thirty days of its launch in the United States sufficient numbers were made available to meet demand in Canada), English copyright does subsist in the Crane design. However, there is no valid assignment of the copyright under English law and Alphalock is not going to get one from Crane now, or assistance in starting a copyright case. So Crane is still the owner of the copyright in the case design (although recent amendments to the law may signify that the copyright is of a short duration, for example, only ten years).

Australia is a signatory of both Berne and the UCC, so copyright subsists by either route. Furthermore, under Australian design law, the commissioner of a design owns the copyright to it. However, under Australian law, if the design is 'industrially applied', as this one certainly was, then copyright lapses unless the design is registered in Australia before it is published. Alphalock misses out again.

A list of current signatories of the Berne and UCC conventions is to be found in Appendix I. It will be observed that the USSR is a signatory of the UCC, but not of Berne, although the latter includes far more European countries. The United States has only very recently joined the Berne Union, so it is possible that works of foreign countries created before its accession will not get the benefit of United States copyright protection, and *vice versa*.

In addition to the Berne and UCC conventions there are a number of bilateral treaties, for example between the United States and Taiwan, and the United States and Singapore, by which nationals of the member countries enjoy copyright recognition notwithstanding the fact that the Asian country in each case is not at the date of writing a member of either of the major conventions.

Are any of the 'moral rights' relevant to the computer industry?

Generally speaking, the answer is no. Again, however, this is a 'national treatment' issue — ownership of foreign copyrights by virtue of the international treaties may bring with it these rights if the work is to be published in a country with such rights.

Accordingly, it should be remembered that these rights often include the right to require that the author be acknowledged, and that no variation of the author's work be published as the unaltered work of the author. It should also be remembered that these are usually inalienable rights of the author.

These rights are much honoured in their complete oversight, and care may have to be taken to check what moral rights, if any, prevail in a country before distribution commences there, as well as whatever other legal considerations this chapter may have provoked!

Protecting copyright

In order to protect copyright interests in works, including technical drawings (even if not protected in your own country they may be protected by copyright in another), computer programs and designs, it is wise to ensure that the following procedures are carried out and maintained:

(1)   All work to be done by contractors (whether inside or outside the organization) should be the subject of a written contract which includes an express assignment of copyright throughout the world; see Section II — Sample Contracts. Take care to provide that if the contractor is using non-employees, there is a written assignment from each sub-contractor.

(2)   Keep a register of all work done, which includes (as a minimum):
    (a)   the name(s) of each person who does the work and what he or she does (in brief, as an *aide-memoire*) — not the employer's name, but that of the individual author(s);
    (b)   the dates between which the work is carried out, or individual sections or revisions as the case may be;
    (c)   the addresses of the authors and their nationality/citizenship.

(3)   Before supplying any product in any country, such as the United States, consult with local lawyers to check whether there are registration requirements or other matters which may enhance local protection.

4 Other Forms of Protection

A special word of warning

In the last chapter we considered the nature of copyright, the most important type of protection for computer software other than the law of trade secrets, or confidential information, considered in the next chapter.

There are other aspects of creative effort which can be protected by legal systems in place in most industrialized countries, and it is the nature and rôle of these which we shall briefly review in this chapter, as well as their overlaps with copyright and trade secret laws. The most important of these is patent law, which we shall leave to the end of the chapter, dealing first with the more obscure or limited forms of protection.

A special word of warning is called for here. The areas of law constituting the subject of this chapter are unusually large and complex. At best we can roughly describe what are the types of legal provisions that may be relevant to the computer industry, and leave the reader interested in more detail to consult a patent attorney, lawyer or a more voluminous text! Most important, however, is that in these areas the non-lawyer can do little in the way of 'self help', and in the event of a practical problem or need arising, the need to consult skilled professionals known to have special expertise in these areas is essential.

Designs

In certain countries, a special, limited form of copyright may be acquired by registration of a 'design', the physical appearance of utilitarian objects, under special designs legislation. A typical definition of a 'design' is 'features of shape, configuration, pattern or ornamentation applicable to an article, being features that, in the finished article, can be judged by the eye, but this does not include a method or principle of construction'.

The legislation is intended to apply only to things of mass production, patterns on materials or on crockery, the designs or shapes of clothing, electrical goods, toys and other consumer articles. However, notwithstanding that designs should contain relevant features which are intended to have *æsthetic appeal* to the eye, they can be very basic, and to the ordinary person quite *unæsthetic*, such as new shapes for light bulbs, toilet bowls or the dial of an ammeter or clock. Thus at first glance the most obvious application of the designs law would be to the shape of or patterns on cabinet or other housing of computer equipment with some *æsthetic* appeal, but in some countries it has been extended to printed circuit board designs and, by logical extension, may even apply to mask works (considered further below).

Registration is only available if the design is new or original, that is, has not been published or used at all in the country of registration prior to the application for registration. This is quite a different test of originality from that for copyright protection, which requires only that the work originate with the author, that is, not be copied.

The duration of the design right is usually shortlived, for example sixteen years instead of the copyright norm of the life of the author plus an additional fifty years, and may be subject to renewals and renewal fees within that period. However, against this a registered design has one major advantage over a copyright work: it enjoys a genuine monopoly. That is, even if someone independently develops the same or substantially the same design as a registered design, without any copying whatsoever, it is an infringement to use that independently developed design, whereas with copyright, one must prove actual copying, direct or indirect, of the original drawing.

The difficulty with this type of protection arises from its obvious overlap with the protection of 'artistic works' by copyright law. Full standard copyright protection extends to such things as the drawings which precede manufacture of almost any article, however humble, and any article which looks to the ordinary person to be the same as the drawing is a 'reproduction' of the drawing. Hence, if it were not for special overlap provisions in the copyright law, if the article is made without the permission of the owner of the copyright in the drawing, it is an infringement of that copyright. This is equally true if the copier never sees the original drawing but only copies an article made by the owner of the copyright to the drawing ('indirect' copying).

In an attempt to deal with perceived anomalies arising from this overlap, different legal systems have devised different provisions for such situations.

In the United States and related legal systems, standard copyright cannot extend to utilitarian or industrial articles as such, although copyright does subsist in the original drawings. So the copying of the article made by the copyright owner from the drawings would not be an infringement of copyright in the drawings. Similarly, the making of a three-dimensional article is not considered an infringement of a two-dimensional drawing, hence even the making of an article directly from the drawings without the permission of the copyright owner would not be an infringement. To infringe the copyright of the drawings, one would have to copy the drawings themselves.

The provisions of English law copyright systems have tended to deal with the same problem by denying certain copyright protection to artistic works which qualify as 'designs' and which have been 'applied industrially' by the owner of copyright (or with his or her permission), thus leaving protection of the industrialized design to the designs law. Copyright is not entirely lost; the overlap provisions create an exception whereby it is not an infringement of copyright to reproduce the design on the same type of article (not necessarily an identical article) as that already produced by the owner of the unregistered design.

The problems with the English law provisions are basically two: what qualifies as a design, and what 'applied industrially' means. Because the standard of 'originality' for standard copyright is lower than for designs, there are works which enjoy copyright but which do not qualify for designs registration; they slip through the net of the designs law. This might even be the case if the design has been 'published' by the copyright owner, and hence disqualified from registration because no longer 'new', but has not been sufficiently published to be 'industrially applied'. What constitutes sufficient industrial application is also unclear. Such intricacies are best explained with an example.

Example

Delilah Disk Systems Pty Limited is an Australian company which produces hard and floppy disk drives for personal computers. It has created a new hard disk product, including not only a new external casing with an attractive design and pattern of air vents, but also a new design of the hard disk subassembly itself, including the shape of the metallic casing of the hard disk. In designing the hard disk subassembly, the Delilah designers have only been motivated by practical considerations, as the subassembly is hidden from human view by the sealed external plastic casing only opened by service technicians.

Prior to release of the new hard disk product, Delilah makes fifteen pre-production products and delivers them without any confidentiality restrictions to certain journalists for appreciation and to its distributors for evaluation and advance orders. One of the journalists warns Delilah of Australian design laws, which provide for the loss of copyright protection for designs which are industrially applied and not registered, so Delilah lodges an application in respect of the external case design of the new product.

Klone Micros is impressed by the success of the Delilah design after release, and decides to take advantage of that success by having look-alike products made in Taiwan, to which it ships one of the Delilah products for reverse engineering and copying by a Taiwanese hard disk manufacturer. The Taiwanese manufacturer is impressed with the Delilah disk subas-

sembly design and adopts this also. At the same time, Klone arranges for a design with features very similar to the Delilah external casing to be applied to a personal computer casing, so that Klone can provide a unified product range. Klone ships its new hard disk and personal computer, which have bigger, less elegant features but basically the same overall appearance as the Delilah product, into Australia where it sells the products as its own, but significantly more cheaply than Delilah's.

Can Delilah do anything about this?

In respect of the external case design, Delilah has a design registration but any action on it would probably fail because the design was 'published' before the design registration application was lodged, that is, it was shown to people under no obligation of confidentiality, and so even if a certificate of registration were issued it could probably be set aside. Further, because the design has been industrially applied and published, it has effectively lost its copyright in respect of not only hard disks but also other goods of the same type, including the Klone personal computer.

However, in the case of the subassembly casing, it would be a very respectable argument under Anglo-Australian law that the design was not registrable as it was purely utilitarian, and so even though it has been industrially applied and published, the drawings for the subassembly have not lost copyright protection. Delilah could therefore prevent the use of the subassembly design, but not the external case design!

There are other anomalies with the design laws arising perhaps because these laws are typically older and less attuned to modern circumstances, such as the curiosity under the English law systems that the rules regarding ownership of designs are different from those of copyright, ownership vesting automatically in the commissioner of the work, not the author or his or her employer.

Because of anomalies such as these, in the United Kingdom, the overlap provisions were virtually eliminated in 1976, resulting until 1988 in a dual régime of protection. Until 1988, if one chose to register a design, one obtained the benefit of the monopoly but a limited duration of protection. However if one chose not to register, one enjoyed full copyright protection, less than a monopoly, but lasting much longer and less prone to the vagaries of the designs law. A similar situation existed until recently in New Zealand. However, recent developments have caused the whole area of the copyright/designs overlap in the area of works 'industrially applied' to come under review again in both of these countries, resulting in a reversion to limitations on the extension of copyright works to designs.

The United States' method of dealing with the copyright/designs overlap appears to have many merits absent from the English law method, that is, before amendments in the United Kingdom itself in the 1970s. The United States law appears to permit the theft of the fruits of the skill and creativity of industrial designers who are not aware of design registration laws, by the copying of, for example, case designs without penalty. However, such antisocial activity is limited or prevented by powerful unfair competition or unjust enrichment laws, preventing the presentation of another's product as one's own, so that the major risk appears diminished.

However, the best solution of all would appear to be the abandonment of designs registration laws altogether, and thus the need for overlap provisions, with all their anomalies, short terms of protection and uncertainties of application. Copyright protection should be extended even to utilitarian or industrial articles, notwithstanding the long duration of copyright, as market forces will surely prevent any person from attempting to gain effective protection over the design of any article that has outlived its commercial life.

Such a step would have a further advantage. One of the drawbacks of design registration laws is that they fall outside the international copyright system discussed in Chapter 3. Further, works which enjoy copyright in one country often have lost their protection in a design registration country, which seems to undermine the purpose and benefits of the international system. Such international protection as there is rests in conventions such as the Paris Union, which only allows a period of grace within which to lodge design registration applications, a poor substitute indeed.

Unfortunately, world trends are at present not heading in such a logical direction.

Semiconductor chip design protection

Semiconductor chip design protection is another area in which special legislation has been introduced, or is being considered, in several countries. This is a problem restricted to countries with active semiconductor chip manufacturing industries, and so not surprisingly the initiative has been taken with the United States and Japan, whilst WIPO is considering a general standard model for legislation, most particularly with European countries in mind.

The concern is, of course, with the masks which are designed, miniaturized and used to 'engrave' layers of semiconductor material with ultra-violet light, in order to build up intricate, tiny and multi-layered electrical circuits, or with the physical appearance of these circuits themselves. In some countries it was felt that such masks or the corresponding circuits could not qualify as 'artistic works' under copyright law, or 'designs' under design laws, because they are not made to be seen, but to be miniaturized beyond human vision unaided by the microscope (although this objection has never troubled those dealing with curiosities such as pages of poetry inscribed on a pinhead!). In addition, features of American copyright law restrict copyright protection for utilitarian works.

The products of the processes and materials, the masks and the silicon chips themselves, are not obviously the proper subject matter for the protection afforded to ideas, that is, the law of patent and trade secrets. This is because they are not novel, and, usually, they are published — at least in the sense that it is possible to 'reverse engineer' silicon chips (usually with some effort and expense, but the will and resources to expend prodigious amounts of both are not lacking in the computer industry).

The United States *Semiconductor Chip Protection Act* of 1984, seen by many as a response to increasing use by Japanese industry of United States chip designs, was enacted to ensure protection of some kind, both in the United States and internationally, for integrated circuits of all types.

Before the enactment of the United States law, the approach taken by most countries had been to attempt to reinterpret the existing laws and conventions in order to see whether they extended to the subject matter. As discussed in Chapter 3, there are a number of international conventions which deal with the protection of intellectual property, the most important of these being the Berne Union and the Universal Copyright Convention.

The Berne Union and the UCC

The Berne Union, for example, which the United States has only just joined, establishes a union for protection of 'literary and artistic works', including:

> every production in the literary, scientific and artistic domain, whatever may be the mode or form of its expression, such as . . . works of drawing, painting, architecture, sculpture, *engraving and lithography*; *photographic works to which are assimilated works expressed by processes analogous to photography*; works of applied art; illustrations, maps, plans, sketches and *three-dimensional works relative to* geography, typography, architecture or science. [Emphasis added.]

Under Articles 2(6) and 2(7), such works 'shall enjoy protection in all countries in the Union', but it is a matter for the legislation of each country of the union 'to determine the extent of the application of their laws to works of applied art and industrial designs and models'. The latter provision continues:

> works protected in the country of origin solely as designs and models shall be entitled in another country of the Union only to such special protection that is granted in that country to designs and models; however, if no such special protection is granted in that country, such work shall be protected as artistic works.

Finally, Article 5(2) provides that the exercise and enjoyment of copyright 'shall be independent of the existence of protection in the country of origin of the work'.

From the foregoing provisions, it would appear clear that the Berne Union is capable of interpretation to require member countries to protect integrated circuits under copyright law.

If this were correct, no new international treaties would be needed. As members of the Berne Union legislate or gain interpretations in favour of protection of chips, protection must be granted to foreign nationals in the same way as copyright in books or records is recognized internationally.

A curiosity arises that, during this period of uncertainty in relation to silicon chips, if one member of the Berne Union decides, by means of its judicial system, that its copyright legislation extends to protect silicon chips and mask works, then it is necessary that those works produced by citizens of other members of Berne countries will enjoy copyright in that member country, whilst not necessarily being certain of enjoying copyright in their country of origin. The reverse is also true, of course: a work may be considered to enjoy copyright in one country, but it is far from clear whether it will enjoy copyright in the other.

Japan, a Berne Union country, may have confused the issue somewhat by introducing its special semiconductor chip protection law. Is this a 'work of applied art' and/or 'industrial design [or] model'?

The Universal Copyright Convention, to which the United States is also a signatory, is rather different from the Berne Union, in that it is far less specific in relation to the works to which it extends. It refers to 'literary, scientific and artistic works, including ... engravings ... '. Furthermore, under the UCC, a member is obliged to protect 'artistic works' of a foreign national only if it offers that protection to its own nationals. This rather different approach means that it is a matter for each member country to decide the extent to which it will implement the UCC in this instance.

US semiconductor chip act

In the United States in the early eighties it was generally accepted that the United States *Copyright Act* (Title 17) would not apply to useful articles, it would apply only to separately identifiable artistic features. Amidst differences of opinion between the Judiciary Committees of the US Senate (which favoured amendment of Title 17) and the House of Representatives (which favoured special legislation), the United States legislature enacted the *Semiconductor Chip Protection Act* of 1984. Recognizing that masks will soon become obsolete, but believing that semiconductor chips will for the foreseeable future possess a layered structure, Congress chose to protect the topological arrangement of the layers which form the chip.

Protection under the Act is for ten years and it depends upon questions of nationality, first commercial exploitation and, importantly, international considerations. Mask works must be registered and to this end must be deposited with the United States Copyright Office. It is possible, however, to make a limited 'identifying' deposit if there are trade secrets associated with the mask work. The most extraordinary provisions relate to 'reverse engineering', and a form of compulsory licence, considered below.

An important section is 912(a) which states that nothing in the *Semiconductor Chip Protection Act* will affect any right or remedy held by any person under the *Copyright Act* or the *Patents Act*. Thus the problems which arise from the interaction of the designs law and the copyright law in common law countries will not occur in this context. It is therefore still open to a chip producer to bring a claim in the United States for copyright infringement of a mask work. If a court could be persuaded that, contrary to popular opinion, Title 17 does in fact protect semiconductor chips then the provisions of the *Semiconductor Chip Protection Act* would be to some extent otiose, except for the benefit of certainty gained in the interim.

The most radical sections of the *Semiconductor Chip Protection Act* are those dealing with reverse engineering. The ramifications of the provisions are still being assessed. For the first time in intellectual property protection, the taking of vast amounts of protected property is expressly sanctioned without any particular limitation as to the amount taken.

Under the copyright laws of common law countries, as well as those of say Japan and Taiwan, it can be said that a 'pure' form of reverse engineering is permissible. Such reverse engineering would be where a chip was examined and its functions and specifications written down. If these functions and specifications are then passed to a team which have not seen the original chip but who are asked to design a chip conforming to the noted functions and specifications, it can be said that nothing more than ideas used in the construction of the chip have been used and there is no property in ideas. Presumably the chip produced would be identifiably different from the original, but even if it were not, this should not qualify the rights of the reverse engineer.

In formulating the reverse engineering provisions, the United States Congress accepted the practice of the United States chip industry of allowing substantial use of a competitor's product design in the development of a new product. This process has been dubbed 'creative copying'.

The test for distinguishing legitimate reverse engineering and chip piracy is two pronged. If the second chip is substantially identical to the first chip there is a conclusive presumption of infringement. If the second chip is only 'substantially similar', then the second prong comes into play. To establish non-infringing similarity once the second chip has been identified as substantially similar, it must be established by 'competent documentary evidence' that the copying competitor had expended substantial energy and resources in the development of the second chip in addition to copying some aspects of the original.

This approach was adopted on the basis that it is relatively easy for a knowledgeable person to distinguish legitimate reverse engineering and the Courts would not be faced with a monstrous problem in deciding whether a particular chip was actually an infringement. It was thought that chips are at one end or the other of a spectrum between legitimate reverse engineering and chip piracy and that very few fall into the grey area between. The obvious problem with such a specific approach is the potential for technological change to render the Act obsolete. If a chip were to be completely reverse engineered by a computer, there may be no documentary evidence to show except a new design, and a job log which merely shows that the computer was doing something for a certain length of time.

There are also special reciprocity provisions by which mask works made in foreign countries giving protection to US mask works may be entitled to protection in the US under the US law.

The Japanese law

As already noted, Japan has introduced its own law. This was introduced primarily to take advantage of the reciprocity provisions of the United States law. It protects circuit layouts and gives the creator a sole use right which may be transferred (provided the transfer is registered) to a third party. Protection is for a period of ten years after registration.

There is nothing to prevent registration of identical layouts unless copying can be proved. This is similar to copyright law which, unlike patent law, does not grant monopoly in a work. Further, like the United States law, reverse engineering is permitted. An infringement occurs when, for a business purpose, the chip is produced, transferred, leased, exhibited or imported without authority. While lack of knowledge is a defence, an infringer is subject to three years' gaol or a fine. The damages are presumed to be the profits of the infringing party, although a greater amount can be claimed.

Other laws and conventions

A number of countries, particularly in Europe, have now introduced laws for protection for chips, and the EEC Commission has issued a directive on protection. The EEC directive is intended to establish an adequate and coordinated system of legal protection for chips throughout the EEC and to help EEC member nations obtain registration under the US Act. The directive includes the following points.

- Protection may be through national copyright laws or by specific statutory provisions.

- Protection should be for at least ten years but not more than fifteen years.

- Reverse engineering will not be considered as an infringement, but once substantial copyright is demonstrated, someone relying on the reverse engineering defence will have the burden of establishing that their own topography is indeed an original creation.

Notwithstanding the poor record of new intellectual property conventions, the World Intellectual Property Organization (WIPO) has proposed an international treaty on the topic. The WIPO treaty does not mandate a special law, but the main provisions are quite close to the United States and Japanese laws. Provisions include the points below.

- Each contracting state will grant the members of other contracting states the same rights it grants it own nationals.

- Teaching, research and reverse engineering exceptions are included.

- No formalities beyond deposit and registration may be required.

- Registration may not be required earlier than two years after initial commercial exploitation.

- Protection would be extended to intermediate forms and non-electrical (for example) optical functions. This is a broader formulation than both the United States and Japanese laws.

It may be that, over time, those who are granted reciprocity status under the United States law will form a *de facto* convention for the protection of the semiconductor chips. This may require modifications of the United States and Japanese laws towards the European and/or WIPO standards, and concessions on the part of European lawmakers towards the United States system of protection. This is indeed a rapidly developing area of the law.

Patents

What is a patent system?

Patents, like registered designs, are monopolies granted by the government for a limited period, typically sixteen or twenty years depending on country. However, far more potent than designs, they do not merely give a monopoly in a particular embodiment of a creative idea, they grant exclusivity in an idea, an invention, howsoever it may be expressed.

There may be several justifications for a patent system, and the conflicting nature of these justifications explains the wide diversity of patent systems throughout the world, each system reflecting the importance given to one or more of these different justifications. For example:

- the most obvious purpose of a patent system may be as a reward to inventive effort, although the system equally rewards those who may accidentally hit upon a good idea with little effort and those whose inventions result from the immense research and development that may be deployed by the modern industrial enterprises; and patent systems do not always differentiate in their rewards between inventions of great social benefit, and relatively minor improvements in existing technology — in fact, until relatively recent times, an evaluation of the 'inventiveness' or otherwise of an invention was irrelevant to the granting of a patent in most legal systems;

- a more likely purpose of the patent system is to attempt to ensure that new technologies are disclosed on a public register, so that all those involved in an industry may observe the developments that are being made, although they may not use them for a certain period, after which they fall into the public domain — yet most legal systems do little to force the inventor to disclose the 'heart' of the invention, procedural and other laws appearing almost to encourage the most obtuse and general descriptions of the invention, or at worst to allow the inventor to conceal the key to true commercial success, to maximize subsequent licensing or to prevent 'avoidance' engineering;

- yet another purpose may be simply to provide a register of those with the relevant technology, in order to enable those interested in acquiring or using the technology to make approaches for necessary assignments or licences.

As a result of these conflicts, different countries have quite different criteria for the granting of a patent. For example, the West German and Dutch systems are most rigorous in their examination processes, requiring high standards of disclosure of the essential nature of the invention as a condition of grant, but resulting in a very far reaching protection against articles or processes different from, but functionally equivalent to, the invention described in the patent, whereas there are no examination procedures at all in the national systems of Belgium and Italy, and no powers of rejection of an application in the French system. United States and English based systems may be found between such extremes.

In this section, we shall consider the median position, as it is this position to which, with growing 'internationalization' discussed further below, patent systems around the world are tending.

In such a median system, because of the extraordinary breadth and power of a patent, the right is reserved for inventions which are

- genuinely new, and
- clearly and precisely described

and the scrutiny afforded to each application is detailed, careful and protracted, to ensure so far as possible that these basic requirements are met.

Who may apply?

Obviously, the inventor should be the proper applicant. This should mean that another person who has 'stolen' the idea from the inventor is not entitled to be registered as the owner, and the true inventor is entitled during the application or for a short period after grant to challenge the application with a view to being substituted as the registered proprietor in due course. However, it should be noted that in some countries, the person entitled to be treated as the 'inventor' may really be the first person to use the invention in that country, not the inventor at all, or a person deriving the invention from the inventor.

In addition, it should be noted that most patent systems protect the first *applicant*, not necessarily the first inventor. With today's heavy competition in closely allied or identical fields of research and development, it is not infrequent that more than one person will devise the same inventive solution to a well understood problem. In this case, the first applicant will be entitled to proceed to registration, although the earlier inventor may be entitled to defend an action for infringement. This creates great pressure to lodge applications as early as possible, which can lead to problems as the inventor may feel pressed to lodge an application before the invention is fully 'ironed out', or properly understood, and this may lead to attacks upon the application or validity of the patent as being wrongly claimed or specified, or give competitors the opportunity to avoid the strict terms of the patent as it fails to specify the 'heart' of the invention. This may lead also to there being different owners of patents in different countries, for substantially the same invention.

Of course, the inventor may assign his or her rights to the invention prior to the application, or an employer may be entitled to the invention by virtue of its being devised 'in the course of employment' (see Chapter 2), as a result of which the applicant will be the assignee or other person entitled to ownership.

Genuinely new inventions

An invention can be one or both of two things, a process or a thing. That is, it may be a method of doing something, such as a method of generating an NTSC colour signal from analogue input, or it may be a thing, such as a disk controller device, or a circuit. In either case it must have one essential ingredient: it must not have been invented by someone else before, or be part of the 'prior art' before the date of application. Many countries also require that it constitute a genuine inventive step above that part of the common general knowledge of those skilled in the area of the invention in the country of application, a subset of the 'prior art'.

What it cannot be is a scientific formula, a mathematical principle, an algorithm, a scheme for performing a mental process, 'bare' information or a 'mere' discovery — many ways of excluding pure information with no industrial application, such as an appreciation that a solvent is necessary to prepare a surface of a circuit board, without the discovery of a new solvent for this purpose, or a new way of achieving the same end. Also, policy considerations frequently prohibit patenting of methods of treatment of the human body, or inventions the disclosure of which will be prejudicial to national security.

Finally, an invention can hardly be something which does not work at all, such as a perpetual motion machine, although the Patent Office will not examine too closely the efficacy of every invention. 'Inutility' may also be a ground of revocation of a patent after grant, or it may be a fatal ambiguity or a lack of complete disclosure of the invention.

What does 'new' mean?

'Novelty' is a fundamental requirement. The invention can be a novel *combination* of previously known components (such as the components of a sailboard in the troubled patent for windsurfers), or a newly discovered *extension* or *use* of something previously known (here penicillin provides an example, the famous drug was not patented, but it resulted in many patents for new ways of manufacturing it, with better yields and so on, and new forms with special applications). However, the new thing or process, or combination, extension or use cannot be 'described by the prior art'.

What is this 'prior art'? It is the information on the subject matter of the patent that has been published prior to the patent application (or possibly even included in prior patent applications, even if published *after* the invention, an artificiality designed to minimize the risk of two patents covering the same invention). This may even mean a photograph of the invention, or an article embodying the invention, given to any person not under an obligation of secrecy, provided a person familiar with the technology (not an expert) could see the essential features of the invention in the photograph or article. It also means documents which are not normally studied by those in the industry, such as other patent applications, scientific journals, and in some patent systems may even include such material from foreign countries, unless very obscure. However, sometimes the invention must be clearly shown only in a single piece of prior art; one cannot collect such materials together in order to create an artificial 'mosaic' that is said to describe the invention.

Surprisingly, what the prior art does include in most countries is revelations made by the inventor himself or herself prior to the patent application, except in very limited circumstances! This can lead to terrible misfortunes; in one famous case a photograph of a prototype was published before the patent application was lodged, and the court decided that the nature of the invention could be observed in the photograph. Canada and the United States are a little more generous to the inventor in this regard, in order to ensure protection is extended to the proper inventor.

In addition, novelty can be lost if the invention is 'used' prior to the application, that is, commercially exploited in some way, even in secret, but such use is normally limited to the country of application.

This places a tremendous onus upon inventors who believe that they have a valuable idea, but need capital to develop the idea into a complete patent application, and to prosecute the application, to maintain secrecy whilst promoting the invention to potential investors.

Obviousness

In addition to the requirement of novelty, some countries also impose a requirement that the work not be 'obvious', that is, clearly and unambiguously signposted by material generally available prior to the application.

This requirement has two qualifications which are very important in practice.

(1) The material to be considered is not all the prior art, as in the case of the enquiry into novelty. It is only that material which would be available and generally known by a person skilled in the area of the patent application, but by no means an expert. Such material may be 'mosaiced' in a manner not permissible in respect of novelty, but only if and to the extent that such a determinedly pedestrian individual would regard that as obvious. The material does not include obscure materials, and may not even include prior patent applications. applications.

(2) Again unlike the enquiry into novelty, the material considered will only be that generally available *in the country of the application.*

As for what 'obvious' may mean in practice, this is difficult to evaluate. However, it should be borne in mind that courts may ask 'if it was so obvious, why wasn't it thought of before?', showing a clear scepticism of use of this requirement with the benefit of hindsight.

Clear and precise description

A patent application consists of two parts, the 'claims' and a 'specification'.

The claims list the inventions claimed by the inventor, often starting with the very broadest description and reducing to the most particular inventive elements, so that claims may be eliminated during the examination process, or in litigation, yet still leave some part or parts of the invention in a valid patent. In addition, and for the same reason, the invention may be claimed variously as a thing and a method, for example, as both a colour video generation device and a method of generating a colour signal from analogue input.

The specification is meant to disclose clearly to one "skilled in the art" (relying again on this prosaic fiction of the capable but uninventive technician'), that is, knowledgeable in the subject matter of the invention, what the invention is, and must be carefully worded to be clear, unambiguous, and supportive of the claims. The specification should be quite detailed, and may include a description of the ideal embodiment of the invention, as well as diagrams.

However, it is often the case that the inventor omits, if possible, the 'best method' of applying the invention, and this may make the difference between commercial viability and worthlessness of the invention. Inventors must be conscious of the fact that a successful invention, because it is published for all the world to see, is immediately the subject of attempts to 'engineer around' the precise words of the claims and specification, and hence holding back the 'best method' may be a device for keeping a technological edge, or give an advantage in licensing negotiations. Such knowledge also ensures that patent applications can be agonizing in their attention to detail and apparent repetition, in an attempt to cover every possible angle.

The procedure for granting of a patent

Once the patent application is complete, it will be subject to examination by skilled personnel in the Patent Office, who will search out the 'prior art' for themselves, and may ask questions, make objections, impose requirements and ultimately either accept or reject the application for publication. Once published, any person in the world can lodge objections to the patent, and this may involve complex administrative proceedings. In the process, patent claims may be eliminated or modified, or a patent application may be split, if the Patent Office is of the view that more than one invention is described.

Finally, if the patent application survives this gamut, letters patent will be granted and the grant will be published, subject to payment of further fees. The patent will be subject to renewal fees during its term, failure to pay which will result in its lapse.

Patents may sometimes be extended beyond the maximum period specified by law; however to justify such an extension, a patentee must explain why he or she has not been adequately rewarded during the period of grant. Accordingly, regard is usually given to preventing circumstances such as wars, but in recent times courts have been more prepared to take into account long periods of delay in exploitation caused by government safety procedures, or other regulations affecting the patented invention.

With such difficult and complex procedures, patent applications typically take a long time to process, and are very costly. If an inventor is serious about seeking patent protection, a patent attorney should be engaged to advise on the patentability of the invention, to conduct a preliminary and later detailed examination of the prior art, to prepare the application in the light of that prior art, and to deal with Patent Office enquiries and procedures. Patent attorneys are technically skilled in their various disciplines and are specially qualified by the Patent Office to prepare and prosecute patent applications, as a result of which they have a monopoly amongst professional advisers in this area; the inventor should not rely on himself or the Patent Office (which is also entitled to prepare patent applications) to conduct a patent application.

Petty patents

In an effort to simplify the patent system, and/or extend patent protection to inventions of lesser stature than those which should be the subject of the full patent system, there have been introduced in many countries modifications of the patent system, permitting 'petty patents' or 'utility patents'. These are intended to be simpler applications, perhaps with only one claim and, as a result of their lesser requirements, result in a much shorter grant of monopoly, for example, a maximum of seven years. Unfortunately, the systems of petty patents or utility patents have not always had the beneficial effects of speed, cost and availability for which they were designed.

Infringement

The monopoly rights granted by a patent are considerable. The patentee has the exclusive right to make a patented article, or to use a patented method, and even to exploit commercially such articles and methods, as well as to licence others to do the same. In some systems the patentee may even have rights to prevent possession of a patented article for purposes contrary to his or her own. Such rights are so broad in fact, that courts have found it necessary to 'imply' a licence granted by every patentee to a purchaser of patented goods so that the purchaser may exercise the patent in order to repair the goods!

Having regard to such broad powers, it becomes very important to interpret patents carefully when infringement is claimed.

It is not possible here to go into detail on this large body of law. However it should be noted that there are basically two different philosophies in respect of the interpretation of patents.

The English system requires that the alleged infringing article embodies the 'essential integers' of the invention actually described in the patent. If the patent requires a particular expression of the invention, and does not catch functional equivalents, then an article which has been designed around the patent so as to do the same thing but not include one of these 'essential integers' will not be an infringement, although a mere 'colourable substitution' of 'mechanical equivalents' will not prevent an article or process from being an infringement. Such subtle distinctions can be hard to put into practice; in a famous case in which a patent described the invention as requiring the movement of a component from rear to front, it was found not to be infringed by a device which moved the same component from front to rear.

This requires of those drafting patent applications that they go to great lengths to generalize their claims, in an attempt to cover every possible permutation of the invention, to set the bounds of the monopoly as broadly as possible. The limit to this activity is defined by the sanction of invalidity of any claim which is too broad in its scope.

By contrast, the German system permits a claim of infringement to be made when the alleged infringing article is clearly contemplated by the invention described in the patent. Such a system is more likely to encourage a disclosure of the essence of the invention in the patent.

International aspects of patents

There is no such thing as an international patent — every patent is a national grant, and must be applied for and prosecuted separately in the country of grant. For this reason, seeking any sort of international coverage is a complex and costly business. Selective targeting of countries seen to be important to the patent is essential in minimizing costs and administrative burdens.

In addition, many countries which would wish to have an effective patent system are unable to afford or recruit the highly skilled bureaucracy necessary to administer a full, searching and examining patent system.

Various international treaties have sought to reduce these difficulties, both for inventors and countries new to a full patent system.

One of the earliest of these, the Paris Union, has been mentioned before and will be referred to again in relation to trade mark rights. As well as setting certain basic standards for the patent systems of member countries, it gives a twelve month period of grace in which to lodge patent applications in other member countries after the initial application in a member country. If it were not for this, after making the initial application and permitting it to be initially advertised, one would be precluded from further applications in other countries because the original application would have become part of the prior art!

A further treaty, the International Patent Cooperation Union, or PCT, attempts to advance the cause of internationalism a little further by:

- permitting an initial application to be made in one member country naming any other member countries, in which case if the application proceeds it is automatically treated as an application in each of those countries with the same date as the initial application (the application must still be dealt with individually in each country however); and

- making provision for 'International Search Offices', including the United States, Japan, Australia and the European Patent Office in Germany, any one of which may receive an initial application under the Union (in its language only), after which it may conduct a search of the prior art and may produce a report on such matters as whether the invention is inherently patentable, on novelty and obviousness, for use by other national patent offices in due course,

with the purpose of streamlining and reducing the cost of international patent applications.

In Europe, further attempts at 'internationalizing' the patent system have resulted in a European Patent Convention, whereby European nations have agreed to further cooperation in processing patent applications in member countries, and most advanced of all is the Community Patent Convention, which creates an 'EEC Patent', a single application resulting in a patent for the entire European Economic Community.

Membership of the PCT Union is listed in Appendix II, and of the Paris Union in Appendix III.

Patents and computer programs

The law in respect of the patentability of computer programs has followed a similar course in most countries.

It is the requirements of novelty and inventiveness which eliminate most computer programs from patentability, even the most creative or clever. Rarely are they anything more than an assembly of familiar components, doing something well known but not done in quite the same way before. Although this sounds like the basis of an invention, rarely is this the case.

It appears, however, that, properly specified and claimed, a computer program may be patentable, either as an integral part of a device, or as part of method or process claims. This may be more so in countries where petty patents or utility patents have been introduced, with their lower level of inventiveness and hence shorter protection.

Generally speaking, however, letters patent are not available for computer programs, nor are they suitable for the protection of computer programs, because the cost and rigidity of the patent system make it inherently impractical for dealing with the highly fluid, ever changing things which computer programs tend to be.

Licensing

The patent law of most countries requires no formality for the assignment or licensing of patents, although to be registered an assignment or licence must be in writing.

It is of importance to note in international licensing agreements that an exclusive licence generally gives the licensee the right to commence legal action for patent infringement in its own name, usually subject only to minor procedural rules; that is, unless the parties to the licence expressly agree to the contrary. Incidentally, an 'exclusive' licence in this context means exclusive *even of the patentee*, that is, even the patent owner must agree not to exercise the patent rights. Of course, the patent licensed must be a patent of the country in which the licensed acts are to be carried out; we noted above that patents are national, so it is no use having a United States patent in Germany!

It is common for patent licences to deal with a number of related issues in the same document — most notably, access to confidential information not disclosed in the patent as to such matters as best materials, methods, marketing and other matters both technical and commercial. Care should be taken, however, to avoid breaches of anti-trust laws, which frequently bear upon provisions quite common in patent licences.

For example, 'tying' arrangements, conditions of a licence which require the licensee to obtain his materials from the licensor or some third party, or which may even limit the persons to whom the licensee may supply, may be illegal or require modification to be made legal. Another common provision, a 'patent pooling' or 'assignment back' condition, by which the licensee agrees to assign to the licensors all developments of the patented invention, is sometimes regarded as anti-competitive.

Because the monopoly powers of the patentee are so great, there are many opportunities for using that power in a manner contrary to the competition law policies of the country of the patent: pricing, exclusivity, customer sharing, lock outs and so on. For general considerations in this area, see Chapter 10.

Finally, it should be noted that there are frequently provisions in national patent laws for compulsory licensing in certain circumstances, usually failure by the patentee to exercise the patent rights in the country for a certain period of time. These provisions tend to be outdated in an international licensing environment, where the centralization of manufacture in one country could well bring benefits to the patent country in terms of cost and availability which could not be achieved if the patent were exercised in that country. To maintain some fairness, however, there are tribunals established to determine the conditions of licence, including royalties. These provisions are, however, rarely utilized.

Sui Generis Protection Laws

In what may appear to have been a knee-jerk reaction to the issue of protection of computer programs, and other products of the computer industry, some countries have introduced purpose-specific legislation to provide the protection feared lacking in existing laws. An example is provided by the semiconductor chip protection laws of the United States being forced upon other countries.

The problems with such purpose-specific legislation are

- it tends to provide a short term of protection, rather than the standard periods: the life of the author plus fifty years in the case of copyright, or sixteen or more years in the case of patents, as there is a common misconception that because some products of the computer industry have a short commercial life, all such products are so restricted — an assumption time is proving to be false and in any event a restriction not considered relevant for all other ephemeral articles, such as railway timetables in the case of copyright;

- it tends to provide for a registration system which is extremely inappropriate and inconvenient for products which are subject to continuous change;

- unlike copyright or patent, it tends to provide for inflexible definitions, which may be appropriate for the technology of today, but is likely to be more difficult to apply in ten years, whereas standard protection systems tend to operate on flexible generalizations;

- it creates overlap problems with existing legislation, inevitably leading to anomalies and intractable interpretation difficulties, such as we saw with designs legislation; and

- it creates a special category of protection which may fall *outside* the international system of intellectual property protection, resulting in reciprocity problems between nations, and unfairness where foreign works or inventions which would enjoy protection if brought within the standard systems of protection lose protection because of the exclusion of such works or inventions.

5 Confidential Information and Trade Secrets

Why do courts protect 'confidential information'?

'Three things', said the English Chancellor, Sir Thomas More in the sixteenth century, 'are to be helped in Conscience: Fraud, Accident and Things of Confidence'.

So saying, the ill-fated Lord Chancellor illustrated the breadth of the personal duties which have, by one means or another, become legally enforceable in the laws of most nations. In some countries this duty is enshrined in the criminal law (such as s.317 of the Taiwanese Criminal Code). In most countries, however, one cannot rely on the criminal law, and a duty of confidentiality must be enforced, or damages for breach of that duty must be claimed, in civil action.

For many years in English law it was thought that the obligation arose because of a sort of contract. In other words, it was thought that when a person revealed to another some secret, it must be that the disclosure was conditional upon a promise, express or implied, not to betray that confidence.

Of course, that may be true in many cases, but sometimes the rules of contract and 'implied terms' (see Chapter 7) plainly break down — for example, if the secret information is accidentally uncovered by a competitor or, for that matter, stolen, by an act of 'industrial espionage'. Furthermore, there are cases in which 'innocent third parties' receive the information from a malefactor, but are genuinely unaware of the duty of confidence that attaches to the information in the first place.

We will look at these individual issues a little more closely later but, in general terms, the solution to these problems was found in the Lord Chancellor's words mentioned above. That is, the law in this case is not concerned with the niceties of contract law, it is concerned with the duty of 'confidence', and 'conscience'. So it is only concerned with whether the information is *genuinely confidential*, and whether at the time it was initially disclosed *that confidentiality was evident to the recipient*.

Why has the law developed in this way? We said in Chapter 1 that the law will not always stretch to general moral obligations, without the aid of special statutes. No doubt there are many historical and sociological reasons. Some cynics might say of the English law that it arose because of the English passion for royalty — the 'leading case' concerned the private diaries of Queen Victoria which had fallen into the hands of an engraver who wished to reproduce the charming drawings that the late Queen had enshrined in the diaries for family use only. However, the most important reason for the law of confidential information arising in almost every country is the necessity to the free working of the business world that confidential information can be disclosed without fear of losing the commercial advantage of it.

Without this protection, business would freeze. For example, a patent protects a truly novel idea or invention, but frequently the patent expresses itself in a range of possibilities, and the most is achieved from the patent only by knowing the most advantageous means of exploiting it. These ways of getting the most out of the patent are usually closely guarded secrets, and it is common for licensors of patents to insist on disclosure of this information. Without such disclosure, the patent may not be commercially viable, and failure to disclose this information could defeat the purpose of the patent system, namely the dissemination of new technologies (see Chapter 4).

The example of patent law also illustrates something of great importance to the nature of confidential information, that is, it may consist of well known components, but its value, and hence its confidentiality, consists of the special way familiar components have been put together.

In addition to non-patentable inventions and processes, there are many other types of information which do not qualify for protection under other legal categories. Copyright, for example, only protects the form in which ideas are expressed, not the ideas themselves, and is thus rarely sufficient. In the case of the computer industry, obvious examples which spring to mind are source codes and flow charts which, although obviously not patentable, and unlikely to be copied as such, are things which a competitor may be very interested in having.

When is information regarded as confidential?

Before embarking on this question, it must be made clear that the information for which protection is sought must be reasonably identifiable. It is simply not enough to claim confidence in vague and broad categories of commercial knowledge, such as 'the customer base', 'business policies' or 'product directions'. To claim the assistance of a court, an aggrieved party must, in effect, be able to give a written description of the information claimed to be confidential, in terms precise enough so that the court, and the party to be restrained, can know what it is that can be used, and what it is that cannot.

Once the confidential information is identified, the issue of confidentiality essentially depends on whether the information has been previously disclosed to others, or even a single person may be enough, without any obligation of secrecy.

Disclosure to employees, within reasonable limits, does not undermine this status, because employees are always bound by a very broad obligation of confidentiality (see Chapters 2 and 5), but disclosure to contractors is another thing entirely because, as we have seen, there is not necessarily any implied term of confidentiality in an independent contractor's relationship with a principal. Likewise, disclosure to any number of customers, so long as each is aware of the duty of confidentiality, will not necessarily result in the information falling into 'the public domain'.

Example

Beta Silicon is a manufacturer and distributor of advanced integrated circuit technology, including processors and very large memory chips. It resolves with Gamma Scientific Instruments to develop a new hand-held information storage and calculating device for certain scientific and engineering purposes, which will use large memory capacity chips to store mathematical and engineering data and have the capacity to process information on an LCD screen with graphics capability, and so on. Both companies are publicly listed, and so information concerning the joint venture is extremely market sensitive until the two have completed product development and feasibility studies. The following events occur:

(1)   the two companies approach a number of potential components suppliers to discuss pricing and product development issues; all requests for tender should be stamped 'Confidential', but the President's secretary misses one or two, which accordingly go out unmarked.

(2)   All employees of each of the companies (some sixty in each) are notified of progress on this vital project.

(3)   The two companies consult with their lawyers and patent attorneys, discussing in detail the product design with a view to lodging patent applications in all major industrialized countries; their advisers are very doubtful concerning the patentability of the device, but patent applications are lodged — the patent registers are of course public records.

(4)   There are rumors of a possible merger, which affects share prices dramatically, as a result of which the companies are asked for an explanation from the relevant stock exchanges. They consult with their brokers and the stock exchange is notified of their plans but requested not to publish until the companies' plans are further developed.

(5)   A press release is prepared awaiting an announcement, but is accidentally sent by the President's secretary to a small industry newspaper, the Silicon Herald. A short time later the President, whilst enjoying cocktails with friends, loudly complains of his secretary's carelessness and the editor of the Silicon Herald is present to hear of her indiscretion.

Beta and Gamma wish to prevent the Silicon Herald from publishing the press release. Can they do so?

The disclosure to potential suppliers, although widespread, should not limit the confidentiality because of the notification of the secrecy of the information being disclosed. This is compromised by the secretary's first oversight, but because the oversight was limited to only one or two suppliers, and because they probably regarded it as confidential anyway, or would be aware that confidentiality had been imposed on other prospective suppliers, this would not necessarily disentitle Beta and Gamma to their relief. Disclosure to employees should not adversely affect the two companies' rights, because of the employees' legal duties of confidentiality and their relatively small numbers. Likewise the disclosure to the patent attorneys, legal advisers and stock exchanges because of their legal obligations of confidentiality, although nothing was expressly said to limit them.

However, the filing of the patent application and the indiscretion of the President pose difficult questions. Lodging a patent application necessitates permission to publish the application in the ordinary course (see Chapter 4) — this is so with any public record. However, patent applications are usually not published for quite a long time after being lodged, so the information may be regarded as confidential until at least the date of formal publication. Even then, only those few who read patent office publications may be aware of the application. The President's carelessness may be the real undoing of the companies — but it still may be that such disclosure, again being so limited, and perhaps only being comprehensible to those like the editor of the newspaper who know the background, will not be sufficient to prevent Beta and Gamma from pulling back the press release.

The above example illustrates to what extent information may indeed be distributed and still retain confidentiality. It really is a matter of degree!

Information can lose its confidentiality, notwithstanding all the above precautions, if the person claiming the benefit of confidentiality has failed to enforce diligently that confidentiality, or even if an employee has carelessly, or maliciously, published the information — in that case, the 'owner' of the information may lose all rights in relation to the information, except against the employee, because the information was already published (even if the owner was unaware of this at the time).

The American *Restatement of the Law of Torts* (Article 757) gives the following review of relevant considerations regarding the issue of whether information is or remains confidential:

"(1)   the extent to which the information is known outside [the] business;

(2)   the extent to which it is known by employees and others involved in [the] business;

(3)   the extent of measures taken ... to guard the secrecy of the information;

(4)   the value of the information to [the business] and [its] competitors;

(5)   the amount of effort or money expended by [the business] in developing the information;

(6)   the ease or difficulty with which the information could be properly acquired or duplicated by others (that is, by their independent endeavours)."

How is confidentiality made known?

As already indicated, the best method of imposing an obligation of confidentiality is to ensure that the recipient knows of it, preferably in writing (although this only assists in *proof*, and is not a requirement). There is no need for a contract — a letter, or even a stamped warning in a visible place, will be sufficient.

However, the obligation of confidentiality may arise even where there is no express warning given. If it is obvious to the recipient of the information, or would be obvious to any reasonable person in the position of the recipient, then that person will be equally bound by the duty of confidence.

The issue is resolved then by reference to the circumstances in which a person was receiving the information — that is, whether he or she should have realized that the information was confidential. If the manuals were clearly marked 'confidential' that would probably determine the issue. One can rely on the nature of the computer industry as a whole — whether in this industry the kind of information in question is such that one would expect it to be confidential, or not. For example, source code is almost invariably regarded as highly confidential, but user manuals rarely, if ever. In the case of technical manuals, one would probably conclude that they were the sort of information which is kept in house for employee technicians only.

The fact that confidentiality may be imposed without any direct, express warning has a very important consequence. It enables 'third parties' to be bound by the duty of confidence, that is, people who have no contact with the owner of the confidential information, but may obtain it through someone else. We consider this further below.

An equally important corollary is that information which is not genuinely confidential at all cannot gain some sort of *de facto* protection simply by being described as confidential, or stamped with any number or any colour of warnings!

Does the law prevent use of confidential information, as well as disclosure?

The protection of confidential information would not be very effective if it only prevented disclosure. Clearly, the usual purpose of taking trade secrets is not to give them or sell them to competitors, but to use the information for the taker's own advantage. For this reason, the court will restrain by injunction even the use of information gained under an obligation of confidentiality, otherwise than in conformity with the original purpose for which the information was given.

Example

April Rice has thought of an excellent method for regulating irrigation and other agricultural management aspects of grain production and conceives that a program for executing the method would have a good market. She goes to see Exceptional Software, Inc. and offers to disclose this method in return for involvement in product development and marketing and a royalty. Exceptional agrees to this, and Rice discloses the method. Work on initial product design begins; however, after a few months, conflicting product development forces Exceptional to abandon the plan and Rice, disillusioned, loses interest. A year or two later, however, Exceptional acquires the rights to modify and distribute a farm management package produced by Farm Management Products, Inc. and when the Exceptional version of the product is released it includes a grain irrigation and management module in which April recognizes some of the crucial aspects of her own idea.

In this example, there can be no doubt that April may take action against Exceptional. It is plain that the idea was her own, and it was disclosed in circumstances in which it must have been obvious that the information was confidential — Exceptional did not know it already and they agreed to pay a royalty for it! Rice cannot get back her right to be consulted in product development, nor can Exceptional diminish its liability to her on the basis that they did not receive the benefit of her advice in product development, because they cannot gain a benefit from their own decision not to honour their obligations of confidentiality.

Finally, it should be recognized that the court may not grant an injunction preventing the continued distribution of the Exceptional Farm Management package, or even that part which embodies Rice's confidential information, because that will help nobody and would only be destructive. So the court would be likely in this case to order Exceptional to pay the agreed amount of royalties in respect of the number of packages

*already sold, and a capitalized lump sum in lieu of future royalties —
unless the parties can themselves agree on a method to deal with the future.*

*Had Rice herself been in competition with Exceptional, and
producing a product of her own, the court may well grant an injunction, unless the information or the method is so public by virtue of Rice's own
product that it would be silly to order Exceptional not to do what anybody
else who sees Rice's own product can do.*

*Of course, the court will grant an order to prevent Exceptional from
disclosing anything about Rice's method that remains confidential, if it is
likely to remain so.*

This example shows the effect of the general law on duty of confidentiality, but could equally be based on the contract that existed between Rice
and Exceptional.

In the next section, we shall examine how the duty of confidentiality extends beyond a contractual relationship, and accordingly the true
power and importance of the duty of confidentiality.

Prevention of the use of confidential information by third parties

As we have already seen, one of the exceptional features of the duty of
confidentiality is that it may be used to prevent use of the information.
This is not a power available in the law of copyright, for example, which
only controls copying, publication, translation and other such forms of
exploitation, but any individual may *use* a copyright work to his or her
heart's content, so long as it does not involve copying, publication,
translation and so on.

Another feature of this far reaching power, considered necessary
to preserve the integrity of the duty of confidentiality, is that it reaches
out to affect recipients of confidential information with whom one may
have had no relationship, whether contractual or otherwise, at all.

For example, in the case of Exceptional Software and April Rice
considered above, even if Exceptional, instead of using the idea itself,
had disclosed it to the supplier of the Farm Management package in joint
product development meetings, then Rice would have had the same
rights against Farm Management, Inc. as she has against Exceptional,
notwithstanding that she had no contract with Farm Management. A
similar conclusion applies to information improperly obtained by
listening devices or by industrial espionage of other types.

Let us consider another example to make this clearer.

Example ——————————————————————————————————

Iota Limited is the manufacturer of a range of large systems and peripherals. Its best and largest customer with many installed sites is Heavy Engineering Limited (HEL). In fact HEL's system service and support requirements are so substantial that Iota has supplied HEL technical staff with technical support manuals including detailed logic diagrams and other materials necessary for service and support, so that HEL can do most of its necessary technical support without calling on Iota's less than adequate resources.

HEL acquires a number of supposedly transparent tape drives from System Peripherals Limited but on installation there are a number of compatibility problems arising from recent operating system and hardware developments of Iota's products. System Peripherals gains access to Iota's technical manuals whilst attempting to instal its tape drives at HEL, which enable it to overcome the difficulties quickly.

System Peripherals upgrades its products and commences hard selling to Iota customers, using HEL as a reference site — the System Peripheral products are much cheaper than the equivalent Iota range.

Here there is no question of claiming against HEL, at the least for reasons of customer relations, but possibly also because HEL may not have been aware that System Peripherals gained access to the manuals. System Peripherals employees may well have stumbled on the manuals and simply assumed they were available for use on the HEL project, and subsequently passed on what they learnt to management at Systems. For this reason, Iota is concerned only whether it can inhibit System Peripherals in its use of the information gained from the manuals — and Iota has no contract to rely on to do this.

The answer depends upon the two simple questions referred to in the preceding sections: is (or was) the information genuinely confidential?', and 'was it disclosed in circumstances in which Systems was, **or should have been**, *aware of that confidentiality?'. The answers to both these questions depend on the circumstances.*

Here HEL itself appears to have obtained the information without restriction, but if Iota can show that it made HEL aware that the manuals were released to it as a concession only, and were considered confidential, then that would be sufficient to preserve the status of the information. But as for Systems, obviously, Iota was not around to warn Systems personally concerning the use of the manuals.

The issue is resolved therefore by reference to the circumstances in which Systems came upon the information — that is, whether Systems should have realized that the information was confidential. As indicated above, in the case of Iota's internal technical manuals, one would probably conclude that they were the sort of information which is kept in house for employee technicians only.

As a result, Iota probably would have a claim against Systems. Again, whether Iota will be granted an injunction preventing Systems from selling its upgraded product at all will depend on the 'justice and

*convenience' of the situation as it stands before the court. However, a
significant factor in favour of Iota, if it has acted promptly and not delayed
so long that 'the cat is out of the bag' already, will be that continued use of
the information by Systems probably entails an ever expanding wave of
disclosure of the information in Systems' own technical manuals, to
distributors, OEMs, and so on, so that an award of money alone may not
adequately compensate Iota for its loss of market position.*

Reverse engineering — the 'springboard test'

It is a frequent defence to a claim of breach of confidentiality that what
was done did not exploit any trade secret obtained from the claimant, but
used independently available information, or even if the trade secret was
used, it was information which could have been obtained from independent sources anyway.

Courts have often been sceptical of defences such as these when
the person alleging them has taken the time and trouble to find out the
claimant's trade secrets in the first place, and then alleges that he or she
did not need them anyway. Sometimes the cleverest solutions to
problems seem simple and obvious only in hindsight.

Specially difficult problems are raised by so called 'reverse
engineering'. Genuine cases of reverse engineering involve the study of a
product in order to determine its design strengths, followed by creation of
a new product which takes advantage of those same design strengths. As
long as no copyright or patent rights are infringed, there is nothing wrong
with this activity, because it is obvious that anything which can be
discovered from inspection of a generally available product cannot be
confidential.

However, if a person finds out from the original manufacturer a
method of producing the product cheaply which is not generally known,
and cannot be devised from inspection of the product, he or she may be
prevented from using that knowledge to produce the article in question.
It is said that the recipient of the information has had the advantage of a
'springboard' into the technology, gaining a competitive advantage
without any research and development cost.

This may lead to an anomalous situation where a recipient of
confidential information is bound by his knowledge in a way that other
manufacturers who independently derive this information are not. To
overcome this anomaly, courts which have jealously preserved the
obligation of confidence may yield to the practical compromise of
ordering the payment of damages or a royalty only, instead of prohibiting
outright the use of the information.

Restraint of innocent third parties

In the example of Iota and Systems Peripherals given above, an important issue was whether Systems was aware of the confidentiality of the information at the time it received it. What if the information has already been passed on to someone else, for example an OEM (Original Equipment Manufacturer) or distributor, who is completely unaware of Iota's interests?

This is a difficult issue for the law. In English law, it has been resolved by looking back again to the words of Sir Thomas More, and the demands of business. It is the primary concern of the courts that the confidentiality of the information be preserved if that is still possible and therefore an injunction will be issued to restrain use or disclosure of the information by a completely innocent third party.

However, questions of fairness arise when the 'innocent third party' has *paid* for the information. For example, in the case of Systems Peripherals and Iota, above, if an OEM company had paid Systems Peripherals for the right to repackage its Iota compatible product and use the technical manuals which incorporate Iota's technical information, can that OEM be prevented from gaining the benefit of what it paid good money to receive? The OEM, of course, would be unaware of the claim of Iota in respect of the information.

In this sort of case, the answer the law gives may vary from country to country. In most countries, the court will acknowledge the overriding importance of the obligation of confidence. In English based legal systems, it is said that confidential information is not property, like an automobile or a piece of land, or even like copyright, it is merely the subject of a personal duty, and hence the principle of a '*bona fide* purchaser for value without notice' is not applicable. In the United States, confidential information, or trade secrets, have been regarded as intangible property, like copyright, but nevertheless in some cases the courts will still prevent the use of the information by an innocent third party who has paid for it.

When is the duty of confidentiality no longer binding?

In the preceding sections, it has been explained that it may not matter if information which is regarded as sensitive has been disclosed to numerous people, as long as all the people to whom the information is disclosed are bound by an obligation of confidentiality, and that obligation is diligently maintained.

Of course, the more people to whom information is disclosed, and the less careful the controls, the harder it becomes for any court to believe that the information could still be genuinely confidential, even if stamped 'Confidential'. There is no way of effectively controlling the information once it has been released in this way, and no amount of stamping of documents as 'Confidential' or of confidentiality or non-disclosure agreements will be of any use.

Why cannot there be a contract not to disclose the information, even if it is already in the public domain? Such a contract cannot be enforced by any of the remedies available to the court — the court will not award damages because no further damage can be suffered by disclosure of already public information, and the court will not award an injunction because that would be an exercise in futility.

Are there other circumstances in which the information which is or was confidential may be disclosed?

It is often said that there may be justifications where a duty to inform the public may be more important than the duty of confidentiality. This is usually raised by journalists and user groups, who may also claim an entitlement to publish arising out of constitutional or other rights to 'free speech'.

The claims of journalists and interest groups of 'public interest' are generally not considered a good enough reason to break a confidence. Of course, in the case of criminal offences, and where there may be danger to life or property, it may be obligatory to disclose this information — but only to relevant authorities, and only if one is sure that this is necessary.

Example

ABC Limited has just released a new mainframe product, the Apex 6. Shortly after release, an internal product evaluation report on the product is extremely critical of the product, recommending major product redesign. This report somehow finds its way to the desk of Jules Guttersnipe, a reporter with a major computer industry weekly, Systemweek, who proposes to write an article based upon its revelation. ABC becomes aware of Guttersnipe's intentions when he asks the President of the ABC Apex Users Group for comment.

Can ABC Limited do anything about this potentially damaging disclosure by Guttersnipe to the world, or by the President of the Apex User Group to other interested users experiencing problems with their immensely expensive equipment? Does it make any difference that the poor performance of the Apex 6 may have an adverse effect on the profitability of major public companies using the equipment?

Notwithstanding the interest of future buyers of the Apex 6 systems, or the existing users, or their shareholders, to have the benefit of the report, ABC is entitled to take court action to prevent the disclosure. Needless to say, ABC is equally entitled to prevent copying and publication of the report itself, by virtue of its copyright in it.

Who can rely on the obligation of confidentiality?

It is obvious the obligation of confidentiality is owed to the person who gives the information. Obvious, but this may lead to conclusions that many in the computer industry overlook.

Example
_____

The Service Bank Limited has acquired a new banking system and point of sale and banking terminals. It embarks upon an ambitious program to produce a leading edge automatic teller service which it intends will give it a significant competitive edge on its competitors. To that end, it engages a systems analyst and an analyst/programmer, as well as several program-mers to create necessary controlling software. These are engaged as contractors only, not as employees.

Having designed and developed the product for Service Bank, the systems analyst and analyst programmer appreciate the great commercial advantage in it and seek lucrative engagement elsewhere, at another bank.

Having been so foolish as not to deal with the contingency with a proper contractors' agreement, can Service Bank do anything about their threatened competitive edge?

The prospects may not be good for the Service Bank. The confiden-tial information devised by the contractors was supplied by them to the Bank, not the other way around, so that, depending on the precise nature of the information, it may be that it is the bank that owes the duty of confidentiality to the contractors.

A person who has given confidential information is entitled, of course, to disclose it to anybody he or she chooses, unless there is an express, or implied, term in a contract imposing confidentiality — but any lawyer will advise that, except in the employment environment, implied terms are not safe ground.

Of course, the contractors are bound by an obligation of confiden-tiality in respect of anything they learn from the bank, but that should not necessarily inhibit them doing their work in the new contract!

This example reinforces the warning in Chapter 2 concerning the differ-ences between employees and contractors. Employees during employ-ment not only have an implied duty of confidentiality, but, as we saw in Chapter 2, their implied duty of good faith to the employer means that their creative thoughts must be exercised only for the benefit of the employer. In other words, an employer automatically gets the benefit of 'ownership' of the confidential information that an engager of contrac-tors does not (without a special contractual arrangement).

Employees and contractors

Finally, the problems of Service Bank in the above example in relation to limiting contractors (and employees) after their contract (or employment) comes to an end must be considered.

As already explained, an obligation of confidentiality does not depend on contract, and so it survives both the contractor's and employee's engagement. However, what is confidential must be distinguished from the general pool of knowledge and experience which an employee is entitled to take with him or her in order to earn a living.

Example —————————————————————————————————

Pearl Chu is a Contract Manager with XYZ Contractors Limited, a company involved with retaining and supplying contractors for short terms. Over a period of years, she grows to understand the business very well, builds a good rapport with a number of contractors whom she gets to know personally, and develops her own reputation. The time arrives when she decides to set up business on her own account, with some friends. After leaving XYZ and taking a short holiday, she contacts all the contractors she remembers and invites them to do business with her when their present contracts are finished. She does not need a list to do this, and didn't take or memorize any before she left XYZ.

Can XYZ do anything to prevent this serious invasion of its business and goodwill? It is unlikely. Getting to know people, to know the business, is inevitable, especially for a senior employee. Unless XYZ can show some particular confidence that is being abused by Ms Chu, then XYZ will not be able to give a court sufficient information to enable it to formulate a fair and reasonable injunction order which protects that confidence but does not prevent Ms Chu from exploiting the skills and knowledge that she has built up during her time with XYZ.

To achieve this sort of limitation after an employee's or contractor's departure, it is necessary for XYZ to have an effective and binding contract by which the employee or contractor has agreed not to do certain things, to compete, with XYZ after employment.

This is referred to as a 'restrictive covenant' and its principles are discussed in Chapter 2. In short, to do this effectively, in the case of either an employee or contractor, there must be a written agreement setting out the precise limits of the competitive behaviour prohibited to the employee or contractor, the geographical area in which such conduct is prohibited, and the duration of the prohibition. Each of these restraints must be *reasonable*, and overreaching by the employer may well result in the agreement being void and of no effect whatsoever.

The exploitation of confidential information

From what we have said, it will be plain that we recommend in all businesses the following:

(1)   Identify the information that is considered genuinely confidential and important to the business.

(2)   All such information should be clearly marked as confidential — on the outside of disks and tapes, or the covers of documents. A procedure should be established whereby as new documents are generated (new product information, internal reports, minutes of meetings and so on), they are marked also. The only way to ensure compliance with such procedures is to ensure that they are not excessive — there is no need to weigh down an organization.

(3)   In addition, at any time when any such information must be disclosed to any person outside the organization (including contractors working within the organization), there should be clauses added to an agreement, or a new agreement, imposing express undertakings of confidentiality and ensuring that all material embodying that information is returned when it is finished with.

(4)   Compliance with these procedures, and the undertakings from outsiders, should be constantly reviewed.

(5)   The status of 'documents' and other materials marked confidential should also be regularly reviewed so that the materials which are no longer confidential are not made the subject of onerous conditions.

Too often companies will take steps to ensure equipment that is lent out is maintained and returned, but fail to take the same steps with much more valuable information!

As for employees or contractors likely to be in a position to acquire (or themselves generate) information which is sensitive to the business, they should be asked to execute undertakings in respect of such confidential information and, within reason, be restrained after engagement from participating in business where such information is likely to be used. It is preferable that such undertakings be executed *before* employment or the contract commences (see Chapter 7 where this is discussed).

6   Unfair competition and trade mark law

The old law — free competition

It has been a long tradition of the law that it is primarily concerned with preventing, or punishing, attacks upon property, land or physical objects, or upon the life or limb of law abiding citizens. Outside the area of enforcing contracts, or related commercial relationships between business people, the law was loath to deal with more intangible injuries that may be incurred in business, or with purely economic losses. *Laissez-faire* economic philosophies prescribed that economic survival of the fittest, and perhaps the roughest and dirtiest, trader would ensure the greatest benefit to the community in the long run.

Famous examples of the workings of this tradition are instructive and, perhaps, even entertaining. In the famous case of Mogul Steamship Co. Limited v McGregor, Gow & Co, the English House of Lords was asked to decide whether the conduct of a group of shipping companies in aggressively cutting their prices with the sole and deliberate objective of driving a competitor out of the business was a wrongdoing that the Court would order to cease or for which damages could be claimed. The House of Lords said it was not. Comments of Lord Justice Bowen of the lower court, the Court of Appeal, best sum up the reasons for this:

> What, then, are the limitations which the law imposes on a trader in the conduct of his business as between himself and other traders? There seem to be no burdens or restrictions in law upon a trader which arise merely from the fact that he is a trader, and which are not equally laid on all other subjects of the Crown. His right to trade freely is a right which the law recognizes and encourages, but it is one which places him at no special disadvantage as compared with others. No man, whether trader or not, can, however, justify damaging another in his commercial business by fraud or misrepresentation. Intimidation, obstruction, and molestation are forbidden; so is the intentional procurement of a violation of individual rights, contractual or other, assuming always there is no just cause for it ... But the defendants have been guilty of none of these acts. They have done nothing more against the plaintiffs than pursue to the bitter end a war of competition waged in the interest of their own trade ... The substance of my view is this, that competition, however severe and egotistical, if unattended by circumstances of dishonesty, intimidation, molestation, or such illegalities as I have above referred to, gives rise to no cause of action at common law. I myself should deem it to be a misfortune if we were to attempt to prescribe to the business world how honest and peaceable trade was to

be carried on in a case where no such illegal elements as I have mentioned exist, or were to adopt some standard of judicial 'reasonableness', or of 'normal' prices, or 'fair freights', to which commercial adventurers, otherwise innocent, were bound to conform . . .

Notwithstanding his Lordship's views, subsequent lawmakers have proved less reticent to regulate trade, by legislation such as anti-trust laws discussed in Chapter 10, under which this case may today have been dealt with very differently.

An even earlier weakening of the pre-eminence of tangible property in the law was the introduction of copyright laws and patent monopolies, 'intangible property' which could only be damaged by 'unfair' competitive activity.

In large part however, the hesitancy, or conservatism, of the law reflected a real concern with the vagueness of the damage alleged to have been suffered. Courts did not wish to create a rod for their backs by creating a remedy when it would be impossible to quantify the money lost by virtue of the conduct complained of.

Early exceptions — 'passing off', defamation and injurious falsehood

One of the earliest intangible proprietary interests recognized by the law of English based legal systems without statutory assistance was the notion of 'goodwill' in a business, a concept familiar to us today. Goodwill in one sense is the difference in the purchase price between a business as a going concern, including its assets, and the purchase price of those assets alone. It is well understood that there is a substantial difference, representing the reasonable assurance of continuing income after the purchase due to the reputation developed over time by the seller of the business. Thus 'goodwill' and 'reputation' are associated, and the law has gradually come to recognize that there is nothing uncertain or vague about the damage suffered when a trader has goodwill and reputation damaged or misappropriated by another.

The law of 'passing off' developed to prevent competitors from damaging, or wrongly attempting themselves to take advantage of another's goodwill and reputation.

As well, the notion of injury to the reputation of a person, or a business, by reason of telling of lies, has been developed by way of the law of 'defamation' ('libel' and 'slander') and 'injurious falsehood'. However, very strict limitations are placed upon these remedies, which are discussed further below, because there the law is concerned less with saleable assets — a person cannot sell his or her reputation in the same way that he or she may sell a business.

The point of distinction between the law of passing off and the law of defamation (and injurious falsehood) is that the former is concerned with, in essence, the 'stealing' of another's reputation, whereas the latter is concerned with the malicious wounding of that reputation without reference to apparent gain. However, the two streams of law have become so much broadened with the passage of time, that they appear to overlap in many places.

In some countries, such as Taiwan, laws such as 'passing off' and some of the other civil remedies discussed here have not developed, and recourse must be had to the general law of fraud, or criminal law, unless specific statutory unfair competition laws have been introduced.

'Passing off' in more detail

The law of passing off is sometimes referred to as the law of 'common law trade marks', because so often the goodwill and reputation of a business is associated with its trade marks. It is important to recognize that there may be rights in a business with unregistered trade marks by virtue of substantial goodwill and reputation.

The classic conduct which the Courts will restrain by injunction, and may punish with an order to pay damages, is the selling of products of one trader representing those products as those of a competitor — that is, typically, 'riding on the back' of the competitor's reputation. This is known as 'switch and sell'.

Example

Literal Limited is a prominent supplier of magnetic media, and has recently released the new 'Memory Extra' line, double sided diskettes, in a blaze of publicity, but does not manufacture all its products, including three and a quarter inch disks, which it purchases from another manufacturer. There is neither a 'Literal' nor 'Memory Extra' trade mark registered or applied for by Literal.

Computer Supplies Limited is in the business of mail order supply of inexpensive computer consumables. It advertises widely in the computer press as follows:

> *Special offer: Genuine Literal "Memory Extra" 31/4" diskettes up to 50% off recommended retail price'*

and specifies prices for various quantities.

Customers who order the product from Computer Supplies receive unmarked diskettes, which Computer Supplies has obtained cheaply from another supplier.

Literal undoubtedly has a right of action against Computer Supplies. Even if the goods supplied by Computer Supplies are identical in origin and quality to those supplied by Literal, this would be irrelevant to

Literal's right of action. Literal has expended time and money to ensure that it has a good reputation for quality, reliability and support for its products, and it is this, as much as the products themselves, which the customer buys when placing an order.

Incidentally, the consumer may also have an action for breach of contract (see Chapter 7), or even fraudulent misrepresentation (see Chapter 8) in these circumstances, but is unlikely to take any action because of the small injury involved.

Conduct which is likely to damage the goodwill and reputation of the principal trader, whilst not necessarily substituting different goods or services, may be equally actionable.

Example

In the above case, instead of supplying cheap unmarked diskettes, Computer Supplies does supply genuine Literal diskettes, but out-of-date, single-sided stock, which it has obtained through a bulk stock clearance sale of a former Literal dealer. The old stock is delivered accompanied by a guarantee that these diskettes are of the same quality as the new 'Memory Extra' diskettes and may be formatted as double sided, which is true — there is nothing special about the 'Memory Extra' diskettes other than the publicity.

This should make no difference. Although the goods are now marked with Literal's name, Computer Supplies is still taking advantage of Literal's advertising of the 'new' product range, to sell the old product range in its place.

Even if Computer Supplies now changes its advertising to say its diskettes are only 'as good as Memory Extra', or 'Memory Extra quality', Literal may still have a right of action. This is a much more difficult question as it is a matter of degree. If the advertising makes it clear that the Computer Supplies' diskettes are not Literal diskettes, or not 'Memory Extra' diskettes, as the case may be, then this would not amount to 'passing off'. However, if the use of the Literal name were unduly prominent, so much so that it could be said that Computer Supplies was really using Literal's name to attract orders from the customers who do not read the 'fine print', then this may amount to a misappropriation of Literal's goodwill.

*Also, if the comparison made were untrue, and the Computer Supplies' diskettes were in fact of inferior quality, then this would amount to a false statement concerning the quality of Literal's diskettes: in effect, that Literal's diskettes: are as **bad** as those of Computer Supplies. Accordingly, by so damaging Literal's reputation, Computer Supplies would be guilty of 'passing off'. Such conduct may even constitute 'injurious falsehood'.*

These examples give rise to the issues relevant to most 'comparative advertising', by which the qualities of one's own products are drawn out, or highlighted, by reference to attributes, or deficiencies, of the goods of other suppliers. In general, subject to quirks of the trade mark law in some countries referred to below, such activity is lawful, as long as it is done carefully, and fairly.

The appearance of things

The law goes further than merely dealing with trade marks. A person may pass off his goods as those of another in ways other than by using familiar trade names and marks, and it is in this area that the general law exceeds the law relating to registered trade marks. That is, goods may deceive a purchaser simply by virtue of their appearance, referred to as their 'get-up', or 'trade-dress'. This includes the colours, shapes and designs of packaging, for products presented to customers in a package, and the shape, colour and designs of products themselves — as long as these are shown to be sufficiently well known to be *distinctive* of the aggrieved supplier, so as to suggest instantly to consumers that supplier, *and no other*.

Example

Red Micros Limited manufactures and sells personal computers of the most distinctive appearance — the casings are a rich red color with black key caps on the keyboards. In addition, the keyboard may be attached to the CPU (Central Processing Unit), in which case the whole form is a wedge shape with bevelled edges which, in conjunction with the arrangement and spacing of air cooling vents, gives a very streamlined appearance. The Red Micros' advertising relies heavily on this appearance with a 'better Red than dead' theme. Competitive Computers wishes to introduce a 'Red-compatible' computer, which is smaller, cheaper, has additional features (such as function keys and a numeric key pad), but operates most of the popular application software used with Red computers. To reinforce the 'Red compatibility' message, the computer casing is also a red colour, and it has a general wedge shape, but it is less stylish than the Red product design, and the keyboard is not detachable, although the key caps are black.
Can Red Micros prevent the sale of this product?

The answer to this question depends very much upon the nature of the likely purchasers — would they be deceived by the appearance of Competitive's product? No doubt the Competitive product has Competitive's trade mark on it, but if it is a consumer product purchased 'off the shelf', then it may be that such customers are less discerning and may be deceived by the general 'get-up' of the product so as to think it is an extension downward of the Red product range. Such customers are less likely to examine the product information on the back of the box or on packaging or manuals to ascertain the fact that Red Micros is not the manufacturer. On balance, one would probably conclude that this conduct of Competitive's does amount to passing off.

This example also illustrates the area in which the law of passing off overlaps with the law of copyright and designs discussed above in Chapters 3 and 4. If the shape of the Competitive product were sufficiently similar to the original drawings for the Red product, then Red may also, in some countries, have a claim for breach of copyright. Similarly, in relation to computer programs which appear to imitate the 'look and feel' of a competing product, an area of claim may well be a claim for 'passing off' in addition to, or instead of, difficult copyright claims as discussed in Chapter 3.

Services

Another significant aspect of passing off law, which set it apart from the law of registered trade marks in most countries until comparatively recent times, is that it gives a remedy when services, instead of goods, are supplied, in a manner which attempts to take advantage of another trader's goodwill and reputation. Again, the reason for this may be the concentration on the value of the goodwill of the business, as opposed to what the business does.

Example

Solutions Services Limited is in the business of bureau processing, including time sharing CPU time for online applications. Solutions uses only 'Alphabet' computer systems and terminals, equipment and operating systems, supplied by ABC Computers Limited.

Because of the hardware it favours, Solutions decides to change its name to 'Alphabet Solutions' in relation to its bureau business and, after checking with the local Trade Marks Office and Companies Office and finding that neither ABC nor anyone else has registered the name as a trade mark or business name, proceeds to do so. It is not a minor factor in Solutions' decision that it is aware of ABC's interest in establishing a subsidiary to provide bureau services using its own equipment, of course.

Can ABC do anything about the conduct of Solutions?

If ABC is able to establish that the name 'Alphabet' has become synonymous with it in this marketplace, and that the conduct of Solutions will deceive its customers into the belief that it is providing the 'Alphabet Solutions' service, not Solutions', then ABC may be entitled to an injunction to prevent Solutions from continuing with its plan, notwithstanding that Solutions is carrying on a business of providing services, not selling hardware as in the case of ABC up to this point.

Distinction, deception and damage

Before leaving the issue of 'passing off', it is necessary to reinforce the limitations of the law, some of which have given rise to the statutory developments in this area, first in the area of registered trade marks, and later in the area of 'Unfair Competition Law'.

First, the mark or get-up must be truly distinctive of the goods or services of the person alleging passing off. In other words, it must be possible to prove that the typical customer of those goods or services would recognize the mark or get-up and identify it with that person and no-one else. There are some important consequences of this:

(1)   *Present reputation*

The reputation of the mark or get-up must be in the present, not in the past. If the mark or get-up has not been used for some time, it may well be that customers would not expect that the new goods or services would originate from the person or company who used to use it. Furthermore, if the mark or get-up has been abandoned, the competitor may well be able to say that the person claiming the reputation has no interest to protect, and hence shouldn't be granted a remedy.

(2)   *Local reputation*

The reputation must be present in the country in which it is claimed customers are being deceived. Fame in the United States or in France, may be irrelevant to a claim of passing off in Australia, or some other distant place. In a world of international communications through film, radio and television, this inevitably results in a certain level of awareness in most countries, but it may not be sufficient to amount to such distinctiveness and reputation that customers will be deceived. In any event, if the person making the claim of passing off does no business in that country, again it may be argued that he, she or it has no interest to protect or be damaged.

(3)   *Not common names or descriptions*

It is unreasonable to expect that any person can gain such an overwhelming reputation with a name or get-up which is common to many. For example, place names such as 'Silicon Valley' or Paris, or common or descriptive words, letters or acronyms used in the industry, such as 'CPU, 'PCB' or 'BASIC', unless very special circumstances intervene.

(4)   *Common field of activity*

It is difficult to establish that reputation in one sphere of activity gives sufficient basis for a claim that customers of entirely different goods or services will be deceived — or, to put it another way, that the person claiming deception really has anything to lose. Immense fame in horse-breeding or restaurants is hardly a basis for a claim that customers buying personal computers given the same name as the stud or restaurant will be deceived into the belief that the computers are produced by the horse-breeder or restaurateur!

(5)   *Reputation with actual customers*

The relevant people to be deceived are the actual customers of the goods or services. It is not enough for a mainframe supplier who is very well known to the "man in the street" to say that another supplier is using a very similar brand name, logo or get-up and the man in the street is deceived by this, because the *actual purchasers of mainframes themselves* may have no doubts as to the supplier with which they are dealing. 'Passing off' was not intended to be a law for the protection of *consumers* generally, but rather a protection for suppliers.

Another way of looking at all these issues is to remember that to establish passing off it is necessary to show that customers are *deceived*, not merely *confused*, and that injury to goodwill is really being suffered or threatened. If customers are not actually deceived in the relevant place, whether because the famous name is a foreign one, or has not been used for some time, or is common to many suppliers, then no complaint can be founded on this old law of passing off.

Licensing and 'common law trade marks'

Passing off protects the reputation of a trader established through the use of a distinctive name, logo, get-up and so on. One of the perhaps unexpected corollaries of this in many countries has been that the law has logically concluded that one cannot sell, or license away, one's reputation. One can sell a business, and the reputation goes with it, but one cannot sell or license the reputation on its own. In other words, as a general rule 'common law marks', as opposed to registered trade marks, cannot be sold or licensed.

For example, if a baker has developed a famous brand of bread, which is unregistered, he or she cannot simply license other bakers to put that brand on their bread — the baker must either sell the bakery, or supervise the licensees so closely that the bread may still be regarded as being produced by him or her.

It is possible, therefore, to license the use of a mark only if the licensee is to maintain a substantial connection with the owner of the reputation, such as through the provision of raw materials and quality control, but in many countries even this activity is subject to considerable theoretical and legal restrictions. If one licenses a common law mark without keeping within these restrictions, it is more than likely that a court may decide that a mark or get-up has ceased to be distinctive of the original supplier, that it has been 'muddied' as an indicator of origin, and hence has no value whatsoever.

Of course, this would be a major impediment to modern trade, especially international trade, and leaves in considerable uncertainty new forms of business such as franchising and merchandizing. 'Passing off' is indeed a creature of the Victorian commercial world.

This is one of the several reasons for the introduction of the modern law of registered trade marks.

Registered trade marks

The old law of passing off has shown disadvantages, although it has proved much more flexible than commercial law. It has proved capable of dealing with subtle issues such as goodwill, and the 'get-up', or packaging, and 'look and feel' of products, and in many countries remains the only manner of protection of goodwill in a business providing services. On the other hand, legal history has shown that it can be inordinately costly and difficult to prove reputation, especially for foreign concerns, and the old law has not always met the requirements of modern licensing.

However, if a trade mark, a name or logo, has been registered in a country under its trade marks law, then the registered proprietor is relieved of what is often the heaviest burden in any passing off action, that is, proving the existence of goodwill and reputation associated with the name, logo or get up. All that need be proved is that the defendant is using that trade mark, or a mark deceptively similar, in relation to the same goods or services in respect of which the mark is registered.

In addition, registered trade marks usually may be licensed, subject to certain restrictions to prevent 'trafficking'.

What is registrable as a trade mark?

Borrowing from the old law of passing off, a trade mark must have the following basic qualities:

(1)   it must be a word, or a picture ('logo') or combination of both;

(2)   it must not be descriptive of the goods (or services) in relation to which it is registered;

(3)   it must be distinctive, or capable of becoming distinctive, of the trade mark owner; and

(4)   it must be original to the applicant for registration and not in any way deceptive.

In short, ideal trade marks are those which are purely invented words, with no reference to the character, quality or origin of the goods/services in respect of which they are registered — marks such as 'Apple' or 'Exxon' are exceptional examples.

A word, a picture, or both

This needs little explanation, but it should be noted that a number of attempts have been made to register as trade marks the shape or colour of objects, such as the famous shape of the Coca-Cola bottles, and the familiar (to some) colours of certain medications.

These are usually found not to be trade marks, and can only be protected by the law of passing off or consumer protection laws (see below).

Another point to be noted is that usually an original drawing may be easier to register than a word, because a drawing is less likely to be confused with other drawings, whereas words can often create difficulties. For this reason, it is sometimes easier to register a word/picture combination, for if the word is rejected, it may remain part of the trade mark as registered, subject to a 'disclaimer' by the owner.

Another interesting example of this requirement is that trade mark authorities are very cautious about registering letters, which may then be used purely descriptively — such as 'PCB' which may simply mean 'printed circuit board', or any of the myriad of acronyms favoured by the computer industry.

Descriptiveness

Trade mark registrations must specify the types of goods/services in relation to which they are or will be used and an application will be rejected if a word mark merely describes those goods/services, their geographical origin, or any qualities that may be claimed in the goods. For example, purely laudatory words such as 'Perfection' will always be rejected, even if already famous, and 'Huggars' was rejected in relation to shoes because it described a snug 'hugging' style of footwear — it did not matter that the spelling had been changed, so that the word appeared to be invented.

The law is careful not to create monopolies in words which are commonly used in an industry. 'Laser printer' would be rejected for printers, 'Disk 800' for disk drives. Other words may be sufficiently changed to be distinctive, such as the famous example of 'Memorex', or to be so unspecific as to be of no concern, for example 'triangle' could presumably be registered, notwithstanding an origin in the 'Technology Triangle' of North Carolina.

Distinctiveness

'Distinctiveness' is the notion that a word or logo must be capable of indicating a particular supplier, and not be capable of another signification. In some areas, this may simply be another side of the 'descriptiveness' issue — thus the word 'Good' cannot be considered distinctive of a single trader, because many people will wish to describe their offerings as good for something or another!

In a similar vein, place names are usually not registrable, especially places such as Paris, London and New York — 'Paris software' has as little chance of registration as 'Paris perfume'. For similar reasons, trade mark authorities are very cautious concerning surnames.

Other words can lose their distinctiveness through overuse — 'Laminex' is a famous example. 'Software' may once have been a classic 'invented word' suitable for a trade mark, but time and use have turned it into a common word.

Originality and deceptiveness

A trade mark should be applied for by the person or corporation that first devised or used it, the 'author' of the mark. This requirement assists foreign entities, enabling them to oppose an application for registration of their marks by local traders, even if they have not yet used the mark in the country of the application.

In addition, the mark applied for must not be deceptive. Even if the mark has not already been registered by someone else in the class of goods or services in respect of which the application is made, its registration may be refused if it is already associated with that person or corporation, so that its new use would deceive customers. This also may be true if the mark itself is not deceptive, but its actual use by the applicant is deceptive.

How does a trade mark get registered or removed?

Application

An application must be filed in the country in which protection is sought. In the United States, not only is there a federal system of registration of trade marks, but also the individual states maintain their own registers. The federal system may only be used for marks which have been used (or, following recent amendments, are intended for use) in trade between the states or in trade overseas.

The application must show exactly what the mark is, perhaps whether it will be limited to certain colours and so on, and describe with reasonable precision the goods for which the mark will be used.

For ease of administration, all possible descriptions of goods are divided into classes. A separate application must be made for each trade mark in each class of goods. The numbering of the classes, and what they include, varies from country to country, but there is an international standard (administered by WIPO), in which the classes most commonly of interest to the computer industry are those numbered 9 (all manner of technical and scientific equipment) and 16 (books and similar goods).

In addition, the Register of Trade Marks may be divided into as many as four parts, labelled A, B, C and D.

Parts A and B are for normal trade marks, A is generally for trade marks which the Trade Marks Office considers as 'inherently distinctive'; Part B is generally reserved for lesser marks, concerning which the Trade Marks Office may have reservations, but which are regarded as 'capable of becoming distinctive'. It should be noted that a mark which is deemed descriptive, however famous, may be considered to be incapable of ever becoming distinctive. In some countries, this distinction is not maintained — for example, in Singapore, where a foreign trade mark can be registered in Part B regardless of its qualities as a trade mark, provided it has seen two years' use in a foreign country.

Part C, if available, is reserved for 'certification trade marks', marks typically reserved for industry associations that allow members who have special standards to use the mark, for example 'Champagne' for wines, 'Stilton' for cheese and the 'Pure New Wool' mark.

Part D, if available, is for marks so famous that use for any other goods would be deceptive — for this is a purely defensive registration, and countries which maintain such a facility will impose very strict standards for applicants.

An application may have to be accompanied by, or subsequently supported by, a number of other documents, such as proof of use or intended use, proof of overseas filing (see below), certification of nationality of the applicant and/or powers of attorney for local agents.

Before filing an application, it is wise to check the Register of Trade Marks, and applications for trade marks, which are public records, in order to be sure that nobody before has had the same bright idea.

Trade marks are examined and granted in order of application, and if another person is first in time, the later application is doomed to failure.

Examination

After a period of time, sometimes a very long time, an officer of the Trade Marks Office, usually called an 'Examiner', will consider the application and will comment on the application and seek clarification of a number of issues. At this time, the applicant may be advised of a prior registration with the same class, or the risk of confusion with a trade mark registered with respect to another class of goods as a risk of deception. In addition, the Trade Marks Office may indicate concern that a mark may be descriptive or defective for some other reason. Also at this time any formal requirements absent from the application may be called for.

The issues raised by the Trade Marks Office are not final, and correspondence may follow in which the applicant explains away the problems, or makes concessions such as disclaiming descriptive words or agreeing to transfer the application to Part B of the Register.

At this stage, it is very useful to be familiar with the trade mark law, as many Examiners' queries may be readily disposed of if the concerns upon which they are based are well understood and may be met with explanations based on examples from decided cases.

Publication, opposition and registration

If the Examiner's queries are satisfied, or are disposed of through the administrative appeals procedures that may be available to applicants dissatisfied with a Trade Marks Office decision, the application will be published in public documents readily accessible to the public and, more particularly, trade mark attorneys. At this point any person feeling aggrieved by the proposal to register the trade mark, for good commercial reason, may lodge an opposition to the registration of the trade mark, and any dispute arising from opposition may be heard by an official of the Trade Marks Office, after hearing the arguments of both sides.

If no opposition is filed, or the opposition is dismissed, the mark will be registered upon the payment of a further registration fee.

The United States practice of using '®' next to *registered* trade marks, and '™' in relation to *unregistered* trade marks, or trade marks the registration of which is pending, should be observed elsewhere with caution. Such a notice in relation to registered trade marks is not required by the law of most countries. It is easy to adopt the practice of using these symbols wherever an American has done so, even when the same mark has not or cannot be registered in the country of use and it is usually a breach of the trade marks law to represent falsely that a mark is registered.

Removal

Once registered, the trade mark is placed on a public register which may be examined by any person. The mark will be struck off the register for non-payment of fees from time to time.

In addition, there are certain limited circumstances in which a registered trade mark may be struck off the register, such as if it can be established that the original registration was obtained improperly, or if subsequent to registration the mark has ceased to be used (has been 'abandoned') by the proprietor, or has ceased to be distinctive or has become deceptive for some reason. Rights to seek the removal of a registered mark because of events subsequent to registration, other than abandonment by the registered proprietor, are sometimes severely circumscribed after the passage of some years, when the mark may be 'deemed' to be distinctive.

Non-use, or abandonment, is the most serious danger to trade marks which are subjected to extensive licensing programs, even between related corporations. In answer to any claim for infringement of a trade mark, in addition to denying infringement, an alleged infringer will invariably seek to strike down the registration itself, and frequently the Achilles' heel of the registered proprietor will be careless licensing practices.

Licensing and 'Trafficking'

Licensing of registered trade marks, without disposing of the business along with the mark, is expressly permitted. It is even possible to register trade mark licences, and in certain countries it is even provided that use by a registered licensee, or 'registered user', is deemed to be use by the registered proprietor, the significance of which will be clearer shortly.

However, there are strict conditions placed upon licences that may be registered. The most important of these is that the registered proprietor must retain a degree of quality control although in practice far less is required than appeared to be the case under the old common law. Thus, a registered user may procure components or ingredients otherwise than from the registered proprietor, provided there are in place recipes or standards with which the user is required to conform. In the case of subsidiaries of a trade mark proprietor, this degree of control is usually assumed, and a subsidiary may even be registered as a user without there being an agreement in place.

The difficulty often arises where a company other than a subsidiary is using the mark, such as an independent distributor or even a parent or sister company, without a registered User Agreement.

Example

Fragrant Software Systems, Inc. ('FSS') is a New York corporation specializing in accounting software for various vertical markets, including the hotel industry. It is a wholly owned subsidiary of a diverse Delaware corporation, Fragrant International, Inc. ('Fragrant International'). FSS has a growing international business, and over the years has taken the protective step of registering its trade mark, the word 'Fragrant', in many countries, including the United Kingdom.

As a result of increasing interest in Fragrant Software in the EEC, Fragrant International establishes a subsidiary in Eire ('Fragrant Eire Limited') for the purpose of packaging, warehousing and distributing the Fragrant products, and appoints an independent distributor in London, England ('Distributor Limited').

In the background, a chain of hotels based in Hong Kong and called 'Fragrant Hotels' has increased in fame and fortune. Its success is based in part upon its methods and style, including a software package for controlling reservations, accounts and so on. It franchises independent hotels wishing to join the chain and take advantage of its reputation, including in its franchise a licence for its software, which it calls 'Fragrant Hotels System Software'.

FSS, the registered proprietor of the trade mark 'Fragrant' in relation to software, sues Fragrant Hotels representatives in the United Kingdom for breach of its trade mark. The defendants cross claim, seeking expungement of the 'Fragrant' trade mark, alleging non-use on the part of the registered proprietor, FSS.

What prospects has FSS in its action?

FSS and Fragrant International may well be facing serious difficulties. How can FSS say that it has used the mark in England? The product distributed in England is made by Fragrant Eire, which is not a subsidiary of FSS but of its parent corporation. Even if it can be said that FSS exercises de facto *control over its parent as a result of some 'common purpose' of a group of companies, the only company which can be seen to have used the mark in England is an unrelated company, Distributor Limited, whose only agreement is an unregistered agreement with the parent corporation.*

In this example, all the problems of FSS would have been overcome had it entered an agreement with Distributor Limited for use of the United Kingdom trade mark in relation to goods made by Fragrant Eire, and registered that agreement. It would also have been prudent to enter and register an agreement between FSS and Fragrant Eire, even though they are related companies, concerning the use of the mark in the production of the software packages. Naturally, the terms of the Distribution Agreement would be too confidential to be placed on a public register. Therefore, even though there are usually provisions in the relevant law for maintaining confidentiality of registered agreements, it is usual to enter a harmless side agreement containing only provisions relevant to the trade mark, and registering just this agreement.

It should be noted that it is not mandatory that one register a licence agreement in respect of a registered trade mark. An unregistered licence will be binding on the parties. However, only by registration, will the use by an unrelated licensee be deemed to be the use of the owner of the trade mark, hence relieving the owner of doing anything itself in the country of the trade mark to ensure that its trade mark is free from the threat of expungement. Otherwise, if the use by the licensee exceeds the limits imposed by the common law, the non-use by the owner, combined with the use by the licensee may be such as to cause the mark to be expunged, and may even entitle the distributor to be treated as the 'true' owner in the country of use!

Infringement

The rights of a registered proprietor of a trade mark are infringed if another person uses the mark, or a mark deceptively similar, in relation to the same goods as those in respect of which the mark is registered.

'Use' for the purposes of infringement should be use as a trade mark, in other words comparative advertising where the trade mark is merely used to identify the competitor's goods is not necessarily an infringement.

There is usually no defence once unauthorized use of a registered trade mark is proved, except in the case of Part B marks only, in which case it may be a defence that no actual deception of anyone took place. This is not a defence in the case of Part A marks.

Example ───────────────────────────

In the case of Fragrant Software, considered above, assume that FSS is able to prove use in England, and now discovers that a small maker of games and novelty software has called a new product 'Flagrant Hotel'. Would this be an infringement?

Probably this would be an infringement. The words 'Flagrant' and 'Fragrant' are very similar, 'l' and 'r' are easy to stumble over. Unless the description of goods in Class 9 used by FSS was very narrow, so as to exclude games software, which is very unlikely having regard to normal trade mark attorney practices, there can be no doubt that the 'Fragrant' and 'Flagrant' products are in the same class of goods, that is, software. Assuming that the 'Fragrant' mark is registered in Part A, which is likely as 'Fragrant' hardly bears any relation to the character or quality of software applications, then it is no defence that nobody wanting to purchase the Fragrant accounting package would be deceived into buying the games package!

FSS may be entitled to extensive remedies, such as damages or an account of the Flagrant profits, as well as an injunction to prevent further sale, and may even in some countries have rights to call for the seizure and destruction of the Flagrant product.

International protection

Trade mark laws are national. There is no equivalent of the international copyright conventions discussed above to give automatic trade mark rights in foreign countries.

However, the Paris Union, to which many countries are party (see Appendix III) does provide a system in which if a trade mark application is lodged within six months of the original filing in another member country, then the later application will be treated as having been lodged on the earlier date, which may be useful in defeating unrelated applicants attempting to gain some advantage by beating a wealthy foreigner to its own mark!

In addition, the Paris Union requires member countries to have adequate anti-counterfeiting laws, and to respect famous foreign marks in the registration process. The Union is sufficiently broad in this respect perhaps even to contemplate that famous, but unregistered, foreign marks should be respected in member countries, and this may signify protection for 'common law marks' also. This conclusion appears to be reinforced by the words of the Union which require to be forbidden conduct which is liable to mislead the public as to 'the nature, the manufacturing process, the characteristics, the suitability for their purpose or the quantity of any goods'. These words have become the basis for the introduction of 'unfair competition' laws in member countries, but this has not necessarily expanded the scope of recognition of famous foreign marks to any appreciable extent.

Further provisions of the Union include requirements that the laws of member countries include strict powers of enforcement, such as procedural laws enabling search and seizure of allegedly counterfeit goods, and their ultimate destruction.

Defamation and injurious falsehood

In addition to the law of passing off, commercial use can occasionally be made of the old law of defamation and 'injurious falsehood', sometimes known as 'trade libel' or 'product defamation'. However, it should be noted that there are no international standards governing this area of law, and the existence and nature of these remedies varies enormously from country to country.

Defamation consists of telling an untruth about another person, which is such as to bring the victim into public ridicule or contempt. The defamation may be written (then it is called 'libel') or spoken (then it is called 'slander'), but it must be 'published' that is, written or spoken to another person who is free to disclose it to anyone he or she chooses. The more widely the defamation is published, the greater may be the damage suffered and to be compensated. By and large, also, the matter spoken or written must be untrue, or be such as to be likely to suggest something untrue in the mind of the receiver of it although truth is rarely a complete defence, as the law is largely concerned with the prevention of unfair damage, in respect of which truth may be a mere excuse for malice. It may be sufficient in some cases if the matter spoken is neither true nor false, but is uttered with 'reckless indifference' to its truth.

It is not possible here to explain in any detail this exceptionally complex area of law, but it should be remembered that in some countries, in addition to the above matter it may be necessary to prove 'malice', and it is almost always very difficult to prove the state of mind of the alleged defamer. In addition, there are a number of defences, such as 'qualified privilege', which are available to a person such as a newspaper publisher but also lesser mortals, who may defame another person inadvertently in discussing a matter of importance to the recipient of the information. In the United States, and some other countries, there may also be complex arguments based on the constitutionally enshrined right of 'free speech'.

Another issue raised by defamation is the amount of damages to be awarded which may be very great, but if the person defamed is a person of not very high reputation in any event, may be as little as a penny.

'Injurious falsehood' is an antiquated common law 'tort' — available in fewer countries than is defamation and almost entirely subsumed in other, more modern remedies, including even passing off.

It consists of the making of false and malicious statements concerning another's products or services. In England, there is no longer a requirement to prove malice.

Again, a statement may be false by implication.

Example ——————————————————————————————————

Spivelex Software and Hardware is a dealer in consumer computer products; and Gerhardt Spivelex is its owner. He is a dealer for Macro Applications Pty. Limited, a software supplier. Macro releases a spreadsheet/word processing product called Superspread (Version 1.0) but after a short time realizes it has serious problems and releases a new Version 1.1 with instructions to dealers to upgrade existing customers at no charge; and apply for a credit of the cost price to Macro. Spivelex immediately sees an opportunity for gain here, and it continues to sell its remaining inventory of Version 1.0 with a sticker over the version number saying 'Enhanced Version 1.1', putting the same sticker on products brought in by customers for upgrade (unless they have detected the problems in the old version!). When one existing customer returns after receiving this treatment to complain, Spivelex says 'It's Macro's fault. They must have supplied the old Version 1.0 under the new version label. I do not think Laura Rogers (Macro's well known Managing Director) cares what happens to users'.

Does Macro or Laura Rogers have any claim?

In this case, in addition to committing all manner of other wrongs, Spivelex has, by knowingly placing the stickers on the Version 1.0 diskettes and supplying them to customers as Version 1.1, committed an 'injurious falsehood', and is liable to pay Macro for any loss the latter can show to have been incurred, or it is likely to incur in the future, as a direct result of Spivelex's conduct. Proving malice may be a problem in some countries, but in this case the fact that the placing of the stickers on the diskettes amounts to a blatant lie, and especially having regard to the terrible statements made by Spivelex concerning Macro and its Managing Director, should be sufficient to show at least a reckless indifference to truth in this instance.

An interesting issue may be raised by Spivelex's comments concerning Laura Rogers — is this slander? On the one hand, it appears to be merely a statement of what Spivelex thinks (for one reason or another) may be true. In addition, it appears to be a statement made to a concerned customer and hence may enjoy 'qualified privilege'. However, it must be considered quite likely that a reasonably minded customer would interpret this observation in its context as being a criticism of Ms Rogers, and it would appear that it has been uttered in circumstances where Spivelex knew and intended that conclusion and did not care whether it was true or not. Finally, such a statement appears to be one that, if spread in the industry, is such as to give Ms Rogers a bad name and hence likely to affect her standing in the community and possible future employment — hence damages awarded may not be nominal. The difficulties and uncertainties of defamation law are such, however, that no firm conclusion can be drawn.

One continuing aspect of importance for this area of law is in the area of credit references and ratings. It has been the law of most countries for some time that false and improper slurs upon a trader's credit worthiness, such as suggestions that the trader is unable or refuses to pay bills on time, or is insolvent or bankrupt, may well be defamatory conduct.

The above summary of defamation and trade libel law should show that this arcane law is not firm ground upon which to rely in the event that one feels attacked by competitors and, except for personal attacks upon one's worth or reliability, should be regarded with caution as a commercial weapon, or even a shield. In addition, many people are frustrated by the law's apparent concentration, even fixation, upon rules and procedures, rather than the merit or common sense of the situation.

The new law — consumer protection

In many countries, such as the United States, Germany, Australia and New Zealand to name but a few, there have been introduced new, far reaching laws, whether in the guise of consumer protection, or 'unfair competition' law which is designed to prevent undesirable trading conduct, including false, misleading or deceptive statements made concerning the supply of goods or services. Sometimes, this law is introduced as a response to the Paris Union referred to above.

The power of these provisions lies in the fact that they may be used by one trader against another. In addition, it is clear that the prohibitions are set aside from the restrictions of the old common law actions. So, for example, no proof of goodwill is necessary, although this may often be a necessary feature of the evidence of likely deception. The nature of the deception is different, too, from that required for a passing off action, not being limited to the origin of the goods or services.

An interesting example of the application of this legislation was provided by the Apple cases, in which Apple Computer Inc. has sought to prevent the worldwide distribution of Apple II clones. In addition to its copyright case, Apple in many countries alleged conduct misleading and deceptive to consumers in the sale of Apple II clones (which were Apple 'lookalikes') with Apple II User Manuals. Apple alleged that this conduct amounted to false representations of an association or other relationship with Apple — for example, consumers may have thought that the Apple II clones were genuine, but cheaper, versions of the Apple product, even though the clones were clearly inferior in every way. Apple has frequently succeeded in these claims.

Finally, unlike the law of registered and unregistered trade marks, it is often irrelevant whether the complainant bringing an action provides the same goods or services as the alleged infringer.

Trade descriptions and customs laws

In some countries, additional remedies may be available in relation to false trade descriptions on goods. Typically, these remedies will arise from administrative procedures or criminal laws which restrict the importation or sale of any goods to which a false trade description is applied. A 'trade description' may be a notion broader than a trade mark, and relate to any matter which is false or misleading appearing on, or in, goods. This may be wide enough to cover trade marks programmed into memory to display on power-up, and may overcome the doubts under the trade marks laws which arise when ROMs, printed circuit boards, or computers without monitors are imported with no visible trade mark otherwise in use.

Customs laws also occasionally permit the seizure of counterfeit goods, usually goods bearing false trade marks, but occasionally also goods breaching copyright or patent laws.

Summary

The law has come a long way since the Victorian days of the Mogul Steamship Company and its economic problems. With the law of passing off and defamation being augmented first by registered trade mark laws and then by the new consumer protection laws and unfair competition laws, there is now a great deal of protection available against unfair business practices, but at the same time there are still many pitfalls for the careless trader.

7 Contracts

The importance of contracts

Contracts are a part of every business transaction, whether purchasing a box of diskettes or arranging for software development which will last for years. The nature of a contract is often not understood, even by sophisticated business people.

It is quite common to hear a business person say "we can do this deal without a contract"; what they almost certainly mean is that they feel that a formal, written contract is not necessary. There is often a misapprehension that if there is only a 'deal' there are no legal issues involved, and hence no need for the expense of a lawyer, whereas if there is to be a formal written contract, a lawyer has to be consulted.

Contrary to this view, an arrangement is a contract if it satisfies certain criteria, no matter what name the parties may give to their understanding. An 'Agreement', a 'Mortgage' or a 'Licence' are all contracts.

Contracts can take many different forms. The legal definition of a contract is probably very different from what a non-lawyer would expect. A contract drawn up by a lawyer, which indicates the parties precisely, and has a proper looking execution clause, where people sign, and which is headed 'contract', is easily recognizable as a contract. Some less easily recognizable forms of contract might be an oral agreement, or a contract constituted by an exchange of letters, or even a combination of both. These informal types of contract are almost invariably indistinguishable in law from the formal documents created by lawyers, and every bit as binding.

There are as many different types of contract as there are different forms of human endeavour. Two transactions which have a similar result can actually be quite different depending upon the contracts which cover the different transactions. A supply of software, for instance, can be either by way of sale or licence; in both cases the user ends up with a copy of the program to use on his or her computer.

Because of this, it is very important for those involved in business to understand the borderline between discussions, negotiations, 'selling' and all other preliminaries, and the binding contract. It is even more important that, knowing where this borderline may lie, those involved then know how to make sure they understand one another clearly — so that their transaction does not end in dispute, regardless of whether a dispute ends in court, for disputes are not a recommendation for future business.

The reason that lawyers, and others, are called upon to draw up formal agreements is to ensure that the terms of an agreement are certain, or as certain as may be possible in any human transaction.

A contract should provide a framework for an entire transaction, to cover as many circumstances which may arise as possible. No contract can hope to cover all contingencies, but disputes can be largely avoided through well drafted contracts which at least provide for the resolution of issues, even if they cannot foresee what those issues might be.

What is a contract?

A contract is not at all dependent upon a single form; a contract can be wholly oral or hundreds of pages long, detailing all conceivable contingencies. Contracts can also be in a mixture of forms, perhaps constituted by a series of letters together with some oral terms or a series of documents linked together by a 'master agreement'.

The test of whether or not there is a contract between two or more parties depends upon the actions of the parties (including what they say and what they write). It does not necessarily depend on whether each party thinks that his dealings constitute a contract, provided the essential elements are present, although it is always possible for the parties *expressly* to agree that their arrangement does not constitute a binding contract, perhaps pending a formal document being created. In the absence of any agreement that the arrangement is not binding, if the following elements are present, there will be a binding contract:

(1)   an *offer*, which is *accepted*;

(2)   *consideration* for the promises given (although this is not required in some countries, such as Japan and Taiwan); and

(3)   *consensus* as to the subject and all major aspects of the contract.

Offer and acceptance

For there to be a contract there must be a firm 'offer' by one party which is 'accepted' in its precise terms by another.

Everyone who claims some knowledge of the law of contracts is familiar with the English case of *Carlill* v *Carbolic Smoke Ball Co.* and so no chapter on contracts would be complete without it. This case illustrates how little is required to constitute offer and acceptance.

Example — Carlill v Carbolic Smoke Ball Co.

The Carbolic Smoke Ball Co. advertised that it would pay £100 to anybody who caught influenza after using its infallible preventative against that disease — a 'smoke ball' — in the specified manner; the advertisement stated that the company had deposited £1000 with its bankers as a show of faith.

Ms Carlill contracted influenza after using one of the smoke balls and sued for the £100 when the defendant refused to pay. She said that there was a contract constituted by the offer of £100 on the conditions laid out in the advertisement, provided she used the smoke ball.

In its efforts to avoid payment, amongst other things, the company said the advertising was merely exaggerated advertising, a 'mere puff' which no-one could seriously take as an offer in a contractual sense, and further that since the 'offer' was made to no particular person, but to the world at large, then it could not result in a contract between the company and any individual.

The court held that there was a contract. By buying the smoke ball Ms Carlill accepted the offer made, even though it had been made at large. In addition, the advertising was clear and unequivocal: more than a 'mere puff', it was an offer to be acted upon. Ms Carlill had fulfilled her side of the contract when she used the smoke ball in the specified manner, and now the company had to perform its side of the contract.

It is clear from this example that the notion of contract is far distant from that of a bargain struck in the marketplace between two traders, face to face.

However, in construing a course of dealing to determine whether or not there is a contract it is important to distinguish mere negotiations, or an 'invitation to treat', from a complete offer and acceptance.

An offer must be unequivocal in its terms and capable of acceptance without modification. An offer may contain certain conditions, such as the conditions in the case of the Carbolic Smoke Ball offer above, that is, that the offeree purchase a smoke ball and use it in a certain way — conditions of payment of money are, of course, the usual terms of the offer. Likewise, an acceptance must be unequivocal and unconditional, or any conditions attached must be accepted in turn unequivocally.

An 'invitation to treat' is legal jargon for merely informing the potential 'other party' to a contract that one is in the market with or for certain goods or services — it is a request for an offer to be made. A request for tender/proposal (RFP) is a classic invitation to treat; the answer to an RFP may be, in contractual terms, an offer but it is not possible to 'accept' an RFP and form a contract.

Consideration

In English law based systems 'consideration' is a further requirement for a legally binding contract. 'Consideration' is merely something, anything, given in return for a promise, the price for the promise, in effect proving that something more than good intentions are involved.

A mere promise to do something is not enforceable as a contract unless it is given in return for consideration. In other words a bald statement such as "I'd be happy to lend you the system for a month's trial" does not constitute a contract and if the party making the statement fails to deliver the system it cannot be forced to do so, at least under the law of contract.

The consideration, or price, need not be something tangible, it may be a mere promise in return; "I will give you this software if you promise to stop using that software" is a perfectly binding contract, if accepted by the other party. The consideration need not even be very substantial, like money or some other worthwhile thing; the same promise, big or small, can be bound for the price of a grain of salt.

Consideration can, in legal language, be either executory, executed or past. The difference between executed and executory consideration is not terribly important as they are equally effective forms of consideration. Executory consideration is constituted by a promise made in return for a counter-promise; consideration is executed when the promise is made in return for the performance of an act. It is important, however, to distinguish both executed and executory consideration from 'past' consideration.

Past consideration is a misnomer because past consideration is, at law, no consideration at all. Any contract based upon consideration which is past will not be enforceable. Simply put, past consideration is something that the promissor has already done or is already obliged to do anyway. This is so even though the promise may be related to the earlier transaction, as long as it is *exactly the same*. A person seeking to enforce a contract must be able to prove that his/her promise or act (depending on whether the contract is executed or executory), together with the promise of the other party, constitute a single transaction.

Example ───

Panda Business Systems sells to Delphic Oracles Limited a computer system and its Grisly Accounting System software, Version 1.6, after having demonstrated the hardware and software combination operating successfully on Panda's own site. The contract is a standard form, acceptance takes place automatically upon delivery of the hardware and cannot be rejected, but the contract specifies delivery and operation of the hardware and software within three months. The Grisly accounting package is a relabelled third party product.

Panda delivers the hardware, but has a great deal of difficulty with its installation and commissioning; certain components malfunction and Panda experiences an acute difficulty in obtaining replacement components.

In the meantime, Panda has a great deal of difficulty with its supplier of the Grisly package, which has ceased supply of Version 1.6 and replaced it with Version 6, at a much higher price. After even more delay, Delphic threatens legal action and Panda's director of sales goes to Delphic's general manager and in the course of discussing support of the system generally says 'Don't worry, provided you agree not to take legal action on any of these claims, we will lend you a Version 1.6 straight away, until we get this thing sorted out'. Panda does this — but Delphic is unable to use the software because the hardware fails again and Panda is unable to get the hardware into operation until six months later when it obtains the necessary components.

Can Delphic now sue Panda for failure to get the hardware and software up and running on time? Panda says that in return for it supplying the otherwise unobtainable Version 1.6, Delphic promised not to take any legal action over the delay. Disregarding all the many legal possibilities presented by this case, it would appear that Panda cannot rely on this promise of Delphic, because it only promised to do what it was already contractually committed to do, that is, supply Version 1.6 — the consideration was past. Had it promised to give one cent instead, Delphic's promise may have been enforceable.

Similarly, if to appease Delphic Panda had promised after the sale, and before any threat of litigation, to make its own system available as a backup site, this promise would have been unenforceable against it, simply because Delphic would have given no consideration for the promise, however morally compromised Panda may have been.

The results in these cases may be quite different in jurisdictions where consideration is an irrelevant, or a lesser, factor in contract law.

Consensus

In reviewing the issues with which lawyers may be concerned in dealing with the formation of contracts, it must not be overlooked that throughout the world what is really being asked is whether there has been agreement, or consensus, between two or more people, evidenced by these various factors. Notwithstanding the presence of any of these factors, if it is apparent that the parties have not come to agreement on any matter considered essential, then it is extremely unlikely that there is a legally enforceable contract (although there may be other grounds of liability, based on deception or negligence, considered below in Chapters 8 and 9).

There are several quite common circumstances in which this can be an important issue.

The first is where the parties are talking 'at cross purposes', and any agreement is vitiated by the fact that there is a misunderstanding or mistake as to some fundamental matter. This is considered further in the next chapter under the heading of 'Mistake'.

The next type of circumstance is where what has apparently been agreed is so uncertain that it is not possible for a court to enforce the obligation. Courts will do their best to construe vague or ambiguous agreements, and may take evidence as to what the parties intended by certain words, or infer certain implied terms into the contract, but where there is irreconcilable ambiguity, then the parties must be taken not to have agreed and the apparent promise may not be enforced.

Finally, there are the cases where the parties exchange correspondence or sign a document entitled 'Heads of Agreement', 'Memorandum of Understanding' or any of numerous misleading titles, which may or may not include some wording to the effect that it is 'subject to contract' or otherwise anticipates some formal writing to be created by lawyers.

A document with a title such as this is a reasonably common phenomenon. It is important to recognize, however, that there is no such thing as half a contract. Either there is agreement between the parties or there is not. If a "heads of agreement" is signed which is clearly nothing more than a statement of intention, and the parties acknowledge that there is more to be agreed and settled in writing, *even if they intend themselves and each other to act in accordance with it*, there is no contract between the signatories. In general, if one party fails to do anything recorded in the document, there can be no suit for breach of contract by the other party.

If, on the other hand, the document is quite complete and clear in itself, and any later contract is merely intended to record the agreement, 'dot the i's and cross the t's', then notwithstanding that the parties intended later to replace the heads of agreement with a more formal document the parties are bound to act in accordance with the heads of agreement, however bald and unpalatable it may be in its lack of protections such as warranties, absence of provision for ownership of developments and uncertainty in the event of breach or default. If a more formal document is never entered into it will be this document which continues to govern the relationship.

Example

Ablative Absolutes Inc. requires an accounts receivable module to be added to its accounting system. The financial controller approaches the general manager of Software Developers Inc. and at the heart of their conversation is the following exchange:

"If I pay you your usual rates will you develop an accounts

receivable system for my business?" To which the manager of Software responds: "Certainly. I'll get our lawyers on to it as soon as possible." There never is a written agreement as anticipated by these remarks and Software commences work.

Is there a contract?

This oral exchange probably represents a binding agreement, notwithstanding that the terms of the agreement are extremely uncertain in a commercial sense. What is the rate of payment? When is it to be paid? What exactly does the system have to do? It may be that both parties have exactly the same idea as to what is required for an accounts receivable system for that business in which case the programming effort can proceed to a successful conclusion. More likely, however, is a disagreement about precisely what should be included in the system, how it should interface with other portions of the user's system, when it should be completed, whether there is to be acceptance testing, what warranties are given, whether maintenance is available, who will own the copyright of the completed system and so on.

A court could probably read 'implied' answers to these questions into the unwritten agreement. 'Implied terms' are discussed further below, but in this case, the implied payment terms will be Software's standard rates, as long as they are 'reasonable'; there is no completion date, but it will be 'within a reasonable time'; Software will obey the 'reasonable' instructions of Absolute; Software will retain ownership of the development, because there is no agreement in writing; the software will be 'reasonably fit for the purposes' for which it is designed; and so on. With hindsight, these may not be seen as very satisfactory to one or both parties, but they do give 'commercial efficacy' to an arrangement that was clearly intended to be acted upon.

On the other hand, had the parties not been clear about whether Software was intended to supply a standard package or create something quite new, or there was some other circumstance which suggested disagreement as to some fundamental aspect of the agreement, then there would be no enforceable agreement, and the foreshadowed formal contract would be a factor in this conclusion.

In some circumstances, such as these, even if there is no contract at all, the law sometimes permits unpaid suppliers of goods or services to recover a reasonable payment. This is a right of action called '*quantum meruit*' or '*quasi* contract' considered further below.

Is a written document ever required?

Contrary to the general rule considered above, sometimes an agreement cannot be enforced *unless* it is in writing.

There are many examples of these, among the earliest being those required to be in writing by the English *Statute of Frauds* of 1677, the successors of which legislation still require, *inter alia*, agreements for the sale or lease of land, and guarantees by one person of another's debts or other performance of obligations, to be recorded in some form of writing and signed by the parties.

More important for present purposes is the requirement of many copyright, patent, trade mark and designs laws, which require that assignments and certain other dealings be in writing and signed by the owner of the right assigned or licensed. The significance of this has been considered particularly in Chapters 3 (Copyright), 5 (Patents) and 6 (Trade Marks), above.

Most recently, many credit transactions, and dealings in intangible rights, have been the subject of legislation requiring writing, usually to protect those who may be adversely affected.

Conversely, in some countries a document in writing, which is optional, may overcome what would otherwise be an unenforceable transaction. In English law, a promise 'under seal' in a deed need not show any agreement at all, nor any consideration — it may simply be a set of 'bare' promises, or 'undertakings'. A deed must be under seal, which means for a company that the company seal must be affixed or for a person that the document be 'signed, sealed and delivered' rather than simply executed.

Deeds are a way of making what would otherwise be an unenforceable promise binding on the promissor. It is for this reason that deeds are often used to terminate existing contracts, or disputes. In such a situation, because neither party admits to being in the wrong there may be no act being done which could be regarded as consideration. A document such as this is known as a 'deed of release'. A deed may even be signed by one party only (a 'deed poll'), and delivered to the promisee, and be just as binding.

Quasi contract

Even where there is no contract, the law will impose an obligation to pay money in certain limited circumstances. In effect, if someone does work for another person at his or her request, or if someone supplies goods to another following a request to do so, or if someone lends money to another person, or gives money labouring under a mistake, *even though there is no agreement whatsoever as to what should be paid or repaid in these circumstances so there cannot be a contract*, then the law *assumes* there is an obligation to pay a *reasonable* amount for the goods or services, or to repay the money (sometimes with interest).

The claim for reasonable payment for goods or services is called *'quantum meruit'*.

Sometimes, such a claim may be in addition or is the alternative to a claim for damages for breach of contract, where it is feared that the circumstances may be such that a claim under the contract would fail. This can be an area of great usefulness for this remedy, as the following example illustrates.

Example

There is a contract between A, a corporation, and B, a programmer under which the programmer is 'to be paid $4000 on delivery of a fully operational file comparison system'.

A informs the programmer, after work has been commenced, that there is no longer any need for such a system and that it would no longer accept delivery of one.

B stops work. Can he sue A?

In this case, B cannot require A to continue to engage his services, because the courts will not enforce an obligation to use or accept services of a personal nature, that is, requiring a particular person or corporation to give ongoing services which require a working relationship to be stable.

B can sue A for 'repudiating' their contract, that is, for breach of the contract, but must then prove his damages, that is, what his profit would have been had he been permitted to finish the project. However, if this is done, it may be that he would have made a loss, or would never have been able to complete the program. B can still sue in quantum meruit. *This claim would be independent of the original contract and would not represent any agreement reached between the parties, it would simply compel the defendant to compensate the plaintiff for the work already done.*

It should be noted, however, that this is not a very useful remedy if the facts of the case are extremely complex. Also, it is not a remedy in circumstances where the only reason for the non-payment or non-completion was the would-be claimant's own fault.

Terms of the contract

Whatever the form of contract, once it can be established that there is a contract — that there is an offer, acceptance and consideration — it is important to establish what the terms of the contract are. Terms can be either express or implied. Express terms are the easier to deal with as they are the ones which the parties actually discussed and decided to include in the contract.

Express terms

Where there is a written contract, in English law systems, a court will presume that the words contain the entire contract and are not to be varied by any oral terms. It is often a difficult question for a court to decide whether a contract has been wholly reduced to writing, and therefore oral terms ought to be excluded, or whether the contract is intended to be partly oral and partly in writing. As with all such questions the answer can be sought only in the intention of the parties. Contracts drawn up by attorneys generally have an 'entire agreement' or 'merger' clause stating that there are no oral terms to ensure that only the written contract is relevant. Examples of such clauses are set out in the sample contracts in the second part of this book.

Thus, where a contract has been formally drawn up, a court will normally conclude that the words constitute the entire statement of the rights and duties of both parties *and will not listen to evidence from either party as to what one of them thought was, or should have been, included* (other than, perhaps, evidence as to the meaning of technical terms, or evidence as to a mutual mistake, or a printing 'slip' in the contract). An important matter to be considered in deciding whether or not oral terms form part of a contract is whether or not an oral statement has been followed by a reduction of the terms to writing. If they have, the written terms will generally be preferred in construing the contract. If for example there is an oral statement that response times will be no more than five seconds but a written contract specifically states that response times will be better than eight seconds the vendor will be obliged to provide only the eight second response times.

It is extremely important to be aware of the difference between a term of a contract and a mere representation. Many a computer user has decided to buy a system on the basis of promises from a salesperson that the system will be able to accomplish some wonderful things, only to find when it does not perform in that way there is no requirement in the contract that it do so. To form part of a contract both parties must have intended that a statement form part of the contract; it is not enough that they merely discussed it in coming to an agreement (although the law of 'misrepresentation' including a contract, and related matters, discussed in the following chapter, may provide a remedy).

If a contract is shown to be wholly in writing then the express terms of the contract are those which appear in the document.

If it has been established that a particular contract is partly oral and partly in writing it is then a difficult question to determine whether a particular oral statement is or is not a term of the contract or merely a representation. One of the important factors in deciding the question is the timing of the statement. A representation made in the early part of the negotiations and not thereafter repeated is unlikely to form part of the contract. On the other hand a representation made after the contract has been formed cannot possibly form part of the contract. An assertion by a vendor, made after some software has been delivered and paid for, that the software can perform a certain function will not form part of the contract.

One somewhat surprising factor which must be examined is whether the person making the statement had any special knowledge or skill in the subject matter of the contract. If the person making the statement is in a position to know the truth of the statement a court will be more willing to infer an intention that the statement form part of the contract. Thus a statement by the vendor of a mainframe that the CPU processes at three MIPs (million instructions per second) is more likely to be held to be a term of a contract than an assertion that the CPU is extremely reliable.

Implied terms

Not surprisingly, a contract, whether written or oral, does not, perhaps cannot, *expressly* provide for every contingency. How often does it happen that, when the unexpected arises, the parties to a contract would say: "Well, had you asked us at the time what would happen if these circumstances were to arise, we would obviously have said . . . ".

In such a case, courts say that the unspoken assumption of the parties must be an *implied* term of the contract. By this means, the law attempts to give commercial efficacy to everyday business transactions.

Such implied terms may arise in several ways, from industry practice, from the individual circumstances of a particular agreement, or by virtue of statutory regulation of commerce.

1. Industry practice

Perhaps an example of a term implied by virtue of industry practice may be found in most software development contracts. Most software development contracts do not assign copyright, nor do they specifically license the software to the end user; therefore it could be said, on a literal reading of the contract, that the user who is paying for the development of software has neither copyright in the developed program nor even a right to use it. However, it will always be an implied term of such a contract that the user has a right to use the program; along with that right there may also be a duty to keep source codes confidential. The implied right to use the software probably will not extend to grant the user a right to sub-license the program.

In addition, as in all industries, there are in the computer industry certain accepted usages which are familiar to everyone in the industry. These accepted usages are supposed to govern contracts which involve the computer industry; both parties to the contract are assumed to understand those terms and accept that they are part of the contract. For example, the concept of 'project manager' of a software development project is well understood, if somewhat difficult to define, and so it is not normally necessary to provide a definition in the contract. Also, there may be terms, in some cases very important terms, which are imported into the contract from its context.

2. Terms implied by the courts

There are no limits to the terms to a contract that may be implied by the courts if they feel it necessary — that the parties *must* have agreed on the matter had they been asked *at the time of entering the contract*, not, of course, with the benefit of hindsight.

Examples include a term in all contracts to provide services that the services will be rendered in a careful and 'workmanlike' manner, that a place of work will be safe for the work to be performed, equipment to be used will be safe, and so on. Another example is '*force majeure*', that is, if some external event occurs rendering performance of the contract impossible, such as government prohibition, war, or destruction of the subject matter of the contract by an 'act of God', then neither party will be liable to the other, however absolute the obligations to be performed.

Further, perhaps extreme, examples of terms implied by the courts, occasionally with less than rigorous logic, may be found in respect of employment contracts in Chapter 2 above.

3. Implications by statute

Terms can also be implied in contracts by statute. In many cases, these are merely intended to codify the general law. For example, in most countries there is a term implied by Sale of Goods legislation or a Commercial Code which imposes on every contract of sale of goods implied warranties as to:

(a)   ownership of the goods being sold;

(b)   fitness of the goods for the purposes for which sold (if made known to the seller, whether expressly or by implication — for example, if the seller knows very well what the goods will be used for, because it is obvious from the goods, such as magnetic media, or because of the seller's knowledge of the buyer's business), if the buyer relied on the skill and judgement of the seller;

(c)   general 'merchantability' of the goods, meaning fitness to be sold at all;

(d)   'quiet possession' of the goods and that the buyer will get title 'free from encumbrances' — in practice it is almost always sufficient to rely upon the condition as to ownership and possession without having to deal with these two implied warranties;

(e)   conformity with description, or sample, where goods have been sold in that manner.

Such warranties were implied into contracts for the sale of goods by the courts well before their being enshrined in statute, and, just as in the general law, the Sale of Goods and Commercial Code laws have generally allowed these terms to be excluded or modified by express agreement, which they often are. In recent times, warranties such as these have been extended to contracts other than merely those for the sale of goods, including loan, lease or hire of goods, and the supply of services. Furthermore, consumer protection laws have tended of late to make these warranties inexcludable, or modifiable only within narrow bounds.

The difficulty with all 'implied terms' is that invariably they are only mentioned when the parties are in dispute, at which time it is virtually impossible to get agreement either as to the existence of the terms (except when imposed by statute) or as to their meaning.

For this reason, it is generally considered safer by lawyers to define expressly, and in writing, agreement on as many issues, or potential issues, as possible, and to exclude all other terms. For example, lawyers will often include a specific '*force majeure*' clause in a contract much more favourable to one of the parties than the general law — it is for this reason that the 'boilerplate clauses' at the end of a contract should always be examined carefully by the parties. The courts will never imply a term contradictory to any matter expressly agreed to by the parties, and will do so only cautiously if the parties have expressly agreed that all implied terms are excluded absolutely.

Exclusion clauses

The parties can always expressly overrule implied terms, or limit or exclude liability for breach of the whole or any part of their contract, in their agreement. If, for instance, the parties adopt a definition of the role of the 'project manager' which is quite different from what is normally thought of by that term, it is the definition in the contract and not the commonly accepted one to which the parties will be bound. That is, however, subject to any applicable legislation which may not permit such an exclusion or limitation of any implied term, or liability for any default.

However, any exclusion clause must clearly and unequivocally apply to exclude the term otherwise implied, and any ambiguity in such a clause will be read *against* the party claiming to benefit from it.
Note: No contract terms, including exclusion clauses, can be of any effect unless they are in the contract. Terms introduced after the moment of contract will be ignored.

Example

Strelitzia Systems is a supplier of sophisticated aircraft engineering design software, which it licenses, instals and customizes to aircraft designers' and manufacturers' requirements. Each system's licence fees are approximately $250 000, accompanied by associated services and maintenance.

Because of its high exposure to claims of defects in the software or its installation, Strelitzia takes out professional indemnity insurance with Iris Insurances, whose policy is expressed to cover 'any liability, howsoever arising, in respect of the negligence of [Strelitzia] . . . '.

Strelitzia agrees to supply and instal its software to Aspidistra Aviation Industries under a contract which includes the following exclusion clause: 'Under no circumstances shall Strelitzia be liable to [Aspidistra] in respect of any loss or damage, howsoever arising, in respect of any breach of this agreement by Strelitzia or any other agreement or obligation, even if notified of the possibility of such loss or damage, beyond the licence fees paid or payable hereunder by [Aspidistra].'

After the contract has been entered, but before supply of the software or the commencement of work by Strelitzia, Iris advises Strelitzia that in its opinion Strelitzia's standard contract is seriously deficient, and requires Strelitzia to send a letter to Aspidistra requiring an amendment to its exclusion of liability, adding the following sentences beforehand:

> *All terms and representations, whether express or implied, whether by statute or otherwise, whether as to merchantability, fitness for purpose or otherwise, are hereby expressly excluded and negated except to the extent expressly set forth herein. [Aspidistra] further acknowledges and declares for the benefit of Strelitzia that it has not relied on any representation or other conduct of Strelitzia in entering this Agreement except as expressly set forth herein, but has relied entirely on its own judgment and evaluation of the System.*

Strelitzia advises by this letter that unless Aspidistra agrees to the amendment, it would be unable to commence work because of inadequate insurance cover. Aspidistra responds with its consent to the amendment.

Following installation of the system, there is found to be a serious error in the computations of the system, resulting in a design fault which in turn leads to destruction of an Aspidistra aircraft and cancellation of substantial orders for Aspidistra aircraft. Aspidistra sues Strelitzia for breach of implied terms of 'merchantability' and 'fitness for purpose' in the contract, negligence and misleading conduct, and Strelitzia lodges a claim under its policy with Iris.

In answer to Aspidistra's claim, can Aspidistra rely on either the initial 'exclusion clause' in the contract, or the subsequent 'amendment'? The answer is probably 'no' in each case.

The exclusion clause as it originally stood will be read strictly against Strelitzia, and its effect will probably be limited to express terms of the original contract, not the statutory implied terms. In addition, it does not refer to liability in negligence or under unfair competition laws, and so cannot extend to these areas of liability, which remain in effect unlimited.

The amendment sought to correct this oversight. However, Strelitzia cannot rely on it as it did not become part of the contract. The reason for this is that it was introduced after the contract was entered, and a new 'mini' contract would be required to change the terms; Aspidistra received nothing in return for the reduction in its rights, Strelitzia was already contractually obliged to supply and install the product and so its agreement to continue was 'past' consideration.

In the event that Strelitzia is found not to have been negligent, but to have broken the implied terms of contract and/or to have (unwittingly) misled Aspidistra, can Iris rely on the terms of its policy to exclude liability to Strelitza? This is a more difficult issue for Strelitzia. Again, if the indemnity clause can be regarded as attempting to limit liability to negligence and exclude breach of contract or statute, it will be read against Iris if that is possible. It may be argued that the exclusion only extends to deliberate or commercial breaches of the contract, or deliberate breaches of statute, but that the indemnity should and does extend to negligent breaches of contract or statute. However, this seems to be stretching the bounds of possibility, and Strelitzia may well suffer the consequences of a badly drafted insurance contract.

Attempts to introduce terms after the point of contract are very common, especially in the computer industry. Typically, 'warranties' (usually little more than exclusion clause) and shrinkwrap licenses are packaged out of sight of the purchaser, and found by him or her after opening the product for the first time. As a result, they are usually worthless. Some countries, and some states of the United States, have introduced laws, however, to give at least shrinking licenses some effect — the 'read this before breaking the seal . . . ' words are of doubtful worth otherwise.

'Boilerplate clauses'

Boilerplate clauses could be defined as the clauses which are least read in a contract. Usually they come at the end of a contract, after the substantive parts of the 'deal' have been described. They are the clauses which are found in many contracts; they all seem the same and it is very tempting to take no notice of them.

It is true that sometimes these clauses do little more than re-state the law; a clause which forbids an assignment of the contract without the consent of the other party does not add anything to the legal position. Other boilerplates can actually be wrong or misleading; a clause which forbids amendment of the contract other than in writing ignores the fact that, in general, parties are free to contract as they like and an oral agreement to vary the contract can be binding despite such a clause — it is possible for instance to vary orally the very term which says a variation must be in writing.

It can be a great mistake, however, to ignore these clauses. Sometimes they can be very important in *changing* the legal position of the parties. A clause which seeks to limit the liability of the other party, for instance, may appear like every other limitation of liability clause but on closer inspection it may be an unacceptable limitation, or may even be illegal if it extends to limiting or excluding liability which national law prescribes as inexcludable. Another notorious example is provided by 'force majeure' clauses, which go beyond the general law that permits parties to walk away in the event of supervening circumstances beyond the control of either party, such as 'acts of God', to provide in effect a 'hidden' termination provision for one party in the event that it is unable to perform its obligations for any reason. When drafting a contract the fact that all may not go as planned should never be ignored, and any clause which limits the liability of a party should be examined very closely.

Some boilerplates can be of crucial importance even in the day to day performance of the contract, even if things do not go wrong. Typical of this group of clauses is a clause which states that time is 'of the essence' to the contract, meaning that a failure to perform by a specified time will result in a breach of the contract entitling termination of the contract forthwith. A supplier, or its customer, not aware that such a clause has been included in a contract could be in for a very rude shock when an attempt is made to deliver after the date set out in the contract!

A set of boilerplate clauses is discussed at the beginning of the second part of this book. Not all are needed in each contract. Boilerplates are usually necessary in a contract, when they are intended to provide a method for one party to give notice to another, or to specify events under which a contract can be terminated. They set the overall commercial agreement into a workable framework. The substantive clauses reflect the essence of the deal between the parties, the boilerplates should seek to ensure that that deal goes ahead smoothly.

Breach of contract

Contracts are read strictly when it comes to performance. Subject to any express terms dealing with breach, failure to perform an obligation agreed to be undertaken, unless a mere trifle, entitles the other party to a remedy except in very limited circumstances.

Anybody who has been in business will be aware of how often contracts are breached, trivially sometimes, at other times in a way which is so serious it is no longer possible to proceed with the undertaking.

If a party to a contract acts in breach of that contract the other party may or may not have the right to cancel that contract. Whether or not there is such a right depends upon the seriousness of the breach, and the time at which it occurs. If time is not of the essence in the contract, delivering a program one day behind schedule would not give rise to a right of termination. If, however, a program which was to take one month has not been completed twelve months later, subject to any express agreement on this matter in the contract itself, the user may be entitled to cancel the contract, refuse to take eventual delivery and not pay for the work that has been done. There is a great deal of complex law in this area, which varies from country to country, and the consequences and rights of the parties in the event of a breach should be the subject of legal advice.

Mitigation

Even if there is a right for a party to terminate a contract and claim damages, it is not enough in most cases for that party to simply cease all action and sue for damages. An aggrieved party has a duty to mitigate the damages which flow from the breach. That is, the aggrieved party must take all reasonable steps to lessen the extent of damage suffered. Thus, if a person has a two year contract for service which is wrongfully terminated after six months it is not enough simply to sue for eighteen months' wages; the plaintiff must be able to prove to the court that he or she actively sought another job. It may be that the plaintiff finds it impossible to find an equivalent job and the damages awarded would equal the eighteen months wages; on the other hand the plaintiff may be able to start a new job six weeks later thereby limiting the damages to six weeks' wages. Similarly if printers which do not work properly, unless a relatively simple adjustment is carried out, are delivered to a distributor, the distributor probably has a duty to carry out that adjustment at the expense of the supplier and not simply return the printers and refuse to pay.

Specific performance

In certain circumstances an aggrieved party can sue for specific performance; that is a party to a contract can seek an order from the court that the defendant must perform in accordance with the contract. An order for specific performance is available only where, for one reason or another, damages would not provide an adequate or effective remedy. An order for specific performance will never be granted where the contract is in essence one for personal service — such an order would probably require constant supervision by the court.

Damages

Once it has been established that the plaintiff does have a right to damages the extent of those damages must be assessed. Put simply, to obtain an order for the payment of damages the plaintiff must be able to demonstrate an actual loss and the damages awarded will equal that loss. If the defendant has contracted to deliver twenty computers at a price of $2000.00 each and fails to do so, the measure of the plaintiff's damages will be the difference between $40 000.00 and the cost of the plaintiff obtaining those computers elsewhere.

As far as possible, therefore, the plaintiff is to be compensated with the amount of money which it takes to put the plaintiff in the position that he or she would have been in had the defendant performed according to the contract, provided such losses were reasonably foreseeable at the time of the contract.

In addition, some countries permit further awards of damages to punish a person who has shown reprehensible disregard for the rights of the aggrieved party. The issue of measuring damages has been discussed in Chapter 1 above.

In general, it can often be a matter of great difficulty to ascertain damages; it is not always easy to point to a particular sum of money which has been lost by the victim of the breach of contract. In many cases the losses are in time rather than money but the courts will not always recompense a plaintiff for his or her time; it is always necessary that a plaintiff be able to show the loss of something compensable by money.

Example

ABC Accountants obtain from Accountants Systems Pty Limited an accounts system which is claimed by Accounts Systems to be suitable for the running of an accounting practice. The system they offer will be able to keep track of the cash flow, the monthly balances, the year end figures, the expenses and so on of the clients of ABC. ABC pays an annual licence fee of $20 000, which includes full maintenance.

The system is duly delivered and put into operation. Basically the system works as expected, although ABC notice that there are a few odd errors, not altogether unexpected in a complex piece of software. These errors are brought to the notice of Accountants Systems who promise to fix them; meanwhile ABC, having recognized the errors, is able to structure its accounts in such a way that the errors do not occur, or are able manually to override the errors. As the financial year progresses, however, more errors appear; sums of more than six figures cause errors and balances are not carried forward from one period to the next. It also transpires that there are more errors in the system than was first thought — some had previously gone undetected.

Eventually, in the third year of operation and after numerous attempts by ABC and the supplier to correct the system and rectify the state of ABC's data files, ABC feels compelled to scrap the system and return to a manual system in order to complete critical client work at fiscal year end. In the resulting chaos, one of ABC's clients who paid the firm an annual average of $20 000 in fees, takes its business elsewhere. To keep the other clients happy the partners and staff at ABC work long hours of overtime.

What are ABC's rights? It is clearly too late to rescind the licence contract and recover the fees paid. In any event, this is not a case where one thing was promised and another delivered — a pile of metal instead of a Cadillac. Nor can ABC obtain any order to force the supplier to 'fix' the *system, because this would amount to enforcing an obligation of personal service, or to replace the system, because this would amount to substituting one contract for another, and the court is not in the business of negotiating terms. Accordingly, although ABC is probably entitled to terminate the contract for breach (subject to any special terms in the contract), it is not entitled to recover the whole, or any part, of the $60 000 paid in licence and maintenance fees. Assuming there is no effective exclusion clause, it is only entitled to claim damages.*

In claiming damages, ABC should be able to collect in respect of the lost fees, but only for the reasonable time in which it would be possible to replace the lost customer with new business, and any additional expenses incurred in replacing the computer system; in addition, provided they can prove that the overtime payments were directly related to the loss of the computer system (no small task) they should be able to recover those payments. The extra time put in by the partners, however, may not be compensated at all. Their out of pocket expenses are covered in the first two categories; they have suffered no monetary loss other than that, they have merely put in extra time to earn their money.

Consumer law

The theories of contract described above have been developed over centuries. They assume an equal bargaining position between the parties. While this assumption is valid in most areas of commerce, it is patently not valid in the area of consumer law. The principle of *caveat emptor* (Latin for 'let the buyer beware'), which has governed the law of contract for many years, cannot apply in an age when marketing is carried out by trained professionals and the untrained consumer is faced with a bewildering array of different products. Goods are no longer purchased in circumstances where the purchaser has a chance to assess the individual goods before buying. A modern lifestyle requires a person to obtain a huge number of goods and there is simply neither time nor opportunity to carry out an examination prior to purchase.

It is for this reason that in many countries contract or other laws have been developed to protect the consumer. Certainly not all suppliers of goods or services would try to take advantage of their powerful position with regard to the consumer and many today provide greater protection to the consumer than is required by law, but there will always be some who would seek to avoid taking responsibility for the goods and services they provide.

In general, consumer laws try to differentiate between contracts made with commercial objectives in mind and those made by consumers. 'Consumer' may be defined in terms of the *purpose* of the acquisition of goods or services, or the *value* of the transaction. In the latter case, the law may well have inadvertent application to many business transactions not intended as its primary target. Such laws operate in most cases to make the statutory warranties referred to above inexcludable from the contract, and/or to prohibit clauses limiting liability for breach in any way.

Sometimes, consumer protection laws are designed to apply to certain transactions independently of the contract. For example, consumers, as well as others, may take advantage of 'unfair competition' or 'unjust enrichment' laws in some countries, which give an independent right of action in the event of misleading or deceptive conduct, including advertising or other promotional material, or even statements made in the course of promoting the acquisition of goods or services.

In drafting a contract where the purchaser (or licensee) will be a 'consumer', it is highly important to take account of such consumer protection laws. Suppliers always wish to exclude or limit their exposure for defective products to the maximum extent possible; even when they genuinely wish to do the right thing by their customers, they would rather do so of their own volition than simply by being forced to do so by the law. If it is possible to limit or exclude the provisions of certain statutes, care must be taken to do so accurately.

Manufacturers and Importers

These days, it is more and more rare for the user to obtain goods from the manufacturer of those goods. Often it is the manufacturer (or an importer in its stead) of goods who organizes a national advertising campaign or establishes a trade mark on which the consumer relies. In many cases the actual provider of the goods has no more chance of assessing the state of the goods supplied than the consumer.

In such cases, it is important in drafting distribution agreements that the retail supplier be indemnified against liability under consumer laws arising because of material or information supplied by the manufacturer or importer.

In some countries, it is an additional feature of consumer legislation that the manufacturer (or, where the manufacturer is not within the jurisdiction, the importer) is forced to accept certain liabilities for defective goods. Usually these liabilities cannot be avoided.

Again, therefore, it is very important in any contract between an importer and the actual manufacturer that the importer seek an indemnity from the manufacturer in respect of any liability which the importer is forced to accept. In other words an importer should seek to ensure that the eventual source of any money needed to cover liability to a consumer is the manufacturer (or an insurer).

Controls on contracts

Consumer legislation is not the only way in which parties are stopped from contracting exactly as they, or one of them, may please. In addition, it has been recognized that in more cases than in consumer transactions there may be an unfairness between the contracting parties in terms of their knowledge or economic or other power.

We shall consider in the next chapter one aspect of this, the law relating to misrepresentation. However, many legal systems permit contracts to be set aside completely, or onerous provisions to be removed or modified, in cases of 'oppression' by one party of the other, and the powers of the courts, and what is recognized as 'oppressive', has been extended greatly in recent times.

Under older legal principles, courts could only act if one party had such an emotional hold over the other as to deprive the weaker party of the ability to act independently, such cases generally being confined to close family ties, or the aged or infirm. In addition, the courts could only declare the contract void, not alter it, and hence there was a danger of losing some benefit to the weaker party, as well as the detriment.

It is not uncommon now to find laws that provide in cases where one party has merely economic or informational authority over the other, so as to constitute 'unfairness', that the courts may not only find the contract unfair, but may alter the contract, for example by removing an exclusion clause. However, cases of use of such laws are still not common, and they may be disregarded for most ordinary commercial transactions.

In addition, we have already referred to the law of 'restraint of trade' in Chapter 2 above, where it touches upon employment contracts which unfairly limit or prevent the employee from earning a living after the end of employment. This area of law is much broader, extending to any contract which limits a person from competing freely, for example in sales of businesses, or development contracts. It will be recalled that the law only strikes down restraints which are 'undue', that is too broad in terms of geographical or time limitations, or which prohibit too many activities, in effect preventing the party burdened with the restraint from carrying on useful work in his or her preferred industry or training.

In many countries, this area of law has also been formalized into statute, such laws often extending the power of the court finding an 'undue' restraint of trade to modify the contract to limit the restraint to fairer bounds, rather than leaving the party meant to be benefited with no reasonable commercial protection.

Anti-trust laws considered in Chapter 10 below may also have application.

International controls on contracts

Until relatively recently, there have not been any international controls on the content or interpretation of contracts in international transactions. As we observed in Chapter 1, the treatment of international contracts has been entirely a matter for national laws applied by local courts. Some national laws may be excluded by express agreement between the parties to a contract, or by the selection of another relevant law to govern a contract, whilst others may not be excluded by such parties and will be applied, at least by a court of the country of such in-excludable laws.

In an effort to reach some degree of uniformity on fundamental issues in international transactions, in 1980 the United Nations sponsored a Convention on Contracts for the International Sale of Goods which sets out certain minimal rules for the formation of, and mutual obligations in, contracts *between parties whose respective places of business are in countries which have acceded to the Convention.* Countries which have acceded at the date of writing, or who have committed to do so, are listed in Appendix IV. The significance of this Convention really derives from the accession of the United States on January 1, 1988.

In the absence of an express exclusion of the Convention, the following are the major features of the Convention:

(1)   The Convention only applies to 'sales', not to the licensing, loan or hire of goods, such as software which is commonly licensed. The Convention also excludes from its operation goods bought for personal, family or household use (unless the seller was unaware of this), and certain other contracts.

(2)   The Convention does not relate to 'contracts in which the preponderant part of the obligations of the party who furnishes the goods consists of the supply of services', but this does not mean that if the contract is one to manufacture goods that it does not apply — the Convention makes this clear by exception. Also, if the consideration for the supply of goods consists of services, then the Convention will apply, as the exclusion only applies to services supplied by the provider of goods — such as a software developer who only incidentally may supply media embodying software, or an accountant who supplies paper. Difficult questions may arise, however, in deciding the case of a developer who merely modifies a package.

(3)   The Convention substantially restates familiar rules of 'offer' and 'acceptance' stated above, subject to smoothing out curiosities which have arisen in different countries over time, such as the odd English law rule that an acceptance sent by post is effective from the date it is posted, not the date of receipt — under the Convention, all acceptances are effective upon receipt. There are a number of provisions for offers subject to time limits, the withdrawal of offers, conditional acceptances, withdrawal of acceptance and other matters of detail.

(4)   Provisions included in the Convention relating to the formation of contracts which do not reflect English and American law state that if a price term is not specified in the offer and accepted, then no contract comes into existence. Also, an offer may be irrevocable if it is stated to be, regardless of whether there is any contractual obligation to keep the offer open.

(5)   There are a number of minimum obligations on the part of the seller if no specific agreement is made, including delivery, documentation, packaging, and the standard 'implied terms' referred to above, including fitness for purpose and compliance with sample on the date *when risk passes to the buyer* (even if discovered after that date). On the buyer's part, there is an obligation to inspect goods promptly and to notify the seller of any defect within a reasonable time, *otherwise the right to claim is lost to the buyer*, unless the defects could not have been observed.

(6)   There are rules also for the passing of risk: typically, in the absence of express agreement, risk passes at the FOB (free-on-board) point, unless the goods are not set aside for the contract at that point (as in the case of bulk goods), in which case risk passes when the goods are set aside, for example, by marking of goods, delivery of shipping documents or otherwise. There are further specific provisions dealing with goods in transit, or other cases of delayed passage of risk.

(7)   There are provisions dealing with breach of contract and damages, including the right of a party to suspend performance if the other party loses 'credit worthiness', even if a breach has not occurred at that time. The provisions as to damages embody the principles of damages substantially as discussed in this chapter and Chapter 1 — punitive damages, or damages unforeseeable *at the date of the contract*, may not be recovered. There are even *force majeure* provisions, which are much fairer and more detailed than those included in most written contracts.

This summary is very brief, and does not cover all the interesting and useful provisions of the Convention. On the whole, the provisions are sensible and fair, and are recommended reading before any international transaction.

These provisions are entirely voluntary, both in the sense that there is no obligation for any country to accede and adopt these requirements into its national law, and in the sense that parties to international contracts are entitled to exclude or modify these terms as they wish.

Conclusion

Where one party fails to perform, a dispute may be inevitable. Often, however, disputes arise because the contract between the parties fails to specify all the rights and obligations of the parties. Sometimes contracts are left deliberately vague because neither party wishes to commit itself to a particular course of action or because nobody wants to put in the time necessary to come up with a proper definition of the work which needs to be done. Sometimes too, parties feel that a vague contract will be of assistance to them later on — if a dispute arises there will be nothing in the contract which shows that their interpretation of the contract is incorrect.

It is the experience of the authors that far more disputes are caused by vague contracts than are averted by them. Also, if a contract is vague disputes which arise tend to be more bitter and long lasting; once court proceedings have started each side looks for all possible breaches of the contract by the other, to bolster their claim.

Contracts are important in all sections of the computer industry. There are different requirements for different contracts and each 'deal' needs to be examined for these requirements. There are, as we have seen, only a small number of particular requirements necessary to constitute a contract. Once they have been satisfied the contract can take a number of different forms — from a nicely bound document tied up with red tape to some words written on the back of an envelope, or even a purely oral contract.

8 Mistake and Misrepresentation

Responsibilities and obligations outside contract

In the previous chapter we examined the nature of contracts, written and unwritten. Clear and express contracts, we noted, are the surest means to ensure mutual understanding of the parties and thus the achievement of their goals.

Clear and express contracts are most likely to eventuate when all the issues known by either party to be likely to be of concern are brought out and discussed or negotiated, mature and realistic questions are asked about the unlikely event of one of the parties being unable to perform all or part of its obligations or otherwise being in disagreement at some future time, and the result being written down in a plain and straightforward manner. Lawyers may help in causing the parties to think of, discuss and resolve issues, and to set out the terms of the agreement in a written, and binding, form likely to be understood by judges.

We are not, however, in a perfect world. This chapter, and to some extent the next as well, reviews different aspects of responsibility for flaws, intentional or otherwise, in the contractual process. These 'flaws' include representations or assurances made or given before the contract is made, but which do not find their way into the contract, and simple misunderstandings between the parties which may undermine the whole purpose of the contract.

A note should be sounded before reviewing these areas. Because of the importance of contracts as an expression of what two or more parties have agreed in a free and open commercial environment, courts are extremely cautious in dealing with any claim that a contract, including its exclusion clauses and all the 'boilerplate' clauses discussed in the last chapter, does not accurately and completely express the wishes of the parties at the time the bargain was struck. For example, the so called 'parol evidence' rule will often prevent one party subsequently from claiming that there was some other aspect to the agreement which was not written down, or that the agreement as it stands is not accurate. For this and other reasons, even though the areas discussed below provide exceptions to the 'sanctity of contract', they can be extremely difficult and unreliable areas upon which to rely. This merely reinforces our comment that it is infinitely preferable to have a well thought out contact.

Mistakes

It sometimes happens that parties enter into a contract labouring under a mistake. If that mistake is 'operative', that is, if it had not been made the contract would not have been entered at all, then the courts may allow the party disadvantaged by the mistake to walk away from the contract, if that is still possible. Of course, in many cases it is unreal to say that the disadvantaged party would never have entered the contract had the mistake been realized as, in most cases, if the facts were known this would have affected the terms of the final bargain only, such as the price. In this case it is sometimes said that the mistake must be as to some fundamental term of the contract — one which was critical to the entry into the contract.

The law tends to divide up the nature of such mistakes as follows:

(1)   common mistakes of fact; and

(2)   unilateral (or 'mutual') mistakes of fact: those affecting one party only.

It should be noted that the mistakes must relate to facts, not matters of law, such as the interpretation of a statute or legal characterization of a transaction, a distinction which is not always easy to make.

Incidentally, a 'mistake' in the legal sense is not restricted to a 'misunderstanding'; it can extend to complete ignorance of some material fact. In this sense, the legal meaning of the word 'mistake' is broader than the common meaning.

Common mistakes

The favourite example of a common mistake is the circumstance where a cargo of corn believed to be in transit on board ship is sold by the owner on the strength of the shipping documents; however it has already spoiled and been disposed of by the shipper. In other words, both parties to the contract of purchase believed the goods to exist, or to belong to the seller, when this was not in fact the case. In these circumstances, the court may regard the agreement as a nullity, or permit either party to rescind the contract.

The mistake of fact must relate to something reasonably precise. For example, the mistake in the above example of the sale of the corn relates to the existence or ownership of the corn, not to whether the corn had value or not. If it were otherwise, this remedy to the disadvantaged party would depend on questions of mistake as to the degree of value, which would place courts in an impossible position of being arbiters of value or merit — a position they have assiduously sought to avoid. So, for example, common mistakes presumably would not be a basis for rescission of a contract for purchase of computer equipment if it were alleged that the mistake was that the equipment worked, or worked properly, but it may form the basis of rescinding the contract in the improbable circumstance of there being a common mistake as to an essential feature of functionality of the equipment.

Example

DIM Pty Limited is a member of a worldwide group. Mr Hasty, the Managing Director of DIM, wishes to acquire a modern PABX system for the company in Australia, and is particularly impressed with a new product installed by a related company in Europe, which has the added advantage of being significantly cheaper than anything obtainable in Australia.

Hasty contacts a local company, ABC Optics, which represents the European supplier of the novel PABX equipment but which, as its name would imply, does not carry any telecommunications products of that supplier. Hasty enquires whether the local company will import and sell the product to DIM.

ABC Optics has no experience in telecommunications equipment and assumes DIM can connect the European PABX equipment into the local public switch network. In addition, both Hasty and ABC Optics have assumed that the entire PABX equipment will be subject to a relatively low rate of import duty. ABC accordingly agrees to the proposal, imports the equipment, and delivers it to DIM but, contrary to the assumptions of Hasty and ABC Optics, the equipment is not suitable for connection into the public switch network and, not surprisingly, the telecommunications authority will not license its installation and connection. Last, and unkindest cut of all, on importation the equipment for various reasons is assessed for duty at such a high rate that the landed cost of the equipment is significantly higher than the locally available products.

In these highly improbable circumstances, it may be arguable that the fundamental error of both DIM and ABC as to the connectability of the foreign equipment into the local network was such as to vitiate the contract, or entitle DIM to rescind the contract and seek a refund — although one would imagine a court would be loath to accede to this argument because of the stupidity of Hasty.

It is possible that the same argument may not be raised in relation to the mistaken assumption that the equipment would be licensed for installation by the local telecommunications authority or the error in relation to the import duty — these appear to be errors of law by both parties in relation to the interpretation of the relevant regulations.

Unfortunately, the case law frequently makes it difficult to distinguish one situation from another.

Incidentally, as this was of course a contract for the purchase of goods, DIM may also get the benefit of the ordinary implied warranties in any sale of goods, which were discussed in Chapter 7 above — that is, subject to any exclusions of those warranties by ABC as discussed in that chapter. One of those warranties is, of course, an implied warranty of fitness for the purpose known to the supplier. However, the qualification of this warranty may apply in this instance, namely that DIM and Hasty clearly did not rely, or it was unreasonable for them to rely, on the skill or judgement of ABC Optics in this example. As to the warranty that the goods will be 'merchantable', it would be reasonable in this example to assume that the goods in question are in fact merchantable, that is fit for normal purposes for which such goods are bought, except for the defect of connectability into the public switch network, which is a defect which should have been ascertained on examination prior to the acquisition of the goods. In addition, it should be remembered that DIM, having accepted delivery of the equipment, is probably no longer entitled to return the goods for a refund, but is only entitled to damages, which may or may not be an adequate remedy. In all the circumstances, DIM may have no remedy other than a claim of mistake.

The above example is based upon the assumption that ABC and DIM (through Hasty) suffered from the same mistake of fact — that Hasty had done nothing to ascertain the correct position, and ABC was oblivious to the need to ensure that the equipment could be used for the purpose intended before importing it, notwithstanding its access to the expertise of the supplier.

As mentioned in the above example, this is an extremely difficult area of law, with decisions of courts over many years making fine distinctions which are not always easy to follow. For example, in the illustration given above, it has been assumed that DIM and ABC have made a common, fundamental mistake as to the equipment to be purchased which has the effect that they were agreeing to buy and sell something completely different. However, other cases would suggest that so long as the parties correctly identified the goods they wanted, it is not a mistake at law that the goods lacked some particular quality that was essential to their intended purpose. Sometimes the availability of a remedy may depend on considerations of fairness, such as whether both parties can be restored to the position they were in immediately prior to the contract. In the example given of DIM and ABC Optics, this may be difficult in that ABC may be unable to do anything with the equipment if it is returned.

The mistake of fact may relate to apparently intangible things, such as whether an opinion is honestly held, or whether there is a common belief as to some future event.

Unilateral and mutual mistakes

More often it is the case that only one of the parties is mistaken as to some material facts (a unilateral mistake) or both parties have made incorrect assumptions but as to entirely different matters (a mutual mistake).

In the example given above, it is far more likely that DIM only suffered from the delusion as to the usability of the equipment, and ABC Optics, not surprisingly, did not care one way or the other, making it quite clear that it was only filling an order. In other words, the mistake was unilateral only.

A prospective licensee of software may assume the software has performance characteristics, such as response times, which it will not have in that licensee's system environment, whilst a supplier mistakenly believes that the customer has made or will make arrangements for installation and implementation of the software package. Here both parties are mistaken as to some matter.

Generally speaking, the law gives no remedy in these circumstances. It must be reemphasized that the law does not give a remedy simply because a buyer has an inflated view of the value of a product. This may be a 'mistake' on the part of the buyer but, in the absence of some misrepresentation (discussed below) or express or implied term of the contract (discussed in the previous chapter), it is not a mistake with which the law is concerned. The mistake in question must go to the substance of what is being transacted.

Therefore, in the circumstances where there is one or more unilateral or mutual mistakes of fact, the law has usually been slow to provide a remedy, unless these mistakes have been induced by misrepresentations, or the mistake is the subject of some implied term in the contract, whether by way of statute or by virtue of general principles.

Example ─────────────────────────────────────

ABC Industries Limited is the owner of a HAL 3000 minicomputer, which has had added to it a number of high performance upgrade and interface boards. ABC decides to dispose of the base CPU configuration, but intends to keep the upgrade and interface boards for use with its new hardware acquisition.

ABC advertises the HAL 3000 for sale as 'a HAL 3000 and peripheral equipment (specified) suitable for high performance applications' and specifies a price. XYZ Holdings Limited, an interested purchaser, inspects the HAL 3000 and the offered peripheral equipment in operation on ABC's site and running ABC's applications, and wrongly assumes the upgrade and interface boards will be included. It considers the price very reasonable. XYZ agrees to purchase the equipment and is dismayed when the HAL 3000 is delivered without the high performance boards, but with a functional but lower capacity configuration.

Can XYZ refuse to take delivery of the equipment and/or claim a refund?

The answer is probably no. ABC may have been ambiguous with its advertising: 'suitable for' does not necessarily mean that the equipment includes the added capacity, and ABC may have done nothing to clarify the matter with the demonstration given, but there is nothing to suggest that ABC deliberately misled XYZ, or knowingly permitted XYZ to mislead itself. In addition, ABC was under no legal duty to disabuse XYZ.

It should be noted that there would only be a statutory warranty of fitness for purpose (referred to in Chapter 7) if ABC knew XYZ's purpose for the equipment. In any event, it would be difficult to say the HAL 3000 was not fit for XYZ's purpose if it could be made so with the addition of the appropriate boards!

It is in these areas that there has been considerable statutory intervention in recent years.

Rectification

Before leaving this area of mistakes, we should mention one further type of mistake. Where there is a mistake in the wording of a contract, a simple mistake of words, then a court may order the 'rectification' of the contract, in effect decreeing what has been proved to be the original agreement, so that no party can take advantage of this simple mistake.

This may be a mistake where there is a simple typographical error in the typing up of contracts, such as reference to a wrong clause or paragraph number, or the omission of words or groups of words, which may give a mistaken impression.

Where such a mistake is evident on the face of the contract, or in certain special cases the court accepts evidence of the mistake, the court can order a rectification of the agreement, that is, that the agreement will be treated as if the typographical or other error had not been made.

Representations

In a number of cases, things which are said, or done, before a contract is entered, may be binding on the person responsible for them.

This is often an extremely contentious area in computer industry transactions at all levels, perhaps because those in the computer industry once relied so heavily on a 'clubby' code of honour, which has proved most unreliable in practice and extremely costly. Even those new to the products of the industry have been so awed by technology that they have not dared or thought to question many assumptions and assurances from which they have derived some pre-purchase comfort.

How then do pre-contractual 'representations' become binding on a representer?

We shall consider this first from the perspective of contract, and in the next chapter from the perspective of the law of negligence.

Representations forming part of the contract

Under the general law, a representation made before a contract is finalized could become a part of the offer made, and thereby simply a term of the contract.

Example

POS Computer Systems Inc. supplies point of sale terminal systems, including small portable computer terminals for use as data entry and retrieval devices in the field. In its brochures for the portable computers, POS states:

> *The compact and easy to use PCT 200R series terminals have been 'ruggedized' for use in the field. A strong sealed casing to keep out dust and damp, and environmental specifications for operation in temperatures between −5°C, and 40°C, ensure continual satisfactory operation no matter what the job.*

Farm Fresh Inc. is a large supplier of farm and dairy produce to retailers in desert townships. It requires simple and sturdy portable computers for its truck drivers, to record deliveries, orders, wastage, payment and so on, and for such data to be transmitted to its head office. This necessitates in the ordinary course that the terminals will be used in the cold storage facilities of both the customers and in the vans at temperatures between −5°C and 5°C, and which are damp and humid, and of course in the cab of the trucks or other places where the noonday temperature can rise very high, up to 40°C, or which are very dusty.

Impressed by POS's brochure, Farm Fresh purchases twenty of the PCT 200R series terminals for trial in the field.

The terminals are delivered with a 'POS Customer Warranty Card' which does little more than exclude all conditions and warranties except those which cannot be legally excluded, but for reasons considered above (see Chapter 7) this may be disregarded, as it is first seen by the customer after the point of contract.

Within a short period of use, Farm Fresh finds that the PCT 200R series suffers from an extremely high incidence of error or failures, mainly due to dust entering the device through the keyboard and interfering with connectors, and the extreme temperature fluctuations affecting electrical components.

What remedy can Farm Fresh seek?

There being no effective exclusion of responsibility for the over-confident assurances given in the brochure, these statements became terms of the contract between POS and Farm Fresh — in this case, warranties as to the performance characteristics of the PCT 200R series terminal. This was because Farm Fresh purchased the terminals on the basis of the 'offer' contained in the brochure, and in reliance upon those representations. There is no need for any special contractual words, such as 'guarantee', 'warranty' and so on, nor any special form of contract. In the circumstances, the statements made were probably fundamental conditions of the contract and, since the device was unable to comply at the time of delivery, the contract may be rescinded and the purchase price refunded, or damages may be claimed, which may be more but, because of the trial conditions, would probably be less.

It is important in considering an example such as this, and further issues considered below, to differentiate between a representation or assurance which is solid, substantial and on which it is reasonable to rely, and a 'mere puff'. A 'mere puff', in the language of lawyers, is one of those exaggerations to which all salesmen are inclined, and which any reasonably sensible customer takes with a grain of salt. All the laudatory epithets, such as 'best', 'fastest', 'value for money', 'most reliable', 'state of the art', and so on, up to the more poetic, such as 'the CPU is so rugged it would run on the local beach', or 'this software is perfect for you, it was designed by people in your industry' tend not to relate to any specific, measurable aspect of performance, but to some subjective measure of worth, which may change in emphasis from person to person.

In the example of POS and Farm Fresh above, the praise by POS of its product went beyond the general to the particular, specifying particular environmental extremes within which the equipment would operate.

From POS's point of view, it could have maintained the benefit of its advertising which, no doubt, was generally accurate although not when tested to the limits which characterized Farm Fresh's unusual business, by including any appropriate qualification in the brochure, in the same place or a separate place brought to the attention of readers (such as a footnote saying 'These operating specifications are generally accurate but may not apply in your particular circumstances. You should enquire at . . . ').

Finally, it should be noted that, under the general law of contract, had Farm Fresh purchased the equipment from a dealer, as opposed to POS itself, it would not have had the benefit of a contractual warranty, or even an extracontractual representation, because it would not have entered any contract with POS itself. If the dealer had adopted the representations in the brochure, they may have been incorporated in the contract with the dealer. Thus Farm Fresh would be forced to rely on the law of negligence, or the new statutory remedies under unfair competition laws (discussed further below, and in Chapter 9).

Extracontractual representations

Under the old common law, if a representation was not part of the contract, then it was extremely difficult to make it binding on the representer.

In these circumstances, unless representations were fraudulent or deceitful, courts would only look to representations made prior to the contract in extreme circumstances, and then only as the basis for rescission of contract, and not for damages. Different courts in different countries have varying rules or tests, in relation to innocent, as opposed to deceitful or negligent misrepresentations, for example, it may be required that the representation made must have been significant or 'material', and false, and that the party seeking relief relied upon the misrepresentation in entering the contract.

In most countries, there are three types of misrepresentations for which the courts may give some remedy, namely

(1)   innocent misrepresentations;

(2)   fraudulent misrepresentations, or 'deceit'; and

(3)   negligent misstatements.

Innocent misrepresentations

In general terms, a person will not be permitted to rely on a contract which he or she has induced as a result of a misrepresentation of some material issue.

As we shall see, the remedies available in the case of negligent or deceitful misrepresentations may extend to damages, but in the case of an innocent misrepresentation, rescission or a defence to some claim under the contract will generally be the only relief available.

What is a misrepresentation? It is fundamental to the general law that the representation should be

(1)   a representation of fact, not of law,

(2)   false, and

(3)   inducing the contract.

Again, a representation as to some opinion held, intention, or some future event, can only be regarded as a misrepresentation if the opinion as to the present or the future, or intention, is not honestly held.

A half truth can be a misrepresentation, if, when taken on its own without what remains unsaid, it is reasonable to expect a false impression will result. By and large, silence cannot be a misrepresentation, unless there is some circumstance giving rise to an obligation to disclose the whole truth, such as in the case of trustees or proposals for insurance, which it is beyond the ambit of this book to discuss.

The requirement for inducement is very important. If the person alleging misrepresentation was not aware of the representation at the time of entering the contract, or completely dismissed it (as in the case of most salesmen's exaggerations) he or she can hardly complain. However, the misrepresentation need not be the only inducing factor, as long as it is one.

This may be a very narrow test, that may not give relief to the person who did not rely solely on the misrepresentation, but upon other matters, either oral or based upon the opinion, perhaps misguided, of other people, as well as the person making the false representation. In other words, in the typical commercial transaction, and not least in the computer industry, which has many facets, this type of test may be very difficult to satisfy.

Example

Kappa Financial Systems Limited is a fledgling company in the business of supplying and implementing software for financial institutions, such as banks, insurance companies and so on. It has a financial package of its own written in a 4GL package supplied by 4GL Inc., and is an OEM for the supplier of the hardware and operating system upon which its software operates, that is Megatherion, Inc.

Kappa responds to a request for tender issued by Heavibank Limited of Hong Kong, which seeks a financial package of hardware and software to handle its trading in metals and currency, which will interface with its mainframe financial systems.

In responding to the tender, Kappa submits a complete hardware and software solution, and in complying with the interface requirements relays information supplied by 4GL and Megatherion as to technical matters and future product offerings of each.

During discussions prior to acceptance of the tender, Kappa states that it has and will have full-time during implementation at least one analyst/programmer, two programmers, and a specialist trainer to conduct training in the use of the system. This is very important to the MIS of Heavibank which has suffered in the past from understaffed implementations, grossly slipping time deadlines.

The MIS of Heavibank accepts the tender of Kappa. In accepting the tender of Kappa, the MIS of Heavibank has not relied on her own judgement, but has engaged consultants to prepare the Request for Tender, review tenders submitted and to interview shortlisted tenderers. Kappa was recommended by the consultants for a number of reasons, including their own understanding of the proximity of Megatherion and 4GL's new product offering.

Heavibank and Kappa immediately publish the project with press releases, and send the papers off to their respective lawyers to prepare a contract. The contract, when prepared, makes no mention of the staff levels required of Kappa, because this was not raised in the tender documentation, or of acceptance criteria for the interface, and the contract includes a 'boilerplate' clause excluding all representations and warranties made or given before the contract.

The success of Kappa in the tender to Heavibank greatly impresses other customers with whom Kappa has also been negotiating, and Kappa suddenly finds itself much busier than anticipated and unable to recruit staff suitably skilled in the Megatherion and 4GL environment.

The implementation and training of the Kappa solution starts falling severely behind schedule because Kappa is unable to make available the staff it expected to have free. In addition, the interface produced early in the project is extremely poor, very slow and clumsy in operation, mainly because Megatherion and 4GL have completely changed their direction and have not produced the enhanced products to make this interface easy to operate.

In the absence of statutory remedies, what is Heavibank's position under the general law?

In relation to the staffing of the project by Kappa and implementation deadlines, Heavibank may allege that it relied on Kappa's statements even though the decision to select Kappa did not turn on these statements alone but on many factors, in relation to which it had the independent advice of its consultants.

However, can it be said that the representations made by Kappa were false? Insofar as they related to the future, at the time of making them Kappa accurately represented its intentions.

Exactly the same observations may be made in relation to the interface.

In any event, Heavibank willingly executed a contract disclaiming any reliance on any prior representations not included in the contract. Heavibank may have to live with the fact that its contract did not specify performance standards and timetables. It may get the product and an interface, but not nearly as soon or as effectively as it had expected.

Furthermore, Heavibank cannot make any claim based on the technical deficiencies created by the decisions of Megatherion and 4GL. Neither Megatherion nor 4GL made any direct statements to Heavibank, only to their OEM, Kappa — and accordingly Heavibank is not entitled to take action against them.

Finally, it should be understood clearly that it does not matter in the least whether the misrepresentations are spoken or written, except that it may be more difficult to prove a spoken misrepresentation was made, or what precisely was said.

Remedies for innocent misrepresentation

A serious deficiency in the old law of misrepresentation is that it is essential to it that the misrepresentation at least results in a contract, even if it does not form part of that contract. If there is no contract, there is no remedy.

In addition, we have already commented on the limitation of availability of damages in the case of innocent misrepresentations — the only remedy available may be rescission of the contract, or, in special circumstances referred to below, where the courts recognize the possibility of a collateral contract.

To overcome this limitation, some courts have sought to extend the circumstances in which representations have become terms of the contract — but this approach can nearly always be defeated by an express term in the contract excluding any such unwritten terms, in which case some courts have even gone so far as to find a 'collateral contract'. In this type of analysis, it is argued that the main contract was only entered into in consideration of the pre-contractual promises or assurances — in other words, there is a separate and parallel contract, not affected by any exclusion clause. In this case, courts are seeking clear and unequivocal contractual promises in reliance upon which another contract has been entered. This test, although easy to talk about, may also be extremely difficult to prove and thus again leave many situations without a remedy. However, if the courts permit proof of a 'collateral contract' this will have as a consequence the right to an order in damages for breach of the collateral contract, instead of rescission of the main contract.

In some countries, such as the United Kingdom with its *Misrepresentation Act 1967*, these problems have been overcome in part by statutory modification of the general law of contract. In these cases it is provided that wherever rescission for innocent misrepresentation would have been available, the courts may also now award damages.

The same, or a more generous, result has also been achieved in the *unfair competition laws* of some countries — but in these cases, rather than modifying contract law, a new and independent remedy of damages is provided for any misleading or deceptive conduct, whether resulting in a contract or not.

Negligent misstatements

In certain special cases, a misrepresentation which is innocent, and may even relate to matters other than facts, may give a right to damages. This is the case with negligent misstatements.

As this area of the law has grown out the law of tort, it is really irrelevant whether there is a contract or not. In fact, in most cases there will not be any contract at all, such as in the relationship between professional advisers and their clients, the publication of prospectuses or other promotional documents, or the answers of banks and government authorities to public enquiries. However, in most countries there is no reason why the same principles should not apply to pre-contractual negotiations.

The courts will award damages to a person who suffers loss as a result of reasonably relying on the negligent statements of another, provided the person making the statements had a 'duty of care' to the person suffering the loss. The concept of the 'duty of care' is explained more fully in Chapter 9 below, but in this special area it means that special relationship between

(1)   a person who is in the business of giving advice, an 'expert' or one who has special knowledge and is in the business of giving it out, or a person who takes on that rôle, and

(2)   a person who consults or seeks information from the 'expert' in the course of the expert's business.

In such circumstances, whether the advice or information is given freely or not, it is considered reasonable for the recipient to rely on the giver of the advice or information to be careful, and for the giver of the advice to foresee that the recipient may suffer loss unless the adviser is careful.

It will be noted that the misrepresentation in this case can extend to 'advice' on a course of conduct — clearly well outside the requirement of the contract law that a misrepresentation relate to a matter of 'fact'.

Example

Expert-Ease Systems Ltd is a supplier of hardware and software solutions for the legal profession, specializing in small systems for 'first time users'.

Robert Strain is a salesman for Expert-Ease, but on his business card he is described as a 'Legal Systems Consultant'.

Strain calls upon the small legal firm of Crank & Gristle which he knows has never used any computer system in its business — still using ledgers and journals for its book-keeping, and typewriters for correspond-ence and documents. Strain finds Crank & Gristle a modestly successful firm, with its accounting done by a part-time bookkeeper who comes in once or twice a week to keep the books and issue accounts, and a couple of elderly and very loyal secretaries.

Strain presents himself to the busy partners of Crank & Gristle and, over tea, tells them of the wonders of computerized accounts, time costing, word processing and personal productivity. They are so overwhelmed by this presentation, and by a sense of shame because they have not kept up to date with the new age, that they accept Strain's offer to 'assess their system requirements' and, relying on his advice, they sign an order for £29 500 — the full price of a CPU and four terminals, mass storage, a laser printer and dot-matrix printer, legal accounting and word processing software, in-

stallation, training and manuals (not forgetting Strain's substantial commission!).

Unfortunately, Crank & Gristle do not realize the agonies of putting all their data into the system, without which the training is next to useless, the book keeper has no comprehension of the accounting methods adopted by the new system, and the secretaries find the vagaries of the creation and printing of documents quite beyond them, and resign to well deserved retirement.

In a case such as this, although this example is a highly romanticized version of the facts, an English Court has found that the supplier's salesman had put himself in the position of an 'expert', notwithstanding that everyone involved knew he was a salesman, and that the partners of the law firm reasonably relied on his 'advice'. The advice, therefore, should have been given carefully and impartially.

In such circumstances, Strain should have advised the law firm of the difficulties of computerization, that they were ill-suited to the entirely new way of doing business called for and that the costs may outweigh the benefits.

A warning should be sounded, however. Simply to make a mistake, or to suffer a reasonable lapse of memory, is not *per se* negligent. Negligence, as is explained more fully in Chapter 9, is more than this: it is to fall short of a standard of care which is the minimum that should be expected of any person in the same position.

Negligent misrepresentations may also be caught by the new statutory remedies referred to in the preceding section.

Fraudulent misrepresentation — deceit

This is another area which derives from tort law, instead of contract, but which has extended remedies to situations *including* the area of contracts.

In the case of 'innocent misrepresentations', including negligence, we were really concerned with the remedies available when the mental state of the representer is completely irrelevant. In other words, it does not matter whether the representer *knew* that what he or she was saying was a lie or not.

If it can be shown, however, that, in addition to all the matters set out in the preceding section, he *deliberately* set out to deceive the hearer, then the courts will award damages as well as the remedies of rescission and a defence to a claim under a contract.

However, proof of deceit is always a difficult matter. The courts will not readily give a finding of fact which could seriously impair a trader's business reputation unless the evidence is very cogent indeed, and it is no easy matter ever to prove any person's state of mind for, as one ancient legal commentator observed, 'The devil himself knoweth not the mind of man'.

'Estoppel'

The legal doctrine of estoppel is a curious creature. By it, it was said that a person who changed his or her position in reliance on a false statement of another will be permitted to assert the false statement in defence of a claim by the other. By this means, a person would not be permitted to profit in the courts from the untruth.

This was an important matter in cases such as if A wrongly represents to C that B is entitled to sub-license to C certain software, A will not be permitted to sue for the return of the software on the basis that B was not entitled to supply the software after all.

The importance of the principle is that the false statement in this case is not necessarily made to induce a contract with the representer, but with a third party. Its limitation was that it could only be used 'as a shield and not a sword'. In other words, the false statement could not be relied upon to rescind the contract into which one was misled or, perhaps more importantly, to obtain damages. In addition, the estoppel could only relate to a representation as to some past or present fact, not about something to occur in the future.

As a result of these limitations, some courts have attempted to develop notions of 'promissory estoppel', based upon a reliance on a representation as to the future, and similar extensions, whereby the person relying on the representation could take action, notwithstanding the absence of negligence or fraud. These developments remain of importance in countries such as the United Kingdom where there is still no comprehensive unfair competition law, but in other countries with the benefit of such laws, it is usually a feature of them that they give a right of action for any misleading or deceptive conduct whether resulting in a contract with the representer or not.

Duress and undue influence

The law has long recognized that where a person in a weak position has been prevailed upon by a stronger party to enter into a contract which he or she would not otherwise have entertained, then the weaker party is entitled to have the contract set aside, or defend any action based on it.

However, the traditional law has tended only to recognize such cases where the power of the stronger over the weaker is so powerful, so overwhelming, that the weaker party is virtually deprived of an independent will — hence limiting the application of the law to the cases of the feeble minded, captive or infirm, and, to some extent, cases of deception and cheating.

In most countries, these principles have been greatly extended by statute, although it is still sometimes difficult to find application for these new laws in practice. Under new laws, it is not uncommon to find that courts have a power to set aside contracts, or even to vary their terms, in cases where there has been any undue inequality of bargaining power, having regard to many factors, such as status, financial circumstances, language or educational difficulties and other very general matters.

Statutory remedies

The examples above have highlighted a number of limitations in the law in relation to mistake and misrepresentation.

It is because of these deficiencies that legislation has been introduced in many countries to broaden the remedies available. This may operate either by way of a modification of the existing contract law, such as the *Misrepresentation Act, 1967* of the United Kingdom or alternatively, it may give an altogether new cause of action, such as unfair competition laws in the United States and Australia, and elsewhere, which give a right to sue for damages where a loss or injury results from any misleading or deceptive conduct.

These developments in the law have tended to supervene old legal theories, but the latter remain the law in many countries, and even where the new laws are in place, the old frequently complement and give substance to the new.

Conclusion

This area of law is an unusually complex one. The summary above, both concerning the basis for legal remedies and the legal remedies themselves, is far too brief to be entirely correct for every circumstance, under the law of every nation! In addition, the law of some countries has advanced beyond the position summarized above, while that of others has not yet come so far.

Whatever is the law, many contracts expressly provide that all representations or assurances made or given prior to the contract, and all conditions or warranties not expressly included in the contract, are excluded and denied, or, paradoxically, acknowledged not to have been given or made at all. Frequently, such a provision will be given some effect, and accordingly recipients of important representations in the contractual process would be well advised to remove such a provision or, more sensibly, include an important representation in the contract itself as a term. On the other hand, such exclusion clauses are not always effective, especially in the cases of deceit or negligence, and accordingly suppliers prone to make representations should take care.

9 Negligence

What is negligence?

The law does not give a remedy for every wrong done. As we shall see in the next chapter, this caused some concern in the case of predatory commercial conduct designed to destroy competition, where the failure of the law to respond with a remedy eventually resulted in special legislation regulating 'anti-competitive' conduct.

The common law has more successfully dealt with conduct which has 'accidentally' caused harm — negligence — but within very carefully prescribed limitations. The purpose of this chapter is to consider the nature of the law of negligence, and to discuss some of those limitations.

Originally, the legal system had the time and resources to deal with only physically invasive behaviour, conduct which was there for all to see and to bear witness to, such as taking away or damaging another person's goods or animals, unlawfully occupying land or buildings, striking or threatening another with physical violence, or holding another against his or her will. In criminal law, such conduct would result in prosecution and fines, or worse. By the civil law, the courts could give compensation to the victim, payable of course by the culprit. In English law, these wrongs became known as 'torts' from the French word for 'wrongs' — 'trespass' to goods (damaging or taking them away whilst they were in another's possession), 'conversion' of goods (misappropriating goods when not in another's possession), trespass to land, 'battery' (physical violence to a person), 'assault' (a threat of physical violence), and 'wrongful imprisonment'.

However, the common law also recognized the need to give compensation to those who suffer injury or loss as an indirect or unexpected consequence of the conduct of another, such as the bringing of dangerous animals or explosive substances onto neighbouring property, or leaving premises in a dangerous state of disrepair.

From this latter area arose the tort of negligence. The legal system came to recognize that it is a socially beneficial policy that if anyone should bear the cost of injury arising from carelessness, it should be the person who causes it, even if unwittingly, rather than the person who suffers it. By this means a greater standard of care would be imposed upon those who can take steps to avoid accidents, or, more significantly as time has passed, upon those who may take insurance against the consequences of their negligence or the negligence of their employees and other agents. This area of law has increased enormously in importance with the widespread use of insurance.

One of the great benefits of this area of the law is that there is no need to prove the state of mind of the person causing the damage — the conduct could be deliberate, but that is irrelevant to responsibility. As we shall see, deliberate conduct may lead to greater liability in damages, but proof of a wrongdoer's state of mind is notoriously difficult.

With the growth in the application of the law of negligence, so has it become more important to carefully define its limitations. For example, it was initially only negligence that resulted in physical injury to goods or person that gave a right of action in the court — 'mere' economic loss would not entitle a person to compensation. The development of the law away from this limitation is one of the greatest importance, which we shall examine later. In addition, one can only sue the actual or real causer of injury — if a person is the mere vehicle of someone else's fault (for example, is forced into doing the wrong which resulted in injury) then one must sue that other person, provided he or she is not too 'remote'. Finally, it is not any behaviour resulting in injury which is 'negligent' for the purposes of gaining compensation: a mistake is not always a negligent mistake.

To put these qualifications into a simple formula, or at least simple to analytically minded lawyers, to prove negligence one must show:

(1)   that a person had a *duty of care* to the person seeking compensation,

(2)   what the *standard of care* was to which that person was obliged to conform in the circumstances,

(3)   that that person's conduct was a breach of that standard,

(4)   that the person seeking compensation suffered *damage*,

(5)   that that person's conduct was the *proximate cause* of that damage, and

(6)   that the damage suffered was *foreseeable* by the person at the time of his conduct causing damage.

With such hurdles to cross, it will be clear that a remedy is not always available. Let us examine these hurdles more carefully, to see if the courts have made it easier than it appears.

The duty of care

A duty of care is owed to any person who can be reasonably anticipated to be affected by one's careless actions. It does not matter if one does not know the particular person. So, for example, drivers of motor vehicles have a duty of care to drive safely to other drivers of motor vehicles, and to pedestrians, who can be expected to be on or beside the roadway.

This seems obvious enough, but such a broad statement would not have been accepted a hundred years ago, when it was thought that the categories of relationships giving rise to a duty of care were much narrower and fewer. In 1837 it was said in a case involving the supply of a dangerously defective firearm to a person whose son was injured by it, considered a difficult case as the son was suing, not the father who purchased the gun:

> ... we should pause before we make it a precedent by our decision which would be authority for an action against vendors, *even of such instruments and articles as are dangerous in themselves*, at the suit of any person whomsoever into whose hands they might happen to pass, and who should be injured thereby ... '. [Emphasis added.]

In 1932, a famous case in English law, *Donoghue* v *Stevenson*, gathered the many threads together to restate the law in the much broader terms we know today — it is also a leading case on product liability and illustrates some very important points about the law of negligence. It is such a fine example that, rather than convert the facts to a modern, computer industry setting, we shall leave them as they were.

Example — Donoghue v Stevenson

Miss Donoghue went with a friend to visit a store selling, amongst other things, ginger beer in bottles. Her friend purchased a bottle of ginger beer and gave some of it to Miss Donoghue to drink. As her friend poured the remainder of the bottle into her own glass, Miss Donoghue alleged that she saw coming out of the bottle the remains of a partially decomposed snail, whereupon she was violently ill and not a little distressed.

The question before the English House of Lords was this: could Miss Donoghue sue the bottler of the ginger beer for negligence in allowing a snail to invade the bottle before filling and there remain until a consumer made a nasty discovery?

This was no easy matter. Miss Donoghue could not sue the shopkeeper under the Sale of Goods law discussed in Chapter 7 above because she did not buy the bottle herself and hence was not party to the contract of sale of goods as was her friend (who suffered no injury), and neither she nor her friend could sue the manufacturer for the same reason. Therefore, in those days before consumer protection laws, Miss Donogh-

ue's only chance for compensation was in tort, and she had to establish at the outset that the manufacturer owed her a duty of care.

The court found in favour of Miss Donoghue, saying that there was a general 'good neighbour' principle, that the duty of care extended to any person whom the manufacturer could anticipate would consume the contents of the bottle — there had to be someone and that person was the person to whom the duty was owed, whether party to a contract or not.

The argument against Miss Donoghue was a respectable one. It was this: the manufacturer already had a contractual liability to its customers, such as the shopkeeper, and indirectly through him to Miss Donoghue's friend. How much further could he be expected to be responsible, how many intervening transactions could occur through which he would remain liable?

Substitute computer hardware or software for the ginger beer and the problem becomes a more real one. To what extent is the supplier responsible to ultimate users, or beneficiaries of data processing carried out using the hardware or software? To this question there can be no easy answer, in each case it depends upon the ability, assessed by a court of law, of an average person in the supplier's position (not, you will note, the actual supplier, who may be abnormally short-sighted!) to anticipate the ultimate victim.

What would be the effect upon this duty of care in the case of

(1) a customer of a bureau, where the software licence forbids use of the software in a bureau facility;

(2) a borrower of software where the licence forbids assignment, sub-licensing or other disposal; or

(3) a customer of, say, an architect or doctor using software in his or her practice, where the software licence specifies that the software will be used only for the licensee's internal business purposes?

It may well be, as is so often the case, that the licences in question were poorly worded and under-negotiated, but can it be said that the supplier can reasonably anticipate the ultimate victim in the case of some loss or damage? In general, in these cases, the courts will not impose liability for damage which is too indirect, unless the causer of the injury knew of the relationship, or likely relationship, between its customer and the ultimate victim.

An issue is raised by disclaimers of liability and exclusion clauses in contracts, to which we have referred in Chapter 7, and which we shall consider in more detail below in relation to 'professional negligence' — the issue being whether the relevant provisions have effectively been brought to the attention of the person alleging negligence (not the initial licensee). In part, in the case of shrinkwrap licences, the problem may be whether these licences have any contractual effect whatsoever.

In certain cases, the damage suffered by indirect victims is considered too 'remote', a matter discussed below.

The standard of care

As we have already noted, it is not any behaviour resulting in injury which is 'negligent' for the purposes of gaining compensation; a mistake is not always a negligent mistake.

The standard of care which will be imposed is meant to be appropriate to the circumstances, the nature of the situation, how the injury occurred, and the sort of person alleged to have been negligent. The doctor who stops to help an accident victim does not have the same standard of care as the same doctor seeing the same patient in his or her surgery; the supplier of equipment or software only has to anticipate reasonable use of it, not extraordinary use, testing the equipment or software beyond its limits; and, finally, 'if a person deliberately agrees to allow a blacksmith to mend his watch, it may well be said that he agrees to accept a low standard of skill'.

Example

Medical Expert Systems Ltd ('MES') is engaged in the business of supplying and maintaining computer systems and software for medical practitioners, including a database of medical information, medical terms, drugs, common symptoms and diagnoses, bibliographic information and so on. This information is independently checked by a medical practitioner on the staff of MES with expert consultants, and is regularly updated. Nonetheless, MES warns doctors to exercise their independent judgement, as no such system can be as comprehensive as human knowledge.

Based upon current medical information from a standard source, the database provides certain information on a sedative drug commonly used by medical practitioners as a mild anti-depressant, including major uses, known side effects, dosages and danger signals.

Unknown to MES, and to MES's consultants at the time of the last consultation within the last year, the drug has unusually hazardous side effects in the cases of patients with a newly discovered viral illness which suppresses the immune system of patients.

Relying on the information in his MES database, Dr Omega prescribes the drug to his patient, who is depressed by the onset of this viral illness, as a result of which the patient is severely incapacitated for a long period. At the date the doctor prescribed, the information concerning this problem would have been known by most specialists whom the doctor, or MES, could have consulted.

Can the patient sue MES for negligence because of the deficiency in the information in the database?

There is no doubt that MES would have a duty of care to patients of doctors using its system. However, although it is difficult to decide such a case in such a general way, it seems that the standard of care that would be imposed upon MES would be to prepare its database with diligence and care, to update it regularly and to warn doctors not to abrogate their own responsibilities to the 'expert system'. The burden on MES is very high, it would be permitted small errors, but would be expected to be reasonably correct and thorough to cross check with up-to-date sources. However, this was recent information which, although it may have been referred to in obscure specialist research journals, may not have been widely appreciated at the date of preparation of the database.

It is an important policy of the law not to stifle commerce by imposing unrealistic standards, whilst weighing the fact that commerce can insure against such liability and thereby ensure that the cost of injury is not suffered by an individual.

Proximate cause

The action of the person accused of negligence must be the real and proximate cause of the injury suffered. If the real cause is, however, completely unpredictable circumstances, the intervening act of someone else, or is in fact the victim's own doing, then the victim cannot allege that the particular loss was suffered as a result of the negligence of the person so accused.

Example

Epsilon Environmental Conditioning Inc. supplies air conditioning and dust filtration systems for computer rooms. Its biggest market is naturally in the high heat generation mainframes and super computers and their peripheral mass storage systems, which require dust free environments.

Epsilon supplies and instals one of its systems to Facilities Management Inc. ('FM'), which specializes in the maintenance and operation of computer systems of third parties, including Indemnity Insurance Inc. Epsilon is requested by FM to instal a circuit breaker and battery backup to ensure continuity of the air conditioning system in the event of lightning strike (to which the area of FM is prone) or failure of the power supply to FM. Epsilon negligently fails to do so.

During an immense storm, lightning strikes the power line of

Facilities Management and, in the absence of a circuit breaker or backup power supply, the Epsilon system ceases to function, while Indemnity's mainframe (equipped with these safety devices) continues to operate. The mainframe becomes grossly overheated and, after some time, is severely damaged.

During the storm, however, one of FM's employees who has the responsibility for caring for the mainframe, goes out for a hamburger and does not return immediately because he stays out to watch the lightning.

The contract between Indemnity Insurance and FM expressly excludes liability for these sorts of events, even the carelessness of FM's own employee, and so it denies responsibility, blaming Epsilon. Indemnity has no contract with Epsilon, so must sue for negligence.

The real author of Indemnity's injury may be FM's employee, especially if he left the computer room after the failure of Epsilon's system, because he could have shut down the Indemnity mainframe. It may even be no-one's fault, simply a result of an unusually severe storm. However, it is usually not an excuse for a negligent person to say that someone else could have prevented the consequences of his or her own negligence, although in this case the lapse of FM's employee may have been of such a long duration that it genuinely constituted an intervening event.

A more typical intervening event would be one where, using the above example, a certain amount of damage was done by the overheating, but even more catastrophic damage was done to the mainframe by the maintenance personnel brought in afterwards. In these cases the argument that the maintenance people would never have been brought in in the first place if it had not been for the negligence of Epsilon (or FM's employee), is usually dismissed by the courts as spurious, and, however difficult it may be to apportion from the original damage, the original culprit would be liable only for the damage it directly caused, and the maintenance people would answer for the balance.

Foreseeability

A negligent person is only liable for damage caused by his or her negligence which was probable, and foreseeable by any reasonable person in his or her position at the time of the negligence. However, as long as the damage is of the type that may be foreseen, it is immaterial if the extent or value of the damage is far greater than expected.

Example ────────────────────────────

Alpha Computers manufactures personal computers. Due to a design fault, one of the electrical connections has a tendency to overheat, in extreme cases causing hot solder to fall upon the plastic base of the computer and burn through the base. In one particular case, such an Alpha computer is used in the office of a plastics manufacturer, Plastics Limited, where the surface upon which it is placed is a new experimental plastic surface for benchtops which turns out to be extremely flammable. The bench catches fire, resulting in a general fire of such catastrophic proportions that the neighbouring factory of Adjacent Limited is also destroyed. One of the side effects of the fire is that Fast Foods Limited, which runs a nearby cafeteria, is virtually ruined as all its customers from the two factories are not working as a result of the fire.

Can Plastics, Adjacent and/or Fast Foods claim for their losses from Alpha?

Plastics certainly could claim against Alpha. A reasonable person in the position of Alpha designing a personal computer must be able to anticipate that an electrical design fault could result in fire damage, and the fact that this damage was much more than anyone would have imagined, and that it was so severe only because of the unusual conjunction of circumstances in this case, is immaterial. Adjacent is in the same position, even though it was a mere neighbour. Fast Foods, however, suffered 'mere' economic loss, unaccompanied by physical damage, and in these cases the courts of many countries are far more circumspect, often judging such a loss as too 'remote'. Another way of looking at Fast Foods' loss is to say that the company was not injured by the fire at all, but by the consequent events, making its loss one further remove from Alpha's negligence.

The calculation of damages in negligence may be compared to that of fraud, or deceit, another common law tort constituted by deliberate deception resulting in damage. In the case of fraud, the deceiver is liable for all the direct consequences of his or her deceit, whether or not foreseeable.

Negligence and self preservation

An important qualification should be imposed upon the broad statements of responsibility for negligence considered above. There is a responsibility on the part of the victim to take reasonable precautions for his or her own self preservation.

This may be expressed in several ways.

Voluntary assumption of risk

As we noted above with respect to the duty of care, if a person knowingly has his watch repaired by a blacksmith, he cannot complain if the blacksmith does not do the job as well as a watchmaker. However, one would expect the blacksmith to exercise the care of a normal person not skilled in watch repairs — so presumably the blacksmith could still be sued for negligently falling short of that standard.

There have been cases which have indicated that where a person undertakes some particularly hazardous activity, and deliberately ignores safety procedures, then no duty of care is owed at all. These cases have tended to relate to passengers in motor vehicles not wearing seat belts or where the driver is drunk, or to industrial accidents, but perhaps the same notion could be applied to the case of an owner of sensitive equipment who chooses to operate it in an unsuitable environment, or to have it operated or repaired by inexperienced personnel. However, it is probably more correct these days to treat such cases as ones where there has been no breach of duty, or the damage suffered has not been caused by the negligence of the person accused, but by the intervening negligence of the passenger, employee or equipment owner as the case may be.

Contributory negligence

The usual manner in which a lack of self preservation is raised in negligence cases is by way of a defence of 'contributory negligence'.

This is only a defence in the sense that a court is usually permitted to apportion the damage suffered between the plaintiff and defendant, depending on its view of the degree to which the negligence of the victim contributed to his or her own loss. The contribution of the victim theoretically could be as high as 100%, but this is extremely unlikely as this would appear to be more a case of an entirely intervening cause, and hence a finding of no negligence at all on the part of the defendant would be more appropriate.

It should be noted that this defence has nothing to do with any claim of negligence on the part of the defendant to the plaintiff, and hence no consideration of duty of care, standard of care and so on is called for. This defence is purely concerned with the victim's self preservation.

An example of contributory negligence may have been found in the example given in the section on 'Proximate cause', above, had the negligent employee been employed by the customer of Facilities Management, not Facilities Management itself.

Mitigation of loss

After the injury or loss has been inflicted, the victim has a duty to minimize its impact, financial or otherwise.

Thus, if as a result of some negligence the victim suffers the loss of the useful processing of data, the victim must do everything reasonable to obtain substitute processing facilities — the victim cannot simply allow a business to go into decline and claim huge losses of profits. The victim can, of course, add its cost of doing so to the damages claimed.

If the negligent party can show that steps could have been taken to 'mitigate' damages in this fashion, then the victim will only be entitled to the lesser amount of damages that would have been payable had the victim been more careful, as opposed to the actual loss suffered.

It should be noted, however, that courts are extremely cautious of the negligent defendant, with the benefit of hindsight, coming along with all sorts of advice as to how the actual damage suffered as a result of its negligence could have been limited or averted altogether.

'Mere' economic loss

In the examples given above, we have laboured a little to give examples of physical injury being suffered as the result of a negligent act.

The law has always been very cautious concerning the extending of a remedy to any person who suffers 'merely' economic loss (unaccompanied by physical damage) arising from the negligence, as opposed to deceit or other deliberate conduct, of others.

In the case of the injury to Fast Foods 'caused' by Alpha Computers in the example given in the section on 'Foreseeability' above, the rationale given was that the damage was too 'remote' or was 'unforeseeable'. It has also been argued that there is no 'duty of care' in such circumstances, for example in old cases of negligent misstatements. In one such case, *Le Lievre* v *Gould* in 1893, a bank relied upon the certificate of an architect in making a loan and, the certificate having been carelessly prepared by the architect, the bank lost money — yet the court said '[a] man is entitled to be as negligent as he pleases towards the whole world if he owes no duty to them [*sic*].' This case would not necessarily be decided the same way today, as we note in the following section.

Negligent statements

In quite recent times the courts of most countries have recognized a broad principle of liability for negligent misstatements to be derived from the classic professional negligence cases relating to 'professional advisers', such as lawyers, doctors, stockbrokers and accountants, and to statutory authorities having a responsibility to store and disseminate information (such as registries and local government bodies).

That broader principle is that anyone, not just a person in the traditional categories of advisers, who gives advice with the expectation that it will be acted upon will be held liable for foreseeable economic loss consequent upon the giving of the advice negligently.

This general principle is limited by a requirement that there must still exist what was described as a 'special relationship' between the giver of the advice and the receiver of the advice — not anyone receiving advice which is negligently given can sue on it, the person giving the advice must know the recipient in such a way as to expect the recipient to rely upon the advice — the absence of such an expectation may well be shown by a disclaimer of liability.

This special relationship and the nature of the 'business of giving advice' have greatly expanded the significance of this area of liability. So, for example, even if the advice is given free of charge it may be in all the circumstances that the giver of the advice should have realized that the recipient would rely upon it. Even where the information is given freely to a group of people, not just a known individual, for example in the form of a newsletter, it may be that the special relationship of trust in the advice may be created.

In one Australian decision, a bank was held liable for statements recklessly and negligently made in an 'open' letter ('to whom it may concern') written by one of its bank managers. This letter was put into the hands of a customer who later gave it to another bank in the course of a loan application. This case was even more interesting as, before entering into certain large loan transactions with the customer, the second bank sought further details from the first bank which the first bank supplied but with a disclaimer of liability. Notwithstanding this, the court found that the second bank was so affected by the original letter of endorsement that the subsequent disclaimer had no effect upon the liability of the first bank.

Example

ABC Data Processing Pte Limited is a service company which provides the data processing requirements of its parent company ABC Manufacturing Enterprises Limited. ABC Data Processing acquires the services of a consultant company, JustinTime Pte Limited to supply, instal and advise on the operation of a manufacturing process control system. ABC Data Processing is attracted to JustinTime initially by an 'advertising news-letter' circulated to all manufacturers extolling the virtues of the supplier: 'extensive practical experience in manufacturing gives us the knowledge to successfully automate your manufacturing line' and so on. ABC Data Processing obtains further information concerning the hardware and software systems used by JustinTime from brochures and meetings with JustinTime sales representatives, and inspects a successful system installed by JustinTime.

The contract presented by JustinTime and signed by ABC Data processing states:

> The Customer acknowledges that it has not relied on any statement or representa-
> tion of JustinTime, as to the fitness for any purpose of the System or any services to
> be supplied hereunder or any other matter whatsoever, and the Customer has relied
> solely upon its own skill and judgement in the evaluation of the System, the services

> *to be supplied hereunder and any benefits to be gained. To the full extent permitted by law JustinTime hereby disclaims all warranties except as expressly set forth herein, whether as to fitness for any purpose, merchantability or otherwise . . .*

This disclaimer is in bold capitalized type.

The staff appointed by JustinTime to the project in fact have little or no experience in manufacturing processes, inadequately evaluate ABC Manufacturing's requirements, and instal an entirely different system from that seen by ABC Data Processing prior to entry into the contract. The project is a disaster.

One of the interesting features of the problem of the ABC group is that ABC Data Processing is probably unable to sue JustinTime whatever the merits of the contract, as it is not the company which has suffered damage. It is ABC Manufacturing which has suffered the damage, but it is not party to the contract — but that may be a blessing, considering the inadequate job done by ABC Data Processing! Can ABC Manufacturing sue for negligence?

It seems highly likely that it can. JustinTime appears to have set itself up deliberately as an 'expert' and expected ABC Manufacturing to rely on it — it does so to encourage the business; it cannot shirk that responsibility if it has been so successful! Does the disclaimer have the effect of breaking down that reliance? It is submitted that it does not. One consideration is that it was made to the wrong person, that is ABC Data Processing, and may not have been brought to the attention of the victim; another is that it was made so late that one could believe that ABC Manufacturing had been so prevailed upon by the earlier materials, particularly the 'newsletter', that the disclaimer was of no effect.

These developments in the law of negligence are undoubtedly the most far reaching in their implications for the computer industry. For example, it is assumed by many people marketing computer products that all customers look upon computer salesmen as sophisticated used car salesmen. In other words, the customer is on its guard. However, just because a hardware and software salesman is a salesman, this does not preclude him or her from being an 'expert' who takes it upon himself to give advice. In many cases, the illusion of a 'computer professional' giving advice to a customer is fostered by the use of the loose titles such as 'systems analyst' and 'consultant' — no doubt to encourage the confidence of the customer. If the salesman sets himself up as a professional, or a specialist, then he has placed himself in a position of giving professional advice. Having regard to the breadth of the description of the nature of liability in the professional negligence cases, it is no objection, in appropriate cases, that the vendor organization's only remuneration from the activity is making a sale.

Example — Mackenzie Patten v British Olivetti

A salesman representing Olivetti went to a firm of solicitors and advised them that, notwithstanding the small size of the firm's business, the firm would be considerably advantaged by a computerization of its accounting system. As it turned out, experts agreed in court that the solicitors could not have benefited from such computerization and the computer equipment supplied was apparently never used, for this reason. The solicitors argued for liability on three grounds, breach of collateral agreement or warranty, misrepresentation and negligence. Olivetti was found liable only on the first ground and the remaining two matters were not decided. However, in deciding the matter, the court found that the plaintiff's partners were inexperienced in computers and had very reasonably relied upon the 'advice' given by the Olivetti salesman. In the circumstances, the salesman was found to be under a duty of care to advise truthfully and impartially in relation to the subject computer systems.

As a result of decisions such as this a whole new range of potential liability is raised for the computer industry.

Other cases

The caution of the legal system has not been restricted to the areas where bad professional advice is given. It has extended to any area where the loss suffered, for example from defective products, has resulted in purely financial loss, unaccompanied by any physical injury to person or property.

However, courts in most countries have thrown off this limitation. A recent notorious instance has been provided by litigation in the United States in which it has been alleged that Lotus 1–2–3 spreadsheet software embodied defects in structure (having regard to an alleged deficiency in the user documentation) that resulted in incorrect cost/price calculations being made, which then affected a pricing in a government contract and so resulted in a substantial loss being made on the contract. The case was settled, but there does not appear to be any doubt that the duty of care existed, and had the software been defective as a result of negligence, then Lotus would have been liable to compensate the user of the software for its loss.

As the judges of old feared, this may open enormous prospects of litigation in our increasingly software dependent society.

Example

Megatherion Bank is the victim in a very complicated EFT (electronic funds transfer) muddle. It, along with a number of other banks in its province of Delphinia, has engaged the service of an EFT switch network provider, Whist Funds Transfer Inc. to link its ATMs and POS terminals with those of all the other banks' in the network (through each banks' central banking system), so that any Megatherion customer holding a Megatherion Debit Card can access his or her account through the ATMs of any of the other banks in the network. Whist's EFT software is supplied to it by Delta Software.

Megatherion wishes to expand the services offered to its customers to the neighbouring province of Acacia, and so it and Whist enter an agreement with another EFT switch network provider operating in that province, Snap Switch Inc. and one of its customers, Gargantua Bank, whereby the Whist system is linked to Snap's system and thereby to Gargantua's ATM and POS network. Snap's EFT software is supplied to it by Kappa Banking Systems.

There is an obscure error in the Kappa software, whereby when the ATMs are off line (as they occasionally are during the day for various reasons), users of non-Gargantua cards by adopting an unusual procedure, may withdraw up to $500 over and over again, until the ATM is exhausted of cash. This is discovered by a Megatherion customer, who opens a bank account with Megatherion in a false name, and drains a series of Gargantua ATMs before disappearing.

The problem here is that Megatherion's books have been depleted with Gargantua's cash as a result of a fault in software provided to Snap by Kappa! Who pays?

Clearly Kappa owes a duty of care to Snap's customers, but it would not necessarily owe such a duty to Megatherion, whose contractual arrangement with Whist, and then Snap and Gargantua, could not necessarily have been anticipated by Kappa at the time of supplying the software to Snap.

In addition, there may be a standard of care issue here, as no doubt Kappa exercised every care in the preparation and maintenance of the software, cannot be responsible for a small bug discoverable and manipulable only with the rare cunning and expertise of a thief.

Vicarious liability — responsibility for employees and contractors

There is a general legal principle, discussed in Chapter 2 above, that an employer is responsible for the acts of an employee during the course of employment, or ostensibly in the course of employment.

The involvement of contractors in the computer industry raises a complication. In the case of a genuine independent contractor, that is, one who is not rightly perceived as an employee by third parties measured against a bundle of criteria (whether within the organization, engaged full-time, answerable to the direction of the principal, and so on), *the principal is not liable for the contractor's acts of negligence*, except to the extent that such acts of negligence were directed to be carried out by the principal.

The classic cases in this area have concerned doctors working in hospitals — is a hospital responsible for the acts of the negligent surgeon who is merely a visiting consultant?

In other words, there is a dilemma that contractors may well be liable in negligence to third parties and not entitled to pass on any of that liability to the organization that engages them. An interesting example may well be a provider of switching services in an ATM network where there is negligently allowed to be a defect in the switching software, causing customers to lose money from their accounts.

Another example is one in which the contractor writes bad code — so bad as to be negligent, as in the celebrated case of engineering software in which the incorrect value for π was entered, which was used to build a footbridge with all the wrong stresses. The footbridge collapsed with loss of life. Of course, the negligent programmer would be liable — but maybe also the engineering firm, not because of vicarious liability but because it foolishly accepted the output of the program.

The difficulty is that here, unlike with the surgeon and the patient cases, the provider of the switching or programming service knows or can reasonably be expected to know of the potential existence of the ultimate sufferer of physical or 'merely' economic loss, but the victim does not necessarily know of the existence of the provider of the services.

Responsibility of employees and contractors to employers/principals

As mentioned in Chapter 2 above, employees as well as contractors may also be liable to their employer for their negligent acts. In English law, this arises out of what must be regarded as one of the most deplorable decisions of this century: *Lister* v *Romford Ice*, cited earlier. The House of Lords decided that the employee was not merely employed to drive a truck, he was employed to drive a truck with proper care. The employee was not employed to go around running over people, even accidentally. Accordingly, the employee had broken his contract of employment and was liable, in breach of contract, to reimburse the employer in full, and this meant to reimburse the employer's insurance company.

It goes without saying that employees in the computer industry are not employed to write bad code or to buy American A4 forms to suit foolscap insurance policies. The employee cannot rely upon some implied term that the employer would insure against such disasters, as this was expressly negated by the House of Lords in the *Lister* v *Romford Ice* case.

In some countries, the effect of this decision has been overturned by legislation, providing that where an employer is liable to any third party as a result solely of the negligence of the employee (not as a result of its own negligence, for example, by failing to provide a safe system of work), then the employer is disentitled from seeking any indemnity from the employee. The legislation does not necessarily prevent an employer from recovering damages suffered because of an employee's 'breach of contract', however; it only prevents the recovery of monies paid out to third parties as a result of the employee's negligence. So if it is found that *in addition to being negligent*, the employee also disobeyed an express instruction of the employer, then the employee may still be liable in full to the employer.

In addition, independent contractors are by definition not employees at all, so they do not necessarily have the benefit of such legislation. As between the parties to a contracting arrangement, the courts will normally respect the parties' stated intention of independence one from the other. Not only will a contractor's contract be subject to the provisions commonly 'implied' by courts, such as an obligation to perform services in a competent and proper manner; it is precisely this relationship of an independent adviser which falls squarely within the definition of a professional or expert with a special relationship to the 'employer'.

Despite this, it is only in the case of the most 'genuine' independent contractors that one ever encounters arrangements relating to disclaimers of liability, or the provision of insurance.

One can only speculate as to the number of contractors who have sought the benefits of independence without weighing the added exposure to liability, and costs.

Overlap between negligence and other areas

In many countries, 'unfair competition' laws deal with conduct which is considered detrimental to fair trade and to consumers. This often includes 'conduct likely to mislead or deceive', a concept so broad that it is rapidly overtaking allegations of negligence and supply of defective goods in being the most common basis for computer related litigation.

Negligence is notoriously difficult to prove — not every mistake is negligent — and the vagaries of the 'sale of goods' warranties have been discussed in Chapter 7 above; but almost any conduct that leads to an unexpected result for a customer, including the supply of computer hardware and software, seems capable of being subject to a claim under such broad unfair competition laws. For example, in the example given above concerning ABC Manufacturing, rather than trying to establish a duty of care upon JustinTime to ABC Manufacturing (a different company from the one with which it was directly dealing), the appropriate standard of care, and a falling short of that standard, how much easier it seems merely to allege misleading and deceptive conduct, and show that reliance upon JustinTime resulted in loss to ABC Manufacturing.

Sale of goods legislation is very important to suppliers of computer equipment and software because it imposes very broad warranties in respect of goods: usually that they are 'merchantable' and 'fit for the purposes made known to the supplier' before the contract was made.

This legislation has, however, severe limitations:

- it does not always extend to services, even if accompanying goods, which are more often than not the true cause of grief;

- it sometimes applies only to a 'sale' of goods, and hence not to a licence, loan or gift of goods (or services);

- it only applies if a contract is entered into — it does not apply, as the general law of negligence does, to assist an ultimate user who is not a purchaser (or licensee); and

- it is often readily excluded from a contract by express terms, although some states and countries forbid this in relation to some, or all, contracts — at least those with 'consumers'.

In addition, although courts may be familiar with the application of these warranties to animal fodder and tractors, they are not yet necessarily sufficiently experienced in computer products to be able to say what 'fit for the purpose' and 'merchantable quality' means when it comes to software or computer hardware.

These warranties, their strengths and their weaknesses, are considered in more detail in Chapter 7 above.

Insurance

The breadth of the application and complexity of the law of negligence, the generosity of awards of damages, and the commercial importance of this branch of the law have all increased with the availability of insurance.

A conclusion of this chapter should be that, in addition to suppliers of the products of the computer industry, all those with highly specialized skills and expertise who are relied upon to give advice should ensure that insurance is taken out indemnifying them against liability for negligence.

Also, remembering that the insurance industry is as unfamiliar with the computer industry as most other sections of society dealing with it, all those exposed in this area by doing business in the industry should ensure that their policies of insurance cover not only liability in the general area of negligence, but also liability arising from an inadvertent breach of contract (such as breach of implied warranties in relation to goods or services) and careless breach of unfair competition laws (if any). The same non-deliberate conduct may result in liability in all three areas, and it would be unfortunate indeed that the victim's choice of action alone determined whether there is adequate insurance cover, or any insurance at all!

Doctors, lawyers and accountants have been familiar with this burden for some time; computer industry professionals must now recognize that the responsibilities placed on them make such insurance a necessity.

10 Antitrust — Competition Law

The policy of competition law

The old law — freedom of contract

Traditionally, as we have seen, the common law has been concerned with the protection of property and the prevention of violence to the person, as well as with securing specific relationships between individuals, such as in contracts and employment. This it has done by providing remedies such as damages, and occasionally by criminal sanctions. The common law has been cautious in preserving the economic wellbeing of individuals or, looking at the problem with a broader view, taking positive steps to ensure free and open markets within which everybody has an equal chance to compete.

In the nineteenth century, in the age of *laissez-faire* economics, judges and lawyers thought that as long as the law let traders make their contracts, and did not interfere with the decisions expressed in those contracts, then capitalist forces within the economy of the nation would ultimately work to the greatest good of all citizens. A famous lawyer, Sir George Jessel, said,

> If there is one thing more than another which public policy requires, it is that men of full age and competent understanding shall have the utmost liberty of contracting and that their contracts, when entered into freely and voluntarily, shall be held sacred and shall be enforced by courts of justice.

One of the very few exceptions to this policy was the Sale of Goods law referred to in Chapter 7.

The development of competition law

The twentieth century has seen a profound shift in this attitude. In addition to the increasing sentiment that unqualified freedom of trade may lead to unfairness to consumers, there has developed a view that legislative intervention is required to prevent the gaining of or use of economic power to stifle competition.

As early as 1890, the American *Sherman Act* prohibited any

'contract, combination or conspiracy in restraint of trade'. The Act also prohibits 'monopolization' of a market.

These provisions reflect an observation that monopolies, or individuals/corporations with such economic power that they can behave like monopolies without fear of competitive retaliation, are free to charge whatever price they choose, or impose other harsh terms and conditions on their customers or suppliers. Similarly, competitors who are not individually strong enough to behave monopolistically, may gather together to agree that they will charge uniform prices or not compete in other respects — and so have the same economic impact as a monopoly.

Greater interest in this subject has led to a greater sophistication in the economic analysis of anti-competitive conduct, leading on the one hand to an appreciation that the real detriment of such conduct is that it leads to economic inefficiencies in supply and consumption of goods and services, and on the other hand to the view that the law may not itself be a very efficient means of regulating such conduct, but that markets may be more effective in its eradication if left to their own cycles.

This is not the place to consider the economic and philosophical issues raised by competition law, but rather to see how a number of (but not all) countries have created laws to regulate competitive behaviour and how these laws may affect the computer industry.

As the law in each country is very much the product of similar economic arguments, it is applied in very similar ways throughout the Western capitalist world. Developing countries have seen less need for such a degree of legislative intervention and socialist economies tend to have rather different problems and approaches to those problems.

The definition of markets

One economic concept is central to each legal system, and that is the concept of the 'market'. People do not behave as economic creatures in an economic vacuum. Their conduct can only be evaluated in relation to their competitors — or those who would step into the shoes of their competitors if given the opportunity. Accordingly, the law only prohibits anti-competitive conduct in a particular market, and a market is defined by the goods and services offered by an individual and its competitors.

However, this definition is not as easy to apply as it sounds. In one sense, markets may be defined in terms of physical characteristics of goods — like those of microcomputers as opposed to mainframes, although minicomputers and the blurring of distinctions between the hardware characteristics of these make such a distinction difficult. At extremes, the distinction is an easy one: the Apple Macintosh computer does not compete with the IBM System 88. The special characteristics of the latter indicate another possibility — markets may be defined in terms of the special needs of the customers — for example banking customers requiring fault tolerant processors for certain applications. In the world of microcomputers, there may be very little interaction between business customers and educational institutions. A similar observation may be made concerning software, from games and spreadsheets for microcomputers to statistical analysis packages for big systems — but it is even possible that a spreadsheet software/microcomputer combination may be competing with a spreadsheet software option for users of a mainframe workstation.

In addition, markets may be defined geographically — a small business may behave as a monopoly in a remote country area, simply because customers are not prepared to travel to a competitor in a distant location.

All these conflicting factors may make the definition of a market one of the most difficult and confusing issues in seeking legal advice in relation to competition law concerns. These problems often make nonsense of judicial and administrative pronouncements on these issues. One of the most famous of these was the refusal of the European Economic Commission to regard England and Continental markets, such as France, as separate markets for the consumption of scotch whisky — in England, scotch whisky was an accepted beverage with a long history, readily sold but with many competitors in the market, whereas in France, other spirits were the cultural beverage and the sale of scotch whisky required expensive advertising campaigns; yet European authorities refused to accept that the product could be wholesaled at different prices in England and France to take into account these very different market factors.

The computer industry is exceptionally complex in this regard. It is made more so by the broad range of products, both hardware and software, and the fact that customers are from all levels and sections of the community, with all sorts of different uses in mind for each acquisition.

The rule of reason and *'per se'* illegalities

The importance of market definition is that most legal systems incorporating anti-trust law qualify the latter by some sort of 'rule of reason'. That is, although the conduct complained of may be of the type regulated by the law, if it has no anti-competitive effect or intention in the relevant market then it will not be illegal.

On the whole, most markets relevant to the computer industry may be regarded as so intensely competitive that, except for the most powerful players, there should be little concern for most aspects of competition law.

An important exception to this assurance must be observed. That is, that it is generally the law that certain conduct is so anti-social that it is illegal regardless of its effect on competition in the relevant market. Typically, these offences are:

- resale price maintenance and price fixing;
- 'third line' forcing;
- trade boycotts, or 'exclusionary provisions'.

We will consider these very important sanctions below.

How competition law works

Competition law finds expression in a number of different forms. In Europe, it is derived from the deceptively simple language of Articles 85 and 86 of the *Treaty of Rome*, and the individual laws of the various nations; in the United States the law is based upon a number of enactments since the *Sherman Act*, including the *Clayton Act*, the *Federal Trade Commission Act* and the *Robinson Patman Act*, as well as the law of a number of individual states. Japanese and Australian laws tend to follow the United States' model.

The law in each country operates in a dual manner, that is, not only with criminal sanctions, but also with the creation of civil remedies — based upon the assumption that participants in a market will do more to preserve their own interests than any regulatory body will have the resources to do effectively.

Criminal sanctions

Breaches of the law are criminal offences, subject to extremely severe penalties, including very heavy fines and prison sentences. In the United States, individuals responsible for breaches (including responsibility for breaches by a company) may be fined up to US$100 000.00, or be imprisoned for up to three years, or both. Corporations may be fined up to US$1 000 000.00. Similar penalties, although not always so great, may be imposed under European, Japanese and Australian laws. In addition, the competition law authorities of each country have powers to obtain injunctions and other remedies.

The criminal law is administered by administrative bodies responsible for bringing prosecutions. However, bringing prosecutions tends to be a small part of their work. Principally, they gain their objectives by investigation and negotiation with the parties they believe to be engaged in an infringement.

In some countries, the investigative powers of these authorities are greatly assisted by statutory obligations to lodge contracts, or documents evidencing an 'agreement, arrangement or understanding', which may infringe the law, so that they may be studied by the authority. Failure to do this may lead to a variety of sanctions, varying in effect from avoiding the contract altogether (that is, making it inoperative so that it cannot be enforced in the event of breach by one of the parties), to additional criminal liability. In Europe, the powers of the European Economic Commission in Brussels are so broad in this regard that it has issued specific exemptions in a number of categories, including exclusive distribution agreements and patent licences, which must be carefully considered and complied with to avoid undesirable consequences.

Because these rules concerning lodgement, registration and/or clearances of documents vary greatly from country to country, and the topic is far too complex to discuss here for each country, it is strongly recommended that, in the event of any 'agreement, arrangement or understanding' that may invoke any of the areas of law discussed here, specific legal advice should be sought.

Civil remedies

In addition to the criminal sanctions, breach of the competition law entitles competitors to take civil action, that is, to sue the infringer for damages suffered as a result, and/or seek an injunction or other remedy to prevent continuation of the conduct complained of.

This is undoubtedly one of the most effective means of maximizing compliance with the law — competitors are far better at policing the law than governments, and are usually quicker to act in protection of their commercial interests.

The incentive for civil action by competitors is made even more potent in the United States, with the availability of triple damages, but such an incentive is not available elsewhere.

Agreements, arrangements and understandings

The law operates on two types of activity — the conduct of individuals presumably with sufficient market power not to fear competitive reprisal, and the conduct of combinations of individuals. The latter can be a more serious problem for competition law authorities in that, although monopolies are rare, individuals who may be pressed to make a deal with their competitors in tough times are many.

It is important then to be aware that the law operates on any concerted action between two or more individuals, what used to be referred to as a 'combination'. It does not affect formal contracts only, but any 'agreement, arrangement or understanding'.

What is an 'agreement, arrangement or understanding'? It is any situation in which two or more people indicate in some way what each wants and have a mutual understanding that each will comply with the expectations of the others.

It need not be binding or enforceable as a contract — merely a 'gentlemen's agreement' is enough — a situation in which each party expects the other to act in a certain way. A 'wink and a nod' is enough.

Example

At a meeting of the EDP Managers' Association the major item of the agenda is a proposed increase in rates of the major supplier of contractors, Programmers Inc., on a number of widely used programming services, and a lobbying effort to prevent or limit the introduction of the new rates. At the meeting it is generally conceded that the cost pressures are threatening only because of the strength of the supplier and it is noted that competitors should be encouraged. Following the meeting, many members of the Association cease using contractors provided by Programmers Inc. and switch to its competitors.

This conduct may amount to an informal agreement to exclude a supplier of services, and if this is so may be an 'exclusionary provision' as discussed below.

However, there is a difference between a 'tacit' agreement, an understanding, reciprocated by others, that certain conduct will be followed by all parties, and a completely unilateral decision — even if, because of the power of a market leader, such a decision is sure to be followed.

Example

With a currency devaluation, Printed Circuit Boards Limited, is feeling great pressure on its margins and wishes to introduce a 15% price increase 'across the board'. Naturally, it does not wish to see its competitors gain market share, and volume, by this decision, but knows that its competitors are under equal cost pressure. The Managing Director of Printed Circuit Boards advises the Managing Director of each of its major competitors of the proposed price increase, by a letter which seeks no reciprocal assurance. ABC introduces the price change and all competitors follow.

This conduct of Printed Circuit Boards would generally be regarded as a unilateral act, and not an agreement, arrangement or understanding, even though Printed Circuit Boards was confident that its prices would be followed. Some economists argue that failure to respond competitively amounts to collusion on the part of competitors, but, without more, a court is unlikely to agree.

The likelihood of affected transactions taking place is very high in the meetings of trade or industry associations. Such associations can perform extremely valuable functions, such as pooling resources to gather information or to lobby governments and their administrative bodies — but they are also fertile grounds for anti-competitive arrangements. This is such an important area of concern that we deal with it further below, under the heading, 'Meetings with competitors'.

It is also extremely easy to be caught in this net when employees may do things unknown to their employers for which the employer may be liable. There is great pressure on sales employees, and it is not unknown for them to agree with their competitors to 'divide the turf'.

A further difficulty will be observed where it is necessary to register or obtain clearances for 'agreements, arrangements or under-standings' when they are not in writing, and are in very vague terms. In this case, if it is decided to complete forms required by adminis-trative authorities, exceptional care must be taken in describing the arrangement.

Supply and acquire

In this chapter, we use the expressions 'supply' and 'acquire'. Under all areas of law, it can be a very important distinction as to whether goods are sold, or supplied by any other means, such as hire or lease. In addition, it can be very important to distinguish between the provision of goods and the provision of related services. On the whole, competition law acts upon all these transactions without distinction, and accordingly uses the expressions 'supply' and 'acquire' rather than words with special meanings such as 'sale' or 'lease'.

'Per se' illegalities

Something which is illegal 'per se', is forbidden 'of itself' — proof of nothing more than the prohibited conduct itself is necessary for liability.

The 'per se' breaches of anti-trust law are those considered so obviously anti-competitive that judges and lawmakers usually conclude that there can be no, or very limited, justification on the basis of the 'rule of reason', or the absence of any anti-competitive effect or intention. These are resale price maintenance or price fixing, 'third line' forcing, and trade boycotts or 'exclusionary provisions'.

Resale price maintenance/price fixing

This conduct is a favourite of competition law authorities — made more so as the conduct, where present, is usually easily proved — and has con-sistently resulted in very large fines. Generally speaking, competitors are less concerned about this conduct, as insofar as it maintains unduly high prices it causes no harm to competitors who are free to undercut.

Alternatively, the conduct is the result of an agreement between competitors, in which event it may be more serious.

The law prohibits the supply of goods on condition that the goods will not be resold below a certain price. This condition need not be contractual, so long as the supplier makes it known or agrees with the acquirer that goods or services will not be discounted. Refusal or withholding of supply because of an acquirer's failure to agree or because the acquirer has sold or is likely to sell the goods below the specified prices is also caught.

Obviously, the fixing of prices, as opposed to setting a minimum, is forbidden for the same reason — ideally competition law authorities wish price to respond to the forces of supply and demand in a particular market. However, 'Recommended Retail Price' lists are not considered illegal — so long as they are genuine recommendations and are not enforceable or enforced in any way. Such price lists are considered quite useful tools for suppliers to indicate their views of the market to retailers, in such matters as optimum margins.

There is a divergence of opinion concerning maximum prices. It is quite common for suppliers to be concerned that goods or services are supplied to the market at a reasonable price, in order to maximize such matters as production efficiencies and the creation of reputation. As long as these do not operate as price fixing arrangements, it is difficult to see any adverse economic consequence from such conduct, and accordingly the rule of reason usually applies. Caution must be exercised, however, where the competition law authorities are concerned that maximum prices may operate with undue rigidity and inhibit distribution in high cost markets, such as remote geographical areas.

The following example illustrates how resale price maintenance problems often arise.

Example

ABC Architectural Systems markets a sophisticated and complex CAD system for firms of architects, using an indirect distribution network of dealers and OEMs. Because of the complexity of the product, its successful implementation by end users is critical to its success and this requires a high degree of pre- and post-sales orientation and support. ABC therefore requires its dealers to learn about the product, maintain fully trained staff in high quality premises, and purchase a full inventory of consumables and diagnostic and support materials. It is the experience of ABC that, notwithstanding fierce competition, discounting of price leads to a shortage of cash to carry out these necessary pre- and post-sale support obligations. At training seminars, ABC representatives explain this and state that dealers must not sell the package below a certain price which is demonstrated to be reasonable. A dealer discounts the product and ABC refuses further supply.

Clearly here a breach of the law has taken place. ABC can do no more than explain the perils of discounting to dealers. If a dealer discounts, his supply cannot be terminated for that reason. If, however, the dealer subsequently fails to comply with the contractual obligation to provide specified pre- and post-sale support or to undertake certain training, then the arrangement could be terminated for that reason alone.

For this reason, distribution agreements which adequately set out distribution obligations, and which are precise, and can be objectively tested, are extremely important in a distribution system. It is unfortunate that ABC has probably lost a valuable reference site in order to learn this lesson, let alone that there is the possibility of civil or criminal action against it, with substantial damages and/or fines.

'Third line' forcing

This is a special type of exclusive dealing whereby a supplier supplies goods or services on condition that the goods or services of some third party are also acquired.

This prohibition may also affect an arrangement whereby special terms or discounts are only available to the customer if the third party products are obtained.

This rule is easily explained, but not so easily avoided in an industry such as the computer industry, in which a number of hardware and software products of a number of unrelated suppliers are closely linked. This is indicated by the following example.

Example

Grunt Systems is a hardware company which provides high powered CPUs and maintenance service. It has developed a new flexible mini-computer which it calls the GruntCPU; however it does not itself have mass storage systems for the GruntCPU1, relying on third party developers loyal to Grunt products in the past, in particular, Massive Inc.

Grunt has encountered some difficulty in the past with its maintenance service as a result of certain types of third party tape drives being sold as inexpensive alternatives to the Massive, and other, drives — there is disagreement between it and the supplier of these inexpensive alternative drives, TPExtra Inc., as to the cause of the difficulties and failures in the Grunt systems using the TPExtra drives. As a result, Grunt institutes an arrangement whereby it certifies certain third party drives as 'GruntCPU1 Approved', and will only supply its maintenance services to customers using such approved drives, initially only the Massive products. In return for certification and recommendation in this manner by Grunt, Massive agrees to supply certain technical information to Grunt to assist it in the manufacture of its own mass storage devices.

Clearly this amounts to supply of services conditional upon the purchase of third party goods, upon which TPExtra may well take legal action against Grunt. In addition, it should be noted that TPExtra may even take action against Massive, because it appears to have participated indiscreetly in this arrangement.

This problem, as so often with competition law problems, may be overcome by correcting the approach taken — if Grunt had simply rebadged the Massive products (perhaps on consignment to avoid cash flow and inventory problems) and then limited its service to its own products, there may not have been any 'per se' infringement. However, such arrangements, as a form of 'exclusive dealing' (see below) in some jurisdictions have been the subject of careful scrutiny by the competition law authorities, particularly in Europe.

The position is not as clear when there is not an outright refusal to supply, or a withdrawal of supply, but merely an incentive to acquire the third party goods or services, such as discounts on products conditional upon the acquisition of third party products.

Example

The Computer Industry Association provides a number of services to members, such as industry information, lobbying government departments, training courses and so on. It arranges a deal with Magnetic Media Limited in which members are discounted membership dues if they prove purchases of a certain number of tapes, disks and diskettes from Magnetic Media Limited during the preceding year. Magnetic Media Limited pays the Association a percentage of sales to enable it to provide this benefit.

This type of arrangement has been found to be a breach of the law. The Association's services are being provided at a discount on the basis of the forced purchase of goods. It may be that the likely effect on competition would be negligible in cases such as this, but this fact is irrelevant to a breach of the law of this kind.

Special problems arise when there are performance/compatibility issues — in many ways unusual to the computer industry. So, if software is supplied but support is conditional upon purchase of specific hardware or operating systems — or some combination of these — problems with third line forcing may arise even though there are powerful technical reasons why support cannot be provided adequately or at all because the software is not entirely compatible with newer versions of the operating systems or hardware, or the software supplier is not sufficiently familiar with the alternative or later products.

Of course, this is not to say that if a customer acquires software knowing that it will only operate on particular hardware, that any question of anti-trust will arise, but hardware suppliers, for example, have been known to 'push' a particular software application in circumstances where the reasons for the push are not so clear. Often, 'bundling' of products, that is, the supply of the hardware and software 'bundles' together so that only one supplier is evident to the end user, overcomes this problem.

Trade boycotts/'exclusionary provisions'

'Exclusionary provisions' are arrangements whereby competitors agree that none will supply goods or services to, or obtain goods or services from, certain people or types of people. These sorts of arrangements, classically market or customer sharing deals which are the special target of the *Sherman Act*, may include much more common occurrences, such as the following.

Example

The credit controller of ABC Computers is very concerned regarding the increasing debt of one of its dealers, XYZ. He telephones a friend at DEF Systems, a competing hardware supplier, and explains his concern, asking whether DEF Systems has the same problem. Together, they agree to put pressure on XYZ: ABC Computers will supply XYZ on a cash basis as long as DEF Systems does the same.

Clearly this is an illegal arrangement and the employers of both credit controllers would be liable to penalty (as well as civil action from XYZ). Had ABC Computers made the decision on its own, it would not be a breach of this prohibition, but it would have faced the risk that XYZ would simply shift its purchases to DEF Systems.

Again, trade associations are particularly at risk, as they negotiate beneficial terms for all their members, usually conditional upon reciprocated benefits.

Example

A group of motor dealers of Flash automobiles, lacking the resources individually to pay for the development, agree to jointly fund the development of software for the management of their motor dealership businesses. They believe that this will give them all a great competitive advantage over other motor dealers. With this mind, they engage ABC Computers to modify an existing software package in accordance with their requirements and, with their competitive advantage in mind, they make it a condition of the contract that ABC Computers will not provide the same modifications and enhancements to other motor dealers.

This arrangement is probably a breach of the law in this form, this time not because the parties to the arrangement have boycotted a third party, but because they have prevented another person from supplying their competitors — the motor dealers cannot prevent ABC from supplying the same goods or services to other people — regardless of how much they pay for the advantage.

Again, however, in this case, the problem may have been avoided. Had the ownership of the copyright in the modifications and enhancements been assigned to the motor dealers (see Chapter 3 above), then ABC could not have provided the same modifications and enhancements to anyone else (the exclusivity provided by copyright is usually exempt from the operation of the anti-trust laws, unless improperly exploited) — although there would be nothing wrong with ABC using the skills and knowledge of the industry learnt in carrying out the Flash dealers' project in writing new and different modifications and enhancements for other dealers.

Discrimination, exclusive dealing, abuse of market power and other restraints on trade

Apart from the matters considered in the preceding section, each of the restrictions on anti-competitive behaviour involves some definition of the relevant market affected by the conduct and an evaluation of the effect on competition in that market. Needless to say, the effect on competition must be a negative one, although this is not always apparent in the cases dealing with this.

In an industry as competitive as the computer industry, these restrictions should not be unduly concerning, except for the large and powerful corporations. Care should be taken, however, in cases where the market may in fact be very narrowly defined, as in the case of remote geographical locations, or in the case of highly specialized products, such as special software applications, where market dominance may be real.

In short, each of the following categories of restriction usually requires proof of market power. If market power is not present, it is extremely unlikely that the conduct will have the slightest adverse effect on competition.

Discrimination

Discrimination in competition law is the practice of charging different prices, or imposing different conditions of supply (including the giving of discounts), among like customers in the same market.

This can be a very difficult rule to apply.

Example ───

ABC Computer Systems Inc. makes personal computers. Its products are extremely well known and successful in England, where the products virtually 'sell themselves'. However, in France, the product is not well known, and requires extensive and costly marketing to sell it in the face of high quality French competition. To adjust for this difficulty in France, or to look at it another way, to exploit the position in England, ABC's marketing subsidiary in Eire sells the personal computers to French dealers 20% more cheaply than to English dealers.

The key to justifying this price differential may be to establish that France and England are separate markets, that is, the customers in each market are not 'like customers' and so there is no discrimination at all. This seems a likely conclusion in this case, but in Europe price differentiation between markets has generally been adversely regarded by competition law authorities. The European Economic Commission and the European Court have been loath to regard different nations within the EEC as different markets, notwithstanding significant cultural and other market differentials, and have generally regarded any price differentiation, in conjunction with other conduct necessary to maintain the division, as anti-competitive.

The same conduct may be even more difficult to justify in different circumstances, such as a price differential between metropolitan and regional customers in the same country.

Some defences to discriminatory pricing are permitted. However, these are typically very narrow, being price differentials or discounts directly relating to savings in manufacture, distribution, sale and/or delivery costs. A moment's thought makes its clear that such savings are impossible to show in 'across the board' multi-level price structures, because they cannot take into account individual customers, and 'direct' savings cannot include consideration of indirect and fixed overheads. 'Volume discounts' are a vexed issue, and have often been found to infringe anti-trust law, because they are not always directly linked to manufacturing or distribution savings, but are more usually directed to gaining market share.

Example

Magnetic Media Limited has a surplus in production capacity of 5¼ inch floppy diskettes. It normally offers the diskettes in single packs of ten at a wholesale price of $25.00 a box. However, to move the stock and encourage distributor and dealer loyalty, it offers the diskette packs in shipper boxes of ten packs for $225.00 and palettes of one hundred shipper boxes for $20 000.

This is a very common situation which may or may not be regarded as price discrimination. There appears no question of customers coming from different markets, although there have been cases in which distributor

*level customers (wholesalers) have been regarded as a market separate
from dealer customers, that is, retailers. There does not appear to have
been any calculation of such savings (nor could there be) to justify the price
differentials. However, it is difficult to conceive of there being an adverse
effect on competition in such an outdated product with many suppliers in
fierce competition.*

A somewhat easier defence is that the price differential was introduced to
meet price competition of a competitor. Unfortunately, this does not
permit initiating discounting, nor does it apparently permit beating the
price competition.

In addition, in the United States, the *Robinson Patman Act*
expressly permits discounting to Federal Government purchasers.

One of the most difficult features of the law is that it includes in
'discrimination' special terms, which might include special concessions
on a wide range of matters, such as delivery, packaging and credit terms.
The law seems to require a monetary valuation of these concessions,
which is often impossible.

Little more need be said in relation to this type of restriction. It
will be apparent that the absurdity of the law makes it extremely difficult
to deal with.

It should be noted that in United Kingdom and EEC law, there is
no express prohibition of discrimination, except insofar as it is combined
with other anti-competitive conduct.

Predatory pricing/dumping

Predatory pricing, that is, pricing goods or services intentionally low in
order to wipe out the competition or gain market share, is also considered
anti-competitive conduct in some countries.

This conduct may be considered indirectly, in the category of
'abuse of market power', because it will be obvious that it takes
considerable strength in a market to be able to survive a predatory
pricing policy long enough to make any lasting impact on competition —
presumably with the long term goal of being freer to set high prices.

The same conduct is referred to as 'dumping' and is also
prohibited by the international trade agreement known as GATT, the
General Agreement on Tariffs and Trade. Under this Agreement,
member countries must provide means to stop their citizens from
supplying goods in another member country below cost, conduct which is
feared may damage local industries. This provision gained prominence
recently with the dispute between many Western industrialized nations
and Japan, whose manufacturers of DRAMs were accused of dumping
their products below cost in order to dominate the markets.

It is often difficult to determine what is genuinely 'predatory pricing' or 'dumping'. One view is that it may be objectively measured as pricing below the cost of manufacture — although that is a notoriously difficult cost to calculate, often depending upon subjective allocations of fixed overheads, such as rent, and indirect expenses, such as certain types of marketing costs.

Ultimately, the proof of a predatory pricing or dumping claim will depend upon proof of an expressed intention — at the end of this chapter, we will warn against written memoranda, such as minutes of meetings, carelessly expressing anti-competitive sentiments such as 'with these prices we should be able to kill the competition'!

Exclusive dealing

Regulation of exclusive dealing arrangements began with the United States *Clayton Act*, adopted in 1914. Typical examples of exclusive dealing arrangements arise in distribution or dealer agreements, and include:

- requiring the dealer to deal exclusively in the supply of goods or services, prohibiting purchases of competing products;

- requiring the dealer to purchase its total requirements of goods or services from the supplier — even when expressed as a specific quantity of goods, where this is calculated to be the dealers' likely total requirements;

- requiring the dealer to purchase one type of product or service in order to obtain another product or service — this is sometimes called 'tying' or 'full line' forcing, that is, requiring the dealer to buy the unpopular products along with the popular ones in order to ensure a full display to the end user.

The law similarly operates on restrictions on a supplier's freedom to supply other customers in the same market.

Because these are such common restrictions, it is important to remember that their illegality depends upon anti-competitive effect or purpose, which in the computer industry usually only occurs when for some reason the relevant market is defined very narrowly.

Example

ABC Computers is having difficulty in ensuring its personal computers, PC1s, are adequately stocked and supported in country areas where there is a low turnover. Likewise, country dealers consider that they can only afford to stock and support the product if they are exclusive outlets in their region — the customers do not travel to distant country towns to get a cheaper price. Accordingly, ABC enters an exclusive dealership arrangement with

Wagga Computers for the region of Wagga Wagga in New South Wales, Australia.

A competitor of Wagga Computers, Educational Systems of Wagga, has for some time supplied the Wagga High School with educational equipment, including computers, and Wagga High School wishes to instal PC1s because the educational software prescribed by the New South Wales Department of Education for computer education classes has been written for the PC1s.

ABC Computers refuses to supply Educational Systems of Wagga (because of its deal with Wagga Computers) at dealer price or at all. Of course, Educational Systems of Wagga could always buy the product from Wagga Computers.

Because the market here is so small — the region of Wagga Wagga, a remote country town — combined with the customers' peculiar circumstances, it is possible a breach of the law has occurred. Great care must still be taken, however, when considering substitutable products in the same market — normally a market cannot be defined in terms of a specific brand name — obviously other personal computers may be sold in place of the PC1.

Abuse of market power and other restraints on trade

However specific the law in certain areas, there are always 'catch all' provisions which prohibit any anti-competitive conduct. These provisions are necessarily vague.

The *Sherman Act* of the United States is typical of these provisions. On the one hand it prohibits any unreasonable 'contract, combination or conspiracy in restraint of trade' which the courts have interpreted to apply to a wide range of activities, including agreements with competitors relating to prices, terms of supply, promotions, market splitting and 'poaching' of customers.

In addition, the *Sherman Act* prohibits 'monopolization'. The prohibition controls far more than the conduct of a single dominant player in a market — it is addressed to any intentional misuse of substantial market power. Accordingly, great care must be taken as to one's reasons for attempting to prevent the sale of competitive products, or to eliminate a competitor.

A 'substantial market power' is identified using one or more of the following factors:

- market share;
- ability to govern or lead prices;
- market structure — even a small market share, say 10%, may be substantial where no competitor has more than 1 or 2%; or
- the ease with which others may enter or leave the market.

Typically, the greatest likelihood of problems with these laws arises with a refusal to supply. In practice, great care should be taken when refusing supply — one should ensure that one has all the right reasons for doing so; reasons which are mixed, that is, partly predatory and partly legitimate may still result in infringement.

Example

ABC Software Systems Inc. has developed a leading DTP printing operating system for laser printers which has become acknowledged as the best solution in the present market. It licenses the product on the basis of a royalty of $175.00 for each copy made.

DEF Solutions Inc. is considering further development of a competing compatible operating system and a meeting is arranged between the two corporations in order to discuss cross-licensing of key developments in the operating systems. At that meeting the Sales Manager of ABC Software Systems Inc. says to the DEF representatives "If you release this product, we will blow you out of the water!".

DEF releases its product on a royalty basis of $145.00 per copy. ABC immediately drops its royalty to $135.00 per copy. DEF is unable to meet this price and discontinues development of the product.

This somewhat improbable example illustrates that the competitive response of ABC could be regarded as infringing the law merely because of the unfortunate outburst of the Sales Manager of ABC. The example also illustrates a potential problem area — namely cross-licensing agreements: — had such an agreement been contemplated between ABC and DEF, great care should have been taken in its drafting to avoid obvious anti-competitive provisions.

Conclusions and warnings

Before concluding this chapter, two special warnings will serve as the best summary of the issues and concerns of competition law.

Meetings with competitors

Industry trade associations and other meetings with competitors may perform useful functions such as gathering statistics and making industry presentations to the public, to government agencies or to legislative bodies.

These meetings, however, can be most dangerous environments. A trade association is ready-made for consideration of prices. It is not necessary for an agreement to be put into effect or even if it were that it may have some likelihood of 'success'. The mere understanding or agreement is all that is required to constitute a breach. In addition, exclusionary activity, when competitors meet and agree on conduct that disadvantages other competitors not at the meeting or any other person or class of persons, may easily result from such meetings. If this is the case the rules of membership should be looked at closely and special care should be taken when planning to attend such a meeting.

There can be guilt by association where a member is merely present at such a meeting of competitors and takes no active part in proceedings. A tacit understanding amounting to an 'agreement, arrangement or understanding' is easily reached at such meetings or at the social events following.

An employee should attend such a meeting only when there is a clear legitimate need for the meeting and a need for someone to attend. The following safeguards should always be observed in discussions with competitors.

There should be no discussion of the following:

(1)   prices, price changes, price quotes, bids, pricing policies, price differentials, discounts or allowances

(2)   any element of price including freight and credit

(3)   output, capacity, inventory levels or costs

(4)   customers

(5)   territories

(6)   amounts paid for goods and services.

(7)   the exclusion of customers or suppliers from sources of supply or markets or

(8)   plans concerning the production, distribution or marketing of particular products.

Informal discussions before or after meetings should be avoided. An agenda should always be prepared and discussions limited to these matters.

In the event of any discussion occurring which may appear improper:

(1)   leave the meeting or discussion immediately;

(2)   in leaving it should be made clear that the reason is that one is not going to be involved in such discussions and endeavour to have the departure recorded in any minutes taken.

The danger and concerns which must be considered by everyone attending a trade association meeting should raise the question of whether membership is a real benefit in the long term. In the United States it has become necessary to monitor every such attendance and to take extraordinary precautions to protect against liability in these situations. If membership is still necessary, involvement should be limited to non-marketing issues.

Memoranda

As some of the examples given above demonstrate, conduct which might otherwise be seen as innocent can take on anti-competitive overtones with the rash words of individuals within an organization. If legal proceedings are commenced, evidence of these rash words will be used against the persons seeking to defend their conduct, and there is no better evidence than written documents.

For these reasons, great care should be taken that minutes of meetings of trade associations, meetings with competitors, and even internal meetings, as well as internal memoranda, be free of unnecessary, damaging material.

Mergers and acquisitions

One way of avoiding the problems of making agreements with competitors, suppliers or customers, is to take one or all over. As a result, all mergers of companies and acquisitions of businesses (in some countries, over a certain value) may be the subject of review by the competition law authorities, seeking anti-competitive effects or intentions. In many countries, these will be the subject of review and clearance prior to the merger or acquisition and will require lodgement of documents with the authorities.

This can be a very awkward procedure where speed and secrecy are essential — neither speed nor secrecy being strong points of governmental agencies.

This is not the place to deal with the complexities of the law relating to mergers and acquisitions, as procedures and requirements can vary greatly. Accordingly, prior to any takeover or merger, or purchase of a business in circumstances where an effect on competition may result, the participants should ascertain what local requirements are and seek legal advice as to those requirements.

11 Data Protection, Privacy & the Freedom of Information

The nature of the problem

The laws of most countries do not recognize any general right of privacy, whether by way of the common law or by way of constitutional rights; only recently have some countries experimented with privacy laws. Even in the United States, the courts have found that the Constitution of the United States does not recognize any such right.

As long ago as 1890, an American author wrote:

> The intensity and complexity of life, attending upon advancing civilization, have rendered necessary some retreat from the world, and man, under the refining influence of culture, has become more sensitive to publicity, so that solitude and privacy have become essential to the individual; but modern enterprise and invention have, through invasions upon his privacy, subjected him to mental pain and distress, far greater than could be inflicted by mere bodily injury.

However, it is not easy to distinguish between what should and should not be private, shielded from the public view or free from outside interference. If a right of privacy exists, it will be the concern of the law to balance the interests of the public and the private individual. The law permits many invasions of privacy, to gain access to places, or documents, or to prevent individuals from doing as they please. Also, any claim for a right of privacy must also be balanced against a right of the public to be informed and other legitimate uses to which information may be put. As an Australian judge has said:

> 'A society in which there was a total lack of privacy would be intolerable, a society in which there was total privacy would be no society at all.'

The notion of privacy is a subjective one. Some people regard receiving a flood of 'junk mail' as an invasion of privacy, others regard it as just a part of modern living, or even a chance to be informed. Some people regard the security of their information, about themselves and their businesses, as their 'property', which should not be available to anyone else, and should be secure from tampering with by unauthorized outsiders, while others consider that some activities of others are more or less 'public property', fair targets for unauthorized intervention of some kind.

The notion of the proper subject matter for a right of privacy tends to be very selfish — on the one hand people seem voracious for information concerning other people, and anxious to defend their 'right' to have it; yet on the other the same people claim a 'right' to privacy for themselves.

In addition, there are many misconceptions concerning privacy. The secrets disclosed to doctors, priests and journalists do not have such protection at law, although it is often (except in the case of journalists) respected in practice. It is perhaps symptomatic of the control that lawyers and lawmakers have over the legal system (and their arrogance) that generally, information disclosed to lawyers, and information from the workings of governments, have enjoyed special legal protection. The only general exception is the relatively narrow law regarding confidential information discussed in Chapter 5 above.

Ultimately, community attitudes must determine what should be considered 'private' to the individual, business or government; it certainly cannot be left to any one person or interest group in society to decide.

In this chapter, we shall be dealing with three aspects of the problem of privacy relevant to the computer industry:

(1)   the privacy of information in one's own possession, in the sense of its protection from observation, and perhaps tampering, by others;

(2)   the privacy of information concerning the individual which is in the possession of others, the sort of information which people generally regard as not the business of others but which others may regard as part of a very valuable business; and

(3)   the protection desired by regulatory authorities over information which does not concern them directly but is regarded as sensitive to national interests, sometimes referred to as 'transborder data flow'.

Privacy in the computer age

Computer technologies have put into the hands of governments, businesses and private individuals powers enabling them to invade the 'personal space' of others.

The first railroads were short routes connecting local centres; gradually, however, it become an economic necessity to join the routes and make the railroads into a system. Telephone networks also evolved in this way. The reason for such growth is quite obvious — it is cheaper to share use of a larger entity than to build one's own facility. Historically, communications and transportation services have formed natural mono-polies. Automated information files have the same properties as com-munications and transportation, that cause the integrated networks to be self-agglomerating. It is cheaper to share the information by tying together independent systems than by building a very large number of highly duplicated systems.

Government agencies and others have been gathering material about individuals and organizations for many years. Without using computers, this information has tended uselessly to fill filing cabinets. Government agencies did not have the resources or processes to enable collection and collation of this mass of data. However, once this information is computerized it is possible, using sophisticated matching techniques, for two or more databases to be combined. Suddenly it is pos-sible to see all sorts of details about an individual simply by glancing through the database. The database can also be programmed to highlight unusual conditions. There are entirely legitimate uses for carrying out such matching — finding people who are cheating welfare services for instance. But knowledge is power and there are also justifiable concerns that most of the details of the life of an individual are no concern of the state.

It is also possible for computers to be used for 'real-time' surveillance. With an appropriate effort and the will to do so, it would be possible to know the moment a particular EFT (electronic funds transfer) card is inserted in an automatic telling machine anywhere in a particular country, or the moment a particular person obtained a clearance on his or her credit card — and where he or she is at that time.

With such developments, any general legal protection of confiden-tial information has become less effective.

For example, the detailed understanding of a complex business which is only available to the individual and to the legal advisers he or she entrusts with it may be gained by taxation or police authorities without resort to the lawyers' files; they can now acquire the masses of paper which previously would be useless to them in their undigested form, enter data into data storage and analysis systems and produce their own reports.

In addition, technology has rendered obsolete existing laws which go some way to protect privacy. For example, while there is now clear law in most countries that tapping a telephone line and eavesdropping on a conversation without permission is illegal, it has been held that a warrant is not required to eavesdrop on a conversation carried on using a mobile telephone because 'there is no reasonable expectation of privacy' when using such a telephone, so the US *Crime Control Act* does not apply to such conversations.

Similarly the law in relation to access to a traditional mail service is quite clear in most countries; legal access to electronic mail messages is still very unclear. Should electronic mail be treated as nearly as possible as traditional mail or should it have a greater or lesser degree of protection? The essence of this argument is whether electronic mail is thought to replace telephone or traditional mail. Proponents of applying at least a telephone style level of protection to electronic mail argue that electronic mail records provide a whole course of correspondence, making their interception potentially even more damaging than the interception of a single telephone call.

The United States has introduced the *Electronic Communications Privacy Act* to protect the privacy of users of cellular phones, electronic mail and other computer networks. This law requires police to obtain a search warrant before eavesdropping on or tapping into electronic networks. Service providers are forbidden from knowingly disclosing the contents of an electronically stored communication other than to the addressee, although there is a statutory exception allowing disclosure where the contents of a message were inadvertently obtained and appear to relate to the commission of a crime. Both civil and criminal penalties are provided for. While cellular telephones are protected, only the 'wire' portion of a cordless telephone conversation is protected. However, the penalty for intercepting an unencrypted, unscrambled cellular telephone call is only $500; the expressed reason for this being to encourage greater reliance on technical protection — an interesting comment on the whole area of privacy legislation.

In the United Kingdom, a similar piece of legislation is the *Interception of Telecommunications Act* which applies to all forms of public telecommunication systems. Law enforcement agencies may apply for warrants on the usual grounds of national security and the detection of crime as well as the more unusual ground of protecting the economic wellbeing of the United Kingdom. The Act does not cover the interception of data in an in-house network; it applies only to public communications. Also, the Act cannot be used to combat hacking or to stop people recording and decoding the emissions of word processing screens to reconstruct the document being worked on.

Notwithstanding these examples, however, the law in most countries is lagging behind technical developments in data exploitation and communication.

Does anyone 'own' information?

As we have already discussed in Chapter 5, 'information' is not generally regarded as property in itself. A person whose information is 'taken' must generally look to civil or criminal remedies in the general law of confidential information, unfair competition laws, or copyright or patent laws.

'Mere' data

Although it is common, particularly in contracts, to refer to confidential information as being 'sold', this is not strictly appropriate as information is not 'goods'; when information is taken by one person from another (whether with or without permission), the original possessor of that information is not thereby deprived of it. When information is stolen the victim may not even know that he or she has been robbed; when it is 'sold' the 'vendor' will still have the information available, and, in the absence of agreement to the contrary, will be able to continue to use it.

The fact that information is not property has serious implications for conventional law.

Example

John Vandal, a student at a university embittered by his failures in a programming course at the university, has a part-time job doing contract maintenance of personal computers for a maintenance firm. The maintenance firm happens to provide maintenance services to Vandal's university. In the course of his part-time job, he is sent to work on a personal computer of the university. Whilst carrying out his service, which he completes successfully, he enters into a database on a hard disk unit attached to the computer and erases all student records, including his own, as well as other files. He already knows that the staff of the university are very anxious to restore the personal computer, as they have not kept adequate backups. Of course, Vandal does not damage the computer or the hard disk, he merely alters the information stored. He boasts of his deed, and is discovered. What action can be taken?

Under the general law, it is unlikely that any action can be taken because the only property affected, the hard disk, has not been damaged or taken away, and he gained access to it in a perfectly lawful manner. This is so, notwithstanding that the damage to the 'owner' of the information may be greater, or more insidious and long-lasting, if information had merely been altered (to give Vandal passes, not failures, perhaps), and remained undetected.

There are cases which tend in the opposite direction, particularly in Canada, but the mainstream of cases in the United States and the United Kingdom in recent times has come to the conclusion that, in the absence of specific statutes dealing with the conduct complained of, the law provides no remedy if the information affected is not used by the 'thief'.

It seems paradoxical that, had Vandal thrown the computer (with its hard disk) and all available diskettes in sight out of the nearest window into a courtyard pool, or even gained access to the computer without permission (in English legal systems this is a technical 'trespass' to goods, even though no damage is done), legal action could have been taken for the loss or damage to the property, and for the costs of restoring the loss resulting from the physical damage. The disk may be regarded as more valuable if it contained the only copy of valuable information, but this is otherwise irrelevant, and the university would get no compensation for 'irreplaceable' information, because it is not going to spend the money restoring something it cannot restore!

Perhaps a compromise position emerged in the English case of *Cox* v *Riley*, where the appellant succeeded in blanking all sixteen programs on a printed circuit card necessary for the operation of a computerized saw. The appellant had been charged with having committed 'criminal damage'. The questions at issue were whether the programs and/or the card constituted 'property' and whether the card had been damaged. The court held that the program itself was not 'property' as it was intangible; equally the card itself, looked at in isolation, had not been damaged. In finding the defendant guilty the court seems to have reasoned that a new item of property — the card plus the program — had been damaged, in the sense of its physical state being altered to the detriment of the owner. The ruling indicates that the program and the item which holds it cannot be divided for the purposes of analysis any more than paint can be divided from the canvas when assessing a work of art.

Credit/debit data

There is another aspect to the 'property' issue when dealing with computer data, and that is the manipulation of financial data to create 'false' credits.

As we are so familiar with dealing with bank accounts, depositing and drawing 'our' money from a deposit account, it is frequently overlooked that the credits in an account book are not 'our' money at all, they are merely data entries. The data entries are merely records in a commercial relationship with a bank, say, and may themselves form part of much larger transactions. Who has been deceived, and whose property has been affected if, by manipulation of such data, a machine is caused to pay money to the manipulator of the machine? A machine is not a person, and cannot be 'deceived' in the human sense. It should also be remembered that, in most legal systems, banknotes and coins are not property any more than the paper credits and debits — no-one can 'own' banknotes or coins which are in currency.

Example ──────────────────────────────

Juliet Larson approaches an automatic teller machine and notices that it is 'off-line', that is, unable to give information from the central bank database. She is already aware from a previous experience that, in such a case, she can, by going through certain procedures, obtain from it more money than she has deposited with the bank. She takes this opportunity to visit a large number of automatic teller machines, with no intention of re-

paying the money, as she already has tickets to fly overseas for an extended holiday.

Has Larson committed a criminal or civil wrong, for which she may be pursued on her travels?

Unless there is special law covering the situation, or existing laws happen to be wide enough, how can it be said that she has 'stolen' the money, when it was willingly given to her; how can it be said that she has used false pretences when she only 'communicated' with a machine, which is incapable of being deceived in a human sense. She has damaged no property, nor interfered with the physical state of anything she should not have done. It cannot be said that she has obtained the money by false 'instruments', or documents, because no documents were created or used by her, only electrical impulses.

In a case such as this, courts have had great difficulty convicting of criminal charges, and civil charges can be very hard to press when it is considered that by the bank's own defective system it virtually threw the money away on the street.

In one Australian case (*Kennison v Daire*), the logic followed by a bare majority of the court was that, had the bank customer's access card and the personal identification number been used to obtain money from a human teller, the accused could have been guilty of obtaining money by false pretences, not larceny. Because a machine cannot form an intention, the position is reversed with an ATM; the relevant intention of the bank must have been formed before the transaction; very odd reasoning indeed when the bank had no knowledge of the accused at the time of forming its supposed intention and being 'deceived'!

The minority judge found no larceny because the ATM was programmed to pass out money under certain conditions and those conditions were met; the machine was not malfunctioning.

The situation is even more uncertain where a computer system has been used by someone to change the state of his or her balance, but the money is not (as yet) removed. In such a case the villain may have committed no criminal or civil wrong right up to the moment he or she attempts to withdraw money, or otherwise to rely on the wrongly healthy bank balance for some other benefit!

The *Computer Crimes Act* of the state of Virginia in the United States, discussed further below, is an example of a special law containing provisions for these circumstances. It states that not only real property and financial instruments, but also computer data and programs and computer services can all be the subject of larceny (theft), and also deals with the improper manipulation of computer data in order to gain a financial benefit.

Great care must be taken in drafting such legislation, however. If information is property, the implications, particularly for financial institutions, educational institutions and other service providers, whose business it is to disseminate information, could be staggering. Also, there is a danger of blurring the distinction between the criminal law relating to theft, fraud and 'mischief' and the matters which are the proper domain of copyright and patent law. Ideas are a critical social resource and anything which tends to make them the property of a particular person should be carefully considered.

As the cases set out above show, the law is by no means settled on the question of ownership of information. A 'sale' of information is probably better characterized as a contract for the service of disclosing the information and a concurrent undertaking never to make use of that information.

It is important therefore, in any commercial dealing with important data, to evaluate the local laws which exist to protect it.

Hacking and viruses

Any review of the legal principles relevant to the preservation of data in one's own possession would not be complete without a consideration of the most damaging and insidious forces in the computer industry.

'Hacking' is a term used to describe the breaching of computer security systems by those not entitled to do so. Usually, it seems to be done out of a sense of bravado rather than with any malice, or intention to do harm. 'Viruses' are small programs devised to be copied inadvertently, and hence are misnamed or concealed in other programs or data, which either by self duplication or some other means damage or slow the operation of their 'host' systems.

The legal difficulty here is that hackers often seem to gain access to computer systems by telephone connections with the intention of observing but not causing any damage, or of using the system in which they roam merely out of curiosity. Damage may arise accidentally, or the hacker may pose a security risk to government or commercial interests by blundering into sensitive areas.

Two pillars of the legal system are 'intention' and 'damage'. 'Intention' to commit some harm or wrong is still a very important basis for most criminal law. The creation of 'strict liability' offences whereby the prosecution need not prove intention is still only cautious, usually justified only in the case of conduct that is considered self evidently harmful. 'Damage', or at least the likelihood of damage, is very important to civil law, and it will be recalled from Chapters 1 and 9 that it is frequently very important for the damage to be proximate to the cause.

Civil law — is there a right to damages?

Whatever their intention, the creators of viruses usually have no connection with those damaged who incur great expense, loss and confusion as a result of the effect upon their computer systems. The person suffering real commercial damage may be at many removes from the creator who originally did no more than post the program on an electronic bulletin board with the tempting title 'Read Me'.

Example _____

Toby Jugg is a tormented journalist, suffering from a delusion that lawyers are engaged in a conspiracy to undermine operating system standards by the improper application of copyright laws. He often writes on legal matters, and as a result of his work has access to an electronic bulletin board/mail network operated by the local Law Society, which has most lawyers interested in the computer industry as subscribers, including Pompus, Sharpe & Rich. The network has a file transfer facility.

In a misguided attempt at retribution, Jugg modifies a small public domain database application with self replicating components and places it on the bulletin board under the name 'Litigation Support — for MS-DOS Users'. On downloading and opening the file, the self replicating routines are loaded into the user's operating system, where they duplicate on each booting of the system.

Pompus, Sharpe & Rich download the file and, over time, as a result of the operation of the virus, their affected operating systems become increasingly slow, until ultimately they find data files corrupted and lost with system failures. In the case of Pompus, Sharpe & Rich, this has particularly disastrous consequences, as one of the affected micros is used for litigation support in a major case for a client, the Nouveau Hotel Group. When the current file is corrupted and the backup is also destroyed, they are put into disarray, a deadline for filing documents is missed, and they are forced to seek an adjournment of proceedings for which Nouveau Hotels is required to pay the costs, some $85 000, and considerable tactical advantage is lost in the proceedings.

If Jugg is tracked down as the source of the virus, can anyone, Pompus, Sharpe & Rich or Nouveau Hotels, take action against him?

Probably not. Jugg has caused no physical damage to any goods, indeed has not been anywhere near the affected computers, and the loss suffered by Nouveau Hotels (assuming they paid) may be regarded as a too 'remote' and unlikely a consequence of Jugg's apparently petty gesture of protest (see Chapter 9 above, concerning the 'tort' of negligence).

Where the viral effect is unintended, a complete accident, the legal position is even more difficult. The recent case of a student at Cornell who released a virus into the ARPNET network of the Pentagon made headlines around the world. His program was designed to sit in computers connected to the network, examine the security procedures and 'report back' to the creator. Unfortunately the result was that over 7 000 computers were tied up for an unconscionable amount of time, resulting in tens of millions of dollars' worth of computer time being wasted along with the costs of programmer time to get rid of the virus.

In the case of hackers who acquire confidential information, it is quite possible that legal action can be taken to prevent their misuse of the information. They acquire the information in circumstances where the confidentiality of the information must be evident and, as we saw in Chapter 5, this alone is usually sufficient to give a right to take legal action. Of course, this may be cold comfort to the person suffering incalculable commercial loss as a result of the loss of confidentiality.

Criminal Law

The recent trend in the United States has been to concentrate on modifications to the criminal law to deal with hacking and viruses. Currently the only states of the United States which do not have computer crime laws are West Virginia and Vermont. Very few countries outside the United States have any specific regulation.

Example — R v Schiffren & Gold

The defendants were accused of accessing the electronic mail box of the Duke of Edinburgh. The defendants admitted doing the deed, the question was whether in doing so they had committed any crime.

The House of Lords, the highest court in the United Kingdom decided that they had not.

The arguments were quite esoteric, revolving around the nature of forgery and whether in accessing the 'mailbox' the defendants had committed that crime by forging an 'instrument'.

While there was no suggestion that the defendants had any particular ill intent, presumably the result would have been the same had the defendants found messages of an extremely personal nature which they then sold to the newspapers (although his Royal Highness, in a long tradition of royal litigants, may have been entitled to commence civil proceedings for breach of confidence if this had been the case).

When prosecuting hacking in jurisdictions where there are no particular hacking statutes some creative thinking may be necessary. A charge such as 'malicious mischief' or 'criminal damage' may be appropriate, especially in the case of spreaders of viruses.

Example — HM Advocate v Wilson

The accused activated an emergency stop button, causing a nuclear power station to shut down and remain inoperative for 28 hours and was charged with malicious mischief. The cost of alternative electricity generation was £147 000, but no machinery was damaged. The English High Court held that any act which interfered with the enjoyment or profitability of another's property could constitute the offence of 'malicious mischief'.

In a recent American case, an employee of the Kodak corporation activated a shutdown procedure in a computer's communication system, crucial to the commercial activities of Kodak, by legitimately accessing the system and reprogramming it to cease operation. He was found guilty under a specific computer crime statute, but there was considerable argument whether simply altering the programmed state of the machine constituted willful damage to it.

The problem with prosecuting the person who introduces a virus by means of a bulletin board, or some other indiscriminate means, remains however that he or she apparently lacks the necessary intention to cause harm. Similarly, the law has difficulty with the hacker who simply inspects files without changing them.

These examples emphasize the need for careful drafting of legislation to cover these broader issues.

Computer crime laws

To ensure that these new crimes are punishable by the law it may be necessary to introduce particular legislation. Probably the most thorough study carried out recently was by the Scottish Law Commission which identified eight forms of computer abuse as candidates for criminal sanctions:

(1)   the erasure or falsification of data or programs so as to obtain a pecuniary or other advantage;

(2)   obtaining unauthorized access to a computer;

(3)   eavesdropping on a computer;

(4)   the taking of information without physical removal;

(5)   the unauthorized borrowing of computer discs or tapes;

(6)   making unauthorized use of computer time or facilities;

(7)   malicious or reckless corruption or erasure of data or programs;

(8)   the denial of access to authorized users.

The commission formed the view that abuses 1, 5 and 7 were adequately dealt with by the existing law. Abuses 6 and 8 were not covered by existing law and the commission could see no reason why they should be made illegal. Any legislation involving matters 3 and 4 would no doubt lead to information being classed as property and the effect of this would extend far beyond the field of computers. Only in relation to abuse number 2 was the commission prepared to recommend the creation of a new offence.

Another recommendation was that where a person in one jurisdiction obtains unauthorized access to a computer in another jurisdiction courts in both jurisdictions should be competent to hear the matter. We shall refer further to this matter below.

On the other hand, the Virginia *Computer Crimes Act* is quite comprehensive in its breadth. The Act proscribes a wide range of computer-assisted activities; it attempts to prohibit every act of unauthorized computer use. 'Computer fraud' is a specific crime with four elements:

- the use of a computer;
- without authority;
- with intention to commit one of the enumerated crimes; and
- property obtained exceeding a threshold value for a felony or misdemeanour.

The last element leads to two problems: what if no property is actually obtained and how does the court determine the value of property or services if there is no market value?

Under the same law, 'computer trespass' occurs when a computer is used without authority and with the intent to cause one of the following:

- the removal of information;
- causing a computer to malfunction;
- altering or erasing information;
- effecting the creation or alteration of a financial instrument or of an electronic transfer of funds;
- causing physical injury to the property of another; or
- making an unauthorized copy of computer data or programs.

Nothing in the trespass section requires fraudulent intent, so the loan of an ATM card, and disclosure of the password, by one person to another in contravention of the agreement between the bank and card holder could constitute trespass.

The Act sets out four elements of a computerized invasion of privacy as follows:

- use of a computer;

- without authority;
- with intention to examine protected information; and
- the actual examination of protected information.

Generally employment, salary, credit or other financial or personal information is expected to be protected, although it might be that any information which is not a matter of public record is protected.

Theft of computer services, and using a computer with the intent of causing physical injury to an individual, are also outlawed.

In Australia, the state of Victoria has recently introduced the *Crimes (Computer) Act*. It is not an entirely new regime like the Virginia Act; it amends the existing Victorian *Crimes Act* of 1958. The Act states, in part, that it is an offence, by act or omission, to cause a computer system or a machine which is designed to operate by means of payment or identification to make a response that the person doing or omitting to do the act or thing is not authorized to cause the computer system or machine to make.

Rights to control of data

The reference in the recent Virginia legislation to protected personal information leads us to the second area of consideration in privacy related issues.

There has been a great deal of interest recently in the notion of protecting people and companies from the use of information about them, not information which they possess, which they consider personal, and hence in some sense 'theirs'.

One of the reasons for this interest in privacy is the potential for misuse of information and the fact that the person who is the subject of the data in most cases probably does not know what information about him or her is available or who is accessing it. Most importantly, in the absence of special legislation, there is no chance for the information to be verified. Unless particular steps are taken, a person or company might be prejudiced by some incorrect information without even being aware that access had been given to such information.

In addition, errors can creep into databases in a number of ways. Apart from the simple case of wrong information being collected, or the 'right' information being ascribed to the wrong individual, contextual errors are the greatest source of problems. Raw, unevaluated data about an individual might give rise to damaging inferences that a fuller explanation of the underlying events, direct knowledge of the source of the information, or professional analysis of the facts would show to be false. For instance, a record which notes the arrest of an individual which does not also include the fact that he or she was acquitted could give rise to a misleading inference.

Example ───

Ralph Wrench is an ordinary citizen who is prone to excesses of ego. He is contacted by a market research company, Superior Market Intelligence, as part of one of its routine surveys, to provide his views upon a range of consumer goods and his and his family's patterns of consumption, as well as 'standard demographic data' concerning himself and his family, his and his wife's incomes, number of dependants and their ages, affiliations to advertising agencies and so on, so that he may be contacted later for further surveys, focus groups and other activities in Superior's line of business. Wrench rather overstates his income, as he believes it will gain him more interest from Superior for further, remunerated, involvement in its activities. Superior maintains a database with all this information concerning Wrench and hundreds of other people.

Regrettably, Superior falls on hard times, and is placed into liquidation. The liquidator recognizes the value of Superior's data, and offers it for sale to the highest bidder, in accordance with her duties to obtain the maximum return for the debtors of Superior.

Wrench is unaware of this, until he finds that an enterprising official of the Internal Revenue Service has also appreciated the value of the information, and he finds he is dealing with a substantial claim for unpaid taxes on his inflated income.

After expending considerable time and money defending the inquiries of the IRS, Wrench succeeds in his opposition. Can Wrench make any claim for the misuse of 'his' private information.

It is almost certain that he cannot, unless it can be argued that Superior understood the information to be confidential when it received it — which would be less than obvious since Wrench clearly gave it the information upon request for Superior's commercial use. In any event, the amount claimable by Wrench for his damages would probably be too small to justify legal action.

In a United States case, Dunn & Bradstreet included on its computerized information service incorrect information that Greenmoss Builders Inc. had filed for voluntary bankruptcy. Although there was no suggestion of malice on the part of Dunn & Bradstreet, the statement was made as a result of a mistake by an employee and an award of $300 000 in punitive damages was allowed to stand by the United States Supreme Court. But this is a case where a traditional legal remedy is usually available — statements which untruthfully denigrate credit worthiness have long been actionable as defamatory (see Chapter 6).

In most cases, as in our example of Mr Wrench, the remedies available to a person who has personal information misused or mistaken in the manner described above are extremely uncertain or, if available, are so costly to pursue in comparison with the financial loss suffered, if any, that they are unlikely to be sought. In these circumstances, special laws, and an administrative system to enforce them, are required.

Database control laws

The main thrust for privacy legislation has come from Europe. There have been regulations in Europe since the mid 1970s, starting with Sweden in 1973.

The United Kingdom *Data Protection Act* requires that all computer bureaux register a description of the personal data held, the sources from which it is derived, to whom it is disclosed, whether it is transferred outside the United Kingdom and notification of a place where those in respect of whom data is recorded may inspect the data pertaining to them. The Act is drawn up in such wide terms that most organizations which run an in-house computer will be subject to the Act.

The Act applies to 'data held' which is defined as 'the data from part of a collection of data processed or intended to be processed'. Possibly this definition could extend to a structured set of data on a paper form which is intended to be entered onto a disk via a keyboard for further processing.

Data itself is defined as 'information recorded in a form in which it can be processed'. 'Information' is not defined. If a printout is information, and not 'data', then an organization which after processing data kept the printout and erased the original computer based records would not be forced to give a copy of the printout to a data subject under the Act; access is confined to data, not to information.

'Possession' is another word the meaning of which is being debated. If a data user holds data which does not identify an individual but which, if related to other data in the possession of the data user, does enable an individual to be identified, then the data is subject to the Act. If the 'other data' is a mental record, would that constitute 'possession'? What if the 'other data' is collected and held by an individual in another department who does not normally require to have access to the computer based records; is that 'possession' by the organization?

The English law does not, however, apply to manual records, only to those held on a computer. Opponents note that this is an artificial distinction and allows a loophole to those who wish to subvert the principles of the Act. As we have seen above, however, for practical purposes it is the computerized databases which are the greatest threat to privacy and if non-computerized databases were to be included it might lead to the regulation of every filing cabinet in the jurisdiction.

Drawing a distinction between manual and computerized files does create problems, however. The Swedish law when introduced had a similar restriction and for a while people felt constrained to put things on paper to avoid the reach of the Act and there is some evidence to suggest that a similar process is taking place in the United Kingdom at the moment.

As with many areas of the law a certain balance is needed in answering the questions raised by privacy issues. The United Kingdom *Data Protection Act*, for instance, gives health records a special status. Unlike other databases the patient must get permission before access to records will be granted. The perceived problem is that doctors who know that a patient can have unrestricted access to the database will choose not to record certain opinions for fear that they are defamatory or otherwise very sensitive.

The databases of police forces and other security organizations provide a particular problem for privacy laws. In carrying out their function they must gather a wealth of material on certain individuals. The most basic information is the police record. Usually a police record is not available to anybody; not even the fact that an individual does not have a record will be disclosed. Any régime which gives individuals the right to inspect information concerning them which is held on a database must take this into account.

All the reports suggest that a majority of the organizations which should have registered had failed to do so by the specified date. So far there have been few reports of prosecutions for failure to register under the Act. However, there is a report that a policeman in Nottingham has been fined £400 for obtaining information from the Police National Computer for his own use.

It remains to be seen how useful and effective the United Kingdom law is.

Freedom of information — a contrary position?

An interesting twist when considering the new privacy laws is the tendency to encourage freedom of access to information held in government records.

Freedom of information is the other side of the privacy coin. While database control legislation is primarily concerned with ensuring only certain people or a certain class of person has access to data, freedom of information laws allow the public access to government information. A justification for this is that they may enable individuals to ensure information held concerning them is accurate or to determine the basis on which a particular decision was made. However, the laws more usually have been used by political groups and journalists to advance their more public interests.

Sweden is reported to have introduced the first freedom of

information legislation in 1766. The United States introduced its Act in 1966 and a number of countries have followed suit.

Under such legislation a person who wishes to obtain access to a document usually makes a request in writing to the relevant government agency. When making the application it is necessary to provide such information as is reasonably necessary to enable the responsible officer of the agency to identify the documents required.

For business people, a significant concern is whether confidential business information, supplied to the government as a potential customer or for other reasons, may be released in response to such an enquiry. Documents should be exempt if disclosure would reveal information having a commercial value which would be destroyed or diminished by the disclosure. Usually information confidential to third parties cannot be disclosed under freedom of information laws.

Transborder data flows

In a global information environment, it should be borne in mind that freedom of information legislation can work in different ways in different parts of the world.

Example ————————————————————————————

In Norway in the mid 1970s, a Norwegian citizen used a computer terminal in Norway to access an American computer. He was able to obtain, under the United States Freedom of Information laws data concerning NATO bases in Norway. The problem was that while the information was available in the United States it was proscribed in Norway and the citizen was successfully prosecuted under the Norwegian legislation covering official secrets.

A considerable percentage of all the computerized data which is available in the world is on computers located in the United States with the result that local legislation which prohibits access to such information locally may be easily circumvented. Any regulation of transborder data flows or freedom of information must always consider this fact.

On the other hand, the United States must remain aware of its lucrative trade in information; in 1984 it is estimated that total revenues of the United States' on-line information industry were $3.65 billion, of which 25%–33% was raised outside the United States.

Even so there have been attempts to limit the flow of information. In 1987, a directive of the United States Department of Defence attempted to create a new category of 'sensitive' information between classified and non-classified. The attempt was finally rejected as ill-conceived after it was pointed out that any effective controls would have to affect the free flow of information within the United States itself; it was perceived that the free flow of information had been instrumental in allowing the United States to maintain its technological lead.

These are examples of the problem of 'transborder data flow'.

The issue of transborder data flow is, however, broader than this. It could be said also that satellite television broadcast, or even mail or a telephone conversation is a transborder data flow. Generally, the issue of transborder data flows arises when a computer in one country is accessed by, or transmits data to a computer or a computer terminal in another country. In a sense the 'flow' itself is quite unimportant; it is issues such as privacy protection, trade principles and employment which are important.

One of the most potent reasons for an interest in transborder data flows by governments is to ensure that data which may be vital to the national interest is always available. It could be disastrous to find that all the information vital to the banking industry, and therefore the economy as a whole was resident on a foreign computer and subject to accidental or deliberate interference.

The implications for privacy, and indeed national security are as obvious as they are startling. It is the nature of the computer and communications industries at this time that the physical location of a mainframe computer does not necessarily have to be in the vicinity of the users and that for many businesses instant access to data from a number of locations across the world is mandatory. The airline industry, for instance, depends upon constant transborder data flows.

The most striking attempt by any government to control transborder data flows is the United States *Export Administration Regulations*. By these regulations, the United States not only restricts the supply of information which is considered technologically significant, but also any goods which are considered to embody such information, including those produced overseas from what is regarded as United States technology. The restrictions apply at several levels — at their most extreme, the export of defense related goods is absolutely prohibited without express, case-by-case, licences; at their most lenient, the export of quite mundane technologies is prohibited only to certain countries. The law is so wide in its operation that even people considered to be possessed of sensitive information may be subject to restrictions on their movements in certain countries, and subsidiaries of United States corporations in other countries may be subject to limitations on the persons permitted access to their premises. Finally, as the law would be laughable if it could be avoided by export to intermediate destinations for re-export, it seeks to limit re-export from foreign countries also.

The United States is not the first country to attempt to extend the regulation of its national laws to activities outside its borders. The

European Economic Community has for some time permitted its anti-trust and other laws to be enforced upon local entities as a result of the conduct of non-local affiliates. The effectiveness of such legislation is largely dependent, however, on the existence of multinational corporations; related corporations may be made scapegoats for the misdemeanours of their foreign counterparts.

Conclusion

The above review of the issues concerning security of information in the computer age, private and public, serves to emphasize the difficulties the law has experienced in coping with new technologies. Old familiar concerns take on a new urgency under the influence of new circumstances.

It remains to be seen whether lawmakers can respond with a coherent legal response to such a complex of conflicting public and private interests in the power of information.

II SAMPLE CONTRACTS

Introduction

In this section we shall be considering a number of types of contracts typical of the computer industry.

This section does not attempt to be exhaustive of either the number or content of such contracts, but merely to give examples which raise a number of relevant issues, and to illustrate the practical application of many of the legal issues discussed in the first section of the book. For these reasons, we do not attempt to give contract forms drafted for the benefit of both sides to a contract, or with variations favouring one party or the other, or attempting to solve particular problems.

These examples should not, then, be followed slavishly. They should be used merely as a guide to clear and, we hope, precise contract drafting, and to the questions that should be answered in the contract process, which questions should be answered with the further assistance of common sense.

We commence with a review of standard boilerplate clauses (mentioned in Chapter 7 above) which, since they tend to be the least read and yet potentially the most harmful to the survival of a contractual relationship when disagreements do arise, we invite the reader to consider now, and in a little more detail than the other examples given, at the front of these contracts!

A Boilerplate Clauses

Boilerplate clauses are those which appear at the end of the contract and deal with all the boring things which you don't need to think about. The deal has been negotiated and set out in the first part of the contract. The last clauses in one contract look very much like the final clauses in another, and they merely ensure that, should it ever become important, certain procedural issues are dealt with.

However, it is precisely because these matters may be of vital importance should there be a difficulty or uncertainty in the course of the contract, that the full implications of some of these provisions be carefully considered. Drafting these clauses should be carefully thought out — the words may sound comforting, but this may disguise their true effect. Above all, the clauses chosen and their content should be appropriate for the contract in hand — an exclusion or limitation of liability which refers only to goods is of very little use in a contract relating only to the supply of services.

1 Definitions

Definition clauses can be very useful. Once a word is defined, it may incorporate a number of things over and over again, without repeating the various additional components it encompasses. For example, 'software' may encompass machine readable object code and user documentation, 'system' may incorporate a CPU and its operating system as well as certain peripheral equipment. Furthermore, once defined, the word can never mean something else, such as source code in the case of 'software', or applications software in the case of 'system'. However, once defined, such words should never be used to mean something different, such as the machine readable object code or operating system on its own, without qualification. This will only lead to further confusion — for example it is absurd to grant a licence to operate user documentation on a single CPU!

Definitions may be introduced the first time a word is used, or in a separate 'definitions' section. If the latter is used, it is important to create definitions only for important words used frequently in a particular sense, and not to weigh the contract down with definitions of words of little significance, or which are not used at all!

In this example, however, we merely provide some suggested definitions for notions which may be useful in cases of contracts likely to be construed very strictly. It is our practice in the examples which follow to define important words as they first appear in the body of a contract.

Example ───

1.1   *In this Agreement unless there is something in the context inconsistent therewith:*

(a)   *words importing the singular include the plural and* vice versa *and words importing any gender shall include the others;*

(b)   *a reference to a person shall include corporations;*

(c)   *words importing singular number shall include plural number and* vice versa;

(d)   *words importing a gender shall include all other genders;*

(e)   *a reference in this Agreement to all sections of a statute includes all amendments to that statute;*

(f)   *except for the purpose of identification, headings and underlinings have been inserted in this Agreement for the purpose of guidance only and shall not be part of this Agreement; and*

(g)   *expressions referring to writing shall, unless the contrary intention appears, be construed as references to printing, facsimile, lithograph, photocopy and other modes of representing or reproducing words in a visible form.*

2   Intellectual property; confidential information

If the parties have not had reason to deal with these issues specifically elsewhere in the contract, it is frequently a good idea to include them here. In most contracts in the computer industry, intellectual property of one kind or another is involved, and even in a contract for the supply or maintenance of computer hardware or software, it can be that the parties obtain information confidential to each other, even if it is only lying around on desks for technicians to see, or in technicians' manuals for customers to see. These provisions ensure that these issues are dealt with in a minimal manner. They also go some way towards dealing with any export control regulations which may affect any transaction during the course of the contract.

Example ───

2.1   *The Client acknowledges that the copyright in all literary or artistic and other works including computer programs ('Intellectual Property') and related documentation provided to the Client by the Company pursuant to this Agreement at the date of delivery thereof either belongs to or is licensed to the Company.*

2.2   *The Client further agrees that it will not at any time knowingly do or cause to be done any act or thing impairing or tending to impair the right, title or interest of the Company to any Intellectual Property provided for the use of the Client in the period of this Agreement or thereafter.*

2.3   *The Client agrees that except as expressly provided by the Company under this Agreement, the Client's use of Intellectual Property provided by the Company pursuant to this Agreement shall not create in the Client any right, title or interest therein.*

2.4   *The Client shall not disclose or purport to transfer any Intellectual Property to any third party.*

2.5   *The Client agrees to treat as confidential all information received from the Company regarding its clients, financial affairs, present or future business plans and products, not generally disclosed to the public, which the Client may learn in the course of or incidental to this Agreement whether or not it is in writing, and in addition any information designated by the Company as confidential ('Confidential Information'). Without limiting the generality of the foregoing the Confidential Information shall include details of any software, its source code or any flow charts, diagrams or data relating thereto, or its method of operation, access to which may be provided pursuant to this Agreement.*

2.6   *The Client shall not disclose to any person, other than those employees of the Client who need to have that information in order to carry out their duties on behalf of the Client, the whole or any part of any Confidential Information, nor use any part of the Confidential Information for its own purposes, or for the benefit of any third party, except as expressly authorized by this Agreement, or pursuant to any requirement of law, without the prior written consent of the Company.*

2.7   *In addition, the Client shall during the term of this Agreement and thereafter procure that its officers, employees and agents observe and maintain complete confidentiality with regard to all aspects of the Confidential Information, as if personally bound by the provisions of this Clause.*

2.8   *The Company shall maintain each and every part of the Client's confidential information, data and results obtained by it in performance of its obligations under this Agreement in strict confidence for the Client, and the Company will take all action considered by the Company as necessary with respect to the use, copying, duplication, access, security and protection of such information, data and results or any part thereof to satisfy its obligations under this sub-Clause.*

2.9   *Neither party hereto shall be required to keep confidential any information which is or becomes publicly available, is already in the recipient's possession at the time of receipt of this Agreement, is independently developed by the recipient outside the scope of this Agreement, or is rightfully obtained from third parties. In addition, the Company shall not be required to keep confidential any ideas, concepts, know-how, or techniques relating to the performance of its obligations hereunder submitted to the Company by the Client or any person on the Client's behalf or developed during the course of this Agreement by the Company's personnel or jointly by the Company personnel and Client personnel.*

2.10   *In addition to the foregoing, the Client shall not itself export or supply to any third party for export from the country of receipt, or otherwise deal in any Intellectual Property or Confidential Information affected by the export control laws of the United States of America or any other country from time to time.*

3   Termination

It is important to enable the parties to terminate a contract in the event of breach — otherwise, it is possible that a dispute may arise whether the provision breached was fundamental to the contract, the breach of which entitles termination, or merely a right to claim damages. In addition, there are circumstances in which one of the parties may wish to be able to terminate the agreement even if no breach has occurred, notably in the event that there are any grounds to believe that the other party may become insolvent or have a receiver appointed, thereby endangering property (such as software or technical materials) in the hands of the potentially insolvent party which may fall into the hands of a liquidator.

Some termination clauses provide for 'automatic' termination, that is, without notice, on the occurrence of certain events. This is common, again, to avoid the consequences of liquidation or bankruptcy by ensuring the contract is automatically terminated at the earliest possible time. However, it should be remembered that sometimes the triggering events specified often occur in circumstances where no liquidation or bankruptcy is likely to follow — for example a demand for payment not satisfied within 21 days — and it may be very embarrassing to the parties if a contract, such as a licence for software crucial to a business, is automatically terminated without their being aware.

It is usually a good starting point in negotiations for the termination clauses to apply equally to both sides, this at least ensures some common sense.

Finally, it is important to turn one's mind to the consequences of termination, including the return of property and confidential materials. The provision in the example whereby 'neither party will have any liability to the other by virtue of such termination' does not preclude a claim for damages for breach of contract, merely a claim that the termination itself breached any right to continuation of the contract.

Example

3.1   *Either party hereto may terminate this Agreement forthwith upon the happening of any of the following events:*

    (a)   *the other party fails to observe or perform any provisions of this Agreement and fails to remedy such breach within thirty (30) days after written notice thereof has been given to the party in breach;*

    (b)   *the other commits any act of bankruptcy or insolvency or a petition is presented for the bankruptcy or winding up of the other or a resolution is passed for the winding up of the other otherwise than for the purposes of amalgamation or reconstruction;*

    (c)   *the other enters a compromise or arrangement with creditors or a receiver or official manager of the other or of any of its assets is appointed; or*

    (d)   *in the event that any party is a person or partnership, that person or any member of that partnership is declared to be of unsound mind or otherwise incompetent to carry on his own affairs.*

3.2   *In the event that this Agreement is terminated then*

    (a)   *neither party shall have any liability to the other by virtue of such termination;*

(b)   *the Client shall do all such things and execute all such documents as the Company or its attorneys may reasonably request in order to record or give effect to such termination; and*

(c)   *each party shall within seven (7) days of the effective date of termination deliver to the other all documents and other things (including microfiche, magnetic tape, disks or other storage media) embodying any confidential information obtained from the other during the term hereof or before this Agreement and relating thereto, or, in the event that any such information is embodied in valuable property belonging to the receiving party thereof, the receiving party shall certify its obliteration by erasure or other appropriate means.*

4   Warranties and indemnities; exclusion clauses

These provisions exhaustively deal with warranties to be given by a supplier, whilst limiting liability and ensuring the other party indemnifies the other for losses it incurs as a result of the performance of its obligations under the contract, for example a liability to its employees as a result of carelessness of the other party in providing a safe place of work.

Example

4.1   *Services to be provided by the Company hereunder shall be provided in a proper and workmanlike manner.*

4.2   *Except in relation to events described in Clause 4.3 below, if, by virtue of performing its obligations under this Agreement, the Company is held by a Court to have infringed a third party's patent, copyright, registered design, trade mark or trade secret rights or if the Company is advised by legal counsel that the performance of its obligations hereunder is likely to constitute such infringement, then the Company shall promptly and at its own expense:*

    (a)   *procure for the Client the right to continue use of any infringing work;*

    (b)   *modify the Services (without materially detracting from overall performance) so as to avoid the infringement; or*

    (c)   *if paragraphs (a) or (b) cannot be accomplished on reasonable terms, at the option of the Company, remove any infringing work from the possession of the Client or cease to provide access to the work and refund the fees previously paid in relation to that work.*

4.3   *The Client shall indemnify and save harmless the Company against any expense, judgement or loss or infringement (including legal costs and disbursements in defending or settling the claim giving rise to same) of any patent, copyright, design right, trade secret or trade mark which results from the Company's use of or compliance with any design, specification, direction or instruction of the Client or which results in any claim or demand by any person arising out of the provision of the Services.*

4.4   *This Clause states the entire liability of the Company with respect to infringement or alleged infringement of any design right, trade secret, trade mark, patent or copyright in the provision of the performance by the Company of its obligations hereunder.*

4.5   *The Client shall indemnify and save harmless the Company from and against all actions, suits, claims, demands, verdicts, judgements, costs and expenses, legal and otherwise, which may arise as a result of or incidental to the performance by the Company of its obligations hereunder, or any transactions between the Company and a customer of the Client or any other third party either directly or indirectly carried out under or incidental to this Agreement.*

4.6   *Except as otherwise expressly provided herein, all warranties, representations, promises, conditions or statements regarding the Services to be supplied or performed hereunder, whether express or implied, and whether statutory or otherwise including, without limiting the generality of the foregoing, warranties, representations, promises, conditions or statements as to the merchantability, suitability or fitness for any purpose, profitability or any other attributes or consequences of or benefits to be obtained from or in the course of the performance by the Company of its obligations hereunder, except as expressly set out herein or in any attachment hereto, are hereby expressly excluded.*

4.7   *The Client assumes exclusive responsibility for the consequences of any properly executed instructions it may give to the Company.*

4.8   *The Client agrees and declares for the benefit of the Company that it has relied upon the Client's own skill and judgement in entering into this Agreement, and has not relied on any statement or representation given by any person on behalf of the Company.*

4.9   *In the event of any breach of any term of this Agreement, the liability of the Company as a result thereof shall be and is hereby limited to an amount which shall not exceed the total amount paid by the Client hereunder to the date of such breach.*

4.10   *In no event shall the Company be liable to the Client for special, incidental or consequential loss or damage or for any indirect loss or damage including, without any limitation to the foregoing, exemplary or punitive damages or damage to personal property.*

4.11   [Here insert any special provision(s) relating to specific statutory requirements which may be excluded, limited or modified.]

Subject to this Clause all conditions and warranties which would or might otherwise be implied in this Agreement are hereby excluded and negated to the extent permitted by law and this is acknowledged by the Client.

5 Payment

In case this has been overlooked, the method of invoicing and payment should be expressly dealt with. This is so particularly in an ongoing service relationship, otherwise the client may have a different view as to when it expects to be invoiced and to pay, and the supplier cannot rely on any implicit arrangement or understanding in the face of an 'entire agreement' clause, discussed below. In addition, in conjunction with the termination provisions considered above, this provision entitles the supplier of goods or services to refuse to further supply goods or services, to threaten termination, and to charge interest on overdue amounts, in the face of an ongoing refusal or neglect to pay, rather than having to rely on a legal action for the recovery of money, and face cash flow crisis. Finally, the provision permits the variation of charges, which also may not be permissible without express terms.

Example

5.1   *Charges payable by the Client under this Agreement will be invoiced monthly on a retrospective basis* [or as otherwise required by the contract, or agreed].

5.2   *The Client will pay the Company within thirty (30) days of the date of any invoice the total of charges for the services shown thereon. If invoices are not paid within thirty (30) days the Company may suspend performance of all or any of its obligations hereunder as it may elect and, in addition, such unpaid amounts shall bear interest at the rate of two (2) percent per month or such lesser amount as is the maximum allowed by law. The Client acknowledges that such interest is a genuine pre-estimate of the Company's cost of funding such overdue amounts and is not a penalty. The Client shall pay the cost of collection and related costs incurred by the Company for invoices which remain unpaid for thirty (30) days.*

5.3   *The Client shall reimburse the Company for any applicable taxes, duties, fees or amounts in lieu thereof, however designated, paid or payable by the Company and levied or based on the charges levied on the Client or on this Agreement or the provision of any goods or services by the Company pursuant to or incidental to this Agreement, excluding, however, taxes based on net income.*

5.4   *In addition to the charges as stated herein, the Company will invoice the Client for special or unusual expenses incurred by the Company at the Client's specific request or as the result of an omission or error on the part of the Client, and the Client shall pay such invoiced expenses pursuant to Clause 5.2 hereof.*

5.5   *Special or unusual goods and services purchased by the Company on behalf of the Client from a third party will be reinvoiced to the Client with a fifteen percent (15%) handling charge. Requested expedited handling may be subject to an additional charge.*

5.6   *Charges may be varied by the Company at any time. Such variations will be effective immediately they are notified to the Client either orally or by notice in writing.*

6   Amendments (or variations)

Notwithstanding the provisions of clauses such as these, the parties to a contract are quite free to make a different agreement, verbally, later if they so choose. Any simple contract may be made or varied by an oral agreement.

Of course it is often worth including a provision that variations must be in writing if only to encourage those charged with the administration of the contract to commit variations to writing; like all contracts, it is to the benefit of all parties if variations to contracts are in writing.

Example

6.1   *Subject to Clause 5.6* [that is, the provision allowing for the variation of charges above], *no amendment or modification of this Agreement or any provision of this Agreement shall be effective unless in writing and signed by both parties.*

7 Terms to prevail

The purpose of the first part of this provision is to deal with one of the unexpected consequences of the ability for any contract to be varied by subsequent agreement, notwithstanding a variation procedure. This is known as 'the battle of forms', when for example a purchaser's subsequent purchase order with contradictory terms may appear to be accepted by a supplier's delivery docket, and so on, leading to a multiplicity of apparently contractual documents. Such a clause may or may not be successful in this regard.

The second part is relevant to international contracts, in which it is not uncommon for translations of a contract form to be made to assist in negotiations. Unfortunately, standards of translators vary, and serious ambiguities, or direct contradictions, can arise.

Example ─────────────────────────────────

7.1   *In the event of any inconsistency between the terms of this Agreement and the provisions of any purchase order, acknowledgement or other documentation of the Client, the terms of this Agreement shall prevail.*

7.2   *In the event that this Agreement is translated into any language other than* [specify language of original master], *then in the resolution of any ambiguity or difference between the* [specify language of original master] *version and such translation, the* [specify language of original master] *will prevail.*

8 Waiver

The purpose of a 'waiver' provision is again to avoid the consequences of the capacity for any contract to be varied by subsequent agreement. It will be important to both parties to avoid an argument later that, because payment was allowed late on one occasion, or goods or services were permitted to be late or not according to specification on one occasion, that the obligation to pay by a certain date or to deliver further goods or services on time and in accordance with specifications is no longer important, or may not be 'the straw that breaks the camel's back', or has been varied in some way in favour of the defaulting party.

Example ─────────────────────────────────

8.1   *No waiver by either party whether express or implied of any provisions of this Agreement or of any breach or default of either party shall constitute a continuing waiver or a waiver of any other provision of this Agreement unless made in writing and signed by the party against whom the waiver would otherwise be enforced.*

9   Dispute resolution

Parties to a contract may decide, either at the time of contract or at the time of a dispute arising, to have disputes resolved (it is hoped) by various alternative dispute procedures, including arbitration. Of course, at the time of dispute, it is unlikely that the parties will rise above their mutual suspicions to agree on *anything*, let alone the matters which have to be decided to enable an arbitration to proceed. These matters include the identity of the arbitrator (or arbitrators), the place of arbitration, the rules which will govern the arbitration, including whether the laws of evidence will apply and the manner of treatment of experts' reports, precisely what issues will be referred to arbitration, and whether legal representation will be allowed.

If, as a matter of principle, the parties agree that arbitration is the appropriate means of resolving disputes, it is not feasible at the time of the contract to set out in detail all these matters, it being more convenient to adopt some particular arbitration system (of which there are many, from international rules such as those of the United Nations Commission on International Trade Law, the London Court of International Arbitration Rules and the International Chamber of Commerce, to regional and national systems), and have a particular independent body select an arbitrator (there are Institutes of Arbitrators in most countries, but, for reasons referred to below, it may be preferable to select a trusted local computer industry association).

Finally there is a mass of local law governing the conduct of arbitrations, which sometimes permit the exclusion of reversion to legal remedies. These add a further level of complexity to the drafting of arbitration clauses in contracts.

We also have the following words of caution in respect of arbitration in computer industry contracts:

(1)   The theory of arbitration is that, instead of going to a court and having to educate a judge in the ways in which a technical matter is handled, an arbitrator who is familiar with such matters already can give a quicker, cheaper and more informed ruling. For this reason, to be useful an arbitration should be concerned more with questions of fact than questions of law, and therefore disputes on peculiarly legal issues, such as the ownership of intellectual property or the duties of one party to the other in respect to confidential information, should not be referred to arbitration by an inexpert (non-lawyer) arbitrator. However, in most disputes, it can be difficult to disentangle the questions of construction of the contract (a question of law) and disputes of fact.

(2)   Also, the choice of arbitrator can be difficult even for technical disputes. The best choice for an arbitrator is someone who has been involved in projects similar to the one under discussion on his or her own account. It may not be possible in the computer industry to find a person who meets this criterion, has sufficient standing in the industry, and who is prepared to take on the job.

(3)   Furthermore, it should be understood that while parties to a contract may bind themselves to have any disputes resolved by an arbitrator, the decision of an arbitrator may be appealable in a court, and so it is possible that an arbitration will result, in effect, in the case having to be heard twice — once before the arbitrator and then again before a judge if the decision is appealed. Many computer disputes arise because of poorly drawn contracts and there are therefore a number of legal issues which must be resolved. In such a case it is virtually certain that the matter will be appealed in a court.

(4)   A perceived advantage of an arbitration is that the parties do not have to 'stand in the queue' waiting for the court to be available; the matter can be heard just as soon as the parties are ready. However, the bigger and more complex the project the more likely it is that an arbitration will approximate a court hearing, with the same procedural steps that are gone through in court, such as compiling a list of relevant documents and so on, being duplicated in the arbitration.

(5)   Arbitrations can also incur extra expense. While it is possible to save money because an arbitration is quicker than a court hearing, it is also true that whereas the state provides the services of a judge, a venue, a shorthand reporter and other court officers for no charge, in an arbitration the parties themselves must bear that cost.

So, while arbitration does work well for more long-established and conventional industries, such as the building industry, arbitration clauses in computer industry contracts should be treated with great caution.

The sample clause we provide below attempts to use conciliation procedures to bring the parties together (which, if anything, is the most likely to produce results) before resorting to formal arbitration.

Example ───────────────────────────────────

9.1   *Any dispute, controversy or claim arising out of or relating to the performance or as to the meaning of this Agreement, not being a dispute affecting ownership of any intellectual property (herein referred to as 'the Dispute'), the Dispute shall first be the subject of conciliation, administered by* [specify a commercial arbitration body, or mutually acceptable industry body prepared to undertake conciliation and arbitration of disputes] *('the Arbitrator') conducted at* [specify a place, presumably the place of the Arbitrator] *and held in accordance with the Conciliation Rules of the Arbitrator in force at the date of this Agreement. Such conciliation shall commence by either party preparing a Notice of Dispute which sets out the subject matter of the Dispute to be determined by the Arbitrator (but not including all the facts and circumstances relied upon) which shall be served upon the other party and a copy delivered to the Arbitrator with a copy of this Agreement and a request for conciliation and, if necessary, arbitration hereunder.*

9.2 *In the event that the Dispute is not resolved by Agreement between the parties within ninety (90) days of the date first specified for a meeting to be attended by both parties, the Dispute shall be referred to and determined by arbitration, administered by the Arbitrator, conducted at* [specified location] *and held under the rules of arbitration of the* [name rules for the conduct of arbitration of the Arbitrator, or other appropriate rules] *conducted by one or more arbitrators appointed in accordance with the said rules.*

9.3 *The award made by such arbitration shall be final and binding on both parties and neither party shall be entitled to commence or maintain any action upon any dispute, controversy or claim arising out of or relating to the performance or as to the meaning of this Agreement, not being a dispute affecting ownership of any intellectual property, until such matter has been referred to arbitration and determined as hereinbefore provided and then only for the amount or to the extent of the relief of the award.*

9.4 *Offers for settlement or any matter disclosed in the course of any conciliation or arbitration hereunder shall be treated as without prejudice and not an admission of liability or as to any fact. The parties shall use their best endeavours to cause all information disclosed in conciliation and arbitration hereunder to be kept and maintained as confidential.*

10 Force majeure

The *force majeure* clauses are often worth reading simply for an insight into the pessimistic tendencies of the drafter. Their purpose is to extend the rights of the parties beyond those of the general and uncertain law of 'frustration'. Some clauses merely refer to circumstances outside the control of the parties; some of the more esoteric ones go into great detail about floods, famine, pestilence and nuclear war covering half a page with all the things which might act to prevent the contract being performed.

The aim of *force majeure* clauses is to protect both parties in the event of occurrences which make performance of the contract impossible. If, for instance, a computer is to be delivered by a certain date but the supplier is unable to get the machine off the docks due to a protracted strike, the supplier wishes to ensure that it is not held to be in breach of contract for failure to deliver the computer.

Force majeure clauses properly form part of many contracts but they must be examined for their relevance to the particular contract under examination and in the light of anticipated or foreseeable circumstances. Caution must be exercised if the clause may operate as a second termination clause, allowing a party to walk away from its obligations merely if it has become uneconomic for some reason to perform as promised, possibly for a reason totally unrelated to the *force majeure* event. It can be wise, therefore, in a *force majeure* clause to give the party the subject of the *force majeure* event the right only to suspend performance for certain period — such as 60 or 90 days — and the non-defaulting party the option of extending the time for performance or cancelling the contract. A *force majeure* clause may also simply specify that the contract may be at an end, or may be suspended, if one party or the other is prevented from performing its obligations by an event of *force majeure* for a certain period — such as 60 or 90 days.

Care should be taken that, on the occurrence of an event preventing one party from performing, the other is not left with its obligations, such as payment, notwithstanding the delay.

Example
_____

10.1   *Notwithstanding any other provision in this Agreement, no default, delay or failure to perform on the part of either party shall be considered a breach of this Agreement if such default, delay or failure to perform is shown to be due entirely to causes beyond the reasonable control of the party charged with such default including, but not limited to causes such as strikes, lock-outs or other labour disputes, riots, civil disturbance, actions or inaction of governmental authorities or suppliers, epidemics, wars, embargoes, storms, floods, fires, earthquakes, acts of God or the public enemy, computer downtime, nuclear disasters or default of a common carrier ('the* Force Majeure *Event').*

10.2   *Upon the occurrence of the* Force Majeure *Event, the party seeking to rely on same shall not be entitled to do so unless and until it serves notice on the other specifying the event relied upon and specifying a period during which suspension of its obligations under this Agreement will be sought (not to exceed sixty (60) days) and thereupon the time for performance required by both parties under this Agreement shall be extended for such period or the lesser period during which performance of the party giving notice is prevented by the* Force Majeure *Event.*

10.3   *In the further event that the* Force Majeure *Event persists at the end of such period, or a further such event supervenes whereby the same party alleges it is prevented from performing its obligations (or any of them) hereunder, the party seeking to rely on same shall serve a further notice on the other party as required by this Clause, but the party receiving same shall be entitled thereupon to terminate this Agreement forthwith by the giving of notice terminating this Agreement, whereupon the parties shall negotiate in good faith as to the consequences of such termination, including the return of property delivered and not paid for.*

11   Entire agreement

This is probably the boilerplate clause which is examined most often by lawyers; probably every dissatisfied user who has regarded contracts as a mere formality at the commencement of the relationship has a list of promises which, in the opinion of the user, were made by the supplier but which have not found their way into the contract as obligations of the supplier. One of the reasons suppliers seek to have this clause included is to ensure that any such promises do not form part of the contract.

In their shortest form these clauses provide that whatever may have been said before you signed the contract, it is of no consequence unless it is expressly written into the contract. Of course, in Chapter 8 above we have seen that the law may act to prevent anyone from making wild promises and then not standing by them, but we have also seen that it is far better to get the contract right than to rely on the vagaries of the law for redress.

It is important therefore to ensure that the contract accurately reflects the agreement reached between the parties. One should therefore include all the documents which set out the obligations and promises of the parties, such as specifications, replies to request for tender and key correspondence.

It is quite possible to go too far in this direction. There is little benefit in attaching to the contract every bit of correspondence which had passed between the parties. There may be contradictory statements, and all manner of requirements inadequately canvassed, which should be carefully reviewed to decide what has been agreed and what has not, and how that agreement should be expressed.

If this is done, it is sensible and mutually beneficial to include an 'entire agreement' clause in the contract; it helps avoid later confusion.

Example ───────────────────────────────────

11.1   *This Agreement constitutes the entire agreement between the parties regarding the subject matter hereof, and supersedes and replaces all agreements, arrangements and understandings relating to the subject matter hereof, whether reduced to writing or not, that may have preceded this Agreement. The Client acknowledges that no warranties or representations have been given by the Company or any person on behalf of the Company, or relied upon by the Client in entering into this Agreement, nor shall any be implied unless and except to the extent that they are expressly contained in this Agreement.*

12   Severability

In some legal systems, it is possible that if any provision of a contract is illegal, if it infringes anti-trust laws, for example, and it is determined to be of fundamental importance to the parties, or it cannot be determined whether one of the parties would have entered the contract at all without it, the whole contract may be struck down, placing the parties in a very uncertain position. This provision invites a court in this situation to strike out just the affected clause, leaving the rest of the contract standing.

12.1   If any provision of this Agreement should be held to be invalid in any way or unenforceable, the remaining terms and provisions of this Agreement shall remain in full force and effect and such invalid, illegal or unenforceable term or provision shall be deemed not to be part of this Agreement.

13   Governing law (choice of law)

Choice of law clauses set out which law will be used to determine the outcome of a dispute. Usually foreign suppliers will insist that their own domestic law be applied; often they do so without much thought. For example, the law of California may be much more severe for a supplier than the law of most Asian countries — it may prohibit the exclusion of liability in certain cases, whereas in many countries, such as Japan, Hong Kong, Singapore and others, the supplier may absolutely exclude liability.

It should be noted, however, that a choice of law clause cannot determine certain important proprietary issues — as we have seen in Chapter 3 above, local copyright issues will be determined by local copyright laws, because copyright is a national right, similarly duties of confidentiality. Also, choice of law cannot generally control procedural issues, such as the assessment of damages — perhaps a matter of relief to Californian corporations, whose own courts occasionally permit punitive damages!

In this regard, it should be noted that provisions selecting a particular jurisdiction, or selecting a particular remedy, common provisions in American contracts, are not effective in most countries, regardless of the choice of law, as the jurisdiction of the local courts, and their remedies, cannot be excluded. The choice of jurisdiction is usually governed by the location of the party to be sued, as only a court in that location will have any power over that party.

13.1   This Agreement shall be governed by and construed in accordance with the law for the time being of [specify preferred legal system].

14   Notices

There is, in fact, not much which can go wrong with a notice clause, provided it calls for notice to be given to the appropriate people and any 'deeming' provisions are reasonable — often, for instance, notice will be deemed to be given seven days after a letter is posted.

However, difficulties may arise if the drafter of a contract has chosen an antiquated precedent which predates facsimile and electronic mail. If care is not taken, a party may purport to exercise a right — to suspend its obligations by reason of a *force majeure* event, for example — but have failed to do so because it did so by electronic mail when the contract prescribes that notice must be given by mail or telex. Care must be taken to ensure that the customary methods of written communication between the parties are taken into account by the drafter.

Example

14.1   *Any notice required or permitted by this Agreement shall be in writing, and shall be deemed given to the intended party when copies are delivered personally or by prepaid mail, telex, facsimile transmission or electronic mail to the party or, where such a party is a corporation, to a director or secretary of the company, in the case of mail seven (7) days after the date of posting, in the case of personal delivery on the date of such delivery, or in the case of other methods one (1) day after the date of transmission, at the mail address or electronic address or facsimile or telex number noted on the front page of this Agreement. Either party may change its addresses or numbers by a written notice to the other party given in a manner specified by this Clause.*

15   Assignment

Often there is a prohibition on assignment of the contract by one party while allowing the other to assign whenever it wishes to do so. This is particularly true of software licences. This clause should be carefully examined in light of the particular circumstances. It may, for instance, be necessary for a user to be able to assign the licence to a related company within the same group. In a purchase of, say, a point of sale system a user would not wish to find that while the hardware component of the system had been purchased the software component had been licensed and there was a prohibition on assignment. Effectively that may mean that it is impossible to sell the POS system should the need ever arise.

Example

15.1   *The benefits and obligations of this Agreement shall be freely assignable by the Company to any related corporation provided that notice of such assignment is given to the Client and the assignee accepts all the responsibilities and duties to the Client hereunder. The benefits and obligations of this Agreement shall not be assignable by the Client without prior written consent of the Company, which consent shall not be unreasonably refused in the case of a substantial assignee capable of undertaking the financial and other obligations of the Client hereunder.*

B   End User Single CPU Software Licences

Software licences are a peculiarity of the computer industry. Their
original form arose at a time prior to the clarification of the copyright law
such that it was construed or was amended to extend to computer
software in any form. At that time, as software was generally supplied for
big systems only and hence there was always a commercial relationship
between the supplier and the acquirer of software, an acceptable avenue
of protection was provided by contract — and so, rather than sell the media with software embodied in it as other publishers sell a book, the
supplier 'lent', or in legal terms gave 'on licence' or 'bailed', the goods for
the use of the licensee in return for a fee. In contracts of loan, or
'bailment', of goods, the supplier may impose conditions on their use,
including their return at some future time, because he never gives up
ownership of the goods.

Software has since that time developed into more of a commodity:
it is more likely to be supplied 'off the shelf' in a sealed box, whether for
micro- or mini-computers. This has resulted, of course, in the absence of
a commercial relationship between the owner/supplier and the acquirer/
user, and yet the owners typically remain concerned to introduce a
contract, if only to remind the user of the subsistence of copyright and to
attempt to impose however ineffectually in the face of consumer
protection legislation, exclusions of warranties. This has resulted in the
'shrinkwrap licence' with which we are all too familiar.

Also known as 'box-top' licences or 'tear-me-open' licences these
contracts get their name from the method by which their terms are
bought to the attention of the consumer, or the action which is alleged to
constitute acceptance of the contract by the consumer. To gauge whether
this method of licensing is effective, shrinkwrap licences must be looked
at like any other contract. Chapter 7 discusses the basics of contract law,
including offer and acceptance, the essential components of a contract. It
will be recalled that it is essential to a contract that all necessary terms are
present in the offer and acceptance, including, in most countries,
'consideration' for the contract. In the case of shrinkwrap licences, the
entire contractual transaction takes place when the consumer requests
the product, is given it, and pays for it — just as in any supermarket purchase. It may be that the licence terms are bought to the attention of the
consumer after the transaction is characterized by law as a sale of goods,

and hence by the time the consumer opens the outer packaging it is too late to be imposing conditions or detractions on the ownership which has already passed.

The only way of avoiding this consequence is to place the licence terms on the *outside* of the packaging, so that they are available for inspection by customers in the store prior to ordering. This is usually unacceptable for marketing reasons, which only confirms that the supplier is not sufficiently concerned in these cases to characterize the supply as a licence rather than a sale. It is to be remembered that, from the supplier's point of view, it may not be worth going to the effort of imposing licence conditions on the consumer; the protection of the supplier from the general law of copyright may be enough — the supplier does not lose any rights in the software by selling copies of it, any more than a publisher or novelist loses any rights to a novel by selling copies of the book.

The main reasons for attempting to impose licence conditions include:

- as warranty protection — suppliers always wish to limit their liability for any effects in the software to the maximum extent allowed by law, although the ability to do this is severely circumscribed in many countries in respect of supply to consumers;

- to control the use of software — forbidding loans, use in a bureau and re-sale, although these restrictions have a certain unreality about them in shrinkwrap licences; and

- to provide terms under which the software can be returned as a result of defects.

It is interesting to note that certain American states, faced with the problems of enforceability of shrinkwrap licences have introduced legislation to ensure that the terms of such licences are binding on the parties.

Finally, shrinkwrap licences can create further special problems. In standard distribution systems, the software product may pass through the hands of a wholesaler and a retailer before reaching the 'licensee' — and nearly all the distribution arrangements will refer to sales, quite inconsistently with the supposed licence at the end of the chain. As none of the intermediaries can be described as an 'agent' in law, and the licensor does not even receive the licence fee, kept by the retailer as receipts from a 'sale', then how can a licence result? In addition, there can be difficult tax issues a yet unresolved in relation to 'licence fees', particularly in relation to international transactions. For example, in taxation law, licence fees and royalties are generally subject to withholding tax, in the country of payment, upon remission from the country of payment. However, all too often receipts from foreign distributions are treated as receipts from sales of goods, not subject to withholding tax, again in contradiction of the supposedly preferred characterization of the ultimate supply to the end user.

The example given below is essentially a shrinkwrap licence, although an additional section is provided to allow for execution by the licensee if possible. This form provides the basic materials for a licence agreement for a bigger software package.

We make the following comments upon this example:

(1)   Usually the first substantive provision in a licence is the term of the licence. For software which is licensed pursuant to a once only licence fee, a 99 year term is common; the granting of a 'perpetual licence' is discouraged, as in many countries it is argued, with considerable merit, that an owner who gives up his right to return of his goods has ceased to be an owner, in other words, a 'perpetual licence' is really a contradiction in terms, and such a transaction would in fact be a sale. The bigger the software system, the more likely that it will be licensed subject to a continuing right of use fee, usually an annual fee (although monthly fees are also quite common), in which case provisions for payment should be added, such as those discussed in the Boilerplate Clauses section, above.

(2)   Provision should always be included for a single back-up copy to be made, unless the user is supplied with a back-up copy as a term of the licence. In some countries with specific software legislation, the right to make a back-up copy is specifically permitted as an exception to the copyright restrictions, however, in the absence of such a statutory right, the making of a back-up copy is a direct breach of copyright and so the user will have no right to make any back-up copies unless that right is specifically granted in the licence.

In bigger software licences, even a statutory right to make a single back-up would be inadequate, and consideration should be given to granting the right to make multiple back-ups, as in the case of a 'multiple site' licence. Required levels of security in such cases will be different in each case; the appending of copyright notices identical to those on the original is essential to such a provision. Again, additional boilerplate clauses will be required for licences of larger software.

(3)   Usually, source code will not be licensed to the user, but if it is, strict security measures should be enforced by the provider. Again, the boilerplate clauses considered above will be appropriate, but additional provisions giving the software provider the right to enter premises to ensure that security measures are being adhered to may be reasonable.

(4)   It is reasonable to provide a warranty period during which faults arising from defective media will be corrected free of charge. Generally, warranties relating to 'defects' in the software are inappropriate, as no software can be described realistically as 'error free', and the customer should only be concerned that the software functions largely in accordance with the user documentation provided. Even these concerns are not appropriate in licences of small package software, as the products generally do comply with their documentation, and if they do not it is unrealistic to expect a supplier to make customized modifications for an individual user — the user should register with the supplier's support program and receive updates and enchancements as they are developed.

In bigger licences, also, warranty periods generally provide little value — they are generally inadequate on specifics of response times and so on, and are not even 'free' maintenance periods, as their cost must be 'built in' to the licence fee. The acquisition process or development agreement should provide for an acceptance period followed by a maintenance agreement (see C — Software Maintenance Agreements, below). No warranty can be a substitute for a properly negotiated support contract.

(5)   In bigger licences, the contract should provide for the installation of the software by the supplier, including permitting the supplier access on preferred days to carry out this task, and also allow the supplier to remove the software (and all copies) after termination of the licence, and perhaps to charge the user for the costs of removing the software.

(6)   Also in bigger software licences, patent and copyright indemnities protect the user from having to ensure that the provider has the right to provide the software. The development of software is usually a lengthy procedure and the copyright history of most programs could fill a small book. The user does not want to get involved in any fight over the copyright in a program, the user merely wants the right to continue to use the product should its supplier be found not to have had the right to grant the licence. In such a case, the user should be entitled to a right to require the supplier to obtain a licence for its continued use in the event that the supplier is found wanting, and only if this is not possible, the right to damages for the consequent disruption of business.

(7)   Again, in bigger systems, consideration may be given to an express right to transfer the software to a disaster recovery site, whether owned by the licensee or not, in the event that the licensed site becomes unavailable for any reason.

Example

Software Name: ....

Please complete the following and read the attached Terms and Conditions. Completion of and signing this form constitutes an agreement to take the Software named above on licence subject to the attached Terms and Conditions.

LICENSEE INFORMATION

Licensee Name: ....
Licensee Contact Name: ....
Address: ....

LICENSEE AGREEMENT

I have read, understood and agree to all the Terms and Conditions of this Licence Agreement as attached:

....

Licensee Signature

....

Name and Title

....

Date

TERMS and CONDITIONS

THIS LICENCE AGREEMENT IS ENTERED INTO BETWEEN [*name: Licensor*], THE OWNER OF ALL RIGHTS IN RESPECT OF THE SOFTWARE REFERRED TO ABOVE (HEREIN REFERRED TO AS 'LICENSOR') OF THE ONE PART AND YOU, THE LICENSEE, ON THE OTHER.

PLEASE READ THIS DOCUMENT CAREFULLY BEFORE USING THE LICENSOR SOFTWARE THE SUBJECT OF THIS LICENCE.

BY USING THE SOFTWARE, YOU AGREE TO BECOME BOUND BY THE TERMS OF THIS AGREEMENT, WHICH INCLUDES THE SOFTWARE LICENCE AND DISCLAIMER OF WARRANTY.

IF YOU DO NOT AGREE TO THE TERMS OF THIS AGREEMENT, DO NOT USE THE SOFTWARE AND PROMPTLY RETURN THE PACKAGE TO THE PLACE WHERE YOU OBTAINED IT FOR A FULL REFUND.

THIS DOCUMENT CONSTITUTES A LICENCE TO USE THE ENCLOSED SOFTWARE ON THE TERMS AND CONDITIONS APPEARING BELOW.

The computer program(s) referred to above, and related documentation and materials (herein collectively referred to as 'the Software') are licensed, not sold, to you for use only upon the terms of this licence, and Licensor reserves all rights not expressly granted to you. You own the disks on which these programs are originally or subsequently recorded or fixed, but Licensor retains ownership of all copies of the programs themselves.

1   Licence

This licence allows you to

    (a)   Use the Software only in conjunction with a single (1) CPU and solely as an end user (that is, for your own use and not for use by or for others, or for marketing or redistribution, alone or as a component of any other product, to any other person). You must enter into an additional licence agreement with Licensor and thereby obtain a further copy of the Software, before using the Software in conection with any other computer or central processing unit, including systems containing mulitiple central processing units, computer networks or emulations on a mainframe or minicomputer.

(b)   Instal the Software on a hard disk for use in accordance with this Agreement or alternatively, in the event that you do not have a hard disk system, to make one copy in machine readable form for back-up purposes. You must reproduce on the back-up copy the Licensor copyright notice and any other proprietary legends that were on the original copy supplied by Licensor. The Software is protected by copyright law. You are not authorized to make any copies of the Software, except as permitted by this paragraph.

(c)   Transfer the Software (including the back-up copy) and all rights under this licence to another party together with a copy of this Agreement provided you give Licensor written notice of the transfer and the other party reads and agrees the terms and conditions of this Agreement.

2   Restrictions

(a)   You may not market, distribute or transfer (other than in accordance with paragraph 1(c) above) any copy of the Software to others or electronically transfer the Software from one computer to another over a network, either on its own or with or as part of any other product or equipment, without an express distribution licence from Licensor. YOU MAY NOT MODIFY, ADAPT, TRANSLATE, RENT, LEASE, LOAN, SELL, DISTRIBUTE, NETWORK OR CREATE DERIVATIVE WORKS BASED UPON THE SOFTWARE OR ANY PART THEREOF.

(b)   The Software contains trade secrets and to protect them you may not decompile, reverse engineer, disassemble or otherwise reduce the Software to a humanly perceivable form. You agree not to divulge, directly or indirectly, any such trade secrets to any person, unless and until such trade secrets cease to be confidential, for any reason not your own fault.

3   Termination

This Licence is effective until terminated. The Licence will terminate automatically without notice from Licensor if you fail to comply with any provision of this License. Upon termination you must destroy the Software and all copies thereof. You may terminate this Licence at any time by destroying the Software and all copies thereof. Upon termination of this licence for any reason:

(a)   you shall have no right to refund of the whole or any part of the licence fees or other amounts paid for this licence and the Software licensed hereunder (except in the circumstances and expressly as provided in Section 6 below); and

(b)   you shall continue to be bound by the provisions of Section 2 above.
Termination shall be without prejudice to any rights Licensor may have as a result of breach of this Agreement.

4   Limited Warranty

Licensor warrants the diskettes in which the Software is recorded to be free from defects in materials and faulty workmanship under normal use for a period of ninety (90) days from the date of delivery as evidenced by a copy of the receipt. During this warranty period, Licensor will, at its option, repair or replace, free of charge, defective diskettes upon which the Software has been supplied (and if necessary restore the Software thereon) or refund the purchase price of the diskette at no charge to you, provided you return the faulty diskette with proof of purchase to Licensor, or an authorized Licensor Dealer, in the country where the Software was first supplied to you. Licensor shall have no responsibility to repair, replace or refund the purchase price of a diskette which, in Licensor's opinion, has been damaged by accident, abuse or misapplication, or as a result of service or modification by other than Licensor, or an authorized Licensor Dealer. All diskettes replaced under this warranty shall become the property of Licensor.

5   Disclaimer of Warranty, Limitation of Remedies

TO THE FULL EXTENT PERMITTED BY LAW, LICENSOR HEREBY EXCLUDES ALL CONDITIONS AND WARRANTIES, WHETHER IMPOSED BY STATUTE OR BY OPERATION OF LAW OR OTHERWISE, NOT EXPRESSLY SET OUT HEREIN. THE SOFTWARE IS PROVIDED 'AS IS' WITHOUT WARRANTY OF ANY KIND. LICENSOR DOES NOT WAR-RANT, GUARANTEE OR MAKE ANY REPRESENTATIONS REGARDING THE USE, OR THE RESULTS OF THE USE, OF THE SOFTWARE WITH RESPECT TO ITS CORRECTNESS, ACCURACY, RELIABILITY, CURRENT-NESS OR OTHERWISE. THE ENTIRE RISK AS TO THE RESULTS AND PERFORMANCE OF THE SOFTWARE IS ASSUMED BY YOU. IF THE SOFTWARE IS DEFECTIVE, YOU, AND NOT LICENSOR OR ITS DEALERS, DISTRIBUTORS, AGENTS OR EMPLOYEES, ASSUME THE ENTIRE COST OF ANY SERVICING, REPAIR OR CORRECTION THEREOF.

EXCEPT AS SPECIFICALLY SET FORTH IN THIS SECTION 5, LICENSOR MAKES NO EXPRESS OR IMPLIED WARRANTIES OR CON-DITIONS INCLUDING, WITHOUT LIMITATION, THE WARRANTIES OF MERCHANTABILITY OR FITNESS FOR A PARTICULAR PURPOSE, WITH RESPECT TO THE SOFTWARE. NO ORAL OR WRITTEN INFORMATION OR ADVICE GIVEN BY LICENSOR, ITS DEALERS, DISTRIBUTORS, AGENTS OR EMPLOYEES SHALL CREATE A WARRANTY OR IN ANY WAY INCREASE THE SCOPE OF THIS WARRANTY, AND YOU MAY NOT RELY ON ANY SUCH INFORMATION OR ADVICE.

IMPORTANT NOTE: Nothing in this Agreement is intended or shall be construed as excluding or modifying any statutory rights, warranties or conditions which are applicable to this Agreement or the Software supplied hereunder, and which by virtue of any national or state Fair Trading, Trade Practices or other consumer legislation may not be modified or excluded. If permitted by such legislation, however, Licensor's liability for any breach of any such warranty or condition shall be and is hereby limited to either:

(a)   the supply of such part of the Software licensed hereunder again; or

(b)   the correction of any defect in such part of the Software licensed hereunder

as Licensor at its sole discretion may determine to be necessary to correct the said breach.

EXCEPT AS SET OUT IN THIS SECTION 5, IN NO EVENT SHALL LICENSOR BE LIABLE FOR ANY SPECIAL, INCIDENTAL, INDIRECT OR CONSEQUENTIAL DAMAGES (INCLUDING, WITHOUT LIMITATION, DAMAGES FOR LOSS OF BUSINESS PROFITS, BUSINESS INTERRUP-TION, AND LOSS OF BUSINESS INFORMATION OR COMPUTER PRO-GRAMS), EVEN IF LICENSOR OR ANY LICENSOR REPRESENTATIVE HAS BEEN ADVISED OF THE POSSIBILITY OF SUCH DAMAGES.

Except as expressly set out in this Section 5, Licensor's maximum liability for damages arising under this Agreement shall be limited to the licence fees paid by you for that part of the Software supplied by Licensor hereunder which caused the damages or that is the subject matter of, or is directly related to, the cause of action.

6   General

This Agreement will be construed under the laws of the [*name country or state*]. This Agreement contains the entire Agreement between the parties hereto with respect to the subject matter hereof, and supersedes all prior agreements and/or understandings (oral or written). Failure or delay by Licensor in enforcing any right or provision hereof shall not be deemed a waiver of such provision or right with respect to the instant or any subsequent breach. If any provision of this Agreement shall be held by a court of competent jurisdiction to be contrary to law, that provision will be enforced to the maximum extent permissible, and the remaining provisions of this Agreement will remain in full force and effect.

C Software Maintenance Agreements

Usually it is desirable that the Software Maintenance Agreement be separate from the Licence Agreement but that the Agreements be executed together. A licensee of software requiring maintenance who fails to negotiate a sensible maintenance agreement prior to entering into the licence agreement and paying the licence fees, and losing his negotiating positions, is a fool to himself and a burden to others.

The commencement of the Maintenance Contract is usually at the end of any warranty period in the Licence Agreement, although in the previous section we indicated that there is no good reason for this as software warranties and software maintenance are different in nature.

Maintenance usually covers both the fixing of errors in the software and the provisions of enhancements. A definition of the maintenance to be provided may vary with each particular software package, and should be carefully negotiated to ensure that the description of the services is complete and appropriate, to avoid unexpected time and materials charges. In a similar vein, the parties should be quite clear as to the hours of provision of the services, and where they will be provided.

The types of maintenance provided vary. In some cases twenty-four hour a day help desk facilities are necessary; in others a response time to telephone enquiries of twenty-four hours may be sufficient.

A frequent dilemma of software maintenance agreements is whether the maintenance should be continued in respect of outdated versions of the software. On the one hand, the licensee does not wish to be forced to take new releases, particularly if there is a charge involved, if it is happy with the performance of an older, but stable, version. On the other hand, it is unreasonable to require the maintenance provider to keep numerous source codes (and programmers familiar with their idiosyncrasies). It is certainly reasonable to provide the user with a certain amount of time to make the changeover, by permitting one or two releases to intervene before the maintenance provider may advise of its intention not to continue maintenance.

Normally source code is not provided to the licensee. If source code has been provided, it is very important that the contract exempt the maintenance provider from any obligation to maintain software written or modified by the licensee and with which it is not necessarily familiar.

Travel costs and associated expenses may be an important issue, and, depending on the site of the CPU, the agreement may have to go into some detail about the standard of accommodation and sustenance permitted on-site service personnel.

It is highly desirable from the provider's point of view that it has the right to suspend the services in the event of non-payment by the user. If the provider's only remedy for non-payment is to terminate the contract and sue for breach, the provider may be loathe to do so, but a mere suspension which keeps the contract afoot allows much more flexibility.

In a periodic contract it is very desirable to include a clause causing the contract to roll over after the initial term expires. This may place the licensee at a disadvantage in becoming committed to a further year of service (and service fees) inadvertently, so the question of how much notice must be given if one side or the other later wishes to terminate the Agreement often arises.

Example

THIS AGREEMENT is made the   day   of 19
BETWEEN   of
                                            ('The Company') of the one part
AND   of
                                              ('the Client') of the other part

WHEREAS:

A   By Agreement dated   198 ('the Licence Agreement') the Client has been
         granted by the Company a licence to use software described in the Schedule thereto
         ('The Software') on the equipment ('the Designated Equipment') installed at
         certain premises ('the Installation Site') as set out in the Schedule hereto.

B   The Client wishes the Company to provide Maintenance Services (as hereinafter
         defined) in respect of the use of the Software at the Installation Site.

NOW THE PARTIES AGREE as follows:

1   COMMENCEMENT
         This Agreement shall commence on   198   (hereinafter 'the Commence-
         ment Date').

2   PERIOD

2.1   The initial period of this Agreement shall be one (1) year from the Commencement
         Date unless earlier terminated pursuant to the provisions of Clause 9 hereof.

2.2   At the end of the initial period this Agreement will continue in full force and effect
         from year to year until terminated pursuant to the provisions of Clause 6 hereof.

3   MAINTENANCE

3.1   For the purposes of this Agreement the term 'Maintenance Services' includes the
         provision of the following services:

         (a)   Delivery of updated versions and enhancement (if any) of the Software
                  according to specifications produced by the Company during the period of
                  this Agreement.

(b)   The investigation and, to the extent possible, correction by amendment to the Software, of any failure of the Software to comply with the Software Manuals as updated from time to time or as specifically set out in the Licence Agreement if and only if:

    (i)   any failure is demonstrable on the Designated Equipment at the Installation Site;

    (ii)   notice is given to the Company promptly after any such failure becomes known; and

    (iii)   the Software has been properly operated and kept up to date, and, subject to Clause 3.3, not modified by the Client.

(c)   On-site remedial support when issues cannot be resolved by telephone or modem support.

3.2   The Company shall during the continuance hereof provide Maintenance Services to the Client in respect of the use of the Software at the Installation Site and on the Designated Equipment.

3.3   In the event that the Software has been modified or adapted by the Client, or errors are determined to have arisen by reason of the Client's errors or negligence, the Company will use its best endeavours to maintain the Software, including the said modifications or adaptations and errors. The Company shall be entitled to charge the Client, at its then current standard rates for such services, for time spent in investigating or correcting any problem with the Software which is attributable to the said modifications, adaptations or errors. A charge will normally be made only when an unusually large amount of time is needed but any decision to levy a charge pursuant to this clause shall be at the sole discretion of the Company. As soon as the Company forms the view that it shall be entitled to charge the Client for services provided to this clause the Company shall immediately inform the Client of that view. No further services relating to the matters notified will be provided by the Company without the express authorization of the Client.

3.4   The Company agrees to respond whenever possible to all telephone calls placed by the Client to the Company within twenty-four (24) hours for the purpose of determining the nature of the Client's reported error. If the Company is unable to provide a solution to the Client at the time of the Company's initial response, the Company will notify the Client of an estimated correction date within seven (7) days after such initial response or the date on which the Company receives any error documentation requested by, whichever is later.

3.5   In the event that the Client fails to implement any updated version of the Software provided by the Company pursuant to Clause 3.1(a), and the Company subsequently offers to its clients or any of them a further updated version of the Software then the Company shall be entitled, unless it has agreed in writing to the contrary, to cease to provide support for the version of the Software then used by the Client by the giving of twenty-one days' notice at any time, whereupon the Client may by notice in writing to the Company terminate this Agreement at any time thereafter. In the event that the Client elects to terminate this Agreement pursuant to this Clause 3.5, the Client shall receieve from the Company a *pro rata* reimbursement of the Annual Maintenance Rate paid in respect of the then current year of service hereunder, less any deductions for monies outstanding, payable by the Client to the Company.

4   CHARGES

4.1   In return for the provision of Maintenance Services the Client shall make the following payments to the Company:

(a)   the current Annual Maintenance Rate set out in the Schedule hereto or as varied from time to time by the Company ('Maintenance Rate');

(b)   all travel costs and associated expenses incurred in the provision of such services to the Client at a location outside a radius of fifty (50) kilometres from any permanent office of the Company from time to time.

The Maintenance Rate shall be paid within fourteen (14) days of the execution of this Agreement by the Client, and thereafter on each anniversary of such date ('Anniversary'), and the Company shall have no obligation hereunder until receipt thereof. All other amounts payable hereunder shall be payable within fourteen days of the Company's invoice or as otherwise provided herein.

4.2   Prior to any Anniversary of the commencement date, the Company may by notice in writing to the Client vary the Maintenance Rate to be paid on that Anniversary and all subsequent Anniversaries unless further varied pursuant to the provisions hereof.

4.3   In the event that the Client requests the Company to make any updated version or enhancement compatible to the Client's computer system, and the Company agrees to provide such updated version or enhancement, the Client shall reimburse the Company's then current rates for such services.

5   EMPLOYMENT OFFERS
5.1   (a)   Each party agrees during a period from the date of this Agreement to twelve months after its completion or termination that it shall not, without the other party's prior agreement in writing, employ or engage on any other basis than herein or offer such employment or engagement to any of the other party's staff.

        (b)   Each party agrees that if it employs or engages any person contrary to the provisions of sub-clause (a) of this clause, a sum in liquidated damages shall be payable as compensation, which said sum shall be equal to fifty per cent of such person's *per annum* salary immediately prior to the time of leaving the employment of the relevant party.

6   SPECIAL TERMINATION PROVISIONS
6.1   In addition to any other right of the Company to terminate this Agreement pursuant to the terms hereof, the Company may terminate this Agreement or any part thereof by written notice to the Client if the Client's licence referred to in Recital A hereto is terminated in whole or in part for any reason.

6.2   In addition, this Agreement may be terminated at any time and for any reason, or for no reason, by either party by the giving of notice of termination not less than one (1) month prior to an Anniversary of the Commencement Date, whereupon the effective date of termination shall be the Anniversary following such notice.

6.3   In the event of termination of this Agreement pursuant to the provisions of this Clause, the Client shall not be entitled to any refund of any monies paid hereunder in respect of the services to be provided by the Company.

[*Insert Boilerplate Clauses.*]
SCHEDULE

1   The Software: Program Name:
        Current Version/Release No.:
2   Current Annual Charge for maintenance of the Software:
3   Installation Site:
4   Designated Equipment:
[*Insert Execution Clauses.*]

D Hardware Purchase Agreements

At a basic level a hardware purchase agreement may specify the price and the equipment to be brought. The vendor may be required to instal the hardware in which case the user will have to have a duty to provide suitable premises and generally dates binding on both sides will have to be specified. The contract may also provide for partial payments on staged delivery and installation.

Where possible the price should be fixed but in certain cases it may need to be subject to currency fluctuation. Normally the currency fluctuation will come into effect as the exchange rate varies by more than 2% or 5% from the date of the contract and the date of importation of equipment. A purchaser should always negotiate reciprocity before agreeing to this clause so that it gets the benefit of any exchange fluctuations in its favour as well as having to pay extra in the event of an adverse move in the exchange rate. In addition, currency fluctuation clauses should be sensible, they should relate to equipment actually imported which is affected by a currency fluctuation at the date of importation (one cannot rely on the importer paying at that time, but cannot be caught by a fluctuation occurring in a period of delay by the importer in payment), and not, as is so often the case in existing standard contracts which refer only to the exchange rate at the date of delivery, to equipment that has already landed or to fluctuations which occur after landing but before delivery.

It is normally preferable that any software be the subject of a separate agreement. A user has a licence to use the operating system software; this means that any purchaser of the user's hardware will need to obtain its own licence for the operating system software.

It is in the interest of the supplier not to part with title to hardware until payment in full has been received. Should a dispute arise and the purchase price not be paid, the supplier then has the right to repossess the machine. However, it is a general legal principle in many countries that, unless the contrary is expressly agreed, title in goods passes *on delivery, regardless of whether the purchase price has been paid.* So, if the contrary is not provided for in the purchase agreement, if the purchaser refuses to pay (or goes bankrupt), the supplier has no right to retrieve just cents in the dollar in full satisfaction of the debt, while the purchaser can resell the hardware at any price! For this reason, it is very sensible that the contract provide that title does not pass until the entire purchase price of the hardware has been paid. From the user's point of view 'possession can be nine tenths of the law' and a supplier may not wish to go to the trouble and expense of getting a court order for delivery up of the machine; but it is settled law that such clauses can be enforceable.

There is another aspect to this issue of title, frequently overlooked. It is a further implication of the general law in many countries that *risk* also passes on delivery. This means that if the goods are accidently damaged or destroyed, or stolen, the purchaser in possession of them will be responsible. It may have to pay for something of which it does not have the benefit! While a supplier will always wish for title to the goods to pass as late as possible, the supplier will try to have risk pass as early as possible. The user must take careful note of when risk passes and insure against loss from that point. Commonly, risk will pass from the moment of delivery of the computer to the user's site. This is a reasonable compromise as obviously the user will be in control of it from that time. In some cases a supplier will attempt to have risk pass from the moment it leaves the premises of the supplier. A good compromise is to have risk and title pass at the same time.

In common with the agreements discussed in this section it is important that any claims as to the performance of the hardware made by the supplier, in a response to tender, in meetings, correspondence or otherwise, be included in the contract (see A — Boilerplate Clauses, above, in regard to 'Entire Agreement' clauses). It may be possible, even, to annex brochures, if these can provide a measure performance of the contract.

Warranties may be more appropriate in hardware purchase agreements, as they may deal with the quality of materials and workmanship of physical components of the hardware, which may otherwise be chargeable items under a maintenance agreement. However, warranties cannot and should not seek to promise the fulfillment of the wishes of the purchaser; expectations of performance should be dealt with by the acquisition process, and appropriate (objectively measurable) acceptance tests (with retention of substantial payment until acceptance tests are passed). The 'sale of goods' warranties (warranties as to 'merchantability' and 'fitness for purpose', discussed in Chapter 7, above) should also be abandoned, in the interests of all parties, as they are virtually meaningless in the context of computer equipment.

Example _____

THIS AGREEMENT is made the   day of   19
BETWEEN   of
                                        ('the Company') of the
   one part

AND   of
                                                                    ('the Purchaser')
of the other part

WHEREAS:

The Company agrees to sell, and the Purchaser agrees to buy, the equipment referred to in the Schedule hereto (hereinafter referred to as 'the Equipment') upon and subject to the following terms and conditions.

1   Delivery
        The Company will deliver the Equipment to the Purchaser's premises in accordance with the Delivery Schedule set out in the Schedule hereto.

2   Title
2.1   Title to the Equipment and to each part thereof shall not be transferred to the Purchaser (or any financing institution facilitating the acquisition of the Equipment by the Purchaser) until the total purchase price and any other sums due to the Company under this Agreement, including any late payment charge payable hereunder, have been duly paid.
2.2   Payment shall be deemed not to have been made until after any moneys payable otherwise than by cash have been duly collected by the Company.
2.3   Unless and until such payment is so made, the Purchaser will hold the Equipment, and if any part thereof that has been damaged or destroyed and moneys received by the Purchaser in respect thereof, on trust for the Company.

3   Charges and Terms of Payment
3.1   The total purchase price specified in the Schedule hereto will be due and payable as follows:
        (a)   as to twenty per cent (20%) of the total purchase price on signing this contract; and
        (b)   as to eighty per cent (80%) of the total purchase price within seven (7) days of the date on which the Equipment is installed and accepted by the Purchaser as ready for use, such acceptance not to be unreasonably delayed or refused by the Purchaser, or in the event that the Company is of the opinion that such acceptance has been unreasonably delayed or refused, as thereafter notified by the Company to the Purchaser.
3.2   All other sums due to the Company are to be paid within fourteen (14) days of the date of Company's invoice therefor.
3.3   Prices include freight, in-transit insurance charges, customs clearance charges and other import duties and charges of any nature (if any are applicable to the Equipment or any part thereof), local delivery special handling, and any special packing requested by the Purchaser. These charges are estimated and the Company reserves the right to invoice the Purchaser in the event that actual amounts incurred exceed such estimates.
3.4   The Purchaser shall in addition pay all sales or other tax applicable to the acquisition of the Equipment by the Purchaser (if any), or shall provide evidence satisfactory to the Company of any exemption from such taxes.
3.5   In the event that the cost to the Company of any part of the Equipment is increased or decreased as a result of the prevailing selling exchange rate between the [*specify country of origin of Equipment*] and the [*specify country of importation of Equipment*] currencies fluctuating in excess of two per cent (2%) from the rates specified in the Schedule hereto at the time payment is made for such part of the Equipment (provided that it is within a reasonable time after importation of such part of the Equipment), the Company shall be entitled to adjust the prices payable by the Purchaser therefor in accordance with such currency fluctuations, or the Purchaser shall be entitled to require such adjustment accordingly.

4   Site Preparation and Installation

4.1   Prior to delivery, a Company representative shall attend the locations(s) at which the Equipment is to be installed and shall inform the Purchaser of the Company specifications for installation of the Equipment. The Purchaser at its expense will in accordance with such Company specifications prepare its premises for installation of the Equipment and provide all installation facilities, including but not limited to space, electrical power, cable troughs, special cables and connector requirements, communications modems, fittings and the like. On completion of such preparations required by the Company (if any), if requested to do so by the Purchaser and at the Company's expense a Company representative shall visit such location(s) once only and if the location(s) are suitable for installation of the Equipment shall so certify to the Purchaser. In the event further preparation is required, which was specified in the original recommendation of the Company, the Purchaser shall pay the Company's reasonable charges and expenses for all further visits required to complete such certification.

4.2   Prior to delivery of the Equipment (or any part thereof), the Company shall notify the Purchaser of the proposed date of delivery (which shall be during business hours on a business day). Upon delivery, the Purchaser will provide access to its premises and the Company will instal the said part of the Equipment. The installing service provided by the Company will consist of the Company standard procedures and standard Test and Verification routines. Any additional installing service requested by the Purchaser or caused by the Purchaser failing to meet its obligations hereunder will be subject to the Company's then current pricing policies and rates or charges.

4.3   A request by the Purchaser for installation service at a location outside a radius of fifty (50) kilometres from the nearest Company Field Engineering Division or State Capital City office will be subject to the Company's then current Remote Location policies and charges.

4.4   If installation of the Equipment by the Company representatives is precluded by local law, union agreement or otherwise, the Company will supervise the installation and the Purchaser will bear any additional costs caused thereby.

5   Software Products

        The supply of any Software Products by the Company to the Purchaser for use with the Equipment shall be subject to the execution by the Purchaser and the Company of a Licence Agreement in a form satisfactory to the Company, and to the terms, conditions and charges thereof.

6   Documentation and Maintenance Material

6.1   The Company shall provide and supply free of charge all documentation applicable to and normally supplied with the Equipment which shall include a complete set of operator's instructions, installation guide and diagnostic software and any other items specified separately in other documents forming attachments to this Agreement.

6.2   Title to all applicable rights in patents, copyrights, trademarks and trade secrets in all documentation and the information contained therein shall remain with the Company. The Purchaser agrees to (a) protect the Company's rights in all such documentation in a manner consistent with the maintenance of patent, copyright, trademark and trade secret rights, as applicable; (b) not copy such documentation in whole or in part; (c) use the documentation in the Purchaser's data processing operations only; and (d) not sell, transfer, or otherwise make the documentation available to others.

6.3   The Purchaser agrees to make all such documentation readily available at the Purchaser's facilities to the Company service personnel upon request.

6.4   The Company will at all times retain title to all spare parts until incorporated into the Equipment, all tools, and all computer program media and the Company may remove or discontinue usage thereof, as applicable, at any time.

6.5   All the Company test, diagnostic and verification information and routines (on Company or Purchaser owned media), maintenance equipment and maintenance materials, information and documentation are proprietary and confidential items, whether on the Purchaser's premises or accessible by remote enquiry, and are and shall remain the property of the Company and may be removed, or usage thereof discontinued, as applicable, by the Company at any time, or the Purchaser will destroy same upon written request from the Company. The Purchaser agrees to treat and protect such proprietary and confidential items in a manner consistent with the maintenance of trade secret rights and to take appropriate action by instruction to or agreement with its employees who are permitted access thereto to satisfy its obligations hereunder.

7   Liability for Loss or Damage

7.1   The Company will maintain insurance of the Equipment during the period the Equipment is in transit and until the date delivery is made.

7.2   Delivery shall be deemed to be made when the Equipment is delivered to the Purchaser's premises as listed in the Schedule hereto.

7.3   The risk in the Equipment shall pass to the Purchaser upon delivery. The Purchaser accepts the responsibility for insurance from that time, notwithstanding that the Purchaser does not become the owner of the Equipment until payment in full has been made.

7.4   Until final payment is made in accordance with Clause 3 above, the Purchaser shall not move any part of the Equipment from the location to which it was delivered by the Company; nor shall it sell or contract to sell, mortgage, charge, lease, or otherwise dispose of the same or part with possession of the same or suffer or permit any lien or distress to be exercised or levied thereon.

8   Warranty

8.1   The Company warrants the Equipment shall be new and free of any encumbrances and that it is authorized to sell the Equipment, and indemnifies the Purchaser in respect of any losses, costs or damages, which may arise as a result of any default on the part of the Company pursuant to the provision of this sub-Clause.

8.2   The Company warrants that upon payments in accordance with Clause 3 above, the Purchaser will acquire good title to the Equipment.

8.3   These warranties are conditional upon the proper use of the Equipment for the purpose for which it was designed and in accordance with the information supplied and do not cover goods which have been subjected to an unreasonable degree of stress or from or on which the original identification marks have been removed or altered.

9   Default of Purchaser

9.1   Default of Purchaser occurs upon:

(a)   non-payment or non-performance of any obligation of the Purchaser under this Agreement and the continuance of such non-payment or non-performance for a period of twenty-one (21) days after the due date for payment or performance hereunder.

(b)   the Purchaser or any guarantor or surety for the Purchaser being wound up, or otherwise than voluntarily for the purpose of amalgamation or reconstruction, becoming insolvent or bankrupt, having a receiver of its property or assets or any of them appointed, having an official manager appointed, making or offering to make any assignment for the benefit of creditors, entering or offering to enter into a deed or scheme of arrangement or composition with creditors or if any proceedings under any bankruptcy or liquidation or insolvency laws are commenced by or against the Purchaser or any guarantor or surety for the Purchaser.

9.2   If the Purchaser defaults, the Company will have the right to exercise any one or more of the following remedies:

(a)   to declare all unpaid charges to be immediately due and payable;

(b)   to require the Purchaser to make available all documentation and to assemble such parts of the Equipment provided hereunder which have not been paid for in full and to make the same available at a time and place reasonably convenient to the Company;

(c)   to take possession without demand or notice (the right to demand or notice the Purchaser hereby expressly waives) of all parts of the Equipment and documentation, wherever located, as yet not fully paid for by the Purchaser;

(d)   to sell, lease or otherwise dispose of the Equipment publicly or privately;

(e)   to terminate this Agreement in whole or in part; and/or

(f)   to pursue any other remedies existing at law or in equity.

9.3   In addition to any other payment obligations hereunder, the Purchaser agrees to pay to the Company all costs and expenses including reasonable legal fees and costs, incurred by the Company in exercising any of its rights or remedies.

[Insert Boilerplate Clauses.]

SCHEDULE

Equipment Purchased: Price:

Exchange Rate:

Delivery Schedule:

Delivery Locations: (Purchaser's premises)

[Insert Execution Clauses.]

E Equipment Loan Agreements

It is a regrettably commonplace practice in the computer industry to lend equipment without recording the terms of the loan. Subsequent disputes as to the return of such equipment, or its care during the period of loan, are also common.

At law, the purpose of a loan, or 'bailment', may govern rights to demand its return, and the responsibilities of the bailee to care for the equipment. For example, if the equipment is lent in return for some benefit received from the borrower, then there may be implied restrictions on the right to have it returned, and the borrower has a very low responsibility for its care and maintenance.

The purpose of the example given below is to show that a brief document can deal with these issues in a simple manner. Naturally, in the case of more substantial 'loans', such as leases or supply for a longer term in return for a fee, the terms of the contract should be much more substantial, including many of the terms of the Hardware Purchase Agreement and boilerplate clauses considered above, and insofar as installation and implementation of a solution is concerned, development and acceptance provisions referred to below in the sample Installation and Implementation Agreement.

Example

The Company will lend and ship to the Customer the equipment identified and described in Schedule 'A' hereto ('the Equipment'). The Customer's use of such Equipment will be for the following limited purposes only:

[*Here specify purpose of loan.*]
from the date hereof to _____ / _____ / _____ .
The disposition of the Equipment will be governed by the following provisions:

(a)   The Equipment
        The parties agree that the equipment mentioned in this section shall consist of the items listed on Annexure 'A', as amended from time to time (the 'Equipment'). The Customer confirms that it has or will have possession of the Equipment on a 'loan-for-use' basis. The Customer will therefore not use or allow the Equipment to be used in any way except for the above purposes and will allow the Company to remove the Equipment from the Customer's custody or control and will do whatsoever else is necessary to ensure that the 'loan-for-use' character of the

Equipment is preserved and is made known to the Customer's creditors if any claim to the Equipment is or might be asserted by a creditor.

(b)   Return of Equipment
The Customer will return the Equipment lent to it by the Company hereunder forthwith upon

(i)   the completion of the above purposes;

(ii)   the termination of this Agreement for any reason; or

(iii)   the Company's written request to return the Equipment;

The Equipment shall be returned so far as possible in its original packaging, and in the same condition (subject to fair wear and tear) as it is delivered. Any material supplied with the Equipment, including programs and data on magnetic storage media, internal and external, and documentation shall be returned without alteration.

(c)   Ownership, Risk, Maintenance and Other Costs
The Equipment shall at all times remain the property of the Company but all risk of loss and/or damage to the Equipment shall be borne by the Customer and the Customer shall insure the Equipment accordingly. The Customer shall at all times maintain the Equipment in good working order and condition, and shall not subject it to adverse electronic or environmental conditions as indicated in the operating manuals accompanying such equipment. All costs of shipment and handling including reasonable casualty insurance incurred in connection with the return of such Equipment shall be borne by the Company (and shall be pre-paid in connection with the return thereof).

SCHEDULE
THE EQUIPMENT

Product No.	Description	Serial No.

ACCEPTED AND AGREED FOR AND ON BEHALF OF CUSTOMER BY
Name:
Title/Position:

F   Hardware Maintenance Agreements

In the process of acquisition of major hardware items, such as mini-computers, which centralize processing power and increase dependence upon a few items of equipment, the reliability of the equipment will, no doubt, have been considered. Most suppliers are able to supply information, such as median uptime and mean time between failures, which can assist in that evaluation.

The decision as to whether a maintenance agreement should be entered into at all, or whether it is more economical to rely on the provision of services on a 'time and materials' basis, may also be made on the basis of such information. Normally, the decision to enter into a maintenance arrangement will be justified, particularly in the case of hardware critical to the continued operation of an organization, as a form of insurance to ensure rapid recovery of malfunctioning equipment.

In such a case, it is particularly important that the hardware maintenance agreement genuinely provide that level of assurance, and such an objective provides the basis for a decision as to the provisions which should be found in the contract. For example, consideration may be given to extending the hours of availability of part or all of the services, guaranteed availability of a complete inventory of spare parts near to, or actually on, the installation site (including expensive and highly reliable components), maximum response times to emergency 'system down' calls or, in the case of maintenance provided by a manufacturer, carefully devised formulae for maximum downtime of a certain percentage over any given 'window' of time taking into account only critical components of an installation, such as the CPU. All or some of these possibilities may be available, at a cost which will be determined by their need.

Precisely what services, and spare parts, are included in the periodical charge, should be clearly defined. Normally maintenance will be both preventative and remedial and this should be made clear in the agreement. It is difficult sometimes to decide whether preventative maintenance should be compulsory, or discretionary to the maintenance provider. However, it should be remembered that typically electrical components do not require a high degree of preventative care (provided the equipment is located in a dust free and otherwise clean environment), whereas mechanical components, such as print heads, may require more regular attention to avoid catastrophic failure.

Facility for a change in the actual hardware must be included in the maintenance agreement; it is relatively unlikely that a user will keep precisely the same system for years, which may be the term of the maintenance agreement. Of course, any change in configuration may require a different monthly charge which should be catered for. In such a case, the user should perhaps be prevented from altering its configuration to the extent that it has no equipment left to maintain — as this would amount to *de facto* termination, allowing the user to escape its obligation to pay maintenance charges.

It will normally be an important provision as far as the maintenance provider is concerned, that the user not be allowed to carry out any of its own maintenance.

A point of contention between user and service provider will be obsolete equipment. The provider will have the power to decide whether it will no longer maintain certain equipment as it becomes 'obsolete'; as equipment ages and there are less and less users of that equipment it gets harder and harder to obtain spare parts and the technical expertise necessary to carry out repairs. However, the user should be cautious in evaluating these provisions in a contract, as they may enable the supplier to force the user to abandon quite serviceable equipment in order to purchase a newer and more expensive system.

A similar area of contention concerns the continuation of service of a part or the whole of a system by a manufacturer when third party peripheral equipment is added. Frequently, an equipment supplier will have a vested interest in the provision of added peripheral equipment, as the initial system sale may have been significantly discounted in the face of competitive tenders, the supplier anxious to realize higher margins on the later sale of add-on equipment to a user it believes to have little alternative. On the other hand, there may be genuine technical difficulties involved in the addition of third party equipment, and the source of the difficulties, and the resulting costly and unanticipated demand on the maintenance services, can be unusually difficult to determine.

Finally, a maintenance provider may wish to supervise any movement of equipment. The provider will not wish to be responsible for any problems which arise as a result of a relocation of equipment, and it may be wise for the user to ensure that the provider cannot escape any of its responsibilities by making the provider responsible for the move as well.

Example ————————————————————————————————

THIS AGREEMENT is made the   day
of   19

BETWEEN   of
                                                          ('the Company') of the
        one part
AND   of
                                                             ('the Client') of
        the other part
WHEREAS:

The Company has agreed to provide and the Client agrees to accept and pay for
Maintenance Service for the Equipment specified in the Schedule hereto ('the Equipment')
only at the location(s) specified in the Schedule ('the Equipment Location') upon and
subject to the following terms and conditions:

1   Term
        The Term of this Agreement shall commence on the date of execution by the
        Company ('the Commencement Date') and shall continue for a period of one (1)
        year from the Commencement Date ('the Initial Term'), and thereafter shall
        continue until terminated by not less than ninety (90) days' written notice by either
        party to the other.

2   Maintenance Service
2.1   Unless otherwise agreed by the Company in writing, the Company shall provide
        the Maintenance Service eight (8) hours per day between 9.00 a.m. and 5.00 p.m.,
        Monday to Friday inclusive but excluding public holidays in the place of the
        Equipment Location ('the Maintenance Period').
2.2   The Maintenance Services to be provided under this Agreement shall conform with
        the following:
        (a)   the Company shall make all repairs and adjustments necessary to keep the
                Equipment in good working order;
        (b)   any Maintenance services provided by the Company include the supply
                and cost of all labour and all spare parts and maintenance items other than
                where service is necessary due to operator error;
        (c)   the Equipment shall be repaired, adjusted, modified and altered only by
                skilled and accredited representatives of the Company who are familiar
                with the Equipment and who have completed successfully the manufactur-
                er's maintenance training in relation to equipment of the same type as the
                Equipment;
        (d)   remedial Maintenance as a result of failure of the Equipment shall be
                performed at all times during the Maintenance Period upon notification
                by the Client that the Equipment or any part of the Equipment is
                inoperative or malfunctioning;
        (e)   preventative Maintenance as considered necessary by the Company and
                designed to keep the Equipment in good working order shall be performed
                at a mutually agreeable time during the Maintenance Period; and
        (f)   preventative Maintenance shall include any adjustments necessary to
                correct problems which are suffered by other customers of the Company
                and which do or could occur in the Equipment as the Company considers
                necessary
        provided that the Company first notifies Client of the work to be carried out under
        this clause and receives written authorization to enter the Equipment Location and
        proceed.

3   Preventative Maintenance
        In addition to the foregoing, the following provisions shall apply to Preventative
        Maintenance:

(a) the Company shall provide Preventative Maintenance during the Maintenance Period at the Equipment Location at service intervals determined by the Company to effect appropriate repairs and adjustments designed to maintain the Equipment in good working order; and

(b) the Company may request access to the Equipment for the purpose of making technical modifications at no additional charge which it considers desirable for the present or future operation of the Equipment and the Client shall provide access to the Company within fourteen (14) days after the Company notifies the Client that it requires access to the Equipment for such purposes.

4   Remedial Maintenance
In addition to the foregoing, the Company shall provide Remedial Maintenance during the Maintenance Period at the Equipment Location in response to requests it receives from the Client to remedy Equipment malfunctions reported by the Client or located by the Company pursuant to Preventive Maintenance.

5   Exclusions from Maintenance Service
5.1   The Company is not responsible under this Agreement for:

(a) the provision, renewal or maintenance of consumable items supplies, accessories, attachments and any equipment not specified in the Schedule hereto; and

(b) modification of or addition to the Equipment or the configuration of the Equipment made by the Client for any reason or under any separate agreement with the Company, software maintenance, and any costs or services associated with the relocation of equipment.

5.2   The Company is not responsible for providing maintenance to the Equipment if maintenance is required or damage to or malfunction of the Equipment is caused for any of the following reasons:

(a) if the Equipment has been modified or tampered with or the Equipment configuration is altered without the written approval of the Company;

(b) accident, neglect, misuse, operator error, variations and surges of electrical power, fusion, fire, air conditioning malfunction, damage caused in transportation, act of God or any cause other than a cause arising from normal use of the Equipment and not caused or contributed to by any employee or agent of the Company;

(c) maintenance or repair by persons other than authorized Company personnel or agents;

(d) if the Equipment is removed from its place of installation or the Equipment Location is otherwise than in compliance with Clause 7 below;

(e) any improper use of the Equipment including the use of media, consumables or components, failure to comply with the Company specifications, failure to use specified operating supplies or failure to comply with operating instructions by any person other than an employee or agent of the Company;

(f) failure of the Client to maintain proper environmental conditions including air conditioning for the storage and use of the Equipment;

(g) if maintenance to the Equipment is required due to the breach by the Client of any of its obligations contained in this Agreement;

(h) unreasonable refusal to grant to the Company permission to enter the Equipment Location or gain access to the Equipment during the Maintenance Period within a reasonable time after request being made therefor by the Company.

The Client acknowledges that maintenance, if provided by the Company to remedy equipment malfunctions caused by any of the matters specified in this Clause, shall be paid for by the Client at the Company's then prevailing rates for labour and materials.

6   Obligations of the Client

6.1   At all reasonable times and provided the Company has sought and obtained permission of the Client in advance, the Client grants the Company a licence to enter the Equipment Location and access to the Equipment and necessary documentation during the Maintenance Period for the purpose of Maintenance Service.

6.2   The Client shall provide working space and facilities, including heat, ventilation, electric current and outlets for use by the Company, adequate storage for spare parts, and access to equipment, attachments and features requested by the Company.

6.3   The Client shall maintain and record such operating information and usage records as may be reasonably requested by the Company from time to time.

6.4   The Client shall promptly notify the Company of any malfunctions in the Equipment.

6.5   The Client will operate the Equipment in accordance with the Company operating instructions and operator's maintenance and diagnostic routines and use operating supplies specified by the Company.

6.6   Except for the operator's maintenance routines specified in Clause 6.5 herein, the Client will not allow any person other than the Company authorized personnel to repair, maintain or tamper with the Equipment.

6.7   The Client shall comply with all reasonable directions of the Company from time to time concerning appropriate environmental conditions including air conditioning for the operation of the Equipment.

7   Movement of the Equipment

7.1   The Client shall provide the Company with at least thirty (30) days' written notice of its intention to move the Equipment to another location.

7.2   If requested by the Client the Company shall provide its services for the dismantling removal and reinstallation of the Equipment at the new location and the Client shall pay the Company for its services herein at its then current rates for such work.

7.3   If the Equipment is moved and installed at another location by persons other than the Company authorized personnel then the Company shall not be responsible for providing its maintenance services for the Equipment unless the Company is satisfied that the Equipment is in proper operating condition at the new location. Any work conducted by the Company to restore the Equipment to operating condition shall be charged to the Client at the Company's then current rates for such work.

7.4   The Company reserves its rights to revise the monthly Maintenance Charge applicable to Equipment moved to a new location.

7.5   In the event that the location of the Equipment is changed in accordance with this Clause then the new location shall be deemed to be the Equipment Location for all purposes under this Agreement.

8   Variation to Monthly Maintenance Charge

8.1   The charges hereunder have been calculated by reference to the Equipment specified in the Schedule hereto at the date hereof and in the event that Equipment or parts thereof are replaced or removed from service or additional equipment is added, subject to the following sub-Clause 8.2 such charges may be adjusted by the Company accordingly by the giving of sixty (60) days' written notice of such changes to the Client. In any event, the modified charges shall not exceed those imposed by the Company on other of its clients in a situation similar to that of the Client.

8.2   In the event that the Client at any time wishes to remove part of the Equipment from maintenance coverage or amend or alter the Equipment specified in the Schedule hereto, the parties agree that they shall use their best endeavours to agree on the charge applicable to the Equipment as altered or replaced and terms upon which the Company will continue to provide its Maintenance Service. The Company will not be obliged to provide Maintenance Service if the Equipment is amended, altered or replaced and the Client fails or refuses for any reason to pay the charges for the Maintenance Services modified in accordance with this Clause.

8.3   The Client shall at all times give the Company at least ninety (90) days written notice of its intention to remove any Equipment from the Maintenance Service and shall continue to pay the charge applicable to the said Equipment until the expiration of the said ninety (90) day period. The Client shall not by exercise of its rights hereunder be entitled to diminish its liability in respect of such charges by more than fifty percent (50%) until after the conclusion of the Initial Term.

8.4   In addition to its other rights under this Agreement, the Company shall be entitled to increase the charges payable hereunder upon the giving of ninety (90) days' written notice to the Client, provided however that during the Initial Term, such charges may be increased only to cover increased costs to the Company in the provision of its services herein including the cost to the Company of obtaining spare parts.

8.5   Equipment installed at a location greater than a radius of fifty (50) kilometres from the nearest Field Engineering Office of the Company is subject to the Remote Equipment Maintenance Surcharge specified in the Schedule hereto.

8.6   The Company shall, if requested to do so by the Client, use reasonable commercial endeavours to provide the Maintenance Service at hours outside the Maintenance Period and the said Maintenance Service shall be paid for by the Client at the then current Company overtime rates for labour and materials including travelling time to and from the Equipment Location.

8.7   In the event that there is any reduction of the charges payable hereunder as a result of the provisions of this Clause 8, the Client shall not be entitled to any refund of any moneys paid prior to the date of such reduction, including without limitation any prepaid charges for the Maintenance Services.

9   Equipment Obsolescence

9.1   The Company may at any time during the term hereof but after the Initial Term withdraw the Maintenance Service in respect of any part of the Equipment which it deems in its sole discretion to be obsolete, provided at least ninety (90) days' written notice is given to the Client.

9.2   Without limiting the generality of the foregoing, the following matters shall be taken into account by the Company in determining whether to exercise its rights hereunder:

(a)   if spare parts for the Equipment become unavailable or difficult to obtain;

(b)   if the Company determines that maintenance of the Equipment is no longer reasonably practicable by virtue of its operating condition;

(c)   if the Equipment has been operating for a period in excess of five (5) years of single shift use or equivalent. 'Single Shift Use' means operation for only eight (8) hours per day on business days.

9.3   If, following the Initial Term, the Company determines that the Equipment has become obsolete pursuant to the terms hereof, or that for any other reason extensive refurbishment and overhaul is required to the Equipment, the Company shall serve a notice in writing on the Client with its estimate of the refurbishment required and the estimated cost thereof and unless the Client undertakes within thirty (30) days of the date of the said notice that it will (whether with the Company or otherwise) contract for the refurbishing estimated by the Company on terms satisfactory to the Company, the Company shall be under no further obligation to maintain the Equipment.

9.4   In the event that there is any reduction of the charges payable hereunder or suspension of the Maintenance Services as a result of the provisions of this Clause 9, the Client shall be entitled to a refund of a proportion of any prepaid charges for the Maintenance Services in respect of any part of the Equipment removed from the Maintenance Services hereunder.

10   Insurance

The Client acknowledges that the Equipment after the date of initial installation at the Equipment Location is at all times at the Client's risk whether the Equipment is at the premises of the Client, the premises of the Company, or the Company's agents or in transit and it is the Client's responsibility to effect all necessary insurance to the Equipment.

11   Documentation and Maintenance Material

11.1   The Company shall provide and supply free of charge all documentation applicable to and normally supplied with the Equipment which shall include a complete set of operator's instructions, installation guide and diagnostic software and any other items specified separately in other documents forming attachments to this Agreement.

11.2   Title to all applicable rights in patents, copyrights, trademarks and trade secrets in all documentation and the information contained therein shall remain with the Company. Client agrees to (a) protect the Company rights in all such documentation in a manner consistent with the maintenance of patent, copyright, trademark and trade secret rights, as applicable; (b) not copy such documentation in whole or in part; (c) use the documentation in the Client's data processing operations only; and (d) not sell, transfer or otherwise make the documentation available to others.

11.3   Client agrees to make all such documentation readily available at the client's facilities to the Company service personnel upon request.

11.4   The Company will at all times retain title to all spare parts until incorporated into the Equipment, all tools, and all computer program media and the Company may remove or discontinue usage thereof, as applicable, at any time. In addition, all the Company test, diagnostic and verification information and routines (on Company or Client owned media), maintenance equipment and maintenance materials, information and documentation are proprietary and confidential items, whether on the Client's premises or accessible by remote enquiry, and are and shall remain the property of the Company and may be removed, or usage thereof discontinued, as applicable, by the Company at any time or the Client will destroy some upon written request from the Company. The Client agrees to treat and protect such proprietary and confidential items in a manner consistent with the maintenance of trade secret rights and to take appropriate action by instruction to or agreement with its employees who are permitted access thereto to satisfy its obligations hereunder.

[Insert boilerplate clauses.]

SCHEDULE

The Equipment
The Equipment Location
The Charges
[Insert Execution Clauses.]

G   Installation and Implementation Agreements

The installation and 'implementation' of major software systems can be a complex and protracted operation, involving the installer in a diversity of tasks, including coding, training, design of forms, advising on procedures, dealing with third parties (such as telecommunications authorities, and the suppliers of hardware or software components), data capture and verification and testing. A large part of these services will be provided on the client's premises, and will involve access to most sensitive confidential information. Surprisingly, this aspect of the supply/acquisition process is relatively rarely the subject of a complete contract — a contract as much in the interests of the supplier as the client.

The example given below provides a framework within which installation and implementation may be regulated by both parties. The Agreement itself does not envisage any particular services being performed, it provides for individual service authorizations to be obtained by the supplier for each activity, which necessitates that the nature and extent of the activity, and its cost, can be considered and specifically approved in each case. Of course, specific provisions relating to sufficiently foreseen requirements of the installation may be provided for in the contract and, even better, there may be a complete project plan and specification for the completed project — in this case, the contract may come to look more like the Development Agreement considered in the next sample contract. However, it is commonly the case in these situations that the implementation work is very much a 'moving target', as the nature and perceived needs of the client organization develop and change with time and experience of the new software/hardware system, so the framework provided by the following example remains of value.

In general, the success of this system depends upon the existence of a project team from the client's organization that has the ability, and the authority, to consider requests for service authorizations and to decide upon them.

We make the following specific comments in relation to the example given:

1   There is no particular reason to limit the term of this Agreement,

as the Agreement will be effective only so long as there are service authorizations in effect. It is envisaged that the particular service authorizations will contain any applicable time limits. The only factor relevant to the term of the Agreement is that the Agreement cannot be terminated while there are service authorizations in effect.

2   Charges for particular services will be negotiated with each service authorization but it will usually be convenient for all concerned if the provider's standard charges are known and form the basis of any negotiation. The provider will wish to retain the ability to suspend services, rather than cancel them if bills are not paid, and to charge interest on overdue amounts.

3   It may well be that the service provider merely provides a person or a number of people to, for instance, supplement the client's existing DP staff and there must be a fundamental distinction between projects for which the provider is acting as project manager and taking responsibility for completion and projects where the provider is merely providing staff who will perform to the best of their ability.

4   As already observed, the provider's staff will have access to much confidential information of the client, including possibly details of employees' terms of employment, customers, future business plans and other matters. A confidentially provision is most important to the client, so that its data and other information will be kept secret by the provider's staff.

5   The provider will generally wish to retain the flexibility to determine which actual members of its staff provide the services and the client will generally not be in a position to demand any contract be performed only by certain nominated provider employees. However, the client will be anxious that any provider employees who fail to comply with its rules of conduct on its premises (such as the wearing of security identification, smoking, eating or drinking in the work area and so on), or who enter areas of the premises forbidden to them or otherwise engage in misconduct, including perhaps poor work standards, may be removed from the client's premises.

6   The crux of the service authorization is a statement which is as specific as possible as to the services actually to be performed. The actual style of a service authorization will depend upon the kind of services to be provided.

7   The mechanism proposed in the service authorization given in this example provides reimbursement of the provider's costs but allows the client a chance to rethink if it becomes obvious that

there will be cost overruns. As soon as it appears that the estimates are not going to be met, the client may terminate the services but remains liable for services incurred up to the termination.

8   Depending upon the size of the project, the service provider may be in a position to demand that minimum charges be set out. This will be important particularly in large projects where decisions will need to be made constantly by the client, whilst the provider has waiting an employee ready, willing and dedicated to work on the client's project. If the client delays, the provider's dedicated staff member may sit idly, so the provider should be able to charge the client for that staff member's time, notwithstanding the absence of any results.

Example

THIS AGREEMENT is made the   day of   19
BETWEEN   of
                                                          ('the Company') of the one part
AND   of
('the Client') of the other part

WHEREAS:
The Client has requested the Company to supply certain professional services in connection with the installation and implementation within the Client's organization of the System described in the Schedule hereto owned by and licensed to the Client and the Company has agreed to provide such services.

NOW THIS AGREEMENT WITNESSES as follows:

1   SERVICES
1.1   The Company shall provide to the Client certain services including, without limitation, the services of planning, installation, implementation and use of data processing products, making modifications to data processing products, programming and application design and development, systems analysis and design, conversion and implementation planning and training ('the Services') in relation to the System at the Client's locations specified in the Schedule, and as otherwise agreed from time to time under this Agreement.
1.2   The term 'Services' shall include all services authorized under a Service Authorization pursuant to Clause 7.

2   TERM
2.1   This Agreement is effective from the date on which it is accepted by the Company and shall remain in force until either party gives not less than three (3) months' notice of termination to the other. This Agreement may only be terminated when all Services authorized hereunder have been completed or have been terminated in accordance with the provisions of this Agreement.
2.2   Completion of any specific Services or of all Services authorized hereunder at any given time shall not terminate this Agreement.

3   CHARGES
3.1 , The Client agrees to pay the Company's charges for these Services in accordance with the rates and minimum charges which are specified in any applicable Service

Authorization, and for billable travel time of the Company personnel.

3.2   The rates, rate classification and minimum hours specified in any Service Authorization shall be in accordance with those set out in the Company Standard Rates published by the Company from time to time (the 'Standard Rates'). The Standard Rates are subject to change by the Company upon at least three (3) months' prior written notice to the Client.

4   CONTROL AND SUPERVISION

4.1   The Client activities in which the Company personnel assist shall be the responsibility of and shall remain under the supervision, management and control of, the Client.

4.2   All Company personnel shall obey the rules of conduct, the operating procedures for the System and the work to be carried out hereunder and the reasonable and lawful directions of the Client's responsible officers whilst on the premises. The Client shall be entitled to direct that any employee or contractor of the Company shall leave its premises, or require the Company to remove such employee or contractor, because of a failure to comply with such rules, procedures or directions, or any of them, in which case the Client shall forthwith notify the Company, advising of the reason for such requirement, and requesting a replacement. The Company shall as soon as practicable thereafter provide a replacement for the employee or contractor removed from the Client's premises. Any exercise by the Client of its rights under this paragraph 4.2 shall not be deemed a breach or repudiation of this Agreement, or a notice of termination (unless the Client so advises the Company pursuant to Clause 2 above), nor shall such exercise entitle the Client to withhold or abate payment of any fees or charges under any Service Authorization hereunder.

5   CONFIDENTIALITY

5.1   At no time shall any Company employee or contractor enter any premises or part of any premises of the Client, except the Locations (except to use permitted amenities) unless accompanied by a Client employee, unless authorized by a Service Authorization to do so.

5.2   With respect to financial, statistical and personnel data relating to the Client's business which is confidential, is clearly so designated, and which is submitted to the Company by the Client in order to carry out this Agreement, the Company will instruct its personnel to keep such information confidential by using the same care and discretion that they use with similar data which the Company designates as confidential.

5.3   The Company shall not be required to keep confidential any data which is or becomes publicly available, is already in the possession of the Company, is independently developed by the Company outside the scope of this Agreement, or is rightfully obtained from third parties. In addition, the Company shall not be required to keep confidential any ideas, concepts, know-how, or techniques relating to data processing submitted to the Company or developed during the course of this Agreement by the Company personnel or jointly by the Company and the Client personnel.

6   NO RESTRICTION ON PERSONNEL OR SERVICES

In recognition of the fact that the Company personnel provided to the Client under this Agreement may perform similar services from time to time for others, this Agreement shall not prevent the Company from performing such similar services or restrict the Company from using the personnel provided to the Client under this Agreement for performing the said similar services.

7   SERVICE AUTHORIZATION

7.1   The Client shall authorize all Services to be performed hereunder by signing a

Service Authorization ('Service Authorization') substantially in the form of the Schedule hereto.

7.2   Estimates of time or cost shown on a Service Authorization are not guaranteed in any way or to any extent by the Company and do not constitute a contract to perform services for a fixed price. If the Company determines that the estimates will be exceeded, the Company will notify the Client as soon as practicable, and the Client may thereupon terminate the Services, paying only for Services furnished prior to such termination date. Charges will be paid by the Client whether the amount of the charge is above or below the estimate.

7.3   Service Authorizations may include work schedules for the Company personnel. The Company will use reasonable efforts to provide the Services of the Company personnel in accordance with such schedules subject to circumstances beyond the control of the Company. If the Company personnel fail to perform scheduled Services under this Agreement because of illness, resignation or other causes beyond the Company's reasonable control, the Company will attempt to replace such personnel within a reasonable time, but the Company shall not be liable for failure to do so.

8   **EMPLOYMENT OFFERS**

8.1   (a)   Each party agrees during a period from the date of this Agreement to twelve months after its completion or termination that it shall not, without the other party's prior agreement in writing, employ or engage on any other basis than under this Agreement or offer such employment or engagement to any of the other party's staff.

       (b)   Each party agrees that if it employs or engages any person contrary to the provisions of sub-Clause (a) of this Clause a sum in liquidated damages shall be payable as compensation, which said sum shall be equal to fifty percent (50%) of such person's annual salary immediately prior to the time of leaving the employment of the relevant party.

[*Insert Boilerplate Clauses.*]

SCHEDULE

SYSTEM
[*Describe precisely the hardware and software combination to be installed and implemented by the Company.*]

LOCATION
[*Set out the Client's locations at which installation and implementation will take place. Note: Certain activities, such as information gathering and training, may take place elsewhere, but these locations can be specified in the Service Authorizations relating to those activities.*]

[*Insert Execution Clauses*]

SERVICE AUTHORIZATION

NAME and ADDRESS of the Client: Agreement No:

Service Authorization No:

Date:

1   The Work detailed below will be carried out and charges will be paid by the Client in accordance with the Agreement for the Installation and Implementation of Software between the Company and the Client referred to above ('the Agreement') whether the amount of the charges is above or below the Estimated Total shown below.

2   The information below is an estimate only and is not guaranteed in any way or to any extent. If the Company determines that the Estimated Total will be exceeded,

due other than to a change in the Company Standard Rates, the Company will notify the Client as soon as practicable, and the Client may thereupon terminate the Services, paying only for Services furnished prior to such termination date.

1   SERVICES

Category
— Training
— Installation
— Customization Services
— General Support (other than maintenance)
[*Tick one*]
[*Attach details*]

2   ESTIMATED OR SPECIFIC SERVICE PERIOD
From   /   /   To   /   /
Detailed Schedule attached?   Yes/No

3   ESTIMATES OF TIME AND COST
Description of Resource
Hours   Rate
Estimated
(Per Month or Total)
Estimated Total

4   TRAVEL/ACCOMMODATION
Necessary   Yes/No
Estimated Amount

5   LOCATION OF SERVICES

6   MINIMUM CHARGES [*Delete if not applicable.*]
To reflect the fact that the Company will dedicate certain resources to the work covered by this Service Authorization, the Company will invoice a minimum monthly charge equivalent to the cost of:
. . . Project Manager(s)
. . . Systems Analyst(s)
. . . Analyst Programmer(s)
. . . Programmer(s)

The above is agreed to: Accepted by:
By: ....   By: ....
For the Company   For the Client
Name: Name:
Title: Title:
Date: Date:

This estimate may be withdrawn if the Company is not authorized to perform this work within thirty (30) days of estimate. To authorize the Company to perform the service indicated in this estimate, complete and return the Client authorization copy.

This becomes a binding Agreement only on acceptance by the Company at its Head Office. Such acceptance shall be evidenced by the return to the Client of an acknowledgement copy of this Agreement, signed by the Company EDP Manager or his/her designated subordinate.

H Software Development Agreements

Software which is written for a particular application, or specially developed or modified for a particular client's needs, should always have a written contract. It is very important to define precisely what is to be delivered by the developer and the cost of it. If it is intended that the development be completed for a fixed price it is particularly important to make that fact abundantly clear and to specify the scope of the work to be carried out for that price in precise detail. The possibilities for mutual misunderstandings and unfounded expectations are boundless.

Fixed price contracts should always contain a mechanism for determining the cost of variations to the contract; it is almost inevitable in any software development that the client will change its mind during the project, usually because it is only when the system is being developed that the client realizes the full extent of the power available through the computer system, and its limitations. Usually variations to a fixed price contract will themselves be subject to a fixed price limitation, so that once a variation is requested a specification for it is drawn up and the developer submits a quotation for the work. This quotation is then accepted or rejected by the client as in any other software development.

Contracts for development which are not limited by a fixed price should also contain a mechanism for specification of the work to be done, an estimate of cost or a means of estimating costs as the development progresses and for agreeing variations. It is still important to determine precisely the work which the client wishes to be carried out. Too often in development contracts the client is vague about precisely the work that is to be done and variations that have been agreed on and suddenly finds that the predicted cost of the system has doubled. Too often, also, the developer is overly anxious to commence work (and cash flow) and suddenly finds that it is encountering maddening indecision on the part of the client, followed by dispute (and a termination of cash flow!).

The most important feature of this agreement is the specification of the software to be written. If the software cannot be adequately specified at the time the agreement is entered into then the agreement must include a mechanism whereby the specifications can be agreed. No software should be written unless it is pursuant to the specifications which have been signed off by both parties. In general the specifications should be submitted by the party who creates them to the other party for approval. If approval is forthcoming, then those specifications form part of the agreement; if approval cannot be obtained, then the agreement is at an end. Obviously, if the development is to be for a fixed price, then the creation of precise specifications is doubly important.

The other important feature of these contracts is the creation of acceptance tests which must be passed before the development is complete, and milestone payments or final payments to the developer are made. Acceptance tests can specify certain response times under specified load conditions or a specified number of terminals operating, or possibly a demonstrated capability to handle a certain set of transactions, depending upon the nature of the particular software. Whatever the form taken by acceptance tests, they should be objectively measurable, and therefore the formal tests should not be carried out by the client or the developer alone, nor be subject to a personal 'feeling' about performance (such as 'substantial compliance' or 'satisfactory performance').

Payment, whether the contract is for a fixed price or subject to time and materials charges, should, from a client's point of view, ensure that a portion of the money is withheld from the developer until the system has been proved to operate effectively. From the developer's (and the client's) point of view, it is important to have a steady and reliable cash flow to enable the work to be carried out — and also an asurance that milestone and final payments will be made, and not delayed or avoided. Retained moneys can be put into the trust account of a neutral agent or on an interest bearing deposit under the control of both parties or a legal representative. Interest on any money put into such an account can be shared between the parties, or it may be appropriate that interest be payable entirely to the developer to assist its cashflow.

Copyright must be addressed. The contract should be explicit on whether copyright is to be retained by the developer or assigned to the client. As pointed out in Chapter 3, copyright will not be assigned from the developer to the client in the absence of an explicit assignment. If copyright is assigned, the client should require delivery of the source code. If copyright is not assigned, then an express licence from the developer to the customer, in comprehensive terms, is mandatory (See B, Software Licences, above), and it may be desirable to arrange for the source code to be placed in escrow (see K, Escrow Agreements, below). Consideration should also be given to maintenance of the software developed after acceptance — which should be negotiated at an early stage, before the client's negotiating position is entirely lost — and in this regard we note that warranties, in the sense of a 'free' maintenance period, are not recommended.

Having a properly drafted agreement which spells out the rights and duties of both sides is a highly desirable position. It is probably more important to have a commercial arrangement where it is in the interests of both parties to perform the agreement. The sample development agreement below shows a highly structured approach, providing for the writing of specifications and documents being signed off by both parties.

Example ———

THIS AGREEMENT is made the   day   of 19
BETWEEN   of
                                                                          ('The Company') of the
one part
AND   of
                                                                          ('the Developer') of the
other part
WHEREAS:

A   The Company wishes to develop and cause to be marketed a software program or
        set of programs to [*describe basic purpose of software to be developed.*]
B   The Developer is in the business of the development, implementation and
        marketing of software systems.
C   The Developer has agreed to draft specifications and a project plan for acceptance
        by the Company and to proceed with the development of such a system in
        accordance with the specifications and the project plan as accepted by the
        Company.

NOW THIS AGREEMENT WITNESSES as follows:
1   DEFINITIONS
        In this Agreement and in any Schedules or Annexures hereto unless the contrary
        intention appears:
        (a)   'Implementation' means the programming services provided by the
                Developer pursuant to this Agreement and the establishment of tables,
                codes, reference files and editing rules for the Company's reasonable
                requirements in relation to a Project Plan;
        (b)   'Installation' means the supervision of compilation of the Software
                pursuant to the terms hereof and the placement of a machine code version
                of the said programs on the hardware of the Company;
        (c)   'Office Procedures' means all office staff, facilities, *pro forma* and manual
                processes;
        (d)   'Project Plan' means the project plan referred to in Clause 4 as varied,
                amended or added to under this Agreement from time to time;
        (e)   'Related Items' means all information and all manuals, documentation,
                notes, improvements, modifications and alterations prepared by the
                Developer and supplied to the Company under this Agreement;
        (f)   'Response Time' means the elapsed time between a user of the system
                depressing a key which causes information to be transmitted to the
                hardware and, where a response is required, for the first character of a
                response to be received at the terminal of the said user;
        (g)   'Software' means all the computer programs prepared by the Developer
                and supplied to the Company under this Agreement including both source
                code and object code versions;
        (h)   'Specifications' means the specifications developed pursuant to Clause 3
                below, including any variations thereof;
        (i)   'System' means all Software, Office Procedures and Related Items
                developed pursuant to the Specifications.

2   TERM
         This Agreement will take effect from the date hereof and will continue until
         terminated in accordance with the terms hereof.

3   SPECIFICATIONS
3.1   The Developer shall develop draft specifications for the Software and related
         Office Procedures ('the Specifications') which will specify the functions and
         performance of the Software and related Office Procedures.
         The Specifications shall include:
         (a)   the matters set out in Schedule 1.
         (b)   a description of the Related Items to be provided.
3.2   Except in the event that circumstances beyond the control of the Developer, or
         variations in the requirements or other instructions of the Company, which
         prevent the Developer from completing the Specifications within the time allowed
         herein, it is a condition of this Agreement that the Specifications are delivered by
         the Developer to the Company within two (2) months of the date of this
         Agreement.
3.3   Upon delivery of the Specifications to the Company for its approval the Company
         shall within fourteen (14) days thereafter:
         (a)   approve it;
         (b)   reject it; or
         (c)   request variations to and/or explanations of any aspect of the
                Specifications.
3.4   If the Company makes no request within the time specified under sub-clause 3.3
         above or requests variations to the Specifications and, in relation to each such
         request:
         (a)   the Company withdraws such request or raises no further request,
                consequent upon the Developer's reply;
         (b)   the Company and the Developer agree on such variation; or
         (c)   the Company and the Developer agree on any subsequent or consequent
                variation or addition to the Specifications then the Specifications as
                modified pursuant to any such request shall be deemed to be approved.
3.5   Upon approval, the terms of the Specifications shall be and are hereby imported as
         terms of this Agreement. All work carried out by the Developer pursuant to this
         Agreement in respect of preparation of the Specification shall be invoiced to the
         Company in accordance with Clause 11 below.
3.6   In the event the Company requires changes in the Specifications after it has
         accepted the Specifications pursuant to clause 3.3, the Company will inform the
         Developer of the new requirements. The Developer will thereupon draft variations
         to the Specifications which will be submitted to the Company for approval in
         accordance with the provisions of clause 3.3. Such draft variations will include, if
         necessary, a provision for a variation of the date for source code delivery specified
         in clause 7.2

4   PROJECT PLAN
4.1   Upon completion of the Specifications the Developer shall, in conjunction with the
         Company, write a draft project plan for development of the Software ('the Project
         Plan') which will specify the means by which the Specifications will be imple-
         mented as computer programs. The Project Plan shall include:
         (a)   a timetable for implementation and testing of certain milestones which
                may include:
                (i)   Design of the Software;
                (ii)   Design of Office Procedures;
                (iii)   Software Installation;
                (iv)   Programming and Testing;

       (v)   Completion and Delivery of Software Documentation;

       (vi)   Completion and Delivery of Office Procedures Documentation;

       (vii)   Training;

       (viii)   Software Acceptance;

       (ix)   Implementation and Use of the System;

(b)   as far as possible the names, and where not possible, the job description of staff to be allocated or engaged by the Developer to this Implementation, their employment status (employee/contractor, full-time/part-time) and the estimated duration of their allocation to Implementation;

(c)   criteria for acceptance satisfactory to the Company;

(d)   a description of the Related Items to be provided.

4.2   Upon delivery of the Project Plan to the Company for its approval the Company shall within fourteen (14) days thereafter:

(a)   approve it;

(b)   reject it; or

(c)   request variations to and/or explanations of any aspect of the Project Plan.

4.3   If the Company makes no request within the time specified under sub-clause 4.2 above or requests variations to the Project Plan and, in relation to each such request:

(a)   the Company withdraws such request or raises no further request, consequent upon the Developer's reply;

(b)   the Company and the Developer agree on such variation; or

(c)   the Company and the Developer agree on any subsequent or consequent variation or addition to the Project Plan then the Project Plan as modified pursuant to any such request shall be deemed to be approved.

4.4   Upon approval of the Project Plan the Company shall be deemed to have read and understood the Project Plan as approved.

4.5   Upon approval, the terms of the Project Plan shall be and are hereby imported as terms of this Agreement. All work carried out by the Developer pursuant to this Agreement in respect of preparation of the Project Plan shall be invoiced to the Company in accordance with Clause 11 below.

5   VARIATIONS IN PROJECT PLAN

5.1   The Developer shall advise the Company of any circumstance whereby in the Developer's opinion its estimates of time or costs, or the Developer's forecast of the identity, number or nature of staff allocated to or required for implementation, must be or has been substantially varied and the extent or nature of such variation.

5.2   In the event that any circumstance whereby in the Developer's opinion the Developer's estimates of time, cost or milestones specified in the Project Plan approved by the Company must be varied, the Developer shall submit to the Company amendments to the Project Plan, or a new Project Plan, or a subsidiary Project Plan for approval by the Company in accordance with the provisions of Clause 4 hereof, PROVIDED HOWEVER that the amended, new or subsidiary Project Plan shall not be unreasonably rejected nor shall unreasonable variations be requested by the Company.

6   THE PROJECT

6.1   For the consideration herein, the Developer warrants that it shall create the Software in accordance with the Project Plan so that the Software operates in conformity with the Specifications.

6.2   In developing the Software, the Developer will be responsible for directing: g:

(a)   its own employees and sub-contractors hired by it; and

(b)   certain people hired, or arranged for, by the Company.

The Developer will be responsible for the actions and performance of the people referred to in sub-clause (b) as if they were the people referred to in sub-clause (a), save only that the Company will be responsible for the actions and performance of the people referred to in the said sub-clause (b) if they disobey or fail to carry out a direction of the Developer.

6.3   The Company will, on the reasonable request of the Developer, remove from the project any person referred to in sub-clause 6.2(b).

6.4   In providing the services to be performed or procured pursuant to this Agreement, the Developer warrants that all programming and other services shall be provided in a proper and workmanlike manner and at all times in compliance with the standards and procedures for the like programming and services specified by the Company in its manuals and other guidelines from time to time.

7   SOURCE CODE DELIVERY

7.1   When the Software operates in conformity with the Specifications, the Developer shall make the Software available to the Company.

7.2   It is a condition of this Agreement that the Software source code be delivered to the Company, or at its direction, within six (6) months of the date of this Agreement unless otherwise agreed in writing between the parties.

7.3   The Company shall consult with the Developer in relation to variations or extensions of the Software for the purpose of reaching agreement as to the development and the bearing of the cost of such variations or extensions and the terms of supply of same to the Company.

8   OWNERSHIP

8.1   Upon approval of the Specifications pursuant to Clause 3.3 or 3.4, the Developer hereby assigns to the Company:

(a)   all inventions, discoveries and novel designs whether or not registrable as designs or patents which are derived by the Developer from the Specifications;

(b)   the entire copyright throughout the world in all writing (including programs), art works and other copyright work ('the Works') created by the Developer or any Sub-Contractor of the Developer during and pursuant to this Agreement (whether or not in normal business hours or using the Company's premises or equipment) AND FURTHER assigns to the Company the copyright and all other rights of a like nature belonging to the Developer which may be conferred or subsist in any alternations or additions to the works created by the Developer at any future time at the written request or direction of the Company.

8.2   The Developer shall both during and after the term of this Agreement do all such acts and things, and sign all such documents, as the Company may reasonably request to secure the Company's ownership or rights in the inventions, discoveries, designs or copyright works referred to in paragraph 8.1.

8.3   The Developer will ensure that all sub-contractors engaged by it execute a Deed in the form of Schedule 2, such Deed to be delivered to the Company prior to the relevant sub-contractors commencing work on the Software.

9   WARRANTIES

9.1   The Developer warrants that to the best of the knowledge of the Developer the Software and all materials produced by or at the direction of the Developer under this Agreement will not infringe any patent, copyright, trade secret or other proprietary right of any third party. The Developer will indemnify and hold the Company harmless from and against any direct loss, damage, cost, liability or expense arising out of any breach or claimed breach of this warranty.

9.2   The Developer warrants that upon completion of the project the Software will conform to the Specifications.

10   CONFIDENTIALITY

10.1   Each party agrees to treat as confidential all information received from the other which is not information which is already in the public domain, or is not required by law to be disclosed. Each party agrees to disclose such information only to those of its employees or sub-contractors who need to know it for the performance of this Agreement.

10.2   The Developer further agrees that it and its employees will, and it will ensure that its sub-contractors will, observe all reasonable security regulations in effect from time to time at the Company's premises, and will use its best endeavours to comply with the Company's written security procedures for confidential material.

11   PAYMENT FOR SPECIFICATIONS AND PROJECT PLAN

11.1   Upon approval of the Specifications pursuant to this Agreement, the Company shall pay to the Developer the sum of [*Insert payment amount.*]

11.2   The drafting of any variations to the Specifications pursuant to Clause 3.7 shall be invoiced in accordance with Clause 12.2.

11.3   Upon approval of the Project Plan pursuant to this Agreement, the Company shall pay to the Developer the sum of [*Insert payment amount.*]

11.4   The drafting of any variations to the Project Plan pursuant to Clause 5 shall be invoiced in accordance with Clause 12.2.

12   PAYMENT FOR SERVICES

12.1   At the end of each week the Developer shall invoice the Company for the services provided hereunder during the previous week, other than the services referred to in Clause 11.1 and 11.3.

12.2   The invoicing referred to in Clause 12.1 shall be at the rate of [*specify rate*] for each complete day worked under this Agreement. Any other amounts invoiced by the Developer shall be in accordance with the Developer's standard terms and conditions.

12.3   Any sub-contractors hired by the Developer to provide services under this Agreement shall be paid by the Developer. The Company will reimburse the Developer in accordance with this Agreement following presentation of the invoice received from such sub-contractor.

13   REPORTS

13.1   Within two weeks of commencing development of the Software pursuant to Clause 6.1, and thereafter at fortnightly intervals, the Developer will provide the Company with a written report on all aspects of the project.

[*Insert Boilerplate Clauses.*]

SCHEDULE 1

[*Here provide details of the preliminary specification and needs analysis of the Client.*]

SCHEDULE 2

Contractor Undertaking

[*Insert Assignment in the form of K: Copyright Assignment, below.*]

[*Insert Execution Clauses.*]

I   General Contractor Agreements

It is a curious feature of the computer industry that so much work is done by independent contractors, paid by the hour or by the job, rather than employees. It is often the case that these contractors remain for such extended periods in the service of one principal, to all the world appearing in every respect as an employee.

Some of the serious implications which may arise because of this use of contractors, both for the contractors and their principals, were discussed above in Chapter 2.

In the sample given below, we attempt to deal with the following issues:

1   The contractor must be reminded that it is an independent contractor and therefore tax deductions may not be made (although these deductions, whether in the form of withholding tax, income tax or however called vary greatly in their rules of application from country to country), insurance for employees will not extend to his or her benefit, and so on. This also means that the contractor must indemnify the principal for losses caused by bad work or the use of third party materials, matters for which employees are not usually held responsible in practice.

2   The right to termination must be made clear. An employee may usually be terminated on notice, and is only entitled to be paid salary for the period of the notice (plus any special or statutory entitlements). In few countries is an employee entitled to additional damages for 'wrongful termination', at least, not in any significant amount. The United States is a major exception to this general comment. However, in the absence of an express contractual provision, a contractor, although he or she may be terminated on 'reasonable' notice, may also be entitled to claim loss of expected profit from the completed project in the case of a termination without cause.

3   Since contractors are not employees, they should have imposed upon them the obligation to obey the work rules of the 'employer', including the obligation to work certain hours, complete time

records (necessary in any event in the case of a contractor paid by the hour), and any other obligations which the general law imposes on employees, and employers take for granted, such as the obligation of good faith, absence of conflicting employment and so on. Since these are not necessarily imposed by implication on contractors, if they are important they should be added. However, this may increase the liability to taxation or workman's compensation insurance/social security as the contractor agreement begins to appear more and more like a contract of employment.

4   An express assignment of all intellectual property rights, including copyright, is essential, as well as an express commitment to confidentiality, especially in respect of matters disclosed to the principal by the contractor in the course of rendering the contracted services. The issue of an author's moral rights may also be dealt with, as otherwise a programmer may be entitled to acknowledgement in the copyright notice of the completed work. These matters are discussed above in Chapters 3 and 4. Even in countries where an assignment of copyright need not be in writing, and may be 'implied', such as Japan, an express assignment puts the matter beyond the vagaries of the law, and will assist in any registration procedures. Similarly, the contractor must be made aware that he or she may not use sub-contractors — a matter which would otherwise be permissible to a contractor, unlike an employee.

5   As there is an assignment of intellectual property rights, the obligation to deliver source code and all working materials is also essential. It is to be remembered that, although an employee's documentation created during employment must belong to the employer, an independent contractor is otherwise probably entitled to keep working documentation. An analogy may be drawn to an attorney or architect in this regard — the same rules apply to a contractor as apply to these, even though a contractor appears more like an employee working 'in-house'.

The sample contract given below is ideally suited to an individual contractor working on general tasks. It is not suited to specific development projects for which the contractor takes management responsibility and liability for completion on time, within specification and within budget. For the latter, the Development Contract considered above is more suitable, whereas this is more appropriate for *ad hoc* activities. Adjustments may be made for more 'independent' contractors, and for more project driven responsibilities by amendment, however, and here the Schedule of Work referred to below may be used, it being otherwise inappropriate.

Example ───

THIS AGREEMENT is made the   day of   19
BETWEEN: of
                                                (herein called 'the Company') of the one part.
AND: of
                                                (herein called 'the Contractor') of the other part.
WHEREAS:

The Company has requested the Contractor to provide services described in the Schedule hereto (hereinafter referred to as 'Services') according to the schedule of work set forth in the Schedule, which the Contractor has agreed to do upon and subject to the following terms and conditions.

1   CONDITIONS AND PROVISION OF SERVICES
1.1   This agreement shall come into operation on .... 19 ...... and subject to the rights of termination shall continue until terminated pursuant to the provisions hereof. Notwithstanding any other provision herein, either party may terminate this Agreement, with or without cause, by fourteen (14) days' prior written notice.
1.2   The Company shall make available to the Contractor at all times during business hours adequate equipment and such accommodation on its premises as the Contractor may reasonably require in order to perform the Services. It shall be a condition of such availability that the Contractor makes known to the Company its requirements a reasonable time in advance of any equipment, premises or other facilities being required.
1.3   The Contractor shall perform the Services in a proper and workmanlike manner, and shall ensure that at all times whilst on or about the premises of the Company its employees and/or agents conduct themselves in a sober and decorous manner that will not bring discredit upon the Company or cause any nuisance to the Company, its employees or other persons dealing with the Company from time to time.
1.4   The Contractor shall provide the Services at the premises of the Company or such other place or place which the Company may from time to time authorize; and such authorization may impose conditions upon the nature or extent of the Services to be provided in any such place.
1.5   The Contractor's employees and agents will observe the working hours, working rules (including without limitation confidentiality requirements) and holiday schedule of the Company while working on the Company's premises. Upon the Company's request, the Contractor will promptly replace any of the Contractor's employees or agents assigned to perform the Services.
1.6   The Contractor will perform the Services under the general direction of the Company. The Contractor, however, will determine at the Contractor's sole discretion the manner and means by which the services are accomplished, subject to the express condition that the Contractor will at all times comply with applicable law.
1.7   The Contractor is an independent contractor without authority to bind the Company by contract or otherwise, and neither the Contractor nor the Contractor's employees or agents are agents or employees of the Company. The Contractor will maintain workers compensation and disability insurance, as well as adequate insurance to protect itself from and indemnify the Company against claims giving rise to any liability to the Company pursuant to this Agreement.

2   PAYMENT FOR SERVICES
2.1   The Company will pay the Contractor the fee set forth in the Schedule for the

performance of the Services provided that, if milestones for performance and delivery of the results of the Services are specified in the Schedule, the Company shall have no obligation to make any payment specified for such milestone until completion and delivery of that milestone to the Company's reasonable satisfaction.

2.2 In the event of termination of this Agreement by the Company without cause after commencement of work under this Agreement or completion of a milestone specified in the Schedule and prior to completion of the next specified milestone, the Company shall pay the Contractor a termination fee equal to the same percentage of the payment due for the next milestone as the percentage of time passed against the time allowed for completion of the next milestone.

3 EMPLOYEES AND CONTRACTORS

UNDER NO CIRCUMSTANCES SHALL THE CONTRACTOR USE IN THE PROVISION OF THE SERVICES ANY SUB-CONTRACTOR OR EMPLOYEE UNLESS AND UNTIL THE WRITTEN CONSENT OF THE COMPANY HAS FIRST BEEN OBTAINED. A REQUEST FOR THE COMPANY'S CONSENT SHALL BE ACCOMPANIED BY AN UNDERTAKING EXECUTED BY SUCH SUB-CONTRACTOR OR EMPLOYEE IN THE FORM OF EXHIBIT 1 HERETO.

4 CONFIDENTIALITY

4.1 The Contractor will not disclose to the Company or induce the Company to use any confidential information of other persons or companies, including former employees or principals (if any).

4.2 The Contractor shall not during or after engagement by the Company disclose to any person or company any confidential information belonging to the Company or to any other person or company which the Contractor may learn in the course of engagement by the Company whether or not such information is produced by the efforts of the Contractor. Such confidential information includes, without limitation, the works (including computer programs) being prepared by the Contractor pursuant to this Agreement, matters not generally known outside the Company, such as developments relating to existing and future products and services marketed or used or to be marketed or used or rejected by the Company and persons or companies dealing with the Company and also information relating to the general business operations with the Company (including without limitation, sales, costs, profits organization customer lists and pricing methods).

5 THE AUTHOR'S MORAL RIGHTS

5.1 The Contractor authorizes and permits the Company to reproduce and make adaptations to or alterations of any part of any works (including computer programs) being prepared by the Contractor pursuant to this Agreement, without acknowledgment of the authorship or part authorship of the Contractor.

6 WARRANTIES AND INDEMNITIES

6.1 The Contractor warrants no literary or other works (including computer programs, diagrams, flow charts or other work) employed or created by the Contractor in the provision of the Services shall infringe any copyright, obligation of confidentiality, patent or other right or property belonging to or benefiting any third party.

6.2 In the event that in the provision of the Services either of the foregoing warranties is broken by the Contractor, the Contractor shall forthwith upon request being made be the Company provide the Services again to correct such breach and at no charge to the Company. Such remedy to the Company shall be without prejudice to any other right or remedy to which the Company may be entitled, whether at law, in equity or otherwise.

6.3   Notwithstanding the foregoing, the Contractor shall indemnify and save the Company harmless from and against any costs, damages, loss or liability of any kind (including legal costs and disbursements in defending or settling the claim giving rise to same) howsoever suffered or incurred by the Company by virtue of the provision of the Services or any breach of this Agreement by the Contractor. Such indemnity shall extend (without limiting the generality of the foregoing) to any costs, damages, loss or liability (including legal costs and disbursements in defending or settling the claim giving rise to same) incurred by the Company by virtue of any injury or disability suffered by any employee or sub-contractor of the Contractor, whether on the Company premises or otherwise and by whatever legal theory (whether statutory, tortious or otherwise) arising.

6.4   In addition, Contractor will indemnify the Company and hold it harmless from and against all claims, liabilities, damages, losses and expenses, including but not limited to reasonable attorneys' fees and costs of suit, arising out of or in connection with any negligent or wilful act or omission of the Contractor or the Contractor's employees or agents which proximately causes or contributes to (a) any bodily injury, sickness, disease or death; (b) any injury to or destruction of tangible or intangible property (including computer programs and data or any loss of use resulting therefrom; or (c) any violation of any statute, ordinance or regulation.

6.5   The Contractor acknowledges and agrees that it is obliged to report as income all compensation received by the Contractor pursuant to this Agreement, and the Contractor agrees to indemnify the Company and hold it harmless to the extent of any obligation imposed on the Company (a) to pay any withholding taxes, social security, unemployment or disability insurance or similar items, including interest and penalties thereon, in connection with any payments made to the Contractor by the Company pursuant to this Agreement and/or (b) resulting from the Contractor being determined not to be an independent contractor.

7   INVENTIONS AND COPYRIGHT WORKS

7.1   The Contractor assigns to the Company:
(a)   all inventions, discoveries and novel designs whether or not registrable as designs or patents;
(b)   the entire copyright throughout the world in all writing (including programs, flow charts, programmers' notes and other documentation), art works and other copyright work ('the Works') created by the Contractor or any sub-contractor of the Contractor pursuant to this Agreement (whether or not in normal business hours or using the Company's premises or equipment).

7.2   In addition to disclosing any inventions, discoveries, designs or copyright works referred to in the preceding paragraph, the Contractor shall disclose and, if required by the Company assign to the Company any other inventions, discoveries, designs or copyright works devised or created by the Contractor whilst engaged by the Company and which relate or may touch upon the future or present business or products of the Company and its related companies.

7.3   The Contractor shall both during and after engagement by the Company do all such acts and things, and sign all such documents, as the Company or its attorneys may reasonably request to secure the Company's ownership or rights to the inventions, discoveries, designs or copyright works referred to in both paragraphs 7.1 and 7.2 of this clause.

7.4   Nothing in this clause shall prevent the Contractor from making use of portions of the Software produced by the Contractor in another program provided that such other programs perform a substantially different function to the Software.

8   PROVISION OF SOURCE CODE AND DOCUMENTATION BY THE
        CONTRACTOR

8.1   Providing that the Company is not in default of this Agreement, the Contractor
        shall, with the cooperation of the Company, provide to the Company such
        documentation in such form relating to the Works as the Company may require
        from time to time.

8.2   The documentation to be provided by the Contractor pursuant to this Agreement
        will be such that every line of the source code version of the Software will be
        adequately explained. The Contractor will, at the request of the Company, provide
        in writing, such further documentation as is required by the Company.

8.3   Forthwith upon expiration or termination of this Agreement, the Contractor shall
        deliver all the Works (including source code of any program) to the Company and
        in addition the Contractor shall leave with the Company all records, books,
        drawings, note books and other documentation and things pertaining to the Works,
        including any extra features of the Works or the confidential information referred
        to in clause 4 hereof, and further any equipment, tools or other devices owned by
        the Company then in the possession of the Contractor or any sub-contractor.

9   EXCHANGE OF STAFF

9.1   Neither party hereto shall induce an employee of the other to leave that other's em-
        ployment for the purpose of becoming an employee or contractor of the inducing
        party, either during the term of this Agreement or for the period of three months
        after the termination or expiration thereof. In the event that either party engages an
        employee of the other as employee or contractor during the term of this Agreement
        or for a period of three (3) months after the termination or expiration hereof, the
        defaulting party shall pay liquidated damages assessed in the sum of $10 000.00 for
        each such employee so engaged, such sum being assessed by the parties hereto as
        fair compensation for the loss of such employee and the cost of engaging and
        retraining a replacement employee or contractor.

[Insert Boilerplate Clauses.]

SCHEDULE

SERVICES

The Contractor will render such services as the Company may from time to time request in
writing in connection with *[specify nature of work]* including, without limiting, the
generality of the foregoing:

[Specify particulars of work to be done and deliverables.]

CONSULTANT'S FEE AND REIMBURSEMENT

The Contractor shall receive the following fee and reimbursement for its services:

A   Fee: $_____ per _____ [in instalments in accordance with the
        completion of milestones and delivery of deliverables as specified below]. The total
        of all payment hereunder will not exceed $_____.

B   Labour charges for temporary personnel retained by the Contractor if approved in
        advance by the Company, invoiced to the Company at a rate mutually agreed upon
        prior to the start of their assignment.

C   Reimbursement for the following:

        1   Outside services (modelmakers, draftspersons, renderers, graphic artists,
                etc.) at cost, as approved in advance by the Company, if $35.00 or more
                per item.

        2   Direct charges (telephones, blueprints, photographs, reproduction art
                work, etc.) at cost.

3   Travel and subsistence at cost. The Contractor will invoice the Company monthly for services and expenses and shall provide such reasonable receipts or other documentation of expenses as the Company may reasonably request, including copies of time records. Payment terms are Net 30 days from receipt of invoice.

SCHEDULE OF WORK

[*Here specify Milestones and Payment for Milestones.*]
[*Insert Execution Clauses.*]

EXHIBIT 1
[*Insert Assignment in the form of K: Copyright Assignment, below.*]

J Employment Agreements

In Chapter 2 we discussed the nature of general employment law. Every employment is governed by a great deal of general law, which in most countries so strongly favours the employer that an express agreement is rarely required.

There are, however, exceptions. In the United States, employment law increasingly favours the employee, and in many countries new statutory rules give added protection to the employee, particularly upon termination of employment.

In any event, it is often desirable to have an express contract *adding* to the general legal obligations of employee and employer, for example, imposing a reasonable limitation on the nature of the competitive work which may be undertaken by the employee after termination.

In addition, a written agreement may express in clear terms the existing law, or clarify grey areas, so that neither employee nor employer can be in doubt in any of the common areas of concern which arise from time to time — such as ownership of inventions and copyright works.

Finally, a contract may set down clear rules as to the termination of employment and the ground upon which he or she may be terminated, so that the employee does not at any stage develop unreasonable expectations as to the conditions of termination or length of notice to which he or she is entitled. This may save both parties from unhappy and protracted litigation at a later time.

The sample contract given below owes none of its features to any special requirements of the computer industry, but it is useful to complete the picture of relevant contracts we are here seeking to create.

Example

THIS AGREEMENT is made the   day
of   19
BETWEEN   of
                                              ('the Company') of the
    one part
AND   of
                                              ('the Employee')
    of the other part
WHEREAS:

A   The Company is engaged in the business of [*specify broadly the business of the employer, for example: the development, manufacture and distribution of software*]; and

B   The Company has offered the Employee employment for the purpose of assisting it in the carrying on of its business as it may direct from time to time,

NOW THE PARTIES AGREE as follows:

1   Employment and Title
        The Company employs the Employee and the Employee accepts employment commencing as [*specify the position in which the Employee shall commence*] (the 'Position') subject to the terms and conditions contained in this Agreement.

2   Position and Duties
2.1   The Employee's initial duties shall be to [*describe the duties of the Position in broad terms, including where these duties will be carried out*], and all ancillary matters arising therefrom, in which regard the Employee shall take instructions from and comply with the requirements of the superiors to the Employee appointed by the Company from time to time.

2.2   In the performance of his duties in the Position, in respect of his demeanour and conduct whether on or outside the premises of the Company, the Employee shall be subject to and comply with the rules of employment from time to time promulgated by the Company, and shall comply with the lawful directions and management of employees of the Company nominated by the Company from time to time in that regard.

2.3   Subject to the foregoing, the Employee agrees and recognizes that the Company has absolute discretion to make changes in his responsibilities in the Position based on the needs of the Company. Accordingly, the Employee agrees to serve in the Position with such duties and responsibilities that exist as of the date this Agreement is signed, and/or as may later be assigned by the Company. The Employee agrees to devote all of his business time, skill, attention and best efforts to the Company's business and to discharge and fulfil the responsibilities assigned to him by the Company during his employment under this Agreement.

2.4   In addition to the foregoing, the Employee shall at all times be subject to a duty of the utmost fidelity to the Company in all his dealings, shall in all things act for the benefit of the Company and its related corporations, and shall at all times conduct himself soberly and decorously whilst going about the duties of the Position and at all other times when representing the Company, whether in public, on the premises of the Company or otherwise.

3   Employment Relationship
3.1   The Employee understands and agrees that his employment with the Company is for an unspecified duration and constitutes employment at will. The Employee understands and agrees that either the Employee or the Company can terminate this employment relationship at any time, for any reason, with or without cause, upon the giving of four (4) weeks notice, whether in writing or not.

3.2   In addition, the Company has the right at any time to terminate this agreement without the need for any period of notice in any of the following events:
        (a)   the Employee commits any breach of this Agreement, whether capable of remedy or not;
        (b)   the Employee disobeys any lawful instruction given by the Company;
        (c)   the Employee commits any act of dishonesty, or any act of impropriety which in the Company's opinion is likely to bring the Company or any related corporation into the ridicule or disrespect of the public or any person, or otherwise damaging the reputation of the Company or any related corporation;

(d)   the Employee becomes unfit for the Position, whether by virtue of ill health, mental illness, an act of dishonesty or any other reason;

(e)   subject to the allowances of Section 5.2 below, the Employee engages in any employment or profit making activity outside his employment hereunder which has not been first approved by the Company's Human Resources Director in writing and which in the Company's opinion derogates from the Employee's ability to perform his duties in the Position, or engages in any activity conflicting with his duties in the Position.

3.3   The Employee understands and agrees that the Company reserves the right, at its sole discretion, to make personnel changes for its own purposes, without limitation, and without incurring any liability.

4   **Maintaining Confidential Information**

4.1   The Employee agrees at all times during the term of his employment and thereafter, to hold in strictest confidence, and not to use, except for the benefit of the Company, or to disclose to any person, firm or corporation without written authorization of the Board of Directors of the Company, any Confidential Information of the Company or any related corporation. The Employee understands that 'Confidential Information' means any proprietary information of the Company or any related corporation, including (without limiting the generality of the foregoing), technical data, trade secrets or know-how, including but not limited to, research, product plans, products, services, customer lists and customers (including, but not limited to, users or potential users of the Company Products on whom the Employee calls or with whom the Employee becomes acquainted during the term of his employment), markets, software, developments, inventions, processes, formulae, technology, designs, drawings, engineering, hardware configuration information, marketing, finances or other business information disclosed to the Employee by the Company or any related corporation either directly or indirectly in writing, orally or by drawings or inspection of parts or equipment.

4.2   The Employee will not disclose to the Company or induce the Company to use any confidential information of other persons or companies, including former employers (if any), unless permitted or required to do so by the Company in the course of employment.

4.3   The Employee agrees to execute any further document regarding the protection of any information as the Company may request from time to time after commencement of employment in the Position.

5   **Conflicting Activities**

5.1   The Employee agrees that, during the term of his employment with the Company, he shall not engage in any other employment, occupation, consulting or other business activity directly related to the business in which the Company is now involved or becomes involved during his employment, nor will the Employee engage in any other activities that conflict with his obligations to the Company.

5.2   Notwithstanding the foregoing, the Employee shall be entitled without consultation with the Company to participate in any bonus, profit share or other remuneration program provided by corporations related to the Company from time to time PROVIDED HOWEVER that the Employee shall notify the Company thereof so that the Company may comply with any taxation requirements which arise from receipt of such a benefit incidental to the Employee's employment hereunder.

6   **Compensation**

6.1   The Company shall pay the Employee a salary of $ /month.

6.2   In addition, the employee shall be entitled to a taxable car allowance of $ /month.

6.2   The Employee shall receive in addition an annual leave loading of 17% of four weeks' salary (not including benefits or allowances), payable only in December of each year of employment.

7   Benefit Program Included

7.1   Health insurance will be provided according to the Company's Medical Plan from time to time.

7.2   Life and Disability insurance will be maintained by the Company for the benefit of the Employee in such amount or amounts from time to time as the Company may at its sole discretion determine.

7.3   If the Employee is a participant in a Superannuation Plan, contributions will be made by the Company in accordance with its legal requirements and the determinations of the Company from time to time, which may be specific to the Employee only.

7.4   Vacation will be the minimum required by law or as granted by the Company's annual leave policy from time to time (whichever is the greater), and holidays will be in accordance with the Company's holidays in the place in which the Employee is carrying out his duties at the date thereof.

7.5   In addition, the employee shall be entitled to the Company's Sabbatical Leave allowance or statutory Long Service Leave (whichever is the greater) subject to the qualification period and other conditions set out in the Company's Employment Guidelines or the statute (as applicable) from time to time. The Employee agrees that in the event that he is entitled to the Company's Sabbatical Leave allowance under this clause such entitlement shall be in lieu of and not additional to statutory entitlements.

7.6   The Employee shall be entitled to take leave as a result of sickness for a cumulative total of twelve (12) days *per annum.*

8   Variation of Any Terms of Employment, Including Salary and Benefits
        The Company shall be entitled at any time and from time to time to modify, increase, decrease, add to or delete any benefit of or remuneration for employment referred to in Sections 6 and 7 above, other than the salary referred to in Section 6.1, which may be modified only by agreement between the Company and the Employee.

9   Inventions and Copyright Works

9.1   The Employee acknowledges that the following belong to the Company
        (a)   all inventions, discoveries and novel designs whether or not registrable as designs or patents;
        (b)   all writings (including programs), art work and other copyright work created during and in the course of employment (whether or not in normal working hours or using the Company premises or equipment).

9.2   In addition to disclosing any inventions, discoveries, designs or copyright works referred to in the preceding paragraph, the Employee shall disclose and, if required by the Company, assign to the Company any other inventions, discoveries, designs or copyright works devised or created by the Employee whilst employed by the Company and which relate to or may touch upon the future or present business or products of the Company or its related corporations.

9.3   The Employee shall both during and after employment do all such acts and things, and sign all such documents, as the Company or its Attorneys may reasonably request to secure the Company's ownership or rights in the inventions, discoveries, designs or copyright works referred to in both Sections 9.1 and 9.2.

10   Consequences of Termination

10.1   Upon termination of employment, the Employee shall not be engaged whether directly or indirectly, whether by employment, consultancy, partnership or otherwise:

(a)   by or with any customer of or supplier to the Company or any related corporation in the state in which the Employee last worked for the Company for a period of six (6) months from the effective date of termination; and

(b)   by or with any supplier of personal computer hardware or software products competing with the Company in the country in which the Employee last worked for the Company for a period of three (3) months from the effective date of termination,

without the express written consent of the company being first obtained (such consent not to be unreasonably withheld).

10.2   Upon termination of employment, the Employee shall leave with the Company all records, books, drawings, note books and other documents and things pertaining to the confidential information referred to in Section 4 hereof and the works and inventions referred to in Section 9 hereof, whether prepared by the Employee or any other person, and also any equipment, tools or other devices owned by the Company then in the possession of the Employee.

10.3   The Employee's obligations arising pursuant to Sections 4 and 9 hereof, as well as this Section, shall survive the termination of this Agreement for any reason. No purported variation or addition to this Agreement shall be binding on the Company or the Employee unless such variation or addition is in writing and signed by the employee and by the Human Resources Director of the Company.

[Insert Boilerplate Clauses.]
[Insert Execution Clauses.]

K   Assignment of Copyright

The nature of copyright is dealt with in Chapter 3.

A copyright assignment transfers ownership of copyright from an author (or subsequent owner), and the author is only left with any 'moral rights' he or she may have by virtue of the copyright law. Generally, copyright is not transferred by implication, except in the case of works created by employees in the course of employment and certain other limited exceptions. Even where this is possible, as in Japan, an express written assignment is desirable for the avoidance of doubt and to assist in registration procedures.

It is important to ensure that the right materials are specified when copyright in a program is being assigned. It is wise that all related works also be assigned to ensure that protection is as complete as possible.

This form also takes the opportunity to deal with confidentiality in assigned materials, as this is often overlooked. As discussed in Chapter 3 above, an obligation of confidentiality is not always created by the general law for the benefit of the assignee because it is the party to which confidential information is disclosed and is generally assumed to owe the obligation.

Example

THIS ASSIGNMENT is made on .... 19 .....
BETWEEN

(hereinafter referred to as 'the Sub-Contractor') of the one part,
AND: ('the Company') of the other part.
WHEREAS:

A   The Sub-Contractor has been requested to author or co-author additions and modifications to certain computer programs and other works described in the Schedule hereto and create adaptations, notes, flow charts, diagrams, drafts and explanatory memoranda and related literary and artistic works including source and object codes derived from or incidental to the said programs (herein referred to as 'Works').

B   The Company is directing the project pursuant to which the Works shall be created and accordingly the parties wish to ensure that the copyright subsisting in the Works rests with the Company.

NOW THIS DEED WITNESSES as follows:

1   In consideration of the sum of one dollar ($1.00) paid to the Sub-Contractor by the Company (receipt whereof is hereby acknowledged), the Sub-Contractor hereby assigns to the Company the entire copyright throughout the world and all other rights of a like nature subsisting or conferred in respect of the Works by the law in force in any part of the world *AND FURTHER* assigns to the Company the copyright and all other rights of a like nature belonging to the Sub-Contractor which may be conferred or subsist in any alterations or additions to the Works or other literary or artistic works created at any time at the request or direction of the Company.

2   The Sub-Contractor acknowledges that the Works and all and any information relating to the business or data of the Company which may be or has been acquired by the Sub-Contractor are confidential to the Company and the Sub-Contractor shall not divulge, communicate or in any manner publish the Works or information except as the Company may in writing authorize and direct from time to time.

SCHEDULE

Name of Software:

1   ....

2   ....

3   ....

[*Insert Execution Clauses.*]

L Confidentiality and Technology Disclosure Agreements

In disclosing something confidential, such as source codes, it is important that the other party be made aware that it has an obligation of confidentiality. As we discussed in Chapter 5, in most countries this is a duty not dependent for its existence on a contract, but simply on an awareness by the recipient of information that it is confidential. The best way to ensure this, and to be able to prove it subsequently should it become necessary, is to have the other party execute a formal acknowledgement. If that is not practicable, then even a letter, handed to the recipient and read prior to any disclosures being made, provided it is in clear terms, may be sufficient. Naturally, only information which is genuinely confidential, and remains that way, is subject to the obligation.

The sample agreement given below is drawn in very wide terms and seeks to have all the information disclosed by one party to the other the subject of the confidentiality obligation. If this is unacceptable then that paragraph could be replaced by a paragraph which states the parties agree that all information specifically described in a schedule shall be considered confidential.

Caution should be exercised on the part of a person seeking to impose a duty of confidentiality in respect of any limitation which attempts to narrow the class of confidential information to that contained in written form, or notified as confidential in 'writing'. The nature of business secrets, and the forms which they take, are varied — they include information on databases, and casual comments overheard in cafeterias concerning products and customers — and it is unreasonable that a person given access to such information, particularly if accidentally, should not be on notice that such information is secret even though it is not in a document and the supplier, unaware that it has been received, cannot formally notify the recipient of its confidentiality. Naturally, a potential recipient may wish to limit its responsibility, but it may have to understand that such a burden is a necessary incident to its chosen business.

From the discussion in Chapter 5, it will be seen that the wide terms of the obligation stated in this example are little more than a restatement of the law, but those obligations, such as a restriction on use of the information for other purposes without disclosure to a third party, are often unappreciated by the recipient, and it is sensible to bring them to his or her attention. The provision relating to appropriate remedies will have little or no efficacy in many countries, particularly those with English law, as the jurisdiction and remedies of the courts cannot be limited or directed in any way. However, such provisions are common in American contracts, as in the United States they will be given some effect.

Example

THIS AGREEMENT is made the   day of
          19
between   of
('the Supplier')
and   of
('the Recipient')
WHEREAS: [*Here, set out a brief background to the disclosure of the information, for example*: The Supplier is the owner of the copyright in [*type of software*] suitable for use on an Apple Macintosh personal computer ('the Software').

The Supplier has requested the Recipient, and the Recipient has agreed, to develop the Software so that it will be suitable for a general marketing release.

In order to further the agreement of the parties, the Supplier will supply the Recipient with a source code version of the Software and necessary documentation, which the Recipient will keep confidential.

Provided that the Software when developed is of sufficient quality, it is the intention of the parties to enter into an agreement with respect to the worldwide marketing of the Software.]

NOW THIS AGREEMENT WITNESSES AS FOLLOWS: In consideration of the mutual promises set out herein [*and the payment by Recipient of the sum of US$ (receipt whereof is hereby acknowledged)**], and in order to further development of the Software by the Recipient:

1   The Supplier agrees to supply to the Recipient the confidential information embodied in the documentation described in the Schedule hereto. In addition, the Supplier shall make available its technical support personnel and such further documentation as the Recipient shall reasonably require for the purposes stated above [*here insert any limitations on the availability of staff or information, for example:* for a period not exceeding two hours cumulatively over a period of seven (7) days from the date hereof].

2   The Recipient agrees that information disclosed by the Supplier, including information acquired by the Recipient from its enquiries of the Supplier or inspection of the Supplier's property, relating to the Supplier's products, software, research, development, know-how or personnel, as well as information relating to the Software, (all being referred to herein as 'the Confidential Information'), is confidential to the Supplier.

3   Each party agrees to maintain the confidence of the Confidential Information and to prevent its unauthorized dissemination or use; provided however that this Agreement shall impose no obligation on a party with respect to maintaining the confidence of Confidential Information which:

(a)   is at the time of disclosure hereunder, or becomes subsequently without fault on the part of Recipient, generally known or available by publication, commercial use or otherwise; or

(b)   is known by that party at the time of disclosure hereunder.

4   Each party agrees not to use the Confidential Information for purposes other than those necessary directly to further the purposes stated above.

5   The Recipient agrees to return all Confidential Information to the Supplier forthwith upon request being made therefor, howsoever the Confidential Information may be embodied at the date of such request, including but not limited to all computer programs, documentation, notes, plans, drawings, and copies thereof, on microfiche, magnetic tape or disk or any other medium whatsoever. In the event such medium cannot be detached from any valuable equipment, the recipient shall so certify and shall forthwith erase the Confidential Information so embodied and certify its erasure to the Supplier within seven (7) days of the request for return being made by the Supplier.

6   Each party hereby acknowledges that unauthorized disclosure or use of Confidential Information could cause irreparable harm and significant injury which may be difficult to ascertain. Accordingly, each party agrees that the other shall have the right to seek and obtain immediate injunctive relief from breaches of this Agreement, in addition to any other rights and remedies it may have.

7   Nothing in this Agreement will be deemed to be an assignment of the copyright or any invention in any part of the Confidential Information or any thing embodying any part of the Confidential Information, or of the developments carried out by the Recipient.

[*In the event of payment of money for the disclosure, add the following clause:]

8   The sum paid by Recipient shall not be refundable, regardless of whether the Recipient is of the view for any reason that the Confidential Information it receives, or any part thereof, has no commercial value or no commercial value to it, or is not confidential, or any other circumstance. Payment of such sum shall not be regarded by the parties as commercial exploitation of any idea or invention embodied in the Confidential Information, but as fair and reasonable remuneration for the services rendered by the Supplier to the Recipient hereunder.]

[Informal Execution Clauses.]

M Escrow Agreements

Software suppliers are understandably reluctant to release their source code to any user; the law of copyright may be clear but that does not mean that it is easy to enforce. In dealing with a volatile industry, users however are equally wary of committing their business to software which may suddenly become useless due to the failure of the supplier. All software has bugs and some of these bugs become apparent only at a later date. Fixing these bugs requires access to the source code.

The problem is to guarantee the user access to the source code should it become necessary, without the supplier losing control of that code. The solution which has gained some popularity is an 'escrow' arrangement.

'Escrow' is an old legal word which originated with the law of deeds (referred to in Chapter 7). A deed was binding upon delivery, so an escrow agent would be an independent third party who would hold a sealed deed and guarantee its delivery to the intended party once certain conditions were met. In the computer industry, an escrow holder will take a copy of source code (or any other development documentation, such as mask data, PCB film, flow charts, etc.) and, for a fee, keep it in a safe place until there are objectively verifiable circumstances permitting its release to the user.

The circumstances of release to the user should be carefully considered. Obviously, they include the bankruptcy or liquidation of the supplier, a matter upon which neither supplier nor user could differ, although for reasons considered shortly these may be difficult pre-conditions in practice. They may also include the failure of the supplier to carry out requested maintenance within a certain time, and in this case there may be difficult drafting to ensure that such a circumstance does *not* include such a refusal based upon the failure of the user to pay licence or maintenance fees!

A difficulty which has vexed the treatment of escrow agreements has been the consequences of receivership, liquidation or bankrupty of the supplier. In Chapter 7, we commented on the difference between executed and executory contracts, the latter being those in which some-thing remains to be done by one of the parties. It is a feature of the appoint-ment of a receiver, liquidator or trustee in bankruptcy that he or she is permitted to renounce executory contracts which impose a burden or obligation on the business the subject of his or her management. It has been argued that an escrow arrangement, under which the user has yet to receive the source code, can be renounced in this fashion so that the user does not get the benefit of either the ongoing support of the supplier or the source code! For this reason, it is important to structure these arrangements defensively against this interpretation; the escrow holder should not be treated as an agent of the supplier, for example, but perhaps a trustee for the benefit of the user (although this has its difficulties also), and the escrow obligation should not be attached to a contract with continuing obligations, such as a maintenance agreement, but should be part of the original licence, or preferably a separate transaction altogether.

The supplier must also promise to keep the escrow agent supplied with the latest version of the source code. It may not always be necessary to have the right of inspection to verify this, but there is no point in having an obligation on a software supplier to hold the material in escrow if it is not being complied with. Once the supplier goes into liquidation it will be too late to discover non-compliance with the escrow agreement; the user will simply have another right of action against the supplier. The whole aim of the agreement is to protect the user.

It is important to note that, even after the source code has been delivered to the user, the user has rights to use the source code only for the agreed purposes and not for any other purposes.

Finally, as the escrow agent is merely a neutral functionary, it is most important that he is freed from involvement, and liability, in any disputes between the main parties.

The example given below is only the agreement with the escrow agent; for a provision imposing the obligation to establish an escrow arrangement, see the escrow provision in A: Boilerplate Clauses, above.

Example ──

THIS AGREEMENT is made the   day of
          19
between   of
                                                        ('the Licensor')
and   of
                                                        ('the Licensee')
AND: of
                                                     ('the Escrow Holder').

WHEREAS:

A   Pursuant to the terms of a Purchase Agreement dated .... between the Licensor
         and the Licensee ('the Purchase Agreement') the Licensor agreed amongst other
         things to supply to the Licensee certain products being .... made in
         accordance with specifications of the Licensee ('the Products') and to develop such
         software from time to time.

B The Licensor has agreed to maintain the Products and developments created by it from time to time and supplied by it to the Licensee pursuant to the Purchase Agreement.

C Pursuant to the Purchase Agreement, the Licensor has agreed to place the Product information specified in Schedule 1 hereto in escrow, including certain relevant technical information and documentation necessary to manufacture, maintain and enhance the Products and spare parts therefor ('the Information').

D The Licensor acknowledges that in certain circumstances the Licensee may require possession of the said Information and is agreeable to providing the same to the Licensee, through the Escrow Holder holding the same on the terms and conditions hereafter contained.

NOW THE PARTIES AGREE as follow:

1 DEFINITIONS

1.1 Where the context permits:

'the Information' means the technical information and documentation relating to the Products, including source code of all computer programs embodied in the Products and PCB films as described in Schedule 1, and as amended from time to time;

'the Products' means the Products and enhancements and other modifications to any part of the Products to be included from time to time pursuant to this Agreement.

1.2 All other words and phrases in this Agreement shall have the same meaning attributed to them in the Purchase Agreement.

2 DEPOSIT AND STORAGE

2.1 The Licensor shall vest in the Escrow Holder and the Escrow Holder shall accept as trustee one copy of the Information in the form specified in Schedule 1 hereto within thirty (30) days of the date hereof.

2.2 The Escrow Holder shall place such copy of the Information in a suitable container, the nature of which shall have been decided by the Escrow Holder after consultation between the parties prior to its deposit (hereinafter called 'the Container'). The Escrow Holder undertakes that the Container will be stored in a safe and secure place.

2.3 Ownership of the Information shall at all times belong to the Licensor but the Licensor agrees to the Escrow Holder's ownership of the copy of the Information (and replacements therefor pursuant to this Clause and Updates pursuant to Clause 3 below) as trustee for the benefit of the Licensee subject to the terms of this Agreement.

2.4 If the copy of the Information held by the Escrow Holder is lost, damaged or destroyed whilst in the possession, custody, or control of the Escrow Holder, the Escrow Holder shall immediately notify the Licensor and the Licensee and thereupon the Licensor shall forthwith deposit with the Escrow Holder such copies of the Information as are necessary to replace that which has been lost, damaged, or destroyed.

3 UPDATING INFORMATION

3.1 At all times while the Purchase Agreement is in force, the Licensor shall ensure that the Information is kept fully up to date and reflects all debugging, enhancements, modifications, and upgrades effected to the Products and supplied to the Licensee in accordance with the Purchase Agreement and for such purposes the Licensor shall deposit a copy of the source codes, technical information and documentation relating to Updates with the Escrow Holder within seven (7) days of their being so supplied to the Licensee.

3.2   If and as long as any development work is being carried out pursuant to the Purchase Agreement, the Licensor shall deposit a copy of the latest version of the Information relating to modifications of the Products with the Escrow Holder on the fifteenth day of each month.

3.3   All further copies of information deposited with the Escrow Holder pursuant to this Clause 3 (hereinafter called 'the Updates') shall be clearly marked with the date of their deposit. Ownership of the Updates shall, upon deposit, vest in the Escrow Holder as trustee for the Licensee and shall be governed by the provisions of Clause 2 hereof and shall be deemed part of the original Information.

3.4   The Escrow Holder shall confirm in writing to the Licensor and the Licensee safe receipt of the Information relating to Updates and shall place the Updates forthwith in the Container and, if so requested by the Licensor destroy the replaced Information or applicable part thereof.

4   INSPECTION

4.1   The Licensee may at any time, by the giving of seven days' notice in writing to the Licensor and the Escrow Holder, require the Escrow Holder to permit an employee of the Licensee (the 'Inspector') to have access to the information for the purpose of ensuring the Information is in a proper condition to fulfil the purposes of this Agreement.

4.2   The Licensor may appoint an employee of the Licensor to accompany the Inspector at all times while the Information, or any of it, is in the possession of the Inspector and it shall be the responsibility of the Licensor to ensure that the said employee is present at the premises of the Escrow Holder at the time nominated in accordance with Clause 4.1 or at such other time as is agreed between the parties.

4.3   The access granted to the Inspector may include the taking of copies of the Information and loading copies of the Products into a computer for the purpose of testing.

4.4   The Inspector may only be given access if he or she undertakes to keep the Information confidential in the terms of Clause 10 hereof.

4.5   At the conclusion of any inspection the Inspector shall return the Information and/or destroy any copies as appropriate.

4.6   The cost of any such inspection shall be borne by the Licensee.

4.7   If the Inspector discovers any deficiency in the Information the Licensee may give the Licensor notice requiring the Licensor to correct the deficiency, at the expense of the Licensor, within seven days, and in this respect time shall be of the essence.

5   RELEASE OF INFORMATION

5.1   In the event that the Licensor ceases to manufacture, service or support the Products in breach of its obligations under the Purchase Agreement or enters into any composition with its creditors or enters into liquidation, whether compulsory or voluntary (other than for the purpose of solvent reconstruction or amalgamation), or has a receiver appointed for all or any part of its assets or undertaking or ceases business or fails to agree to a reasonable request from the Licensee that further enhancements to the Products be made then, subject as hereinafter provided, the Escrow Holder shall upon written request from the Licensee reasonably acceptable to the Escrow Holder forthwith release the Information to the Licensee, to be used by the Licensee only for the purpose specified in Clause 8 below. The written request by the Licensee shall be in the form of a statutory declaration by an officer of the Licensee setting out in detail the grounds upon which release of the Information is sought and exhibiting such documentation in support thereof as the Escrow Holder shall reasonably require. Prior to releasing the Information the Escrow Holder shall be entitled to take such steps to verify the said statutory declaration and documentation as it deems appropriate.

5.2 In the event that a dispute shall arise as to any of the matters referred to in Clause 5.1 hereof or the fulfillment of any obligations referred to therein, the fact of such dispute shall forthwith be referred at the instance of either the Licensee or the Licensor to a director for the time being of the Escrow Holder whose decision shall be final and binding as between the Licensee and the Licensor.

5.3 Nothing in this Clause shall be taken to limit the right of the Licensor or Licensee to recourse to conciliation, arbitration, or the commencement and prosecution of any legal proceedings under the Purchase Agreement and the reference to and decision of the director of the Escrow Holder shall relate solely to exercise of the Escrow Holder's duties under this Agreement and not as to any substantive matter at issue between the Licensor and Licensee. In performing his or her obligations under this Clause, such director shall not be acting as an arbitrator and shall not be bound by rules of natural justice, procedure or evidence.

6   THE ESCROW HOLDER'S FEES

The Licensee shall pay the Escrow Holder's fees as specified in Schedule 2 hereto for the services rendered herein on the date hereof. The Escrow Holder's fees shall be reviewed annually by the Escrow Holder as at each anniversary of the date hereof and upon notice of the reviewed fees being given in writing to the Licensee, the Licensee shall pay such fees within seven (7) days of the relevant anniversary of the date hereof, and time shall be of the essence of the Licensee's obligations herein.

7   PROPERTY IN PRODUCTS/INFORMATION/UPDATES

Except as provided in the Purchase Agreement or any other agreement between the Licensor and the Licensee from time to time, the intangible property rights in each of the Products, the Information and the Updates and any amendments, additions to or variations thereof, whether permitted or not, are and shall remain those of the Licensor and without limiting the generality of the foregoing it is acknowledged by each of the Licensee and the Escrow Holder that, except as hereinbefore provided, each of the Products, the Information and the Upgrades comprise confidential information and copyright material which is the property of the Licensor and neither the Licensee nor the Escrow Holder shall do, allow, permit or cause to be done, allowed or permitted, whether by act of omission or commission anything which is inconsistent with or in derogation of the Licensors's aforesaid proprietary rights.

8   THE LICENSEE'S PERMITTED USE

In the event that the Escrow Holder releases the Information to the Licensee in accordance with the provisions hereof, the Licensee shall only be entitled to use or procure the use of the Information to manufacture, service and maintain the Products in a manner compatible with the provisions of the Purchase Agreement or to enhance the Products. For this purpose, the Licensee shall be permitted to reproduce, or authorise the reproduction, of the Information by, and disclosure to, a manufacturing, maintenance or service agent for such purposes.

9   LIABILITY OF THE ESCROW HOLDER

9.1 The Escrow Holder shall not be liable to any person whatsoever for the accuracy, description, relevance, completeness, merchantable quality, fitness for any purpose or any other matter relating to the Information and/or any Updates or other information received by it hereunder.

9.2 The Escrow Holder shall not be liable to determine that whatever is deposited or accepted by it for deposit is or is not the Information or the Updates as herein defined.

10   OBLIGATIONS OF THE ESCROW HOLDER

10.1   The Escrow Holder hereby agrees to maintain the Information and the Updates and all information and/or documentation coming into its possession or to its knowledge under this Agreement in strictest confidence and secrecy.

10.2   The Escrow Holder undertakes not to make use of the Information and the Updates other than for the performance of its obligations under this Agreement and shall not disclose or release the same to any party other than in accordance with the terms hereof.

10.3   The Escrow Holder undertakes that its employees and any other person authorized by it to have access to the Information and/or Updates shall sign a written undertaking to observe the same degree of confidentiality and secrecy as the Escrow Holder is so bound hereunder.

10.4   The obligations imposed hereunder shall continue, notwithstanding the release of the Information or termination of this Agreement, until or unless the Information falls within the public domain through no fault of the Escrow Holder or the Licensor.

11   INDEMNITY

The Licensee and the Licensor hereby jointly and severally agree to indemnify the Escrow Holder and hold the Escrow Holder harmless against any and all loss, damages, costs and expenses that may be incurred by the Escrow Holder by reason of the Escrow Holder's compliance in good faith with the terms of this Agreement.

12   TERMINATION

12.1   This Agreement shall be terminated upon:

(a)   the expiration of ninety (90) days from the Escrow Holder giving notice to each of the Licensee and the Licensor of such termination;

(b)   the expiration of ninety (90) days from the Licensee and the Licensor jointly giving notice to the Escrow Holder of such termination;

(c)   the Information being released in accordance with Clause 4 hereof;

(d)   the non-payment of the Escrow Holder's fees as herein provided; or

(e)   the destruction or corruption of the Information as a result of *force majeure* or any other circumstances beyond the Escrow Holder's control.

12.2   Upon termination of this Agreement in accordance with either one or more of Clauses 12.1(b) and (d) hereof the Escrow Holder shall forthwith deliver the Information and Updates to the Licensor.

12.3   Upon termination of this Agreement in accordance with Clause 12.1(a) the parties shall negotiate in good faith the appointment of another party as escrow holder. Failing such agreement, the materials and updates shall be returned to the Licensor.

[*Insert Boilerplate Clauses.*]

SCHEDULE 1

THE INFORMATION

[*Describe in detail the materials to be placed in escrow.*]

SCHEDULE 2

THE ESCROW HOLDERS FEES

[*Insert Execution Clauses.*]

N Reciprocal Back-Up Site Agreements

Often disaster recovery plans rely upon an arrangement between users of the same hardware/operating systems that, in the event of a disaster at either site, the victim of the disaster can use the equipment at the other's site. This is obviously a very sensible and practical solution, but such arrangements are difficult to finalize acceptably, and need to be carefully thought through. One is well advised to put in place an agreement covering a number of essential issues.

The obligation to provide a processing site, with the resultant disruption as new data is loaded and new staff occupy one's data processing centre, must not be underestimated. Therefore, what constitutes a disaster ought to be carefully considered. Neither party wishes to discover that its computer is being used to carry out the overflow processing of the other, in other words, the 'disaster' is simply the fact that the hardware of one party can no longer efficiently cope with the demands being made of it. One method of guarding against this is to specify that processing can take place at the back-up site only when no processing is possible at the other.

The next issue to consider is the specification of the times at which reciprocal access will be allowed. Obviously, the back-up site will be upset if disaster recovery by the other party affects its ability to process its own work, and access may have to be limited to after hours batch processing, or weekend processing. By the same token, if the whole process is going to work, the victim of the disaster will need reasonable access. Naturally, compromise is the essence of these arrangements.

What forms of access will be allowed? For instance, is dial up a possibility? Depending upon the nature of the disaster, and the nature of the two facilities involved, it might be possible for disaster recovery to take place on a bureau basis.

The total number of people allowed on the reciprocal site at any one time should be limited, and such people must be made aware of, and be prepared to abide by, the rules of the reciprocal site, particularly those relating to security. It may also be necessary to limit the 'class' of people allowed access — security may dictate that only DP people have access to the site. This is obviously a very important issue. For most organizations the computer room is the heart of operations and anybody with access to that area potentially has access to very detailed and confidential information about the business. Certain things can be physically locked away and normal security precautions should apply but there may need to be special provisions in the agreement as to what parts of the room there can be access. Within the computer system too there can be restriction on access.

Perhaps the biggest problem to consider is the continuing compatibility of the two systems. Both hardware and software must be taken into account in a provision whereby each party guarantees that it will maintain parallel system acquisitions and upgrades — if either party decides against this, that moment should be the end of the arrangement; the parties should not wait for a disaster to find that they have gone down incompatible paths. As an operational problem it may not be possible for the two installations to be kept exactly parallel over an extended period, but if this is the case there should be provision in the agreement for compatible systems to be available for rapid installation. It is a good idea in this case to provide for regular, say six monthly, trial runs to ensure continued compatibility.

There are certain costs associated with running any computer, the costs of power, consumables, and perhaps the cost of security and DP staff that must supervise the other party's use of the system. It should be agreed who will bear these costs: the costs may be borne where they fall because of the reciprocal benefits of the agreement, or the party causing the additional expenditure may agree to pay all these costs.

There are a number of other issues, which are considered in the following example.

Example

THIS AGREEMENT is made the   day   of 19
BETWEEN   of
                                                                ('Company 1') of the one part
AND   of
                                                                ('Company 2') of the other part
WHEREAS

A   Company 1 is the owner or otherwise in possession of the hardware and operating
        system software configuration described in the Schedule hereto presently installed
        at its premises at [*specify location*].

B   Company 2 is the owner or otherwise in possession of the hardware and operating
        system software configuration described in the Schedule hereto presently installed
        at its premises at [*specify location*].

C   Company 1 and Company 2 have each agreed to share the use of the other's
        hardware and operating system software in the event of total or substantial
        unavailability of its own hardware and operating system software upon and subject
        to the terms and conditions of this Agreement.

NOW IT IS HEREBY AGREED AND DECLARED

1   INTERPRETATION

1.1   In this Agreement unless and to the extent that the context requires otherwise:

'Back-Up Rights' means the right to request and use the hardware and operating system of the other party to this Agreement on the occurrence of a Disaster Event;

'Back-Up Site' means the location of the hardware to be used by the parties following the occurrence of a Disaster Event.

'Commencement Date' means [*specify date from which the parties will be in a position to comply with their mutual obligations*];

'Disaster Event' means an event in which for any reason it is not possible for productive work to be executed on the hardware of the party exercising its Back-Up Rights;

'Minimum Back-Up Configuration' means the minimum configuration specified in the Schedule hereto required by the party exercising Back-Up Rights following the occurrence of a Disaster Event.

2   BACK-UP RIGHTS

2.1   Upon the occurrence of a Disaster Event, the party whose hardware and operating system software is unavailable ('the Affected Party') may give notice to the other party hereto ('the Back-Up Party') that the Affected Party requires the use of the hardware and operating system software of the Back-Up Party.

2.2   In the event that either party hereto receives notice of a Disaster Event from the other party hereto, the Back-Up Party shall make available to the Affected Party no less than the Minimum Back-Up Configuration of its hardware and operating system software for use and operation by the Affected Party in accordance with this Agreement. In addition, the Back-Up Party will make available such of its staff as it may have available and willing to provide the Affected Party with assistance in the use and operation of the hardware and operating system software.

2.3   Upon notification of a Disaster Event by the Affected Party, the Affected Party shall notify the Back-Up Party of the names or descriptions of all persons which it requires to be permitted on the Back-Up Site for the purpose of exercising the Back-Up Rights under this Agreement. The Back-Up Party shall be entitled to object to the number of personnel or to the attendance of particular personnel and shall in addition be entitled to appoint times for the orderly exercise of the Back-Up Rights including installation and operation of application software and related matters. Provided that at all times whilst on or about the Back-Up Site, all such persons so nominated by the Affected Party shall wear any security identification that the Back-Up Party may require and shall comply with all the Back-Up Party's reasonable directions, the Back-Up Party shall provide access to the Back-Up Site to all such persons in accordance with the times and appointment specified and shall allow such persons to use the hardware and operating system software and other equipment supplied by the Affected Party consistent with the Back-Up Party's normal practices and procedures. To facilitate the provisions of such access, the Back-Up Party shall provide reasonable facilities such as, but not limited to, secure storage space, a designated work area with adequate heat and light, and access to a telephone line in accordance with the Back-Up Party's normal business practices.

2.4   On receipt of notice of a Disaster Event, the Back-Up Party shall advise the Affected Party of the times and number of hours of availability of the Back-Up Party's hardware and operating system software. Such times and hours shall be reasonable and adequate for the Affected Party's minimum processing requirements during the period of unavailability of the Affected Party's hardware and operating system software PROVIDED HOWEVER that the Back-Up Party shall make available at least the Minimum Back-Up Configuration and it shall be reasonable for the Back-Up Party to require the Affected Party to use and operate the Back-Up Party's hardware and operating system software outside normal business hours and/or in batch processing mode (where possible).

2.5   The Affected Party shall at its own cost

(a)   procure all necessary consents and/or licences

(i)   to use any application software on the Back-Up Party's hardware at the Back-Up Site following the occurrence of a Disaster Event; and

(ii)   to use the Back-Up Party's hardware and operating system for its own purposes pursuant to this Agreement following the occurrence of a Disaster Event.

(b)   provide all necessary media and consumables, as well as any specialized communications or other equipment it may require in order to exercise Back-Up Rights;

(c)   not in any way damage, interrupt or otherwise interfere with the Back-Up Party's data or processing on the Back-Up Party's hardware and operating system software;

(d)   permit its use of the Back-Up Party's hardware and operating system to be supervised by employees of the Back-Up Party and shall reimburse the Back-Up Party's reasonable expenses in providing such supervision including any overtime payment or allowance required to be paid in such event;

(e)   itself comply, and shall cause its employees or agents entering upon the Back-Up Site at all times to comply, with the reasonable directions of the Back-Up Party, including the wearing of security identification and other security requirements while on the Back-Up Site; the Back-Up Party may require any employee or agent of the Affected Party to leave the Back-Up Site and the Affected Party shall ensure that any such employee to which the Back-Up party objects shall not attend the Back-Up Site;

(f)   pay the Back-Up Party's reasonable expenses incurred in providing the Back-Up Party's hardware and operating system software for use in operation by the Affected Party, including if required an apportionment of electrical and amenities charges, maintenance and support costs and fees, wages and salaries, and consumables calculated in accordance with the Affected Party's utilization of the Back-Up Party's hardware and operating system software as a proportion of the overall utilization of the Back-Up Party's hardware and operating system software during the time of use by the Affected Party. Such expenses shall not include any apportionment of rent or lease payments for the hardware and operating system software or the Back-Up Site itself.

The Affected Party's continued right to exercise the Back-Up Rights pursuant to this Agreement shall be conditional upon compliance with the provisions of this paragraph 2.5, and may be terminated forthwith upon breach thereof.

2.6   The Affected Party shall be responsible for operating terminal devices and telecommunications facilities and for arranging all activities connected with the use and operation of such devices and other equipment required by the Affected Party on the Back-Up Site, other than the Back-Up Party's hardware and operating system software.

2.7   The Back-Up Party shall use all reasonable endeavours to arrange for the physical safety and integrity of the Affected Party's media and documentation whilst on the Back-Up Site.

3   MAINTENANCE OF THE HARDWARE AND OPERATING SYSTEM
    SOFTWARE CONFIGURATION

3.1   In the event that either party proposes to alter the configuration of its hardware or obtain an amendment, upgrade, or new release or version of any part of the hardware or operating system software it shall forthwith notify the other party of its intention whereby the parties may discuss any variation to this Agreement or the annexures hereto or termination pursuant to Clause 4 hereof as the case may be. In the event that the parties hereto agree that this Agreement must be terminated as a result of any proposed changes to the hardware and/or operating system software of either party, then the party proposing such change shall not implement such change until the conclusion of the period of sixty (60) days' notice specified in Clause 4.2 hereof.

3.2   Each party hereto warrants that it shall use its best endeavours to maintain the hardware and operating system software in accordance with the manufacturer's and/or supplier's environmental and maintenance recommendations PROVIDED HOWEVER that nothing in this clause shall constitute any guarantee or warranty that a party's hardware and operating system software will be available for use on the occurrence of a Disaster Event to the other party's hardware and operating system software.

4   COMMENCEMENT AND DURATION

4.1   This Agreement shall commence on the Commencement Date and shall continue until terminated pursuant to the provisions hereof.

4.2   This Agreement may be terminated by either party for any reason, with or without cause, on sixty (60) days' prior written notice, whether or not the hardware and operating system software of the terminating party is being used at the date of such notice.

4.3   In addition, this Agreement may be terminated by notice forthwith by either party after notice specifying a breach of this Agreement and requiring its correction is served by the terminating party and such breach remains unremedied fifteen (15) days after such notice has been received by the party in breach.

5   WARRANTIES AND REPRESENTATIONS

5.1   The Affected Party shall at all times and notwithstanding any assistance, direction or supervision provided by any employee of the Back-Up Party, be and remain entirely responsible for the results obtained from the use of the Back-Up Party's hardware and operating system software. Each party hereto accordingly acknowledges and declares for the benefit of the other that it does not require from and is not given by the other the benefit of any warranty or representation whatsoever as to the hardware or the operating system software (including without limitation any warranty or representation as to the merchantability or fitness for any purpose) or any benefits to be obtained from the use thereof. Neither party hereto shall in any circumstance be liable or accountable to the other for any defects in the hardware or the operating system software unless such defect is caused directly by any wilful or negligent act or omission of the Back-Up Party.

5.2   The Affected Party shall indemnify and save harmless the Back-Up Party and any of its employees or agents from and against any loss or damage suffered by the Back-Up Party, its employees or agents, (including without limitation loss of revenue or income) and any and all liability to any third party (including reasonable legal costs and disbursements) for any loss or damage not the fault of the Back-Up Party arising from or in connection with the exercise of the Back-Up Rights hereunder and the attendance of any persons on the Back-Up Site in order to exercise such Back-Up Rights.

5.3   The Back-Up Party shall indemnify and save harmless the Affected Party and any of its employees or agents from and against any direct loss or damage suffered by the Affected Party (excluding indirect losses including, without limiting the generality of the foregoing, loss of revenue or income) for any loss or damage not the fault of the Affected Party arising from any failure by the Back-Up Party to provide adequate maintenance and support of the Back-Up Party's hardware and operating system software during the term of this Agreement or the variation of the configuration of the hardware and operating system software from that specified in the annexures hereto, including the Minimum Back-Up Configuration without notice to the Affected Party. Such indemnity shall extend only to the cost of locating reasonable substitute back-up facilities where possible.

5.4   Each party hereto warrants and agrees that its exercise of the Back-Up Rights shall be solely for its own benefit and not for the benefit of any third party hereto.

5.5   Each party hereto shall ensure that it has adequate back-up and disaster recovery procedures to minimize the risk of exercise of the Back-Up Rights hereunder and, if exercised, to minimize the duration of use of the Back-Up Party's hardware and operating system software pursuant to this Agreement.

6   ADVICE AND CONSULTATION
Each party hereto shall consult with the other, cooperate in all reasonable respects, supply to the other all information and make available such personnel resources as it may reasonably require to provide the Back-Up Rights and otherwise comply with its obligations hereunder.

7   MOVEMENT OF THE INSTALLATION SITE
In the event that either party intends to move the Installation Site of its hardware and operating system software then such party shall give the other three (3) months' notice in writing of the intended date of such move and shall consult with the other as to any necessary changes in the matter of providing the Back-Up Rights or the requirements of either party caused by such a move.

8   CONFIDENTIALITY
8.1   Each party warrants that it will retain in confidence all data concerning the other obtained in the course of performing this Agreement, and will neither use it nor disclose it to anyone without the express written permission of the other unless such data is in the public domain without any breach of any contract or confidence.

8.2   Neither party shall make any public statements in relation to this Agreement without the prior written permission of the other which permission shall not be unreasonably witheld.

8.3   Each party to this Agreement shall preserve and ensure that its employees and agents preserve the confidentiality of all data, information, documents and material disclosed or entrusted to it by the other party on a confidential basis.
[Insert Boilerplate Clauses.]

SCHEDULE

Company 1 Equipement
Company 2 Equipement
Minimum Configuration
[Insert Execution Clauses.]

O Database / Network Access Agreements

Access to useful data, or to communication network, is one of the new services created by the computer industry, and as we have seen in Chapter 11, it has created some special problems.

The contract permitting such supply typically deals with a number of matters of great concern to the supplier of such access; the user of the service generally is only concerned with continuity of access and quality of the data available. The first issue therefore dealt with by the contract, after the term of the contract and the payment of the supplier's charges, is the shifting of responsibility for the continuity of supply of the service to the user, at least in part, that is the connection by the telecommunications services. The contract also shifts the burden of responsibility for the quality of the data to the user. This may seem less fair, as it is the supplier who is in complete control of the data supplied. However, as we have seen in Chapter 9, the potential liability in negligence of a supplier of information, or under other related laws, such as unfair competition laws, is a serious risk which the supplier of information must do everything possible to minimize — at least to reduce insurance premiums.

Foremost among the issues dealt with by the contract is copyright. Databases enjoy copyright protection either under specific laws, such as the Japanese law granting databases copyright protection, or as a general literary work, a 'compilation'. In that case, the supplier is entitled to remind the user that the data should not be copied, except of course to the extent reasonable to use the service, presumably to make one hard copy at the time of downloading.

Fraudulent access to the network is another vexed issue. Naturally, the user does not wish to pay for, or be responsible for any other consequences of, fraudulent access. On the other hand, the supplier of access has far less responsibility for such access than the user, and has a reasonable expectation of payment.

Example ——————————————————————————————

THIS AGREEMENT is made the   day of   19
BETWEEN   of
                                                    ('the Company') of the one part

AND   of
                                          ('the Customer') of the other part

WHEREAS:

A   Pursuant to an Agreement dated   ('the Licence Agreement') the Customer is
          licenced to use the software package known as [*name of Software Package*] ('the
          Communications Software').

B   The Customer has requested and the Company has agreed to supply certain
          transaction information for use by the Customer with the Communications
          Software.

NOW THIS AGREEMENT WITNESSES as follows:

1   DEFINITIONS
1.1   'The Company System' shall mean the computer system used by the Company
          from time to time to provide the Information.

1.2   'The Customer's System' shall mean the Customer's computer system used by the
          Customer from time to time to receive the Information.

1.3   'The Commencement Date' shall mean   19

1.4   'Information' shall mean the information made available by the Company which is
          more fully described in Schedule 1.

1.5   In this Agreement unless the contrary intention appears all words and terms should
          have the same meanings as those set out in the Schedules.

2   TERM
          Unless earlier terminated pursuant to further provisions herein, this Agreement
          shall come into force on the Commencement Date and continue for a period one
          (1) year and thereafter until terminated by either party on the giving of three (3)
          months' notice in writing. In addition, this Agreement and the licences hereby
          granted shall terminate automatically upon termination for any reason of the
          Licence Agreement.

3   CHARGES
3.1   In consideration of the Company providing the Information the Customer shall
          pay to the Company the Annual Fee and access charges set out in Schedule 2.

3.2   The Annual Fee shall be due and payable on the Commencement Date and
          thereafter on each anniversary of the Commencement Date.

3.3   The Company shall be entitled to adjust the Annual Fee by giving the Customer
          notice not less than ninety (90) days prior to the anniversary of the Commence-
          ment Date.

3.4   If invoices are not paid within thirty days, the Company may suspend provision of
          the Information and, in addition, such unpaid amounts shall bear interest at the
          rate of 2½% per month or such lesser amount as is the maximum amount allowed
          by law. The Customer acknowledges that such interest is a genuine pre-estimate of
          the Company's cost of funding such overdue amounts and is not a penalty.

3.5   In addition to all charges specified herein the Customer shall reimburse the
          Company for any taxes and duties, excluding income tax and personal property
          tax, paid by the Company and which are directly applicable to the provision of the
          Information by the Company.

4   INFORMATION
4.1   The Information will be provided only by standard telephone line/modem
          connection ('the Link').

4.2   Other than a signal from the Customer's System to the Company's System requesting that the Information be downloaded, there will be no access of the Company's System by the Customer's System. The Customer shall be responsible for ensuring that the Customer's System and the Link are used solely for the purpose of obtaining the Information and any improper use of the Customer's System or the Link shall be the responsibility of the Customer.

5   **DUTIES OF THE CUSTOMER**

5.1   The Customer shall be responsible for:

(a)   payment of all charges for access to the Information gained by use of the Customer's network address and password, whether or not the Customer gains any benefit therefrom, including any unauthorized use (unless caused by the neglect or fault of the Company);

(b)   arranging and maintaining with the relevant telecommunications authorities for any permissions required for provision of the Link;

(c)   arranging its own communication facilities in consultation with the Company, including the use and maintenance of suitable computer and communications equipment;

(d)   ensuring that proper steps are taken to ensure security of the Customer's System and the Link;

(e)   ensuring that the Information is used only for the internal purposes of the Customer.

6   **CONFIDENTIALITY AND COPYRIGHT IN DATA AND PASSWORD**

6.1   All parts of the Information obtained by the Customer pursuant to this Agreement are confidential to the Company. In addition, copyright in the Information belongs to or is licensed to the Company for supply to the Customer only. The Customer is only licensed by this Agreement to use the Information for its own internal business purposes, such licence not extending to reproduction of the Information (other than a single download to disk or other storage medium and a single printed copy) or resupply to any person whatsoever.

6.2   In addition, the Customer shall maintain its password used for access to the Information in the utmost confidence in order to prevent unauthorized use and access to the Information.

7   **PERFORMANCE**

7.1   The Company does not warrant the correctness or completeness of the Information. It is the responsibility of the Customer at all times to ensure that such parts of the Information used by it are correct by independent verification means, before any reliance is placed on it.

7.2   The Company shall not be liable to the Customer for any loss or damage suffered or incurred by the Customer arising from or in relation to any alleged failure by the Company to meet any performance specifications or criteria when such failure arises from circumstances not in the control of the Company, including but not limited to: (a) defects in a communication line; (b) any breach of this Agreement by the Customer; and (c) computer failure.

8   **PROPERTY**

All documentation, tapes, disk packs and programs utilized or developed by the Company in connection with this Agreement (except those furnished by the Customer) are and remain the sole property of the Company.

[*Boilerplate Clause.*]

SCHEDULE 1

[*Here specify the data to which the Customer has access.*]

SCHEDULE 2

[*Here specify the charges for access.*]

[*Execution Clause.*]

P   Software Distribution Agreements

Software has two special characteristics, portability and ease of copying, which make it unusually attractive for distribution internationally, as its high value is combined with relatively low freight, insurance and storage costs. With these, however, are often high sales and technical support costs. There are other disadvantages, of course, with the prevalence of unauthorized copying, although such theft denies its perpetrators the advantage of support for the software, and with support access to new, improved versions.

The ease with which software lends itself to distribution, and the special needs of software distribution, demand the inclusion here of a distribution agreement for software.

Software may be distributed in two ways. It may be purchased and distributed as finished goods, or it may be relatively inexpensively manufactured by the distributor itself. The latter method is in fact more like a traditional publishing agreement, and therefore certain special issues must be addressed by the contract, such as the following.

(1)   There must be granted an express right to reproduce the software (as well as any necessary manuals) — however, this right must be carefully circumscribed, as a general licence would permit the distributor to reproduce parts only of the software, perhaps for inclusion in its own products. It may be appropriate to assist the distributor with appropriate materials, such as transparencies and bromides for printing, as well as copy protection software, where necessary. The reproduction right may extend to marketing materials, and technical and marketing brochures.

(2)   There must be granted an express licence in respect of the supplier's trade marks for reproduction on packaging, and express controls on the appearance and quality of packaging and manuals — the placing of trade marks on goods made by the distributor is classic 'use' in trade mark law (as distinguished from a distributor of finished goods, already marked by the supplier, who is merely *displaying* a mark in relation to the supplier's own goods, not *using* it, a fine legal distinction) and unless there is a licence, the distributor may gain proprietary rights in respect of the marks.

Consideration should also be given to registering with national trade mark authorities a user agreement making clear the distributor's status. On the other hand, the distributor must not be permitted to present the software as its own, and the agreement should go beyond a mere licence but require the correct presentation of the supplier's marks.

(3)   Clearly, since the supplier's remuneration is not principally derived from a margin on sales, it is usually based upon royalties. Royalty arrangements are among the most complex and difficult of all to draft, and in the absence of written, clear and comprehensive agreement, among the most likely to result in dispute. Vague expressions such as 'nett receipts' or 'gross receipts', should be carefully defined, specifying the deductions permissible (manufacturing costs, distribution costs, fixed and variable overheads, and so on), and there should be detailed provisions for reporting at regular intervals and the auditing of royalties (the costs of which can be so high, that provisions for cooperation and payment of audit costs should also be dealt with). It should be remembered that the software may not be 'sold', but may be licensed or supplied on other bases which may affect the characterization of moneys taken in by the distributor — a known device to reduce the royalty bearing receipts is to supply the software very cheaply but make up the difference in installation or service charges.

(4)   In international transactions, royalty earnings are almost invariably the subject of taxation in their country of origin, at least withholding tax which is deductible in the supplier's country, the implications of which should be carefully weighed. It is also possible, as the supplier usually requires the supply of the software on licence, that a supplier may be regarded as *prima facie* taxable on the full retail licence fee, which would create very awkward problems.

(5)   In consideration of royalties, it should be recognized that the distributor needs to have a certain number of copies free of royalties (unless that is taken into account in the percentage fixed upon), for the purposes of warranty replacement, promotions (give-aways) and demonstration copies, but care must be taken to place a limit on promotional and demonstration copies, so that they do not become the preferred method of supply, and outnumber copies supplied in a manner resulting in royalties.

(6)   Because of these licences, even greater care than usual should be given to the *term* of the agreement. All agreements should provide for certain minimum performance obligations, failure to comply with which will permit early termination. However, in any contract for longer than one year, performance requirements set

out in a contract can become rather artificial, and consideration should be given to the annexing of the distributor's business plan each year, and making the creation of an acceptable business plan a condition of renewal, the terms of which are made binding obligations.

(7) Careful thought should be devoted to the outlining of the distributor's support obligations. Failure to support adequately the software, commonly the distributor's greatest expense and not the most obviously revenue earning for it, will quickly result in the supplier's loss of reputation. In this area, the different requirements of minor updates (frequently supplied free of charge as they correct small defects), upgrades (frequently supplied for a fee) and entirely new versions (which can be virtually new programs and therefore only be supplied on the basis of repurchase) should be dealt with. It may be necessary for the distributor to have access to part or all of the source codes for the software.

(8) As a supplier in this form of distribution relationship can become somewhat distanced from its market, it is important to introduce regular reporting. This also has the advantage of ensuring a forum for discussion of supplier/distributor concerns, which is the most likely device for the avoidance of dispute in the longer term.

Many similar issues are raised by standard distribution of finished goods. The example given below deals with these issues, but in a very minimal fashion. In all distribution agreements, great care should be taken to add to the respective obligations of the parties to create a customized agreement which precisely reflects their mutual concerns.

Example

THIS AGREEMENT is made the day of 19
BETWEEN: of
(herein called 'Supplier') of the one part
AND: of
(herein called 'Distributor') of the other part.

WHEREAS:

A The Supplier owns or has the right to license and/or arrange the distribution of certain complete computer programs for use in conjunction with [*specify hardware upon which software is used*], and related peripheral products, such computer programs being known as [*name software program, or refer to schedule of products*].

B The Distributor has requested the Supplier to permit it to market and distribute such computer programs in [*specify country or area*] and has submitted to the Distributor a business plan specifying the manner in which it proposes to distribute and support same.

C In reliance upon the representations made by the Distributor, the Supplier has agreed to permit the Distributor the right to market and distribute such programs upon and subject to the terms and conditions of this Agreement.

NOW THE PARTIES AGREE as follows:

1   DEFINITIONS
- (a)   'Business Plan' means the business plan referred to in Recital B above, which is annexed to this Agreement and Marked Exhibit 1, as amended or added to pursuant to this Agreement, or any business plan substituted therefor pursuant to this Agreement;
- (b)   'Effective Date' means the date of execution of this Agreement by the Supplier;
- (c)   'Software' means:
  - (i)   the before recited computer programs and upgrades and enhancements thereof from time to time, and any other computer programs agreed between the Supplier and the Distributor to be incorporated herein; and
  - (ii)   all documentation including (without limitation) all user manuals pertaining to such programs;
- (d)   'Sub-Distributor' means any person or corporation to whom the Distributor grants distribution rights in respect of the whole or any part of the Software in accordance with the terms of this Agreement;
- (e)   'Territory' means [specify country or area]; and
- (f)   'Ordinary Business Hours' means the ordinary hours of trading on business days in the Territory.

2   TERM
2.1   This agreement shall commence on the Effective Date and shall continue for a period of [specify initial term] from the Effective Date, unless earlier terminated in accordance with the terms hereof. Not less than three (3) calendar months prior to the expiration of this Agreement by the passage of time the Distributor may notify the Supplier that it wishes to renew this Agreement for a further period of [specify term], and provided that the Distributor is not in breach of this Agreement and has submitted to the Supplier a new Business Plan to cover the period of such renewal which is acceptable to the Supplier, this Agreement (other than this Clause) shall be extended for a further period of [specify renewal period].

2.2   In the event that this Agreement is renewed pursuant to paragraph 2.1 above, the Business Plan accepted by the Supplier shall be substituted for Exhibit 1 hereto.

3   DISTRIBUTOR RIGHTS AND DUTIES
3.1   *Grant of Licence*
- (a)   During the term of this Agreement and subject to its terms and conditions, the Supplier grants to the Distributor an exclusive, non-transferable right to reproduce, market and distribute the Software and to sub-distribute the Software, limited to the Territory only and only as expressly permitted by this Agreement.
- (b)   The grant herein
  - (i)   is subject to and conditional upon the Distributor obtaining all necessary licences and authorities necessary to enable it to effectively exercise all or any of the rights herein granted in the Territory, including but not limited to any governmental licences or permits, and any licences required in respect of the distribution of related software for use with the Software; and
  - (ii)   does not (by virtue of its exclusivity) operate to restrict the Supplier from incorporating the Software into, or dealing with the Software in the Territory as part of, any other computer product of the Supplier, including without limitation the Supplier software currently developed and being developed by the Supplier.

3.2   *Distribution of Software*

(a)   The Distributor may within the Territory appoint non-exclusive Sub-Distributors of the Software to assist in the marketing and distribution of the Software in the Territory, and shall keep the Supplier advised from time to time of the names and addresses of the Sub-Distributors so appointed. Such Sub-Distributors shall not be granted permission or any right by the Distributor to reproduce the Software, in whole or in part, for any purpose whatsoever.

(b)   The appointment by the Distributor of any Sub-Distributor shall not operate as an assignment of any or all of the Distributor's obligations hereunder, and the Distributor shall remain primarily liable for the acts and omissions of such Sub-Distributors as if they were the acts or omissions of the Distributors.

(c)   The Supplier shall be entitled at any time during Ordinary Business Hours and on reasonable notice to inspect and, if it requests, to copy any writing or other record evidencing the appointment of any Sub-Distributor in order to ensure compliance with this Agreement, and the Distributor shall provide the Supplier or its nominated agents in that regard every assistance PROVIDED HOWEVER that nothing herein shall entitle the Supplier to copy any record or obtain any information concerning prices at which the Distributor sells copies of the Software to Sub-Distributors.

3.3   *Marketing of Software*

(a)   The Distributor at its expense shall diligently seek to develop in the Territory the market for and to advertise and promote in the Territory sales of the Software to the fullest extent and shall make such provisions as it deems adequate to supply the Software in sufficient quantity to reasonably satisfy such market.

(b)   Such advertising and promotion shall at all times fairly and accurately represent the Software in relation to other products of its type and shall comply with any reasonable directions as to content or format that the Supplier may from time to time give to the Distributor in that regard. Copies of all advertising and promotional material shall be supplied to the Supplier in sufficient time prior to publication to enable it to give any specific directions it may have and for such directions to be acted upon.

3.4   *Marketing*

No later than thirty (30) days prior to the start of any calendar year during the term hereof, the Distributor shall, if requested by the Supplier, prepare and deliver to the Supplier for the Supplier's review, a marketing plan for the Software including without limitation, a description of:

(a)   the market trends in the Territory;

(b)   the Distributor's channels of distribution;

(c)   promotional activities contemplated by the Distributor; and

(d)   other marketing activities contemplated by the Distributor.

3.5   *Title*

The original and any copies or versions of the Software, in whole or in part, whether or not incorporated in other software programs, including without limitation translations, partial copies, modifications and updates are and shall be the property of the Supplier or a third party which has licensed its right in the Software to the Supplier. This Agreement shall not convey title or grant any rights of ownership in the Software to the Distributor, nor shall the Distributor grant or purport to grant any rights of ownership in the Software to any third parties.

3.6   *Compliance with the Business Plan*

In the exercise of its rights hereunder, and performance of its obligations, the Distributor shall comply with its representations and performance forecasts in the Business Plan, unless and to the extent that the Business Plan is amended by agreement between the Supplier and the Distributor. As a condition to its agreement to any such amendment, either party may require additions to the Business Plan.

4   TRADE MARKS

4.1   *Permitted Use*

The Supplier grants to the Distributor for the duration of this Agreement the non-exlusive, non-assignable right to use and display the trade marks and the names [*specify only the names and marks essential to the advertising and distribution of the Software*] belonging to the Supplier, only in the Territory and only in relation to the Software subject to the terms and conditions herein contained. Such use shall at all times comply with the Supplier's corporate and/or product identity guidelines from time to time notified to the Distributor.

4.2   *Agreement to Use*

The Distributor covenants and agrees to mark each copy of the Software made by the Distributor with the trade marks and names referred to in the preceding section in accordance with the packaging format of the Supplier from time to time and to ensure that they appear in all catalogues and other promotional material relating to the Software subject always as set forth in Clause 4.3. The Distributor shall not give undue prominence to its own names and marks on such packaging or in such catalogues or other promotional material as against the Supplier, and on the packaging the Distributor's name or mark shall not unless the Supplier otherwise agrees appear other than as a small, discreet notice of the status of the Distributor as a licensee of the Supplier.

4.3   *Packaging Format*

Without limiting the generality of the foregoing the Distributor undertakes and agrees to ensure that all Software supplied by it or its Sub-Distributors is clearly marked in a manner approved by the Supplier disclosing that the Software (as the case may be) is subject to copyright in the Territory belonging to the Supplier, and that the names and marks of the Supplier used by the Distributor belong to the Supplier and are licensed to the Distributor.

4.4   *Formalization*

If the Supplier desires to better secure its proprietary rights in respect of the Software and/or in respect of the names and marks referred to in the preceding sections, the Distributor will when requested by the Supplier and at the Supplier's expense do all such things and execute all such documents as the Supplier or its attorneys may advise to be necessary in that regard.

5   SOFTWARE LICENCE FEES — PAYMENT TERMS

5.1   *Software Licence Fees*

(a)   In consideration of the rights herein granted, the Distributor shall pay to the Supplier royalties at the rate of [*specify royalty rate, for example:* forty percent (40%)] of the Supplier's recommended retail price as published from time to time for each copy of the whole or any part of the Software supplied by the Distributor to any person, whether free of charge or otherwise, PROVIDED HOWEVER that during the term hereof the Distributor shall be permitted to make and supply such numbers of copies of the Software royalty free as follows:

Purpose of Supply	Number *per annum*
fair and reasonable replacements for defective goods supplied *without charge*	not more than 5% of copies supplied
copies of the Software supplied *free of charge* as upgrades or enhancements under regular upgrade and enhancement programs approved by the Supplier	not exceeding installed base
free demonstration copies supplied in the ordinary course of business	twenty (20) only

The Distributor shall be permitted such royalty free copies only on the condition that records are maintained which establish to the Supplier's satisfaction that the copies of the Software claimed to be royalty free have been supplied for the approved purpose.

(b)   Within thirty (30) days after the close of each calendar month during the term hereof, commencing with the month following the Effective Date, the Distributor shall furnish to the Supplier a complete and accurate royalty statement for such month, together with a banker's draft in Australian Dollars for all royalties then due and owing.

5.2   *Reports*
At the election and cost of the Supplier, on or before the sixtieth day after the end of each of the Distributor's Fiscal Years, the Distributor shall deliver to the Supplier certified statements from the Distributor's then regularly engaged independent accountants showing, on an annualized basis, the information previously set forth in the monthly royalty statements. The Distributor's accountants who render the certified statements shall be members of or affiliated with an internationally recognized, independent accounting firm.

5.3   *Audit Rights*
The Distributor shall permit the Supplier and its agents and accountants, on reasonable notice and at reasonable times during normal business hours, to audit, at the expense of the Supplier, the books and records of the Distributor which pertain to the subject matter of this Agreement. In the event that an audit by the Supplier shall disclose any error in accounting by the Distributor, appropriate royalty adjustments shall be paid immediately by the Distributor, or refunded by the Supplier, as the case might be. In the further event that such error is found to be favourable to the Supplier in an amount equal to or in excess of 10% of the amount actually reported for any quarter, the Distributor shall reimburse to the Supplier the cost of such audit. If three (3) or more such errors are disclosed by audits undertaken within the term of this Agreement, the Distributor shall be deemed to be in material breach of this Agreement and the Supplier shall have the right to terminate this Agreement without further notice to the Distributor.

5.4   *Expenses*
The Distributor shall be solely responsible for all costs and expenses (including without limitation all taxes, levies, duties and export or import duties and similar charges of whatever nature, whether imposed by local, state or federal governments or agencies) incurred by it in the marketing, sub-distributing and distribution of the Software.

6   PURCHASE OF GOODS FROM THE SUPPLIER
6.1   *Orders, Terms and Title*
The Distributor may purchase, whether for resupply or otherwise, any Supplier products on its product price list from time to time at such discount as may be

agreed upon between the Supplier and the Distributor from time to time. In addition, the Distributor may purchase from the Suppplier any marketing materials, such as point of sale materials, brochures and product specifications, or packaging materials, produced by or for the Supplier, at cost plus reasonable handling and shipping charges, in order to assist it in the carrying out of its obligations hereunder. All prices shall be FOB the [*specify city of the office of the Supplier*] office of the Supplier, exclusive of sales tax (if any). Orders may be placed upon the Supplier at its address first hereinbefore appearing by telex, first class mail or any other written means, and shall be effective upon receipt of payment in cash or such credit documentation (such as a letter of credit, banker's draft or guarantee) as may be agreed upon between the Supplier and the Distributor from time to time. Title shall not pass in any goods ordered by the Distributor until full payment has been received therefor.

6.2   *Delivery*

The Supplier will use its best efforts to deliver orders within thirty days of the effective date of such orders and the Supplier will endeavour to do all that is necessary to facilitate delivery of Supplier products PROVIDED HOWEVER that the Supplier shall not be liable for any delay in delivery or cancellation of any order arising from the unavailability of any goods ordered or any other circumstance beyond the Supplier's control. The Supplier shall be entitled to allocate orders in such manner as it deems fit.

7   SOFTWARE SUPPORT

7.1   *Enhancements and Upgrades*

(a)   The Supplier will send to the Distributor at no extra charge all enhancements of the Software or any part thereof released to the Supplier's customers. It is the duty of the Distributor to ensure that end-users in the Territory are notified without delay of available upgraded versions of the Software and such versions are to be made available to end-users without delay.

(b)   'Enhancements' and 'upgrades' in this Clause do not include new products of the Supplier, whether or not such new products incorporate the whole or any part of any existing Supplier product, or any features of any existing Supplier product, the subject of this Agreement.

7.2   *Software Corrections*

The Distributor will maintain and support the Software at no charge to the Supplier provided that the Supplier shall provide the Distributor promptly and without charge with such technical advice and assistance as the Distributor may reasonably require to enable it to provide such maintenance and support. The Distributor will promptly disclose to the Supplier in writing any errors, bugs and corrections in the Software of which it becomes aware. The Supplier will use its best endeavours to correct any errors or bugs in the Software as quickly as reasonably possible and supply the correction to the Distributor, whether disclosed by the Distributor or discovered by the Supplier, and shall make no charge for such correction.

8   REPRESENTATIONS, WARRANTIES AND COVENANTS

8.1   *Right to Distribute*

The Supplier represents and warrants that it owns or has a right to distribute the Software in accordance with the terms of this Agreement.

8.2   *Confidentiality of Source Codes*

The Distributor acknowledges that the source codes of the Software and all corrections, ammendments, variations, extensions or additions to such source codes are confidential to the Supplier. Nothing in this Agreement shall entitle the

Distributor to access the whole or any part of the source code of any of the Software.

8.3 *Prohibition of Reverse Engineering, Modification*

(a)   The Distributor covenants that the Distributor will not disassemble or reverse engineer the Software, in whole or in part.

(b)   In addition, the Distributor shall not permit any contractor or third party to have access or gain access to, or work on the Software (or any part thereof) or make any correction, amendment, variation, extension or addition thereto.

9   WARRANTY

9.1 *Selection of Software by the Distributor*

The Distributor agrees with respect to the Software to accept the responsibility for:

(a)   its selection to achieve the Distributor's intended results;

(b)   its use; and

(c)   the results obtained therefrom.

The Distributor further agrees that it has the responsibility for selection and use of (and results obtained from) any other programs, equipment or services used with the Software.

9.2   The Supplier warrants that the Software conforms to the written specifications and descriptions thereof from time to time supplied by the Supplier to the Distributor.

9.3   The Distributor understands and agrees that any solutions, corrections and improvements supplied by the Supplier shall be promptly implemented. The Distributor further recognizes that its failure to so implement such solutions, corrections and improvements may render the Software unusable or non-conforming to its documentation and the Distributor agrees to assume all risks arising therefrom.

9.4   Except as to the express warranty contained above as to conformity of the Software to the appropriate specifications and descriptions, the Supplier makes no warranties or representations, express or implied, in fact or in law, and excludes the implied warranties and conditions of merchantability and fitness for a particular purpose.

[*Insert Boilerplate Clauses.*]

[*Insert Execution Clauses.*]

EXHIBIT 1

Business Plan

Q   Bureau Processing Agreements

Bureau processing takes place when the provider makes available its computer for the use of a remote user. The provider's computer is at its site and, if the services provided include on-line access, the user is connected to the provider's system by communication lines.

The services to be provided will vary from contract to contract. Invariably, potentially one of the most contentious issues which should be carefully covered by the contract is responsibility for the results of processing. Subject to further comments below, if the user has sought out its preferred applications which it specifies to the bureau, and has established its own data to commence with, then the bureau will expect not to be responsible for the performance of the application, or the stability of the data — the contract will appear more like facilities management which is considered in the next example. However if, as is commonly the case, the bureau promotes its services as a total solution, perhaps even collecting, converting and verifying data for use on its own preferred software, then the user should not be concerned in any way with the method by which the services are performed, but only contract for the *result* it expects, and performance criteria will be a major part to the contract.

Whatever services are provided, whether batch or on-line, the quality of processing, the timely completion of batch processing and the response times of on-line enquiries, may be adversely affected by the bureau's management of its hardware/operating system. Not only will it be of great importance to the user of the service whether the bureau maintains a specific minimum hardware/software configuration, and does or does not take advantage of upgrades and enhancements as they become available to improve performance, but also that the bureau does not succumb to the temptation to add extra customers to the processing burden of the system to the detriment of its overall performance. Accordingly, in addition to specifying the services to be provided, what reports need to be printed and sent by courier to the user daily, what transactions must be processed on-line and so on, some attention should be given to requirements of the bureau to maintain its system, and minimal performance levels to ensure the maintenance of basic standards.

In some cases, it may be necessary to provide for education or user support to be provided by the bureau, to ensure that the user's operators can deal with difficulties they may have from time to time. In the example given below, such support is provided by a 'help desk', available between certain hours, and the level of services available depends on the level of fees paid by the user.

In addition, there is a responsibility on the part of the user. The user must be responsible for getting data to be processed to the bureau, in some cases by direct telecommunications link, in others by delivery of the appropriate media, and the bureau can only comply with time restraints if material provided to it by the user is correct (bad data can cause errors in operation) and on time. The user must not burden the system with excessive transactions (without additional fee), and may need to notify the bureau twenty- four hours (or more) in advance, if it wishes to run particular reports which require large slabs of CPU time and so on. If the user has access to the system on-line, it must be prohibited from tampering with unauthorized areas of the software or operating system.

Also, it should be noted that the bureau is merely acting on behalf of the user in providing processing, and therefore the provision of those services should not include responsibility for what is processed, or the results of the processing undertaken in accordance with the user's instructions.

Issues concerning payment for the service are also very important. The two payment system, an amount in advance for a minimum level of processing and related services and an additional amount for additional services in arrears, is desirable from the bureau's point of view as it aids in the bureau's cash flow and it is always desirable when providing a service to be paid in advance. In addition, it should be clear that the user does not receive a refund if the minimum level of processing is not required, as the system must be maintained in readiness, whether used by the user or not, and this involves considerable fixed overheads which cannot be readily diverted to other customers, even if the user does permit the bureau this flexibility. From the bureau's point of view, also, it will always be necessary to be able to adjust the rates. The bureau would prefer to have an unfettered right to do so, but if this is not acceptable to the user, the changes can be pegged to an appropriate index of inflation.

The termination provisions of a bureau processing agreement should be given special attention. If the user terminates the agreement, it is appropriate that there be a long period of minimum notice. The bureau may have substantial equipment ready for processing, and it may take some time to have in place a replacement user, and the replacement process may be costly. Likewise, if the bureau terminates, the user should have a reasonable peiod to put in place replacement processing facilities.

Whoever terminates the agreement, provision must be made for the return by the bureau of the user's material. Depending upon the nature of the bureau processing being carried out, this may include software and data, in both digital and printed form, and possibly even paper and other consumables for which the user has already paid. In the example given below, the user is required to specify what is to happen to the items in the bureau's possession, and failing such specification the provider is entitled to dispose of them.

Confidentiality of the user's information resident on the provider's computer will be of great importance to the user and particular applications may require particular security provisions.

Example

THIS BUREAU PROCESSING SERVICE AGREEMENT is made the
day of   19

BETWEEN   of
                                            ('the Company') of the one part
AND   of
                                            ('the Customer') of the other part

WHEREAS:

A   The Company is in possession of certain hardware, and software for use thereon, referred to in Schedule One.

B   The Customer desires the Company to perform certain processing services in relation to [*briefly describe nature of processing to be undertaken, for example:* on-line order entry and inventory management], the services required by the Customer being more particularly set out in Schedule Two ('the Services').

C   The Company has agreed to provide the Services using the System upon and subject to the terms and conditions more fully set out in this Agreement.

NOW IT IS HEREBY AGREED as follow:

1   Definitions
         In this Agreement, unless the contrary intention appears:
         (a)   'the Commencement Date' means the date of execution of this Agreement or such other date as is agreed between the parties;
         (b)   'the System' means the hardware and operating system software specified in Schedule One, and all ancillary equipment and communications networks associated therewith, as updated from time to time with new equipment and releases of the operating system software; and
         (c)   'the Production System Software' shall mean the software used on the System by the Company in support of the day to day business of the Customer pursuant to this Agreement.

2   SERVICES
2.1   The Company will provide the Services using the System for a period of [*specify term, for example:* one (1) year] commencing on the Commencement Date and thereafter until terminated by either party giving the other three (3) months' notice in writing.

2.2   The Customer shall prior to the Commencement Date:
         (a)   at its own expense instal and make operational on the Customer's premises such equipment as the Company may recommend as necessary in order to access and/or make use of the Services supplied by the Company; and

(b)   deliver to the Company a master and back-up copy of all initial data required for the provision of the Services on machine readable media in a form suitable for use by the System. Failure to do so by the Customer shall not relieve the Customer of any obligations under this Agreement in respect of the payment of fees and charges payable hereunder. It shall be the responsibility of the Customer to retain such further back-up copies of such initial and all subsequent data in such manner and form as the Customer considers necessary for its own purposes.

2.3   During the term of this Agreement, the Company shall maintain or cause to be maintained at its own expense the hardware and software elements of the System within its control by the employment of competent and skilled technical support personnel familiar with such elements of the System, and/or the engaging of reputable third party support contractors.

2.4   The provision of the Services by the Company shall be subject to the condition that no member of the staff of the Customer has any authority whatsoever to alter any of the System software. No person employed by, sub-contracted by or under the control of the Customer shall make any changes to the System software without the consent in writing of the Company. In the event that any changes are made to the said software from a terminal controlled by the Customer, then the Customer undertakes to reimburse the Company at its then current rates for all work required to return the said software to its original condition.

[If the Company must instal any hardware or software in order to provide the Services, it may be prudent to add a time limiting provision, for example:

2.5   In order to provide the services to the Customer, the Company shall within ninety (90) days of the Commencement Date:

(a)   complete the installation and initialization in a form suitable for the provision of the Services of the Software [and Hardware] referred to in Schedule One under the heading 'Software [and Hardware] to be installed by the Company'; and

(b)   obtain and maintain thereafter all necessary licences, approvals and consents, and pay all fees, charges and costs, necessary for the operation of the System and the provision of the Services to the Customer.]

3   SERVICE CHARGES

3.1   On execution of this Agreement, the Customer will pay to the Company a registration fee of *[specify the initial charge, if any]*.

3.2   The Customer agrees to pay the Company's charges for the Services in the manner and in the amounts specified in the Schedule of Rates and Charges ('the Rates') attached as Schedule Three hereto, as modified by the Company from time to time during the term hereof in accordance with this Agreement.

3.3   At the end of each month, the Customer will be invoiced a minimum amount in respect of the Services to be supplied by the Company during the forthcoming month, including a minimum monthly charge payable in respect of the availability of the System for Customer processing, which shall be payable by the Customer regardless of its intention to use the Services or not and which shall not be refundable in whole or in part, regardless of whether the Customer's actual use during any month is less than that necessary to support that charge on a transaction basis. Such amounts are included in the Rates. All charges payable to the Company in addition to the minimum amount as a result of actual utilization of the Services by the Customer will be invoiced to the Customer at the end of the month in which they were incurred.

3.4   The Rates shall not be subject to change by the Company for a period of six (6) months from the Commencement Date, but thereafter are subject to change by the Company at any time and from time to time upon the giving of not less than three (3) months' prior written notice to the Customer.

4   PERFORMANCE BY THE COMPANY

4.1   The Services will conform to the Performance Criteria set out in Schedule Four.

4.2   In addition to any other rights it may have under this Agreement, the Company may by notice in writing to the Customer at any time during the term of this Agreement suspend any services to be supplied by the Company hereunder in any of the following events:

       (a)   if the Customer has access to the System for any reason, whether by on-line access or otherwise, and the Customer attempts to modify any part of the System;

       (b)   the Customer is in breach of any term of this Agreement, including the payment of any moneys; or

       (c)   the Company is prevented from performing any of its obligations under this Agreement as a result of any act, event or cause beyond its reasonable control including, without limiting the generality of the foregoing, unavailability of spare parts or other supplies, acts of God, industrial disputation, war, civil strike, flood, fire, explosion or epidemic.

If the Customer receives notice of suspension under this sub-Clause 4.2, the Customer shall not be entitled to any rebate or refund of any payment made prior to the date of such notice, but in the event only of receipt of notice under paragraph 4.2(c), the Customer shall be entitled to such rebate in the Rates as the Company may determine, based upon the continued availability of any part of the Services during the period of such supervening act, cause or event.

4.3   The Company shall not be liable to the Customer for any loss or damage suffered or incurred by the Customer arising from or in relation to any alleged failure by the Company to meet any performance specifications or criteria, when such failure arises from circumstances not in the control of the Company, including but not limited to: (a) defects in a communication line; (b) any breach of this Agreement by the Customer; (c) equipment failure.

4.4   (a)   In the event that any element of the System ceases to operate or malfunctions so that, in the opinion of the Company, the breakdown or malfunction adversely affects the provision of the Services to the Customer, the Company undertakes to use all reasonable commercial efforts to have the System operational as soon as possible and to follow, as far as practicable, procedures laid down in Schedule Five.

       (b)   The obligations of the Company under this Clause are subject to and conditional upon the receipt by the Company of adequate notice of any defect in or cessation of operation by the System, such that the Company is reasonably aware of the defects in the Services by which the Customer is affected.

5   CUSTOMER DATA

5.1   Magnetic tapes, disks or other media to be furnished by the Customer in order that the Company may provide the Services must be compatible with the System and must be in good condition for machine processing. In addition, the Customer accepts sole responsibility for the adequacy and accuracy of its source data, instructions and procedures and the results obtained therefrom.

5.2   If the Customer fails to furnish its data to the Company in the form and at the time required by the Company from time to time, the Company may not be able to process in accordance with the usual timetable for provisions of the Services set out in

Schedule Four or agreed with the Customer from time to time, but the Company will use reasonable commercial efforts to process the Customer's work if reasonably practicable and as promptly as possible. The Customer agrees to pay for all expenses of the Company incurred by it as a result of the Customer's failure to furnish its data to the Company in the form and at the time required.

5.3   Data submitted by the Customer to the Company for processing shall be transported at the Customer's expense between the Customer's premises and the Company's premises and return, unless specifically included in the Services.

5.4   The Company shall take all reasonable steps to maintain data submitted by the Customer free from corruption, provided however that the Customer shall be solely responsible for recreation of any data which may be damaged, altered or destroyed while resident on the System or in transit between the Company and the Customer by any means.

5.5   Without limiting the particular provisions of Schedule Four, the Company shall at all times maintain back-up copies of the Customer's data from day to day, and in addition shall maintain both 'father' and 'grandfather' back-up copies of such data, but shall not be required to keep any further archival materials for the Customer unless specified in Schedule Four or separately agreed between the Customer and the Company.

5.6   In the event that the Company modifies the System for any reason during the term of this Agreeement, whether its hardware or software elements or both, in order to improve, correct or update the System, the Customer shall render to the Company such assistance as it may reasonably request if any modification and/or verification of the Customer's data is required to enable the Company to continue to provide the Services. The Company shall carry out such modifications to the System with all reasonable expedition, and any suspension in the Services during such modification of the System and Customer data (if any) shall not constitute a breach of this Agreement.

6   CONFIDENTIALITY
6.1   The Company shall maintain each and every part of the Customer's information, data and results in strict confidence for the Customer and the Company will take all action considered by the Company as necessary with respect to the use, copying, duplication, access, security and protection of such information, data and results or any part thereof to satisfy its obligations under this provision.

6.2   The Company shall not permit any contractor or other third party to gain access to or do any work with the Customer's information or any part thereof unless such contractor or other third party gains such access or does such work with written permission first obtained from the Customer.

6.3   The Customer shall keep confidential all information relating to services supplied by the Company, including the Rates, and shall not disclose any such information to any third party without the prior written consent of the Company.

7   CONSEQUENCES OF TERMINATION
7.1   In the event of the termination of this Agreement for any reason the Company will, at the request of the Customer, provide the Customer in a mutually agreeable format and at the Company's then current charges for processing, personnel and other services and consumable items, all of the Customer's records then in the possession of and maintained by the Company, provided that the Company has been paid for all services rendered to the date of cessation. If the Company has not received instructions from the Customer within thirty (30) days of the effective date of termination as to the disposition of the Customer's records then held by the Company then the Company may dispose of such records in such a manner as the Company may determine but respecting the confidentiality thereof.

7.2   In the event of the termination of this Agreement by reason of any neglect or default in the performance of this Agreement by the Customer, the parties agree that the Customer, in addition to payment of all invoices rendered by the Company to the Customer for Services rendered up to the effective data of termination, shall pay to the Company liquidated damages calculated as follows:

(a)   in the event of termination within the initial period of one (1) year, the product of the current minimum monthly charge at the date of notice of termination or, in the absence of notice, occurrence of the terminating event, and the number of uncompleted months of this Agreement; or

(b)   in the event of termination after the initial period of one (1) year, three (3) times the current minimum monthly charge at the date of notice of termination or, in the absence of notice, occurence of the terminating event.

It is mutually acknowledged and declared that such amount of liquidated damages represents a genuine estimate of the Company's cost in loss of establishment costs and reasonable expectation of return thereon, and loss of business and efficient utilization of the System during a reasonable period for seeking replacement business. The Customer shall not be entitled to any refund of any part of such liquidated damages in any circumstances.

8   LIMITATION OF LIABILITY; INDEMNITIES

8.1   The Company shall have no responsibility to determine the authenticity or accuracy of any data or other information delivered by the Customer to the Company, or the accuracy of the reports or other output based thereon and the Customer shall indemnify and save harmless the Company from and against any liability under any claim, judgment, order, award for damage arising from any defects, error, inaccuracy or non-authenticity of any such data or other information.

8.2   The Customer shall be solely responsible for recreation of any data which may be damaged, altered, or destroyed while resident on the Company computer system.

8.3   In addition to its obligations under Clause 4.3 hereof, if the Company shall commit any error or omission in the services, or fail or be unable for any reason to furnish, deliver or transmit the Services to the Customer correctly or at all, or in so supplying, delivering or transmitting the services commits an error or omission or does any act or thing incidental thereto which causes the Customer to suffer loss or damage, the maximum liability or responsibility of the Company shall be: (i) to correct the services; or (ii) supply the services again as the Company may elect, pro-vided always that the Company accepts no responsibility whatsoever unless it receives written notice of any such error or ommission within ten (10) days after delivery of the services to the Customer.

Under no circumstances shall the Company be liable or responsible to the Customer or to any third party for any consequential loss or damage which it or any such third party may suffer or incur by reason of any error, omission, failure or delay in the provision of the Services.

8.4   In no event shall the Company or the Customer be liable one to the other for special, incidental or consequential damages or for any indirect damages including without any limitation to the foregoing exemplary or punitive damages, damage to property or loss of profits.

[Insert Boilerplate Clauses.]

SCHEDULE ONE

THE SYSTEM

[Here describe the hardware and software (including operating system environment) in reasonable detail, including model and version/release numbers.

Include if necessary a heading 'Software/Hardware to be Installed by Company'.]

SCHEDULE TWO

THE SERVICES

The services provided by the Company shall conform to the specifications below. Any modification proposed to such specifications will be binding on the Company only if

(a)   they are in writing; and

(b)   the date on which they become effective and form part of this Agreement is specified; and

(c)   they are agreed to by an officer of the Company duly authorized in that regard and such agreement is noted in writing and signed by such officer.

SPECIFICATIONS

[Here set out in reasonable detail the Services to be supplied to the Customer, for example under the following headings, if applicable:

I   TRANSACTION CAPTURE AND PROCESSING SERVICES
II   ACCESS AUTHORIZATION AND VERIFICATION
III   ON-LINE DATA ENTRY AND RETRIEVAL
IV   BATCH PROCESSING AND TURNAROUND TIME
V   REPORTS
VI   MISCELLANEOUS SERVICES

- Supply copies of original documentation as requested
- Consult on computer-to-computer links
- Access to terminal services

VII   SYSTEM UPTIME

The Company shall maintain availability of the System for access on-line between the hours of 8.00 a.m. and 6.00 p.m. Eastern Standard Time on Business Days in *[specify city]*. In the event of a hardware or software failure which would result in a reasonable standard not being maintained in any one day, on-line processing will be switched by the Company to one or other of the back-up processors, at the Company's discretion, to maintain the above mentioned service level.

VII   COSTS OF TRANSFERRING INFORMATION FROM THE COMPANY TO THE CUSTOMER

Reports produced by the Company may be despatched by courier between 5.00 p.m. and 7.30 p.m. daily or transmitted by electronic means. In the event of an interchange file produced by the Company being unreadable or otherwise in error, on being informed by telephone, the Company will create and despatch a replacement file by the earliest available means. The Customer shall pay for the costs outlaid to third parties of interchanging information, agreed to be provided pursuant to this Agreement, in such form (electronic or otherwise) as shall be agreed between the parties from time to time.

IX   HELP DESK

1   Help Desk Services shall include:
    (a)   telephone assistance with network and host operational difficulties which include the identification of problems with access to the Bureau Services by the Customer and remedial action including but not limited to:
        (i)   informing the relevant telephone company or line provider if the Help Desk believes the fault lies with a telephone company communication line;
        (ii)   logging operational faults and giving status reports on scheduling of operational fault fixes;
        (iii)   informing the Customer if the Help Desk believes the problem to be in the Customer's computer system;
    (b)   telephone and technical support which includes the identification of problems signalled by the Customer in using software running on the Bureau Service and where possible rectification by:
        (i)   suggesting alternative approaches which can taken by the Customer;
        (ii)   duplicating the Customer's problem on the Help Desk terminal;
    (c)   on-site assistance which includes attendance by a member of the Help Desk personnel at the Customer's premises to examine the problems with software running on the Bureau Service or communications between the Customer site and the Bureau Service.

2   Help Desk Services specifically exclude:
    (a)   assistance in writing new programs not currently running on the Bureau Service;
    (b)   problems specifically relating to the Customer's data held on the Bureau Service;
    (c)   assisting a user to connect hardware to the Bureau Service;
    (d)   assistance with software at or below the level of microcode.

3   Help Desk Services will be available only between the hours of 9.00 a.m. and 5.00 p.m. on business days. Help Desk Services will be supplied to the Customer only at its premises as specified in this Agreement.

4   (a)   Level 1 support includes provision to the Customer of a technical newsletter produced by the Company and telephone assistance with network and host operational difficulties;
    (b)   Level 2 support includes Level 1 support and telephone technical support up to a maximum of twelve hours per year;
    (c)   Level 3 support includes Level 2 support and ten hours per month of telephone technical support and provision of the Company documentation on microfiche;
    (d)   Level 4 support includes Level 3 support and on-site technical support up to a maximum of ten hours per month.

5   The Customer agrees to take the level of support noted above and the Customer will pay to the Company the Help Desk fees according to the Company's standard prices for such services. In the event that the hours of Help Desk Services supplied to the Customer exceed those contracted for in this authorization, Customer will be invoiced for such excess services at the Company's then current rate for such excess services. Such excess services will be provided when Help Desk personnel are available.

6   Time expended in on-site assistance shall include the reasonable travelling time between the premises of the Company and the Customer's location(s).

7   This authorization shall be for an initial period of one year and thereafter shall continue from year to year unless terminated by not less than ninety (90) days' notice.]

SCHEDULE THREE

RATES AND CHARGES

1   The services supplied by the Company to the Customer pursuant to this Agreement will be charged to the Customer on the terms and rates specified below.

2   In the event that any fees or charges payable by the Customer and calculated by reference to the number of data/line item entries open during a month are increased, the Company may adjust the Minimum Monthly Charge set out below and the said fees or charges payable by the Customer in the same proportion as the increase in such data/line items.

        [*Here specify the charges for the Services, for example under the following headings:*]

        (a)   Minimum Monthly Charge:
        (b)   Initial Fee:
        (c)   Interchange File Report Service:
        (d)   Transaction Charges:
        (e)   Batch Processing Charges:
        (f)   Miscellaneous:

SCHEDULE FOUR

PERFORMANCE CRITERIA

1   The Company will ensure that, as far as possible, the System meets the performance criteria specified below whenever it is in operation provided that the 'Upper Volume' number of transactions per hour is not exceeded.

2   The Customer may modify the 'Upper Volume' provided:

        (a)   notice of such modification is in writing;
        (b)   such modification is to take effect no less than thirty (30) days after notice is given to the Company; and
        (c)   such modifications are agreed to by an officer of the Company duly authorized in that regard and such agreement is noted in writing and signed by such officer.

3   In the event that the System fails to meet the performance criteria referred to in Clause 1 at least once in each of twenty (20) consecutive business days then the Customer may, at its option, suspend payment of any money due under this Agreement until such failure is corrected, without incurring any additional interest charges or suffering any other liability.

4   Upper Volume:

[*Insert Execution Clauses.*]

SCHEDULE FIVE

DISASTER RECOVERY PROCEDURES

[*Here specify procedures to be adopted by the Company in the event of system unavailability for a specified time.*]

R Facilities Management Agreements

Facilities management is the process of attending to a computer at the service provider's site, mounting and demounting tapes or disks, providing paper to the printer and so on. The attraction of this arrangement can be that the facilities manager may be able to take advantage of economies of scale, or more probably the customer seeks to move its equipment (and perhaps some of its DP personnel) off valuable leasehold space.

While facilities management encompasses many of the same services as a bureau service, it is much more important in a facilities management contract to provide for the care and maintenance of the customer's equipment. For reasons discussed above in relation to the preceding example, the responsibility of the facilities manager for the selection of the hardware and software should be significantly less under this contract. It must be the responsibility of the facilities manager to do nothing to endanger the insurance covering the equipment.

At the commencement of the agreement, the equipment subject to the agreement must be installed and arrangements must be made for notification to the insurers of the location of the equipment. It is possible that the equipment will be acquired directly from the manufacturer and installed on the facility manager's site, or it may be that existing equipment of the customer must be relocated.

The facilities manager should be assured that the licensor of the customer's software has granted permission for it to use the applications and operating system software on the customer's behalf (the terms of most licences forbid use of the software by any other person), and to move the software if necessary to another site.

Needless to say, careful thought must be directed to the termination provisions, and what will happen to the equipment at that time.

Finally, in the example given, provision is made for the transfer of employees of the customer to manage the hardware for the facilities manager.

Example _____

THIS FACILITIES MANAGEMENT AGREEMENT is made the   day of   19

BETWEEN   of
('the Company') of the one part
AND   of
('the Client') of the other part
WHEREAS:

A   The Company is in the business of supplying and operating computer hardware
        and software as part of bureau services from its premises at [*specify the place where
        the facilities will be maintained*] ('the Installation Site');

B   The Client possesses computer equipment presently installed in a computer centre
        at [*specify existing location of facilities*] and at one or more of its ancillary premises,
        remote from the computer centre ('the Remote Sites'). Certain items of such
        equipment, currently installed in the computer centre will be transferred to the
        Company ('the Equipment'). The Client has entered into one or more agreements
        with persons or companies named in Schedule A for the maintenance of all
        computer equipment installed ('the Equipment Maintenance Agreements'). 'The
        Equipment', the 'Remote Sites' and the 'Equipment Maintenance Agreements' are
        described in Schedule A;

C   The Client at the date hereof owns or is licensed to use and operate certain
        Applications and Operating System Software ('the Applications and Operating
        System Software') at one or more of the Remote Sites and has entered into one or
        more agreements with the persons or companies named in Schedule B hereto for
        the maintenance and support of the Operating System Software at the Remote
        Sites ('the Software Maintenance Agreements');

D   In addition, the Client is the employer of certain persons ('the Employees') named
        in Schedule C experienced in the use and operation of the Equipment and the
        Applications and Operating System Software for the purposes of the business of the
        Client; and

E   The Client has requested the Company to take over the operation of the Equipment
        and the Applications and Operating System Software at the Installation Site on
        behalf of the Client, and to use and operate the Equipment and the Applications
        and Operating System Software on behalf of the Client, in conjunction with other
        equipment in the Company's possession ('the Company Hardware') which the
        Company has agreed to do upon and subject to the terms and conditions
        hereinafter set forth.

NOW IT IS AGREED as follows:

1   DEFINITIONS AND INTERPRETATIONS
1.1   In this Agreement and the Schedules hereto, unless the context otherwise requires,
        the following words and phrases shall bear the meaning prescribed in this Clause:
                'Application Software' means the software owned and developed by the
        Client for the processing of Input Data and producing Output Data together with
        all intervening processes, not being the Operating System Software, and identified
        in Schedule E hereto;
                'Batch Processing Services' means those services set out in Part 1 of
        Schedule D hereto;
                'Bureau Service' means the operation and use of the Equipment and the
        Software to provide the On-Line Services and the Batch Processing Services;
                'Business Day' means any day other than any Saturday, Sunday or a public
        holiday;
                'Commencement Date' means [*specify effective commencement date, for
        example:* the date hereof];

'Communication Network' means all telecommunications lines, modems, communications controllers, multiplexors and terminals or other equipment used for the purposes of transmission from any terminal or device on any Remote Site to the Installation Site;

'Contract Authority' means the person nominated by the Client to represent it for the purposes of this Agreement to be the Client's personal point of contact for the Company;

'the Company Hardware' means the equipment used by the Company for the purposes of this Agreement and specified in Schedule F hereto as varied, removed or added to by the Company from time to time during the term of this Agreement;

'the Company Representative' means any person authorized in writing by the Company to represent it for the purposes of this Agreement to be the Company's principal point of contact for the Client;

'the Company's Standard Rates' means the standard rates for services provided hereunder, machine time, labour and materials as set by the Company from time to time pursuant to this Agreement;

'Input Data' means data supplied by the Client for use in the Bureau Service;

'Installation Site' means the Installation Site or such other premises nominated to the Client from time to time as the place of installation of the Equipment and the Applications and Operating System Software;

'Licences' means the licences relating to the Operating System Software between the Client and the Licensors named in Schedule B hereto;

'the Client Data' means the data provided by, processed for and produced for the Client by the Bureau Service for the purposes of this Agreement and includes both Input Data and Output Data;

'the Client Personnel' means any contractor, servant or agent of or appointed by the Client for carrying out any act or doing any thing on the Client's part to be performed or done under or incidental to this Agreement;

'On-Line Services' means those services set out in Part 2 of Schedule D hereto;

'Operating System Software' means the System Software for use and operation in conjunction with the Equipment supplied by the Licensors under the Licences;

'Output Data' means data belonging to the client produced by the Bureau Service;

'Quarter Day' means the last day of March, June and September during the term of this Agreement;

'User Documentation' means user manuals and other documentation applicable to the Equipment and the Applications and Operating System Software, its use and operation.

1.2   In this Agreement, unless the context otherwise requires, the following interpretations shall apply:

(a)   'normal business hours' means 9.00 a.m. to 5.00 p.m. on Business Days.

(b)   'delivery' in relation to data includes where appropriate transmission across the Communication Network from any Remote Site to the Installation Site.

(c)   Clause headings shall not be deemed to be part of this Agreement and shall not be used in its interpretation or construction.

(d)   Where the last day of any period prescribed for the doing of any thing falls on a day which is not a Business Day that thing may be done on the first Business Day following that day.

1.3   In the event of there being any conflict between any term or condition contained in any clause of this Agreement and any Schedule to it, the terms contained in this Agreement shall prevail over those in the Schedule.

2   DELIVERY AND INSTALLATION
2.1   (a)   The Client shall deliver and install the Equipment and the Applications and Operating System Software on the Installation Site before the Commencement Date. The Client shall pay and bear all costs of and incidental to such delivery and installation and provide all necessary labour and supervision.

       (b)   The Client shall make all provisions for any special handling and hoisting requirements for delivery and installation, including the erection of any scaffolding.

       (c)   Delivery and installation shall be at the Client's sole risk and expense. The Client shall repair and make good (or, at the Company's option, pay the cost of such repair or making good) any damage to the Company property or premises, any damage to other property on the Installation Site or on premises in which the Installation Site is located, and to any premises upon which the Installation Site is located, caused by the Client or the Client personnel during or incidental to delivery and installation hereunder.

2.2   (a)   The Client shall give the Company not less than two (2) Business Days' notice of the date and time when delivery and installation is to commence and take place. Such notice shall also specify the number and identity of all the Client personnel that the Client wishes to use in delivery and installation. The Company shall be entitled on any reasonable grounds to object to any person mentioned in such notice or place such limits on the number of the Client personnel to be used, in which event the Client shall not use such personnel (and may substitute other personnel acceptable to the Company) or exceed such maximum number of personnel in such delivery and installation.

       (b)   Delivery and installation under this Clause shall, unless the Company otherwise agrees, commence no later than [*specify latest time by which delivery and installation shall commence.*]

2.3   (a)   The Company shall prepare the Installation Site so that it will accommodate the Equipment and provide adequate storage space for all media belonging to the Client or to be used in the performance of the Bureau Services.

       (b)   The Installation Site shall on and from the Commencement Date conform to environmental, space and power requirements (if any) of the maker(s) and maintainer(s) of the Equipment and the Operating System Software.

       (c)   Subject to the provisions of sub-Clause 2.5 hereof, the Company shall provide access to the Installation Site for the purposes of delivery and installation to the Client personnel approved by the Company at such times as may be agreed between the Company and the Client.

2.4   (a)   The Company shall provide such supervision and direction during delivery and installation as may be necessary to properly complete installation provided that safety and security of the Equipment, the Applications and Operating System Software and the Client Data shall at all times remain the responsibility of the Client.

       (b)   The Client shall pay the Company's Standard Rates for providing any supervision and direction required after the Commencement Date, including any penalty and overtime rates for services provided outside normal business hours.

2.5   At all times whilst on or about the Installation Site all the Client personnel shall wear any security identification that the Company may require and shall comply with all the Company's reasonable directions. The Company shall be entitled to require removal from the Installation Site of any of the Client personnel who fail to comply with such requirements.

2.6   The client shall remove (or at the Company's option reimburse the Company for the cost of such removal) all refuse and rubbish left on the Installation Site after completion of delivery and installation under this Clause.

3   TITLE IN AND CONDITION OF EQUIPMENT AND SOFTWARE

3.1   The parties hereto acknowledge and declare that no title in or to the Equipment or the Applications and Operating System Software shall pass to the Company under this Agreement. Subject to the provisions of this Agreement, the Company shall properly operate and care for the Equipment and the Applications and Operating System Software and shall use all reasonable endeavours to ensure the physical integrity and security of the Equipment and Software from time to time during the term of this Agreement.

3.2   The Client warrants to the Company that each item of the Equipment and the Applications and Operating System Software shall be on the Commencement Date in good working order and condition, free from defects in design, workmanship and materials, and that the Client is entitled to enter into this Agreement in relation thereto, subject only to and excepting such defects notified to the Company by the Client in writing prior to the date hereof.

3.3   The Client warrants that it is the owner of the Applications Software and all rights therein and that it is entitled to enter this Agreement in relation to the Equipment and the Operating System Software. The Client shall indemnify and save harmless the Company from and against any loss or damage howsoever arising, or any claim, demand, action, proceedings and any judgment, award or order consequent thereupon, made or brought by any third party arising from or incidental to the right of possession of any item of Equipment or Applications and Operating System Software alleged or found to be enjoyed by any person other than the Client. Such indemnity shall extend, without limiting the generality of the foregoing, to any costs or expenses incurred by the Company, including legal costs and disbursements, in relation to such loss or damage or claim howsoever arising.

3.4   The Company warrants to the Client that each item of the Company Hardware shall be on the Commencement Date in good working order and condition, free from defects in design, workmanship and materials, and that the Company is entitled to enter into this Agreement in relation thereto, subject only to and excepting such defects notified to the Client by the Company in writing prior to the date hereof.

3.5   The Company warrants that it owns or is entitled to enter this Agreement in relation to the Company Hardware. The Company shall indemnify and save harmless the Client from and against any loss or damage howsoever arising, or any claim, demand, action, proceedings and any judgment, award or order consequent thereupon, made or brought by any third party arising from or incidental to the right of possession of any item of the Company Hardware alleged or found to be enjoyed by any person other than the Company. Such indemnity shall extend, without limiting the generality of the foregoing, to any costs or expenses incurred by the Client, including legal costs and disbursements, in relation to such loss or damage or claim howsoever arising.

4   DEINSTALLATION AND REMOVAL
Prior to the effective date of termination of this Agreement for any reason (including the expiration of this Agreement and any extension thereof due to the passage of time) the Client shall have deinstalled and removed all items of the

Equipment and the Applications and Operating System Software from the Installation Site. The Client shall pay and bear all costs of or incidental to deinstallation and removal of the Equipment and the provisions of Clause 2 hereof shall apply to such deinstallation and removal as they apply to delivery and installation.

5   INSURANCE

5.1   (a)   The Company will carry and maintain in full force and effect during the term hereof insurance protection, naming the Client as an additional insured, in relation to the Equipment and the Applications and Operating System Software.

Without limiting the generality of the foregoing, such insurances shall include public liability (arising from use and operation of the Equipment and the Applications and Operating System Software) and insurance of Equipment and the Applications and Operating System Software against all risks (including negligent or malicious damage, fire, theft, electrical and water damage (including such damage caused by negligence of the Company, its servants or agents), such insurance commencing from the Commencement Date and continuing, subject to renewals from time to time, until the deinstallation and removal of the Equipment and the Applications and Operating System Software or termination of this Agreement (whichever shall first occur).

(b)   Such insurance shall be for an amount at least sufficient to pay out the Company all the revenue it would have received under this Agreement had not any insured risk occurred and shall specify that the Company and the Client shall be parties notified for any purpose under such policy of insurance, including the occurrence of any insured risk, termination or any other notifiable occurrence under such policy of insurance.

(c)   The Company will, upon request, provide the Client with current certificates of insurance evidencing the above provisions, at any time and from time to time during the term of this Agreement. The Company shall provide the Client with not less than thirty (30) days' prior written notice in the event of any intended cancellation, expiration or reduction of such insurance.

6   EMPLOYEES

6.1   The Company shall offer employment to the Employees on and from the Commencement Date and on the terms of salary no less than those specified in Schedule C hereto. Except as specified by Schedule C, such employment, if accepted by any of the Employees shall be on the Company's usual terms and conditions of employment including the right to dismiss any of the Employees at any time or for any reason, upon giving notice required by law. The Company shall have no further obligations to the Client in relation to the Employees except as provided herein.

6.2   Unless and except to the extent otherwise in writing agreed between the Company and the Client from time to time, the Client warrants that, on the Commencement Date, the Employees shall have ceased employment with the Client and shall have been paid or otherwise compensated in respect of all annual leave; sick leave, long service leave or other statutory entitlements and superannuation and other non-statutory benefits and shall have no outstanding unsatisfied claims of any nature whatsoever in relation to their employment by the Client. The Client shall indemnify and save harmless the Company from and against all and any liability of any kind whatsoever and to any person, including, without limitation, any federal, state or other governmental or statutory authority (including labour and industry, taxation and payroll tax authorities) in respect of or arising from or incidental to the employment of any of the Employees by the Client.

6.3   (a)   The Client warrants that each of the Employees has been trained by the Client and is skilled and experienced in the use and operation of the Equipment and Applications and Operating System Software and has satisfactorily completed all relevant user training in relation thereto.

        (b)   The Client further warrants that the Client is not aware of any misconduct or dishonesty of any of the Employees (whether during or before employment by the Client) of which it has not informed and given full particulars to the Company prior to the execution hereof.

        (c)   The Client acknowledges and declares for the benefit of the Company that good conduct, honesty and proficiency are essential to any employment by the Company and the Company will not employ any person who has a bad history in any such matter.

6.4   The Company and the Client acknowledge and declare that the skill and experience of the Employees is important to the Company's performance of its obligations under this Agreement. The Company shall ensure adequate training of back-up staff for the event of unavailability for any reason of any of the Employees or the departure of any of the Employees from the Company's employment.

7   USE OF SOFTWARE AND EQUIPMENT

7.1   (a)   The Client shall pay and bear all licence fees (if any) and any other charges or fees to be paid pursuant to the Licences and shall comply or procure compliance with all other terms and conditions thereof. The Company will cooperate in every reasonable respect and shall use its best endeavours in order to comply with the terms and conditions of licence imposed by such of the Licences of which the Company is supplied with a copy.

        (b)   The Client shall procure the written consent of each Licensor named in Schedule B hereto for the use and operation of the item of the Operating System Software licensed by it at the Installation Site in conjunction with the Company Hardware.

        (c)   Such consent shall expressly authorize the use and operation of such item of the Operating System Software named therein by the Company on the Company Hardware or on such other equipment compatible therewith or of identical operation as the Company may use from time to time hereunder and the making by the Company of such reasonable number of copies for back-up purposes only as the Company may consider necessary from time to time during the term hereof.

        (d)   The Company shall not use any item of the Operating System Software at any place other than the Installation Site or for any person or company other than the Client or otherwise as the Client may in writing direct from time to time.

7.2   In the event that any item of the Equipment is leased, rented, hired or charged:

        (a)   The Client shall pay and bear all lease, hire or rental charges and any other charges or fees to be paid pursuant to such leasing, hiring, rental or charge arrangement and shall comply or procure compliance with all other terms and conditions thereof. The Company will cooperate in every reasonable respect and shall use its best endeavours in order to comply with the terms and conditions of such leasing, hiring, rental or charge arrangement of which it is provided with notice in writing setting out such terms or conditions in full.

        (b)   The Client shall procure the written consent of each lessor, hirer, renter or chargee to the use and operation of such item of Equipment at the Installation Site.

7.3   The Company shall not use or operate any item of the Equipment otherwise than at the Installation Site for the Client or as the Client may in writing direct.

7.4   The Client acknowledges that it has used the Applications and Operating System Software and the Equipment for a considerable period prior to the date hereof and accordingly acknowledges and declares for the benefit of the Company that it does not require from and is not given by the Company the benefit of any warranty or representation whatsoever as to the Equipment or the Applications and Operating System Software (including without limitation any warranty or representation as to merchantability or fitness for any purpose) or any benefits to be obtained from the use thereof. The Company shall in no circumstances be liable or accountable to the Client for any defects in the Equipment or the Applications and Operating System Software unless such defect is caused directly by any wilful or negligent act or omission of the Company.

7.5   The Client shall indemnify and hold the Company harmless from and against any loss damage suffered by the Company (including without limitation loss of revenue) directly or indirectly as a result of the refusal or revocation of any permission, authorization or consent on the Client's part to be procured hereunder or any defect in the Applications and Operating System Software or the Equipment, if and so long as the Applications and Operating System Software and the Equipment are used and operated by the Company in accordance with the provisions of this Agreement.

8   MAINTENANCE AND SUPPORT OF THE COMPANY HARDWARE EQUIPMENT AND APPLICATIONS AND OPERATING SYSTEM SOFTWARE

8.1   (a)   The Client shall be responsible for the provision of all maintenance and support of the Applications and Operating System Software and the Equipment and shall bear all charges and costs therefor.

(b)   The Client shall procure that maintenance and support services to be supplied on-site pursuant to the Licences, the Equipment Maintenance Agreements or the Software Maintenance Agreements shall be supplied at the Installation Site. The Client shall further procure that any off-site telephone enquiry support services provided under any of the Licences, the Equipment Maintenance Agreements or the Software Maintenance Agreements shall be provided to the Company Representative or such other person as the Company Representative may appoint from time to time.

(c)   The Client shall notify the Company of the names or descriptions of all persons which it requires to be permitted on the Installation Site for the purpose of carrying out maintenance or support services in relation to the Applications Software and any services provided under the Licences, the Software Maintenance Agreements and the Equipment Maintenance Agreements. Provided that at all times whilst on or about the Installation Site all such persons so nominated by the Client shall wear any security identification that the Company may require and shall comply with all the Company's reasonable directions, the Company shall provide access to the Installation Site to all such persons by appointment only at such time or times as the Company may agree and shall allow such persons to use such machines, communication facilities and other equipment (as normally supplied by such persons pursuant to the provision of services provided by them) consistent with the Company's normal business practices at no charge, as in the reasonable opinion of the Company are necessary in order to enable such persons to perform services thereunder. To facilitate the provision of such services, the Company shall provide reasonable facilities such as, but not limited to, secure storage space, a designated work area with adequate heat and light, and access to a telephone line in accordance with the Company's normal business practices. The Company shall be entitled to remove any such person on the Installation Site who fails to wear such security identification or comply with the Company's reasonable directions from time to time.

8.2 The Client shall indemnify and save harmless the Company and any of its employees or agents from and against any loss or damage suffered by the indemnified party (including without limitation loss of revenue or income) and any and all liability to any third party (including reasonable legal costs and disbursements) for any loss or damage not the fault of the indemnified party arising from or in connection with the provision of any services under the Licences, the Software Maintenance Agreements or the Equipment Maintenance Agreements and the attendance of any persons on the Installation Site in order to provide such services.

8.3 (a) The Company shall be responsible for the provision of all maintenance and support of the Company Hardware and shall bear all charges and costs therefor.

(b) The Company shall indemnify and save harmless the Client and any of its employees or agents from and against any loss or damage suffered by the indemnified party (including without limitation loss of revenue or income) and any and all liability to any third party (including reasonable legal costs and disbursements) for any loss or damage not the fault of the indemnified party arising from any failure by the Company to provide maintenance and support of the Company Hardware during the term of this Agreement.

9 OTHER CHARGES

The Client shall directly bear and be responsible for the payment of the cost of all goods, services and facilities not provided for elsewhere in this Agreement necessary for the satisfactory operation of the Equipment and the Applications and Operating System Software or any part thereof, including but not limited to:

(a) all peripheral or other equipment installed on the Remote Sites;

(b) installation of data communication facilities between the Remote Sites and the Equipment on the Installation Site;

(c) transport of documents and media between the Remote Site and the Installation Site to the Company premises;

(d) expenses incurred by the Client personnel in visiting the Company's premises or elsewhere for the purposes of this Agreement and operation of the Equipment and the Software; and

(e) forms and continuous stationery and all other consumables and supply items whether supplied by the Company or otherwise required for the operation of the Equipment and the Applications and Operating System Software.

10 SCOPE OF CONTRACT

10.1 In consideration of payment by the Client of prices and charges provided for in Part 4 of Schedule D to this Agreement and subject to and in accordance with the terms of this Agreement, the Company shall:

(a) provide to the Client the Batch Processing services specified in Schedule D, Part 1;

(b) provide to the Client the On-Line Processing Services specified in Schedule D, Part 2; and

(c) use the Equipment, the Applications and Operating System Software and the Company Hardware, except where the contrary is indicated in the schedules hereto, exclusively in the provision of the Bureau Service to the Client.

10.2   The Company shall use all reasonable endeavours to conform to and satisfy processing and delivery schedules requested by the Client from time to time.

10.3   The Company shall take all reasonable precautions to prevent the loss of or improper alteration of the Client's files, records or data.

10.4   The Company shall maintain a high level of security to ensure that no unauthorized person can gain entry to any area under the Company's control where the Client's program files or data are stored or processed and to prevent unauthorized access by terminal devices or otherwise to any files, records or data maintained by the Company on behalf of the Client.

10.5   Upon cessation of the provision of the Bureau Services by the Company and at the request of the Client, the Company will provide the Client in a mutually agreeable format all of the Client's files, records and data then maintained by the Company, and will make available the Equipment and the Applications and Operating System Software for deinstallation and removal at times reasonably convenient to the Company and provided that the Company has been paid for all services rendered to the Client prior to the date of such provision, deinstallation or removal as the case may be.

If the Company has not received within thirty (30) days after the effective date of termination of this Agreement instructions from the Client concerning the disposition of the Equipment, the Applications and Operating Systems Software or the Client's files, records and data then maintained by the Company, the Equipment, the Applications and Operating Systems Software or such files, records and data (as the case may be) may be disposed of by the Company in any confidential manner as the Company may determine.

10.6   The Company agrees that with the authority of the Client except as otherwise required by law (in which event the Company shall make a report of the inspection to the Client in writing), any files, records and data maintained by the Company on behalf of the Client shall be available for inspection by the appropriate regulatory authorities and by the Client's internal auditors and external auditors upon reasonable prior written notice to the Company providing that the Client agrees to pay at the Company's Standard Rates then in effect all reasonable costs incurred in the preparation of files, records and data for such inspection.

10.7   At all times during the currency of this Agreement the Company agrees to price the Company's Standard Rates reasonably having regard to its costs and in accordance with prevailing market rates

11   PERIOD OF CONTRACT

11.1   The contract period shall be for the initial period set out in Part 3 of Schedule D hereto (hereinafter 'the Initial Period') commencing on the Commencement Date.

11.2   The Initial Period and any subsequent period shall be extended for a further period of three (3) months unless either party gives notice of termination to the other no less than three (3) months prior to the end of the applicable period.

12   MODIFICATION OF THE BUREAU SERVICE

12.1   On each Quarter Day during the term of this Agreement the Bureau Service may be amended, added to or changed as hereinafter provided.

12.2   In the event that the Client wishes to remove, enhance or add to the Equipment or the Applications and Operating System Software, then the Client shall give at least thirty (30) days' notice prior to a Quarter Day of any such change.

12.3   The Company shall be entitled, on thirty (30) days' written notice to the Client, to increase or decrease any fees and charges set out in Schedule D hereto as and to the extent required by any change, increase, enhancement, removal or addition in the Bureau Service PROVIDED HOWEVER that in no event shall the charges for the Bureau Service be reduced hereunder beneath the minimum levels specified in Part 4 of Schedule D hereto.

12.4   The Company shall not make any change in the Company Hardware without the consent of the Client, such consent not to be refused unreasonably in the case of any item of equipment which is sound and functionally equivalent to the item of the Company Hardware replaced.

12.5   Any addition or change to the Company Hardware, the Equipment or the Software shall be governed by the terms and conditions of this Agreement as if fully described in the Schedules hereto.

13   ADVICE AND CONSULTATION

13.1   The Client shall consult with the Company, cooperate in all reasonable respects, supply to the Company all information and particulars of its business operations and make available such personnel resources as the Company may reasonably require to provide the Bureau Service and otherwise comply with its obligations hereunder.

13.2   Unless otherwise provided herein the Client shall be responsible for ordering terminal devices and telecommunications facilities and for arranging all activities connected with the installation of such devices and other equipment, equipment and facilities required by the Client on any Remote Site, the use of the Bureau Service and complying with its obligations hereunder.

14   MOVEMENT OF INSTALLATION SITE
In the event that the Company intends to move the Installation Site then:

(a)   the Company shall give the Client three (3) months' notice in writing of the intended date of such move and shall consult with the Client as to any necessary changes in the manner of providing the Bureau Service or the requirements of the Client caused by such move;

(b)   The Company shall during such move be responsible for and shall bear all costs associated with the deinstallation, removal, shipment and reinstallation of the Company Hardware, the Equipment and the Applications and Operating System Software and the re-establishment of all necessary telecommunications and other facilities necessary in the provision of the Bureau Service by the Company; and

(c)   The Company and the Client shall use their best endeavours to obtain all necessary consents and approvals from the Licensors and the owners, hirers or chargees of the Equipment and suppliers of services under the Equipment Maintenance Agreements and the Software Maintenance Agreements in order that the Licences shall continue and such services shall continue to be supplied to the new Installation Site.

15   DOCUMENTATION AND USER AIDS

15.1   The Client shall supply the Company on license with such of the User Documentation as the Company may require from time to time for the use and operation of the Equipment and the Applications and Operating System Software.

15.2   Subject to the contrary provisions of any licence of which the Client notifies the Company prior to the Commencement Date, the Company shall be entitled to reproduce the whole or any part of the User Documentation without prior consent from the Client to the extent considered necessary or expedient by the Company to provide the Bureau Service or otherwise comply with its obligations hereunder.

15.3   (a)   The Client shall notify the Company of any revisions, additions or amendments made or recommended by the Licensors named in the Licences or the suppliers of any part of the Equipment.

(b)   The Company and the Client shall consult on any revisions, additions or amendments to the User Documentation that the Company may recommend.

15.4   The Client shall without charge to the Company provide the Company with any revisions, additions or amendments to the User Documentation supplied to the

Company in accordance with the terms hereof in the same number of copies as the documents supplied by the Client hereunder which it revises or amends.

15.5   The Company shall be permitted by the Client at all times during the currency of this Agreement and at no cost to the Company to use and employ all ideas, innovations, formulæ, processes, know-how and techniques of every kind whatsoever used by the Company in connection with its provision of the Bureau Services and whether developed, submitted or suggested by the Client or by the Company.

15.6   Upon termination of this Agreement the Company will return to the Client any part of the User Documentation in the possession, custody or power of the Company.

16   TRAINING

The Company will be responsible for the training of its staff from time to time in the use and operation of the Equipment and the Applications and Operating System Software. Any training of the Company staff at any of the Remote Sites or other sites of the Client required during the term of this Agreement will be at the expense of the Client and without charge to the Company.

17   LIABILITY

17.1   The Client shall be exclusively responsible for the consequences of:

(a)   any properly executed instructions given to the Company by the Client;

(b)   the Client's failure to access processing services in a manner prescribed by or agreed to by the Company;

(c)   inaccuracies in Input Data.

17.2   The Client acknowledges that it has inspected and is aware of the capacities and functions of the Company Hardware and has satisfied itself as to its suitability and fitness for the Bureau Service and that the Company has not made and does not make or give any warranty, promise or representation as to the suitability or fitness for any purpose of such equipment.

The Company shall use its best endeavours to ensure that such equipment performs the Bureau Service in accordance with documentation supplied by the Client but, notwithstanding any other provision of this Agreement or the Schedules hereto, shall not be liable in any manner whatsoever for any failure of the Bureau Service to perform in strict accordance with the provisions of Schedule D hereto or documentation supplied by the Client relating to the Equipment or the Applications and Operating System Software.

17.3   The Client shall be responsible for auditing, balancing, reconciling and identifying any out of balance or error condition and in the event that such condition cannot be rectified in the normal course of operation in an on-line environment shall promptly notify the Company of the existence of the out of balance or error condition.

17.4   The Client shall be responsible to the extent deemed necessary by the Client for maintaining a procedure external to the Bureau Service for reconstructing otherwise irretrievably lost or altered files, records or data and for recreating original documents or records lost or damaged whilst in transit to or from or at the Company's places of business.

17.5   (a)   The Client shall purchase or rent from the Company or otherwise supply at its own expense a sufficient quantity of magnetic tape or other media to enable at least two (2) generations (the current and immediately preceding from which the current is derived) of all files, records and data maintained by the Company on behalf of the Client to be stored thereon and such magnetic tape or other media shall remain the absolute property of the Client.

(b)   At not less than weekly intervals the Company shall ensure that a copy of the latest version of all the Client's files, records and data maintained and processed in the Bureau Service are stored on the magnetic tape or other media owned or rented by the Client and the Company shall comply with all procedures in the documentation supplied by the Client and all directions of the Client from time to time considered by the Company at its sole discretion to be reasonable and necessary for the preservation and storage of the Client Data on magnetic tape or other media and shall forthwith deliver to the Client or its appointed agents such magnetic tape or other media for safe keeping.

(c)   The Client shall have the right to process the magnetic tape or other media which is the subject of this Clause 17 in any manner necessary to carry on its business and to safeguard the Client's legitimate interests PROVIDED HOWEVER that any such processing shall be at the Client's sole risk and the Company shall not be responsible for any loss or damage incurred by the Client through the use of such magnetic tape or other media by the Client for any purpose.

17.6   The Company shall use due care in the provision of the Bureau Service and shall at its expense correct as far as possible any errors or omissions occurring in its provision of the Bureau Service caused by any negligent acts or omissions of its servants or agents or by malfunction or failure of any part of the Company Hardware or ancillary equipment used by the Company in the provision of the Bureau Service as soon as possible after the Company learns of any such error or omission.

17.7   Except as provided elsewhere in this Clause 17 the Company's sole liability under this Agreement for damages resulting from any breach of this Agreement by the Company or any negligent or wilful default or omission by the Company or a servant or agent of the Company acting in the course of his employment or agency shall be limited to direct monetary losses, and in any event, shall not exceed the amount charged by the Company for providing those services. As a condition precedent to such liability, the Client shall notify the Company promptly of deficiencies in the Output Data or the On-Line Service and, without limiting the generality of the foregoing, such notice shall be given in the case of Output Data not later than 5.00 p.m. on the Business Day following receipt by the Client of the Output Data and in the case of On-Line Services within twenty-four (24) hours of the occurrence of the defect. The Company shall not be liable in any manner under this Agreement in respect of any defect notified later than the times herein specified. The Client also agrees to cooperate with the Company, at the Company's expense and direction, in taking all reasonable steps to recover from any third party any amounts for which the Company is liable pursuant to this Clause.

17.8   The Company shall have no responsibility to determine the authenticity or accuracy of any data or other information delivered by the Client to the Company, or the accuracy of the reports or other outputs based thereon and the Client shall indemnify and save harmless the Company from and against any liability under any claim, judgment, order, award or any damage arising from any defect, error, inaccuracy or non-authenticity of any such data or other information.

17.9   To the full extent permitted by law, all conditions and warranties which would or might otherwise be implied or imposed in this Agreement, including conditions and warranties as to merchantability of goods or fitness for purpose of any goods or services supplied hereunder, are hereby excluded and negated to the extent permitted by law and this is so acknowledged by the Client.

17.10   In no event shall the Company or the Client be liable, one to the other, for special, incidental or consequential damages or for any indirect damages including without any limitation to the foregoing, exemplary or punitive damages, damage to property or loss of profits, even if the said party is advised of the possibility of such damage.

18   CHARGES
18.1   The Client shall pay for the Bureau Service at the rates set out in Part 4 of Schedule D.

18.2   The rates set out in the said Schedule are fixed except for:

(a)   any adjustment necessary to account for the change in royalties or fees payable by the Company for or relating to any software which forms part of the Bureau Service;

(b)   the costs of material and services (including without limitation stationery, magnetic tape or other media, electricity, insurance, rental of the Installation Site and hardware and software maintenance) incurred and which are provided by a third party not a subsidiary of or affiliated with the Company or its related companies, in which case the Company may pass on, at cost and within thirty (30) days of written notice to the Client, any increase in the cost of such material and services. Such price increases may be verified by making available, on request, the relevant invoices.

(c)   charges identified in Schedule D as the labour or materials component of the Bureau Service may be varied by the Company so long as any such variation does not result in such charges after such variation exceeding the affected charges as expressed in Schedule D by a percentage greater than the percentage increase in the rate of inflation as measured by any government published index of inflation for the relevant period for the city or region of the installation site.

(d)   reconstructions of the rates set out in Schedule D caused directly or indirectly by the use made of the Bureau Service by the Client.

18.3   The Company shall invoice the Client each month for all fees, charges and expenses incurred prior to such invoices and not already paid by the Client.

18.4   Payment of the amount shown on any of the Company's invoices forwarded to the Client shall be made by the Client within thirty (30) days from the date of receipt of such invoice unless a *bona fide* dispute exists in which case the undisputed items on the invoice will be paid within the specified period. In the event that the Client fails to pay any amounts when due under this Agreement, the Client shall upon demand pay interest at the rate of one and one half per cent (1½%) per month (but in no event more than the highest rate of interest legally allowable) on such overdue amounts from their due date until the date of payment, provided

(i)   the Company has notified the Client in writing that such amounts are overdue; and

(ii)   the Company invoices the Client for the amounts due for interest within thirty (30) days of receipt of payment by the Company of the overdue amounts.

18.5   In addition to all charges specified herein the Client shall reimburse the company for any stamp duties or the like relative to this Agreement or the services provided hereunder.

19   FILE OWNERSHIP, ACCESS, CONFIDENTIALITY AND SAFETY
19.1   Data files created by the processing of the Client Data are the sole and exclusive property of the Client.

19.2   (a)   The Company warrants that it will retain in confidence all the Client Data obtained in the course of performing this Agreement, and will neither use it nor disclose it to anyone without the express written permission of the Contract Authority, unless such data is in the public domain or obtained from a third party not known by the Company to be in breach of any contract or confidence.

(b)   Neither party shall make any public statements in relation to this

Agreement without the prior written permission of the other, which permission shall not be unreasonably withheld.

(c)   Each party to this Agreement shall preserve and ensure that its employees and agents preserve the confidentiality of all data, information, documents and material disclosed or entrusted to it by the other party on a confidential basis.

19.3   The Company shall use all reasonable endeavours to arrange for the physical safety and integrity of the Client Data from the time of transfer of any data tapes or of transmission from a terminal.

[Insert Boilerplate Clauses.]

SCHEDULE A

The Equipment
[Insert full details of Client equipment to be taken over, including model and serial numbers.]
Remote Sites
[Insert details of locations and equipment which will have access to the main system.]
Equipment Maintenance
[Insert details of third party maintenance organizations responsible for maintenance of the Client equipment referred to above.]

SCHEDULE B

The Licensors
[Insert names (and contact personnel) of licensors of software licensed by the Client and to be used by the Company in the provision of the services.]
Applications
Operating System Software
Software Maintenance
[Insert details of third party maintenance organizations responsible for support and maintenance of the Client software referred to above.]

SCHEDULE C
The Employees

[Insert details of Client employees being taken over by the Company.]

SCHEDULE D
PART 1
Batch Processing Services

I   The services provided are the making available of the Equipment and the Company Hardware in conjunction with the Applications and Operating System Software on the Installation Site for use by the Client from the Remote Sites in accordance with the functions of the Applications and Operating System Software during the term of this Agreement (not including the On-Line Services).

II   The Company and the Client will agree from time to time on a periodical timetable for batch processing runs. The timetable once agreed upon will form part of this Schedule.

III   If it is able to do so the Company will at the request of the Client rectify any Input Data and the Client shall pay the Company at the Company Standard Rates for all additional work carried out by the Company to effect such rectifications in addition to the charges specified in Schedule D for any work carried out by the Company based on the unrectified Input Data.

IV   The Company will use its best endeavours to deliver to the Client the complete results of each batch processing run within two (2) working days of the agreed processing date except for Payroll Processing, which shall be delivered within twenty-four (24) hours of commencement. Should circumstances over which it has no control prevent the Company from achieving this turnaround on any occasion, the Company undertakes to contact the Client on each occasion and no later than two (2) working days after the date on which the work was to be performed to explain the reasons for the delay and to negotiate a new completion date for the work.

V   The Client is responsible for delivery to the Company of all Input Data and non-standard stationery and for collecting the Output Data and security files from the Company. The Client will notify the Company of the delivery service it will use. If requested by the Client, the Company will make available the services of a messenger service for the transport of Input Data and Output Data at the cost of the Client at the then current rate charged by that messenger service.

PART 2
On-line Services

I   The On-Line Services provided by the Company to the Client are as provided by [specify components] of the Software.

II   The On-Line Services in relation to [specify components] will be available on Business Days between 7.00 a.m. and 7.00 p.m. ('the System Hours').

III   By arrangement between the Company and the Client the On-Line Services can be made available with the Company's support at other times subject to payment by the Client of any overtime premium required by the Company from time to time. Any warranty given by the Company in relation to response times does not apply to such extended times.

IV   By arrangement between the Company and the Client the On-Line Services can be made available without the Company's support at times other those listed in Article II of this Part.

V   The Company makes no warranties whatsoever in relation to response times or availability in relation to the On-Line Services at any time and the Client acknowledges that in providing such services the Company does not provide the facility to correct errors or to reconnect the Client to the On-Line Services should a fault occur.

PART 3
Duration

The initial term of this Agreement shall be from the Commencement Date to [specify end of term] whereafter (unless the Company has received written notice to the contrary prior thereto) this Agreement shall continue for periods of three (3) months until terminated with three (3) months notice in writing by either party, such notice ending no later than the end of any such period.

PART 4
Charges

I   Fixed Monthly Base Charge

A fixed charge per month which covers:
- computer room preparation
- provision of air conditioning
- electricity
- insurance
- floor space
- paper handling and storage
- tape storage
- management

BASE CHARGE — $

2   Partly Variable Monthly Charge
    (a)   Computer Operators: 3 shifts ×
    2 Operators 1032 hours per
    month at $27.00 per hour $
    (b)   Data Control × 2 @ 344 hours per
    month at $27.00 per hour $
3   Fully Variable Monthly Charge
    (a)
    (b)
    (c)
4   Minimum Levels
    (a)   The Fixed Monthly Base Charge shall not be decreased.
    (b)   The Partly Variable Monthly Charge shall not be reduced below:
        (i)
        (ii)
    (c)   The Fully Variable Monthly Charge may be decreased by removal of the
    following Equipment at the following times:
        (i)
        (ii)
        (iii)

SCHEDULE E
Applications Software

Introduction
Applications software listed below represents the major applications of the Client. The list is not finite in that special and one time facilities exist within the libraries for various other purposes and these may be processed from time to time.

1   Asset Register
2   Bank Reconciliation
3   Budget
4   Chart of Accounts
5   Creditors
6   Debtors
7   General Ledger
8   Payroll
9   Staff Savings
10 Superannuation
11 Warranty

SCHEDULE F
The Company Hardware

[Insert Execution Clauses.]

Appendix I

Signatories of Copyright Conventions

Universal Copyright Convention (UCC)

Algeria
Andorra
Argentina
Australia
Austria
Bahamas
Bangladesh
Barbados
Belgium
Belize
Brazil
Bulgaria
Cameroon
Canada
Chile
Colombia
Costa Rica
Cuba
Czechoslovakia
Democratic Kampuchea
Denmark
Dominican Republic
Ecuador
El Salvador
Fiji
Finland
France
German Democratic Republic
Germany, Federal Republic of
Ghana
Greece
Guatemala
Guinea
Haiti
Holy See
Hungary
Iceland
India
Ireland
Israel

Italy
Japan
Kenya
Laos
Lebanon
Liberia
Liechtenstein
Luxembourg
Malawi
Malta
Mauritius
Mexico
Monaco
Morocco
Netherlands
New Zealand
Nicaragua
Nigeria
Norway
Pakistan
Panama
Paraguay
Peru
Philippines
Poland
Portugal
Republic of Korea
Saint Vincent & the Grenadines
Senegal
Soviet Union
Spain
Sweden
Switzerland
Tunisia
United Kingdom
United States of America
Venezuela
Yugoslavia
Zambia

International Union For The Protection of Literary and Artistic Works (Berne Union)

Argentina
Australia
Austria
Bahamas
Belgium
Benin
Brazil
Bulgaria
Burkina Faso
Cameroon
Canada
Central African Republic
Chad
Chile
Colombia
Congo
Costa Rica
Cyprus
Czechoslovakia
Denmark
Egypt
Fiji
Finland
France
Gabon
German Democratic Republic
Germany, Federal Republic of
Greece
Guinea
Holy See
Hungary
Iceland
India
Ireland
Israel
Italy
Ivory Coast
Japan
Lebanon
Libya
Liechtenstein

Luxembourg
Madagascar
Mali
Malta
Mauritania
Mexico
Monaco
Morocco
Netherlands
New Zealand
Niger
Norway
Pakistan
Philippines
Poland
Portugal
Romania
Rwanda
Senegal
South Africa
South Korea
Spain
Sri Lanka
Suriname
Sweden
Switzerland
Thailand
Togo
Tunisia
Turkey
United Kingdom
United States Of America
Upper Volta
Uruguay
Venezuela
Yugoslavia
Zaire
Zimbabwe

Appendix II

Membership of the International Patent Cooperation Union (PCT Union)

Australia
Austria
Belgium
Brazil
Cameroon
Central African Republic
Chad
Congo
Democratic People's Republic of Korea
Denmark
Finland
France
Gabon
Germany, Federal Republic of
Hungary
Japan

Liechtenstein
Luxembourg
Madagascar
Malawi
Monaco
Netherlands
Norway
Romania
Senegal
Soviet Union
Sri Lanka
Sweden
Switzerland
Togo
United Kingdom
United States of America

Appendix III

Membership of the Paris Union

International Union for the Protection of Industrial Property (Paris Union)

Algeria
Argentina
Australia
Austria
Bahamas
Belgium
Benin
Brazil
Bulgaria
Burundi
Cameroon
Canada
Central African Republic
Chad
Congo
Cuba
Cyprus
Czechoslovakia
Democratic People's Republic of Korea
Denmark
Dominican Republic
Egypt
Finland
France
Gabon
German Democratic Republic
Germany, Federal Republic of
Ghana
Greece
Guinea
Haiti
Holy See
Hungary
Iceland
Indonesia
Iran

Iraq
Iceland
Israel
Italy
Ivory Coast
Japan
Jordan
Kenya
Lebanon
Libya
Liechtenstein
Luxembourg
Madagascar
Malawi
Mali
Malta
Mauritania
Mauritius
Mexico
Monaco
Morocco
Netherlands
New Zealand
Niger
Nigeria
Norway
Philippines
Poland
Portugal
Republic of Korea
Romania
San Marino
Senegal
South Africa
Soviet Union
Spain

Sri Lanka
Suriname
Sweden
Switzerland
Syria
Tanzania
Togo
Trinidad and Tobago
Tunisia
Turkey

Uganda
United Kingdom
United States of America
Upper Volta
Uruguay
Vietnam
Yugoslavia
Zaire
Zambia
Zimbabwe

Appendix IV

Signatories of the International Contract Convention

United Nations Convention on Contracts for the International Sale of Goods

Argentina
Australia
Austria
China (PRC)
Egypt
Finland
France
Hungary
Italy
Lesotho
Mexico
Sweden
Syria
United States of America
Yugoslavia
Zambia

In addition, Norway has acceded effective from August 1, 1989.

Index